Aircraft Rescue and Fire Fighting

Fifth Edition

Jeff Fortney
Project Manager/Editor

Clint Clausing
Senior Editor

ifsta

Validated by the International Fire
Service Training Association

Published by
Fire Protection Publications
Oklahoma State University

RECYCLABLE

The International Fire Service Training Association

The International Fire Service Training Association (IFSTA) was established in 1934 as a *nonprofit educational association of fire fighting personnel who are dedicated to upgrading fire fighting techniques and safety through training.* To carry out the mission of IFSTA, Fire Protection Publications was established as an entity of Oklahoma State University. Fire Protection Publications' primary function is to publish and disseminate training texts as proposed and validated by IFSTA. As a secondary function, Fire Protection Publications researches, acquires, produces, and markets high-quality learning and teaching aids as consistent with IFSTA's mission.

The IFSTA Validation Conference is held the second full week in July. Committees of technical experts meet and work at the conference addressing the current standards of the National Fire Protection Association and other standard-making groups as applicable. The Validation Conference brings together individuals from several related and allied fields, such as:

- Key fire department executives and training officers
- Educators from colleges and universities
- Representatives from governmental agencies
- Delegates of firefighter associations and industrial organizations

Committee members are not paid nor are they reimbursed for their expenses by IFSTA or Fire Protection Publications. They participate because of commitment to the fire service and its future through training. Being on a committee is prestigious in the fire service community, and committee members are acknowledged leaders in their fields. This unique feature provides a close relationship between the International Fire Service Training Association and fire protection agencies, which helps to correlate the efforts of all concerned.

IFSTA manuals are now the official teaching texts of most of the states and provinces of North America. Additionally, numerous U.S. and Canadian government agencies as well as other English-speaking countries have officially accepted the IFSTA manuals.

ISBN 0-87939-323-8 978-0-87939-323-6   *Library of Congress Control Number: 2008935723*

Fifth Edition, Third Printing, August 2012   *Printed in the United States of America*

10   9   8   7   6   5   4   3

If you need additional information concerning the International Fire Service Training Association (IFSTA) or Fire Protection Publications, contact:

Customer Service, Fire Protection Publications, Oklahoma State University
930 North Willis, Stillwater, OK 74078-8045
800-654-4055   Fax: 405-744-8204

For assistance with training materials, to recommend material for inclusion in an IFSTA manual, or to ask questions or comment on manual content, contact:

Editorial Department, Fire Protection Publications, Oklahoma State University
930 North Willis, Stillwater, OK 74078-8045
405-744-4111   Fax: 405-744-4112   E-mail: editors@osufpp.org

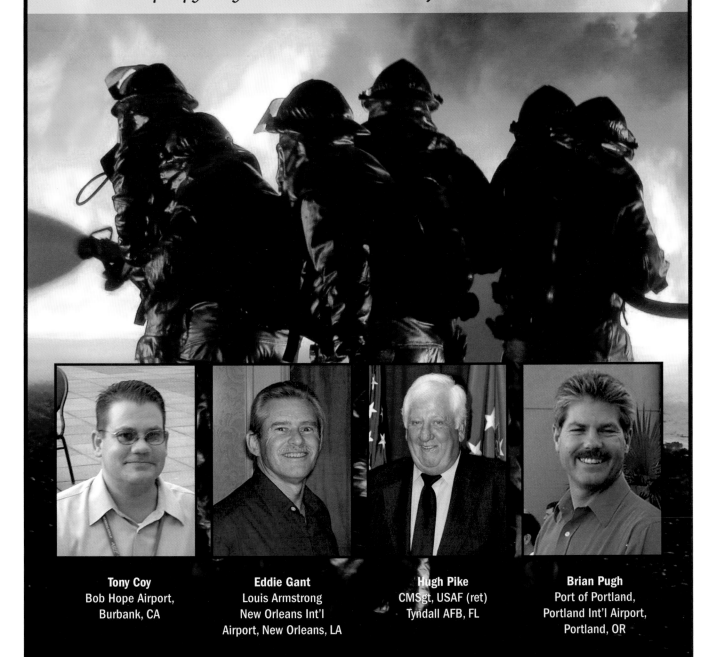

IFSTA's fifth edition of Aircraft Rescue and Fire Fighting is dedicated to the memory of four members of the ARFF community. Their hard work and dedication improved the quality of aircraft rescue and fire fighting services worldwide. They will be missed.

Tony Coy
Bob Hope Airport,
Burbank, CA

Eddie Gant
Louis Armstrong
New Orleans Int'l
Airport, New Orleans, LA

Hugh Pike
CMSgt, USAF (ret)
Tyndall AFB, FL

Brian Pugh
Port of Portland,
Portland Int'l Airport,
Portland, OR

Background image courtesy of William D. Stewart. Images of Tony Coy, Eddie Gant, and Brian Pugh courtesy of Mary Ness. Image of CMSgt (Ret.) Hugh Pike courtesy of the United States Air Force.

Table of Contents

Preface

This fifth edition of IFSTA **Aircraft Rescue and Fire Fighting** presents information for airport firefighters as well as other fire and emergency service personnel who may respond to aircraft accidents/incidents. This new edition has been revised to reflect the changes in aircraft and the advances in aircraft rescue and fire fighting.

Acknowledgement and special thanks are extended to the members of the IFSTA Validation Committee who contributed their time, wisdom, and talents to this manual.

IFSTA Aircraft Rescue and Fire Fighting Validation Committee

Chair

William D. Stewart
BWI Airport Fire Department

Committee Members

Brian Canady
Dallas-Fort Worth
International Airport
Dallas-Fort Worth, TX

John J. Demyan
Lehigh Valley International
Airport
International Association of
Firefighters
Allentown, PA

Samuel R. Feltner
Wright-Patterson AFB
Union, OH

David D. Harris
Lockheed Martin Aeronautics
Marietta, GA

Edwin A. Jones
SMSgt, USAFR
910 CES/DEF
Youngstown ARS, OH

Randy J. Krause
Boeing Fire Department
Duvall, WA

Michael F. Lattanzio
Fair Oaks Volunteer Fire and
Rescue Company
Fairfax, VA

Mark Lee
University of Missouri Fire
and Rescue Institute
Columbus, MO

Robert G. Lindstrom
Will Rogers World Airport Fire
Department
Oklahoma City, OK

Les Omans
San Jose Fire Department
San Jose, CA

Arty Pamplin
Lawton Fire Department
Lawton, OK

Dr. Mark A. Rivero
Las Vegas Fire Rescue
Las Vegas, NV

William A. Parker, Jr.
Manchester Fire Department
Eighth Utilities District
Manchester, CT

Tim Stemple
Lockheed Martin
Fort Worth, TX

David Y. Whitaker
Memphis Fire Department
Memphis, TN

Thomas H. Phalen
Virginia Department of Fire Programs
Glen Allen, VA

Special recognition is given to William Stewart for assisting in the development of our draft chapters and to Timothy Stemple for conducting our technical review. The following individuals and organizations contributed information, photographs, and other assistance that made the completion of this manual possible:

David Bruch, Lehigh Valley Aviation Services
    Civil Air Patrol

Douglas E. Courchene, Fire Chief (USAF Ret.)

David M. DeSanto, DFWIA GIS / IT Department

Jan Doddy, Doddy Photography

East Allen Township (PA) Fire Department:
    Chief Barry Frantz
    Assistant Chief Ray Anthony
    FF Cory Demyan
    FF Josh Smith

Stan Fernandez, San Rafael, CA

J.R. Frasher, Airport Director, Greenville Airport Commission

Gary Hall, East Coast Jets, Inc.

Edwin A. Jones, USAFR

Marty Huffman, Rosenbauer America

Bill Keller, Program Coordinator, Fire Service (Extension West Virginia University,) Morgantown, WV

Captain James Mack, Capital Region Airport Commission

Mary Ness

Sean Quinby, Assistant Chief of Training, Seymour Johnsons AFB, NC

Jessica Parsons, L3 Communications Aviation Recorders

Paul Pestel, Russellville (AR) Fire Department

Scott Ramey, S. D. Ramey Photography

Jeffrey A. Reichmann, Reichmann Safety Services.

John Sileski, Guardian Fire Equipment

Ron Stoffel, Minnesota Department of Natural Resources Forestry Division

Brad Tuttle of 10 Tanker Air Carrier

Dallas/Fort Worth (DFW) International Airport

DFW International Airport Department of Public Safety Fire Department:
    Alan Black, Fire Chief
    John Griffin, Battalion Chief
    John Kendall, Battalion Chief
    Robert Cook, Captain
    Brian Canady, Training Officer
    Victor Azevedo
    John Barzyk
    Chris Coyle
    James Curtis
    Ben Duvall
    Amanda Eads

Darrel Gillis

Greg Harrison

Darren Himes

Ronald Jacobs

Ann J. Joiner

Wes Pruett

Cole Sellers

Todd Smith

Craig Thornton

Anthony Walker

Lewis Warren

Robert White

Greenville Airport Commission

L3 Communications Aviation Recorders

Lehigh Valley International Airport:
  Skip Fairchild, Director of Public Safety
  Dave Bachemin
  John Demyan, Lieutenant

Loudon County Rescue Squad
  Jeremy Mader

Marine Corps Combat Development Command
  David Hooser

Nancy Run (PA) Fire Department:
  Dave Bachemin, Fire Chief
  Tim Foerst
  Jamie Hauze
  Brenden Kammetler
  Kevin McCabe

Richmond International Airport:
  James Nilo, Fire Chief
  Gregory Baylor
  Walter P. Drew
  Kurt Hinrichs
  Adam Matanoski

Rockville VFD
  Christopher Bouie
  Brian Keitz

Rosenbauer America

Stillwater (OK) Fire Department personnel:
  Rex Mott, Assistant Chief
  Trent Hawkins, Fire Marshal

Stillwater (OK) Regional Airport personnel:
  David Lyons
  Tony Chambers

Susan C. Robertson, NHQ
  Photographer, Civil Air Patrol

Tinker Air Force Base (OK) Fire and Emergency Services:
  Michael E. Tuley, Assistant Chief and Fire Chaplain
  Brian Maple
  Daryhl Page

Tulsa Fire Department Station 51 at Tulsa International Airport:
  Rick Phelps, Airport Chief
  Craig Mathews, Training Officer
  Rick Mitchell, Captain
  Mark Dix
  John Forest
  Randall Matheson
  Wendell Hillhouse
  Jon Picard

A special thank you to my fellow senior editor, Barbara Adams, for working with the Aircraft Rescue and Fire Fighting committee during its first meeting.

As always, thanks are extended to the personnel of Oklahoma Fire Service Training for their assistance on this project.

Additionally, gratitude is extended to the following members of the Fire Protection Publications Aircraft and Rescue Fire Fighting Manual Project Team whose contributions made the final publication of this manual possible.

Aircraft and Rescue Fire Fighting Manual Project Team

Project Manager/Editor
Jeff Fortney, Senior Editor

Senior Editor/Proofreader
Clint Clausing

Technical Reviewer
Timothy Stemple

FPP Photographers
Brett Noakes
Mike Sturzenbecker

Production Manager
Ann Moffat

Illustrators and Layout Designers
Clint Parker
Lee Shortridge
Errick Braggs

Library Researchers
Susan F. Walker
Jenny Brock

Editorial Assistant
Tara Gladden

The IFSTA Executive Board at the time of validation of the **Aircraft Rescue and Fire Fighting** manual is as follows:

Introduction Contents

Introduction

Introduction

Today's airport firefighter must be knowledgeable in the many facets of aircraft rescue and fire fighting. In addition to basic fire fighting knowledge, skills, and experience, airport firefighters must learn to use specialized techniques, tools, and equipment in order to mitigate airport emergencies. Aircraft are larger and more powerful than in previous decades, are constructed of new advanced aerospace materials, and as a result, present new challenges to personnel responding to aircraft accidents/incidents. Effective aircraft rescue and fire fighting (ARFF) accident/incident response requires that airport firefighters be familiar with the varied aircraft at their airport as well as with the different features of the airport.

This edition of **Aircraft Rescue and Fire Fighting** provides basic information needed by firefighters to effectively perform the various tasks involved in aircraft rescue and fire fighting. It also serves as a reference for other emergency responders likely to be involved with aircraft accidents/incidents.

Purpose and Scope

Purpose: This manual provides basic information firefighters need to effectively perform the various tasks involved in aircraft rescue and fire fighting. Written for all fire protection organizations, the manual discusses the use of structural and specialized aircraft fire fighting apparatus and equipment, civilian and military aircraft, and the theory and practice of aircraft fire fighting and rescue operations.

Scope: The information contained in this manual is intended to meet the requirements contained in the 2010 edition of NFPA® 1003, *Standard for Airport Fire Fighter Professional Qualifications*, as published by the National Fire Protection Association. Additional material addresses the airport fire fighting apparatus covered in Chapter 9 of the 2009 edition of NFPA® 1002, *Standard on Fire Apparatus Driver/Operator Professional Qualifications*. Key parts of NFPA® 402, *Guide for Aircraft Rescue and Fire-Fighting Operations* (2008 edition), and NFPA® 403, *Standard for Aircraft Rescue and Fire-Fighting Services at Airports* 2009 edition), are also covered in this manual.

> **NOTE:** Material in this manual includes those subjects included in the training requirements of Federal Aviation Regulations (FARs) 139.315, 139.317, and 139.319.

Notice on Use of State and Province

In order to keep sentences uncluttered and easy to read, the word "state" will be used to represent both state and provincial level governments. This usage is applied to this manual for the purposes of brevity and is not intended to address or show preference for only one nation's method of identifying regional governments within its borders.

Key Information

Various types of information in this book are given in shaded boxes marked by symbols or icons (sidebars, information, key information, and case histories). Smart Operations tips and What Does This Mean To You notices are given in boxes indicated by a safety-alert icon. See the following examples:

Sidebar

Atmospheric pressure is greatest at low altitudes; consequently, its pressure at sea level is used as a standard. At sea level, the atmosphere exerts a pressure of 14.7 psi (101 kPa) {1.01 bar}. A common method of measuring atmospheric pressure is to compare the weight of the atmosphere with the weight of a column of mercury: the greater the atmospheric pressure, the taller the column of mercury.

Information

Some experts make this differentiation: Acids are corrosive, while bases are caustic. In the world of emergency response; however, both acids and bases are called corrosives. The U.S. Department of Transportation (DOT) and Transport Canada (TC), for example, do not differentiate between the two. Any materials that destroy metal or skin tissue are considered corrosives by these agencies.

Key Information

Volatility refers to a substance's ability to become a vapor at a relatively low temperature. Essentially, volatile chemical agents have low boiling points at ordinary pressures and/or high vapor pressures at ordinary temperatures. The volatility of a chemical agent often determines how it is used.

Three key signal words are found in the book: **WARNING, CAUTION,** and **NOTE.** Definitions and examples of each are as follows:

- **WARNING** indicates information that could result in death or serious injury to industrial fire brigade members. See the following example:

- **CAUTION** indicates important information or data that industrial fire brigade members need to be aware of in order to perform their duties safely. See the following example:

- **NOTE** indicates important operational information that helps explain why a particular recommendation is given or describes optional methods for certain procedures. See the following example:

NOTE: *Vapor* is a gaseous form of a substance that is normally in a solid or liquid state at room temperature and pressure. It is formed by evaporation from a liquid or sublimation from a solid.

NFPA® Copyright Permission

One of the basic purposes of IFSTA manuals is to allow fire service personnel and their departments to meet the requirements set forth by NFPA® codes and standards. These NFPA® documents may be referred to throughout this manual. References to information from NFPA® codes and standards are used with permission from National Fire Protection Association, Quincy, MA 02169. This referenced material is not the complete and official position of the National Fire Protection Association on the referenced subject which is represented only by the standard in its entirety.

Qualifications for Aircaft Rescue and Fire Fighting Personnel

Chapter Contents

Key Terms

NFPA® references for Chapter 1:

NFPA® 1003 (2010)

4.1	4.3.3	5.3.9
4.2	4.3.4	5.4.3
4.2.1	5.1	
4.2.2	5.1.1	**NFPA® 1002**
4.3	5.1.1.1	**(2009 - Chapter 9)**
4.3.1	5.1.1.2	9.1
4.3.2	5.1.1.3	9.1.1

Federal Aviation Regulations (FAR):

139.315(a)	139.315(d)	139.319(l)
139.315(b)	139.315(e)	
139.315(c)	139.319(i)	

Qualifications for Aircaft Rescue and Fire Fighting Personnel

Learning Objectives

After reading this chapter, students shall be able to:

1. Describe the history of aircraft rescue and fire fighting.

2. Identify organizations that are relevant to aircraft rescue and fire fighting.

3. Describe the roles and responsibilities of relevant organizations.

4. Discuss the basic requirements for aircraft rescue and fire fighting personnel.

5. Identify basic facts about aircraft rescue and fire fighting training programs.

6. Explain the general training requirements for aircraft rescue and fire fighting personnel.

Chapter 1
Qualifications for Aircraft Rescue and Fire Fighting Personnel

Case History

Modern aircraft rescue and fire fighting (ARFF) services and personnel protect millions of people as they fly worldwide each year. The evolution of ARFF has been a long, slow process since the early years of human flight. It was only five years after the Wright Brothers first powered flight at Kitty Hawk, North Carolina, when the first aircraft crash fatality occurred. On September 17, 1908, Orville Wright and U.S. Army Lieutenant Thomas Selfridge were airborne when one of the aircraft's propellers broke free. The aircraft lurched to the right and, at a height of approximately 75 feet (23 m), went into a nose dive. The crash pinned both men in the aircraft's wreckage. Orville was freed first and later, after much difficulty, the more seriously injured Selfridge was pulled from the wreckage. Orville Wright lived to fly again but Lt. Thomas Selfridge died that day from the injuries he'd received.

Prior to responding on any emergency, aircraft rescue and fire fighting personnel must have a minimum standard level of knowledge and skills to deal with aircraft operations and emergencies. Since ARFF personnel will likely encounter rescue, mass-casualty, fire fighting, and hazardous materials (haz mat) operations, this chapter outlines the training needs and competence level for the duties assigned to ARFF personnel. A basic knowledge of these skills is critical in helping to ensure firefighter safety as well as the safety of others. Quite often, techniques used to rescue passengers are unique because aviation accidents can pose an extreme set of circumstances never previously encountered and difficult to recreate in a training scenario.

The need for Crash Fire Rescue (CFR) dates back to 1903 when the Wright Brothers carried with them ½ gallon (1.9 L) of gasoline contained in a tank twelve inches (305 mm) long and three inches (76 mm) in diameter. In those early days, since landing speeds were very low, most airport accidents were survivable. When a major accident which involved fire did occur, the occupants were usually killed by the impact rather than from an ensuing fire.

It was not until World War II that any real effort was made in the CFR field. Aircraft design changed from the biplane to the monoplane – from a single piston engine to multiple turbo prop engines and subsequently jet engines. Large quantities of fuel were now being carried in the wings and fuselage. Large numbers of relatively inexperienced aircrews, rapidly thrown into combat together with uncertain weather conditions, accounted for a significant number of accidents requiring CFR to become a priority overnight.

Figure 1.1 A late 1950s U.S. Air Force Type O-6 Cardox Crash Fire Rescue (CFR) truck which carried 4,000 pounds (1 814 kg) of carbon dioxide (CO2). *Courtesy of Douglas E. Courchene, Fire Chief (ret.) and Assistant Chief Sean Quinby, Seymour Johnson AFB, NC.*

The enthusiastic response of the emergency crews and the relatively small area of the airports – runways approximately 3000 feet (914 m) long for fighters and 6000 feet (1 829 m) long for bombers – resulted in a surprisingly high rescue capability. Rescue crews were often housed at the base of or adjacent to the control tower. This location combined with highly trained personnel provided an excellent response capability, despite the fact that extinguishing agents and equipment used at the time would currently be considered highly ineffective.

Following Word War II, CFR was almost forgotten by the civil aviation world. Fortunately the military services continued research, but at a diminished level. Because of that research, military fire trucks improved in size, speed, and discharge capability **(Figure 1.1)**. Additionally, carbon dioxide (CO2) gave way to protein foam. Meanwhile, civilian airports experienced little progress, except at a very small percentage of the major terminals. With the advent of commercial jet aircraft that contain large passenger and fuel capacities, some interest was aroused regarding CFR and civilian progress was resumed. The Federal Aviation Administration (FAA) was formed over concerns about the safety of civil aviation in the Federal Aviation Act of 1958 after a series of midair collisions.

Those who remained in aviation in a civilian capacity remembered the catastrophic aircraft fires that were experienced in flight operations during World War II. Initially CFR services ranged from elementary to non-existent, and many lives were lost in aviation accidents because the flight crews, who often survived the crash, were trapped in the wreckage and unable to escape. Commercial airports after the war did not learn from these experiences. The emergency services provided, if any, were ineffective. In a survey taken by the Air Line Pilots Association (ALPA) in 1968, of the 530 commercial airports in the United States, over half of them still had no emergency services based at the airport. They relied on structural equipment from the nearest town. Even today, many airports have no aircraft rescue and fire fighting (ARFF) resources onsite and depend on fire and EMS services from surrounding communities.

The real changes and improvements to civilian ARFF services began in the 1960s and 1970s. The International Civil Aviation Organization (ICAO) and the National Fire Protection Association (NFPA®) began to develop standards and guidelines regarding ARFF. The NFPA® published the first such standard;

NFPA® 403, *Aircraft Rescue and Fire Fighting Services at Airports*. Since then, both the NFPA® and ICAO have developed and updated a significant amount of ARFF related materials.

Prior to 1973, the FAA relied on each individual airport to determine how to provide ARFF services. In 1973, the Federal Aviation Administration created Federal Aviation Regulation (FAR) Part 139, Certification and Operations: Land Airports Serving CAB – Certificated Air Carriers. This document identified five indexes that specified the types and minimum quantities of extinguishing agents, as well as the number of ARFF apparatus for airports that serve passenger aircraft. It also addressed response times, emergency notification, communication, airport emergency planning, training, and fire fighting equipment. At the same time, the FAA allowed funds available from Airport Improvement Program (AIP) to be used to fund over 90% of the purchase of required ARFF vehicles, agents, and equipment. FAR Part 139 has also been modified and expanded several times in the past thirty years. In addition to the FAR changes, in the mid 1980s, the FAA changed CFR to ARFF to avoid confusion with other aviation terminology as it related to the Code of Federal Regulations (CFR).

ARFF has continued to evolve through the years to meet the ever changing needs of the aviation industry. The ARFF service has responded with the introduction of new apparatus, extinguishing agents, and procedures **(Figure 1.2)**. New aviation technological advances include replacing aluminum fuselages with composite fuselages. These lightweight materials are stronger and more resilient to the stresses of flight. Since composite materials are light, aircraft can be designed and constructed much larger, which enhances the challenges of an already demanding profession.

Understanding how an ARFF department fits into an aviation emergency response picture will allow the ARFF firefighter to realize that they are first responders and a critical link in the response chain. This chapter introduces the ARFF firefighter to the organizations that provide valuable assistance during an aircraft accident or incident.

> **Code of Federal Regulations (CFR)** — Formal name given to the books or documents containing the specific United States regulations provided for by law; complete body of U.S. Federal law.

Relevant Organizations

ARFF personnel should be familiar with a number of organizations that deal with air transportation in the United States and other countries. Some of these organizations develop standards; others are regulatory in nature, while oth-

Figure 1.2 A modern Aircraft Rescue and Fire Fighting (ARFF) apparatus. *Courtesy of Rosenbauer America.*

ers are investigative organizations. In the United States, the Federal Aviation Administration (FAA), the National Transportation Safety Board (NTSB), the Transportation Security Administration (TSA), and the National Fire Protection Association (NFPA®) each have an impact upon aviation and the ARFF community by creating standards and regulations. The Air Line Pilots Association (ALPA), Association of Flight Attendants-CWA (AFA-CWA), Joint Aviation Authority (JAA), International Air Transport Association (IATA), International Civil Aviation Organization (ICAO), Accident Investigations Branch (AAIB), American Association of Airport Executives (AAAE), and United Kingdom Civil Aviation Authority (CAA) serve in similar capacities in other countries and internationally. The following sections provide background information on each of these agencies, as well as websites which provide more information about their interaction with the ARFF community.

Federal Aviation Administration (FAA)

The Federal Aviation Administration is a subdivision of the U.S. Department of Transportation and is involved with the regulation of civil aviation. The FAA issues the Federal Aviation Regulations (FARs) as well as Advisory Circulars (ACs) and Cert Alerts, intended to provide guidance to the airline industry. Examples of these include FAR 121, which outlines the regulations for commercial aircraft operations and FAR 139, a large portion of which outlines the requirements for ARFF protection at airports.

FAA Advisory Circulars

The following Advisory Circulars are of particular interest to ARFF Personnel.

— 150/5200-12B – Fire Department Responsibility in Protecting Evidence at the Scene of an Aircraft Accident

— 150/5200-18C – Airport Safety Self Inspection

— 150/5200-31A – Airport Emergency Plan

— 150/5210-6D – Aircraft Fire & Rescue Facilities & Extinguishing Agents

— 150/5210-7C – Aircraft Rescue & Firefighting Communications

— 150/5210-13B – Water Rescue Plans, Facilities, & Equipment

— 150/5210-14A – Airport Fire & Rescue Personnel Protective Clothing

— 150/5210-15 – Airport Rescue & Firefighting Station Building Design

— 150/5210-17A – Programs for Training Aircraft Rescue & Fire Fighting Personnel

— 150/5210-18 – Systems for Interactive Training of Airport Personnel

— 150/5210-19 – Driver's Enhanced Vision System (DEVS)

— 150/5220-4B – Water Supply Systems for Aircraft Fire & Rescue Protection

— 150/5220-10D – Guide Specification for Aircraft Rescue and Fire Fighting Vehicles

— 150/5220-19 – Guide Specification for Small Agent ARFF Vehicles

— 150/5230-4A– Aircraft Fuel Storage, Handling, & Dispensing on Airports

In addition to writing regulations, the FAA conducts research on a variety of fire safety related topics and systems involving aircraft, ARFF vehicles, and extinguishing agents. Free aircraft accident and incident data is also available from the FAA.

FAA certification inspectors will conduct annual inspections of FAR Part 139 regulated airport fire services and conduct a response test. FAA funding is available for purchase of ARFF vehicles, agents, and equipment, as well as building approved ARFF fire-training facilities. The FAA released three computer based ARFF training programs for recurrent training of airport firefighters. A wide variety of informational handouts and videos are also available from the FAA regarding airport marking, communication, ground movements, and other information of interest to ARFF personnel. These materials can be obtained from most FAA Flight Standard District Offices (FSDO). The FAA investigates aircraft accidents including accidents and incidents not investigated by the National Transportation Safety Board. Further information about the FAA and its programs can be found at its web site at www.faa.gov

National Transportation Safety Board (NTSB)

The National Transportation Safety Board is an agency of the U.S. Department of Transportation tasked with determining the probable cause of aircraft accidents as well as incidents involving other modes of transportation. Depending on the size and nature of the incident, ARFF responders may interact with numerous representatives from the NTSB. After conducting an investigation and reporting their findings through a formal public hearing the NTSB publishes accident reports which are available to ARFF personnel. Other free items of interest include the following:

- Annual reviews of aircraft accidents
- Aviation accident databases
- Safety reports
- Special reports
- Assorted other publications

Valuable insight can be gained regarding accident response by visiting the NTSB website, www.ntsb.gov.

Transportation Security Administration (TSA)

The Transportation Security Administration is a component of the U.S. Department of Homeland Security and was established following the events of September 11, 2001. TSA is responsible for the security of the national transportation systems (highways, buses, railroads, mass transit systems, ports and airports) within the United States. To ensure dangerous materials and weapons are not brought onto transportation vehicles, TSA agents should act as follows:

- Screen passengers and cargo.
- Inspect luggage and transportation vehicles.
- Vet and credential transportation workers who might require access to secure areas.
- Provide air marshals.

Further information about the TSA and its programs can be found at its web site at www.tsa.gov.

National Fire Protection Association (NFPA®)

The NFPA® is an organization concerned with fire safety standards development, technical advisory services, education, research, and other related services. Its members come from the educational, product, response, and scientific sectors of the fire protection field, both private and public. The NFPA®'s primary service is the development of technical consensus standards. The NFPA®, which was organized in 1896, also develops fire training and public fire education materials. Information about NFPA® and its activities can be found on its web site at www.nfpa.org.

NFPA® Standards

Although there are others, the following are the NFPA® documents of particular interest to ARFF personnel.

— NFPA® 402 – Guide for Aircraft Rescue & Fire-Fighting Operations
— NFPA® 403 – Standard for Aircraft Rescue & Fire-Fighting Services at Airports
— NFPA® 405 – Standard for the Recurring Proficiency of Airport Fire Fighters
— NFPA® 407 – Standard for Aircraft Fuel Servicing
— NFPA® 412 – Standard for Evaluating Aircraft Rescue & Fire-Fighting Foam Equipment
— NFPA® 414 – Standard for Aircraft Rescue & Fire-Fighting Vehicles
— NFPA® 422 – Guide for Aircraft Accident / Incident Response Assessment
— NFPA® 424 – Guide for Airport / Community Emergency Planning
— NFPA® 1002 – Standard on Fire Apparatus Driver / Operator Professional Qualifications
— NFPA® 1003 – Standard for Airport Fire Fighter Professional Qualifications

Air Line Pilots Association, International (ALPA)

The Air Line Pilots Association, International (ALPA) is the largest airline pilot union in the world and represents 61,000 pilots who fly for 40 U.S. and Canadian airlines. Known internationally as US-ALPA, it is a member of the International Federation of Air Line Pilot Associations. ALPA representatives are involved in a variety of safety related activities and often interact with ARFF responders as they conduct accident investigations. ALPA also has an extensive number of airport liaison representatives at many U.S. airports. Additional information can be found at www.alpa.org.

Association of Flight Attendants (AFA-CWA)

The Association of Flight Attendants-CWA (AFA-CWA) is the world's largest labor union for flight attendants. AFA-CWA represents over 55,000 flight attendants at 20 airlines. AFA-CWA is significant to ARFF because flight attendants are the crewmembers who are most likely to be tasked with fire suppression or medical emergencies while aircraft are in flight. Also, like ALPA, AFA-CWA representatives are involved in a variety of safety-related legislative initiatives and are often present during accident investigations. Additional information can be found at www.afanet.org.

Joint Aviation Authority (JAA)

The Joint Aviation Authority represents the civil aviation regulatory authorities of various European States. It is associated with the European Civil Aviation Conference (ECAC). The purpose of the JAA is to develop and implement common aviation standards and procedures. Further information about the JAA and its programs can be found at its web site at www.jaa.nl/index.html.

International Air Transport Association (IATA)

The International Air Transport Association is a global trade organization that represents almost 260 airlines. IATA publishes the "Technical Instructions for the Safe Transportation of Dangerous Goods by Air". Information about IATA and its activities can be found on its web site at www.iata.org.

International Civil Aviation Organization (ICAO)

The International Civil Aviation Organization is a component of the United Nations. Its mission is to develop and adopt standards and approved practices for international civil aviation that relate to ARFF, air navigation, unlawful interference of air traffic, and border-crossing procedures. Similar to the FAA, ICAO publishes information and recommendations regarding required numbers of ARFF vehicles, agent quantities, response times, and other ARFF related operations. Further information about the ICAO can be found at its web site at www.icao.int.

Air Accident Investigations Branch (AAIB)

The Air Accident Investigations Branch is part of the United Kingdom's Department of Transport. The AAIB investigates civil aircraft accidents and other serious incidents within the United Kingdom. Additional information about the AAIB and its programs can be found at its web site at www.aaib.dft.gov.uk/home/index.cfm.

United Kingdom (UK) Civil Aviation Authority (CAA)

The Civil Aviation Authority is the United Kingdom's regulatory authority for aviation. The CAA is responsible for regulating all UK civil aviation functions to include airspace policy, safety regulations, economic regulation, and consumer protection. Information about the CAA and its activities can be found on its web site at www.caa.co.uk.

Transport Canada (TC)

Transport Canada is an organization that is similar to the United States NTSB. TC is responsible for establishing transportation policies, programs, and goals pertaining to air, marine, rail, road, emergency response, and accident investigation as determined by the Government of Canada. The TC web site contains information similar to the NTSB web site. http://www.tc.gc.ca/en/menu.htm.

International Aviation Fire Protection Association (IAFPA)

The International Aviation Fire Protection Association was formed in 2000 by a group of airport/municipal fire service professionals and industry specialists. It serves as a professional and fraternal association of international airport, municipal, and military fire and emergency services professionals. The IAFPA promotes the exchange of information, study, and improvement of aircraft rescue fire fighting and airport facility fire protection. IAFPA publishes a digital magazine several times a year that has a wealth of ARFF related reports and information. Every year, the IAFPA also conducts several conferences and training activities at various international locations. Further information on the IAFPA can be found on the Internet at www.iafpa.org.uk

Aircraft Rescue and Fire Fighting Working Group (ARFFWG)

The ARFFWG is a non-profit international organization dedicated to the sharing of aircraft rescue and fire fighting information between airport firefighters, municipal fire departments, and all others concerned with aircraft fire fighting. ARFFWG is comprised of ARFF professionals from around the world. The ARFFWG is very involved in many government, industry, and private committees and projects, where ARFF is an issue. ARFFWG publishes ARFF News and have a video lending library, as well as conduct regional and annual training conferences. Like the IAFPA, the ARFFWG is an excellent networking opportunity. Additional information about the ARFFWG and different membership options and benefits can be found at www.arffwg.org.

Aircraft Manufacturers

Aircraft manufacturer's websites provide excellent information about aircraft including aircraft "Crash Charts" designed to outline the basic information ARFF responders need to know relating to specific models of aircraft. A complete list of all the aircraft manufacturers in the world and associated web links is available at http://en.wikipedia.org/List_of_aircraft_manufacturers.

American Association of Airport Executives (AAAE)

The AAAE is a professional organization for airport management. The AAAE offers or co-sponsors emergency response and ARFF related training conferences. ARFF training lesson plans, images, videos, power point presentations, and other information can be downloaded from their website. AAAE utilizes Airport News and Training Network (ANTN), which has many programs directed at or of interest to ARFF personnel. Airports that are a member of ANTN get continuous programming via satellite. The individual programs can also be purchased in a video or digital format. Information from the AAAE can be accessed at their website at www.aaae.org.

Other Relevant Organizations

For a membership fee, the Aviation Fire Journal (AFJ) offers a bi-monthly, digital magazine with ARFF related articles, aircraft accident case studies, ARFF department profiles, and other information. The AFJ also distributes all the aircraft incident related information via email from the various news media wire services in the form of the Air Crash Rescue News. For additional information access AFJ at, www.aviationfirejournal.com.

AirDisaster.Com (www.airdisaster.com) offers reports on recent aviation disasters, thousands of downloadable images of past aircraft accidents, cockpit voice recorder transcripts and recordings.

The Aircraft Owners and Pilots Association (AOPA) Flight Safety Foundation offers aircraft accident data bases and statistics, annual overviews of accident statistics and trends (Nall Report), featured monthly accident case studies, and aviation related web links. AOPA can be contacted at www.aopa.org/asf/.

AirSafe.com (www.AirSafe.com) offers information on aviation accidents and fatal events by aircraft and region. It provides safety information regarding U.S. airline fleets, as well as data analysis, air safety links, personal safety, and aviation safety.

Entry Level Requirements

The National Fire Protection Association identifies the job performance requirements for airport firefighters in NFPA® 1003, *Standard for Airport Fire Fighter Professional Qualifications*. Other regulations pertinent to ARFF firefighters include those from the Department of Transportation (DOT), the Code of Federal Regulations (CFR), Title 14, Part 139, *Certification and Operations: Land Airports Serving Certain Air Carriers* (commonly referred to as Federal Aviation Regulation [FAR] Part 139 or 14 CFR Part 139), and the International Civil Aviation Organization (ICAO) *Airport Services Manual*, Part 1, Chapter 14. When possible, training programs also should conform to the applicable recommendations of pertinent Federal Aviation Administration (FAA) Advisory Circulars (AC). ACs are not requirements but rather suggested or recommended guidelines.

Before candidates are accepted into ARFF training programs for aircraft rescue and fire fighting, they must meet certain basic entrance requirements to be in compliance with NFPA® 1003. General requirements of this standard specify that every candidate must:

- Meet the minimum educational requirements established by the AHJ
- Meet the age requirements established by the AHJ
- Meet the medical requirements of NFPA® 1582, Standard on Medical Requirements for Fire Fighters or of the AHJ

In addition, prospective ARFF personnel need to be in good health and physically fit to perform adequately as airport firefighters. The authority having jurisdiction (AHJ) shall develop and validate physical fitness requirements that meet appropriate legal standards. According to NFPA® 1003, before being certified as an ARFF firefighter the candidate must also be certified as a Fire Fighter I and II in accordance with NFPA® 1001, *Standard for Fire Fighter Professional Qualifications*, to include meeting the appropriate training and certifications required in NFPA® 472, *Standard for Competence of Responders to Hazardous Materials/Weapons of Mass Destruction Incidents*

ARFF personnel may also have to respond to medical emergencies. These incidents can range from a single-person medical emergency to a multiple-casualty or mass-casualty incident. Therefore, it is important for ARFF personnel to have the appropriate emergency medical care training. The FAA requires at least one individual with a minimum of 40 hours of emergency medical care training be available during air carrier operations. The AHJ may choose to exceed this requirement.

When dealing with a large number of victims, ARFF personnel should utilize a rapid assessment and triage system and be familiar with the parameters necessary to treat and transport multiple victims. When working in this environment, firefighters may be at risk for exposure to blood, bodily fluids, and other potential infectious materials (OPIM). People infected with diseases and viruses such as hepatitis and HIV create contamination concerns for emergency personnel. Subsequently, ARFF personnel must also know the techniques for

Department of Transportation (DOT) — Administrative body of the executive branch of the state/provincial or federal government responsible for transportation policy, regulation, and enforcement.

Authority Having Jurisdiction — Term used in codes and standards to identify the legal entity, such as a building or fire official, that has the statutory authority to enforce a code and to approve or require equipment. In the insurance industry it may refer to an insurance rating bureau or an insurance company inspection department.

protection from related biohazards. More information concerning emergency medical care is given in the IFSTA/Brady Fire Service First Responder and Fire Service Emergency Care manuals.

ARFF Training Programs

Airport firefighters need to understand the causes of aircraft accidents and incidents, factors contributing to accidents/incidents, and mitigation of those conditions. Through practical exercises ARFF personnel should learn to operate apparatus and equipment and use them to their fullest potential.

A comprehensive training program for ARFF personnel — whether assigned to an airport or another type of station that supports ARFF operations, including mutual aid agreements, — is critically important to a firefighter's effectiveness in dealing with aircraft emergencies. Only through pre-incident training can firefighters reduce the likelihood of making costly mistakes during aircraft accidents/incidents **(Figure 1.3)**. High-quality continuing education and training enable ARFF personnel to acquire and maintain the knowledge, skills, and abilities essential for them to fulfill their mission safely. NFPA® 405, *Recommended Practice for the Recurring Proficiency Training of Aircraft Rescue and Fire-Fighting Services*, contains the recommended performance criteria for maintaining proficiency and effective aircraft rescue and fire fighting services.

In many cases, airline companies and other airport agencies are willing to participate in and provide resources for ARFF training activities. There are several types of training an ARFF firefighter may receive:

- *Cadet (recruit) training* — Initial training received prior to being assigned to a company

- *On-the-job training* — Learning while performing the day-to-day work requirements under supervision of more experienced firefighters

Figure 1.3 ARFF personnel during a live fire training evolution.

- *In-service training* — Proficiency training such as classroom study, hands-on skills exercises, and live fire drills conducted within the firefighter's own fire department
- *Special courses and seminars* — Extension programs, conferences, short courses, workshops, correspondence courses, or programs in recognized professional schools

Firefighters are not limited to any one of these types of training. In fact, firefighters are apt to be more successful if they participate in more than one of these.

ARFF Training Requirements

Aircraft rescue and firefighting personnel must meet the requirements of Fire Fighter II as defined in NFPA® 1001. They also must meet the requirements of first responder operational level as defined in NFPA® 472 and the job performance requirements of NFPA® 1003. The requirements contained in NFPA® 1003 are divided into three major duties: response, fire suppression, and rescue. These duties, along with those specified in FAR Part 139 and in ICAO *Airport Services Manual*, Part 1, Chapter 14, require that the airport firefighter be able to demonstrate knowledge and skills in the following subjects:

- Airport familiarization
- Aircraft familiarization
- Safety and Aircraft Hazards
- Communications
- Extinguishing Agents
- Apparatus
- Rescue Tools and Equipment
- Driver/Operator
- Incident Management
- Airport Emergency Plans
- Strategic and Tactical Operations

The remainder of this chapter provides a brief overview of these subjects. Each of these topics is discussed extensively in the subsequent chapters.

Airport Familiarization

Firefighters can begin learning about their airport through training classes and by studying the overall layout of the airfield on grid maps. However, classroom training and looking at maps alone do not provide all the necessary information. A firefighter must physically tour the airport grounds and learn the airport features, including the following:

- Control tower
- Runway layout
- Vehicle standby positions
- Critical instrument landing system (ILS) areas
- Airport buildings and hangers
- Maintenance and storage facilities

Mutual Aid — Reciprocal assistance from a neighboring fire and emergency services agency to another during an emergency based upon a prearrangement between agencies involved and generally made upon the request of the receiving agency.

Response — Call to respond.

Fire Suppression — All work and activities connected with fire extinguishing operations, beginning with discovery and continuing until a fire is completely extinguished.

Rescue — Saving a life from fire or accident; removing a victim from an untenable or unhealthy atmosphere.

Instrument Landing System (ILS) — Electronic navigation system that allows aircraft to approach and land during inclement weather conditions.

- Drainage systems
- Water distribution systems

An airport firefighter must also be able to identify airport structures and terrain features that may affect, limit, or prevent the response capabilities of ARFF vehicles or that may present a hazard to vehicles responding to accidents or incidents on the airfield. When responding to aircraft emergencies away from the airport, ARFF vehicles may be required to depart the airport through other-than-normal exits or areas. Therefore, personnel must know the locations of emergency exit access as well.

Airport firefighters should also be familiar with systems used to identify runways and taxiways. Because there are so many activities occurring simultaneously at an airport, there must be a way of managing vehicle and aircraft movements. Traffic-flow procedures, airport pavement marking and signing systems maintain vehicular and aircraft control.

All airports have target hazard areas that an airport firefighter must be able to identify. These include the following:

- Fuel storage and distribution systems
- Terminals
- Baggage areas
- Parking structures
- Hangars
- Transportation systems
- Aircraft maintenance facilities **(Figure 1.4)**
- Dangerous goods storage and handling areas

When involved in an emergency, aircraft carrying hazardous materials/ dangerous goods may be directed to a predetermined designated isolation area on the airfield. The airport firefighter must know these locations and the response routes to them in accordance with ARFF and or Airport Operations Area (AOA) policies and directives.

The need for security at an airport is the responsibility of all airport employees, especially in today's environment of terrorism. At some airports, performing security duties is part of a firefighter's job. Therefore, firefighters must be familiar with the rules and regulations governing security on their airport.

Figure 1.4 Aircraft maintenance hangars can provide a wide range of hazards.

Aircraft Familiarization

Airport firefighters must be familiar with the types of aircraft using their airport so that they can plan for specific hazards and prepare to mitigate such situations. They must also be familiar with aircraft construction features and materials as they relate to forcible entry, rescue, and fire fighting operations.

An airport firefighter must be able to identify the aircrew, passenger locations, and capacity for each type of aircraft using the airport. ARFF personnel must also be able to locate and operate normal entry and service doors, emergency exit openings, cargo and avionic compartment openings, access to concealed spaces, and escape systems and evacuation slides of each aircraft. When normal entry is not feasible, a firefighter must be able to locate and gain entry through forcible entry points on the aircraft. For military aircraft, it is important to be familiar with canopy and seat-ejection systems as well as weapons and explosive devices.

A firefighter must be familiar with the types of aircraft components and the systems found on aircraft at their airport. These include:

- Aircraft construction and construction materials
- Engines
- Shutdown procedures
- Fuel systems
- Oxygen systems
- Hydraulic systems
- Electrical systems
- Fire protection systems
- Auxiliary power units (APU)
- Aircraft radar systems
- Landing gear, brake systems and wheel assemblies
- Lavatory and waste systems and waste

ARFF personnel should be able to identify the flight data recorder (FDR) and cockpit voice recorder found in aircraft. Both the digital flight data recorder (DFDR) and cockpit voice recorder (CVR) assist in the investigation of the accident, and are key items for the investigation authorities **(Figure 1.5 a and b)**. Firefighters should know the procedures to follow upon locating these devices to guard them against further damage.

Canopy —Transparent enclosure over the cockpit of some aircraft .

Flight Data Recorder (FDR) — Recording device on large civilian aircraft to record aircraft airspeed, altitude, heading, acceleration, etc., to be used as an aid to accident investigation.

Digital Flight Data Recorder (DFDR) — Digital recording device on large civilian aircraft to record aircraft airspeed, altitude, heading, acceleration, etc., to be used as an aid to accident investigation; commonly referred to as the "black box".

Cockpit Voice Recorder — Recording device installed in most large civilian aircraft to record crew conversation and communications and is intended to assist in an accident investigation to determine probable cause of the accident.

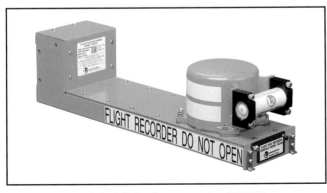

Figure 1.5a A digital flight data recorder (DFDR).
Courtesy of L3 Communications Aviation Recorders.

Figure 1.5b A cockpit voice recorder (CVR).
Courtesy of L3 Communications Aviation Recorders.

Safety and Aircraft Hazards

The airport firefighter faces many real and potential hazards in and around aircraft accidents/incidents. Although an aircraft incident may not always involve a fire, a firefighter must be aware of other hazards associated with the aircraft. ARFF personnel must understand the effects that hazards such as burning fuel, toxic smoke, aircraft wreckage, and biohazards pose to themselves, the victims of the accident, and the fire fighting equipment. ARFF personnel should focus on the aircraft cabin doors and emergency exits as a means to remove trapped occupants.

Figure 1.6 Because of the dangers of fighting aircraft fires, ARFF personnel should wear proper protective clothing and self-contained breathing apparatus (SCBA).

The environment in which airport firefighters must work requires that they be provided with approved personal protective equipment (PPE). Proper training in the use of protective clothing and positive-pressure self-contained breathing apparatus (SCBA) is mandatory **(Figure 1.6)**. Just as important as knowing how to don and use protective equipment is understanding its limitations and being able to identify common hazardous respiratory environments. Firefighters should train in SCBA use in low visibility environments and should be able to demonstrate breathing techniques used under emergency conditions, including assisting other firefighters, conserving air, and using the bypass valve. The firefighter should also be able to maintain, clean, inspect, and reservice breathing apparatus.

Finally, traumatic injuries suffered by the victims in aviation related accidents can be extremely gruesome and horrific. The department should have in place a critical incident stress management (CISM) program to mitigate the effects stress imposes on response personnel during and after these incidents. Also, ARFF personnel must be aware of the assistance available to them to help cope with the results of post-incident stress.

Communications

The expedient and accurate handling of fire alarms or aircraft emergency notifications is a significant factor in the successful outcome of any incident. Aircraft rescue and fire fighting communications include notifications of emergencies sent to the telecommunications center (communications center), notifications by the center to the proper, fire fighting forces, and information exchanged at the scene. ARFF personnel must be able to identify the procedures for receiving single and multiple alarms and know how to use the alarm-receiving equipment housed in the communications center.

Mutual aid agreements may be necessary for certain responses. The airport firefighter must know the procedures for notifying and requesting these

Critical Incident Stress Debriefing (CISD) — Counseling designed to minimize the effects of psychological/emotional post-incident trauma on those at fire and rescue incidents who were directly involved with victims suffering from particularly gruesome or horrific injuries.

Critical Incident Stress Management (CISM) — A comprehensive crisis intervention system composed of 7 elements: pre-crisis preparation, a disaster or large scale incident, defusing, critical incident stress debriefing, one-on-one crisis intervention/counseling, family/organizational crisis intervention, and follow-up/referral mechanisms. (http://www.icisf.org/inew_era.htm)

resources. Mutual aid companies may use radio frequencies that are different from those of the airport fire department so the firefighter must be able to identify these radio frequencies as well. A predetermined communication plan is highly desirable to interact with outside resources.

ARFF vehicles responding to an emergency site may require clearance from the control tower to proceed into or through certain areas of the airport. Once on the scene, ARFF personnel must be able to provide an initial status report and may, at times, communicate directly with the flight crew of the emergency aircraft. ARFF personnel should understand how to use the aircraft flight and service interphone system. All ARFF personnel must be able to use and understand hand signals for aircraft rescue and fire fighting, in order to communicate with aircraft crewmembers as well as with other firefighters **(Figure 1.7)**. Airport firefighters should know hand signals for marshalling and parking aircraft and for communicating with aircraft crew members.

Extinguishing Agents

An airport firefighter may come into contact with fires involving many types of combustible materials: seat coverings inside the passenger compartment, exotic metals in engine assemblies, the aircraft's hydrocarbon fuels and onboard oxygen systems, and others. Depending upon the material burning and the size and location of the fire, different situations may require different types of extinguishing agents, application techniques, devices, and equipment. Understanding the classifications of fire is important to a firefighter because each class has its own extinguishing agents and techniques.

Apparatus

An airport fire department may have many different types of apparatus, each of which carry fire suppression systems and extinguishing agents; hoses, nozzles, and accessory fittings; and a wide variety of rescue tools and equipment. ARFF personnel should be trained to activate the fire suppression systems and use an assortment of turrets, handlines, and extending/elevating waterways. A firefighter must be able to identify each hose, nozzle, and adapter, know the purpose of each, and know their location on ARFF apparatus. They also must be familiar with how to deploy and utilize various tools and equipment for effective fire fighting. Airport firefighters must be totally familiar with all aspects of operating the ARFF vehicles at their airport **(Figure 1.8)**.

Figure 1.7 An ARFF firefighter giving hand signals during a training evolution.

Figure 1.8 An ARFF apparatus driver/operator practicing aircraft approach techniques.

ARFF apparatus are designed to deliver mass quantities of fire fighting agents, but they have a limited capacity. Therefore, agent application, conservation, and management are important to successful ARFF operations. When ARFF vehicles deplete their agent supply, they must be able to refill as quickly as possible. Firefighters must be capable of establishing a resupply point using hydrants, other static water supplies, and/or water tenders (tankers).

Rescue Tools and Equipment

A variety of tools and equipment is available for gaining access into an aircraft and rescuing its occupants. Which tools are actually needed depend on the type of aircraft, its position, and the skills of the ARFF personnel. Understanding the limitations, safety considerations, operational characteristics, and capabilities of all available tools will assist the firefighter in selecting the right tool or piece of equipment for the job. A complete and thorough understanding of the basic types of tools used in aircraft rescue and fire fighting also ensures that the firefighter can perform when needed. Forcible entry is a learned skill that begins with a thorough knowledge of aircraft construction, interior arrangement, systems, and materials **(Figure 1.9)**. Firefighters must remain current on the construction features of aircraft and the locations and operating features of doors, hatches, and windows. Emphasis should be placed on utilizing all available aircraft exits to remove passengers when ARFF personnel respond to a crashed aircraft.

When airport firefighters cannot gain access into an aircraft because the normal means of access have been compromised, locked, or blocked, they must force entry. Selection and use of the appropriate tools is imperative to gain access into an aircraft. ARFF personnel may have to use rescue tools once inside to disentangle and extricate trapped occupants from interior wreckage and collapsed fuselage sections. Caution must be exercised in utilizing power tools, and or friction (non ferrous tools) causing machinery to avoid a possible interior/exterior ignition.

Driver/Operator

The fire apparatus driver/operator is responsible for safely transporting firefighters, apparatus, and equipment to and from the scene of an emergency or other call for service. They must be thoroughly and regularly trained in driving in all the types of terrain, weather, low visibility, and off road conditions

Figure 1.9 ARFF personnel practicing forcible entry techniques.

encountered on or around the airport. The driver/operator must also ensure that the apparatus and the equipment it carries are ready at all times.

In general, driver/operators must be mature, responsible, safety-conscious adults. Because of their wide array of responsibilities, often under stressful emergency situations, driver/operators must be able to maintain a calm, "can-do" attitude under pressure. Psychological profiles, drug and alcohol testing, and background investigations may be necessary to ensure that the driver/operator is ready to accept the high level of responsibility that comes with the job.

To perform their duties properly, all driver/operators must possess certain mental and physical skills. Not every firefighter is capable of becoming a driver/operator. The required levels of these skills are usually determined by each jurisdiction. NFPA® 1002, *Standard for Fire Apparatus Driver/Operator Professional Qualifications*, sets minimum qualifications for ARFF vehicle driver/operators in addition to those already set forth in NFPA® 1003.

Fire apparatus must always be ready to respond. Regardless of whether the truck responds to an emergency call once an hour or once a month, it must be capable of performing in the manner for which it was designed at a moment's notice. In order to ensure this, certain preventive maintenance functions must be performed on a regular basis. Performing routine maintenance checks can prevent most apparatus or equipment failures and in most fire departments it is a requirement for driver/operators to perform these checks.

Airport Emergency Plans

A plan of operation should be created so that appropriate procedures can be developed and resource needs identified before aircraft accidents/incidents occur. Such a plan addresses the need for a coordinated and structured response to emergency situations within the local jurisdiction. The plan should be as complete and detailed as necessary to ensure that all involved agencies are aware of their roles and responsibilities under various conditions.

Incident Management

To ensure safe and effective aircraft rescue and fire fighting operations, ARFF personnel must understand and use an incident command system (ICS) for all drills, exercises, and daily operations. The National Incident Management System - Incident Command System is the prescribed system for use in the United States. NIMS-ICS is a system of procedures for controlling personnel, structures, equipment, and communications so that all responders can work together toward a common goal in an effective and efficient manner. NIMS-ICS is designed to be applicable to all incidents. Such organization is extremely important because the airport fire department's work often involves life-threatening situations and working with other agencies. Thus, any lapse in organization could have serious consequences for victims and firefighters alike.

Strategic and Tactical Operations

Airport firefighters should know standard operating procedures (SOPs) as they relate to aircraft emergencies. This is necessary to select strategies and tactics for controlling the emergency and bringing it to a successful conclusion. Emphasis should be targeted at assisting occupants from the aircraft while utilizing all available means to complete this task.

Strategy — Overall plan for incident attack and control established by the incident commander.

Tactics — Methods of employing equipment and personnel on an incident to accomplish specific tactical objectives in order to achieve established strategic goals.

Standard Operating Procedures (SOPs) — Standard methods or rules in which an organization or a fire department operates to carry out a routine function. Usually these procedures are written in a policies and procedures handbook and all firefighters should be well versed in their content. A SOP may specify the functional limitations of fire brigade members in performing emergency operations.

Because tactical operations must be implemented quickly, pre-emergency decisions are best made in the training room with the understanding that they can be adjusted as needed on the fire ground. Many of the emergency scenarios ARFF personnel will encounter can be preplanned prior to an incident. It is important that ARFF departments research, develop, and implement standard operating procedures to minimize confusion on an incident scene.

ARFF personnel also need to be skilled in basic assessment procedures. Early recognition of the need for mutual aid assistance, as well as the speedy requesting, and responding of needed off airport resources is critical. The success or failure of the emergency can be determined in the first minutes of the response **(Figure 1.10)**. Tactical decisions regarding approach and setup must be made during the initial response. Standard Emergency Response Plans (SERPs) are a good starting point or blueprint to work from. SERPs help organize and coordinate multi agencies response to assure everyone is on the same page. Airport firefighters also need to know how to adapt and use structural rescue and firefighting equipment for ARFF applications. Furthermore, ARFF personnel must include tactics for aircraft evacuation when assessing an emergency.

Figure 1.10 Rapid application of fire fighting agents during an aircraft fire is critical to saving the lives of aircraft passengers and crew. Here, ARFF driver/operators practice agent application techniques.

The success or failure of a fire fighting team often depends upon the skill and knowledge of the personnel involved in initial attack operations. A well-trained team of firefighters with an attack plan and an adequate amount of extinguishing agent, properly applied, can contain most fires in their early stages. Failure to make a well-coordinated attack on a fire may allow the fire to gain headway and burn out of control.

Summary

ARFF personnel must be highly trained and prepared to provide aircraft rescue and fire fighting capability at airports around the world. These personnel should be familiar with the various organizations that are relevant to the ARFF mission as well as the basic requirements and training necessary for becoming an ARFF firefighter. This chapter discussed a variety of relevant organizations within the United States as well as those from other countries. It outlined the basic entry requirements for ARFF personnel found in such NFPA° standards as 1002, 1003, and others. It also identified the specific topics that personnel must be trained and certified in to become ARFF firefighters.

Review Questions

1. Which NFPA° standard was the first to address aircraft rescue and fire fighting services?

2. What is the responsibility of the Transportation Security Administration (TSA)?

3. List several basic requirements for aircraft rescue and fire fighting personnel.

4. What is in-service training?

5. What are some target hazard areas with which an airport firefighter must be familiar?

6. What is a digital flight data recorder (DFDR)?

7. What is automatic aid?

8. Why is fire fighting agent application, conservation, and management important to successful operations?

9. Who is responsible for making sure that the fire apparatus and the equipment it carries are prepared?

10. What is the purpose of a Standard Emergency Response Plan (SERP)?

Airport Familiarization

Chapter Contents

Divider page photo courtesy of DFW International Airport - ITS/GIS Department

Key Terms

NFPA® references for Chapter 2:

NFPA® 1003 (2010)
5.1.1.3
5.2.1
5.2.2

**NFPA® 1002
(2009 - Chapter 9)**
9.1.2
9.1.3
9.2.2
9.2.3

Federal Aviation Regulations (FAR):

139.319(a)
139.319(b)

139.319(c)
139.319(d)

Airport Familiarization

Learning Objectives

After reading this chapter, students shall be able to:

1. Discuss the two basic types of airports. (NFPA® 1003, 5.2.1, 5.2.2)

2. Describe various airport traffic patterns. (NFPA® 1003, 5.2.1, 5.2.2)

3. Explain airport runway and taxiway designation systems. (NFPA® 1003, 5.2.1, 5.2.2)

4. Discuss airport lighting, marking, and signage systems. (NFPA® 1003, 5.2.1, 5.2.2)

5. Explain airport design. (NFPA® 1003, 5.1.1.3, 5.2.1, 5.2.2, 5.2.4)

6. Discuss ARFF fire stations.

Chapter 2
Airport Familiarization

Case History

At 23:50 hours on June 1, 1999, American Airlines Flight 1420 crashed 24 seconds after touching down at Little Rock National Airport in Little Rock, Arkansas. Severe thunderstorms with high winds and wind shears were passing through the Little Rock area that night. The aircraft, a McDonnell-Douglas DC-9-82, overran the departure end of runway 4R and struck part of the airport's instrument landing system (ILS) localizer array. It then penetrated the airport's perimeter chain link fence, crossed over a rocky embankment, and struck the support structure for runway 22L's approach lighting system. The aircraft broke apart and came to rest in a floodplain that was 15 feet (4.6 m) below the level of the runway. Eleven people were killed, 45 were seriously injured, and 65 received minor injuries.

Due to the bad weather, limited visibility, and miscommunications, ARFF crews had to search for the crash site prior to conducting fire fighting and rescue operations. The ARFF station was equipped and staffed with three apparatus and four firefighters. The limited visibility and unknown location of the aircraft resulted in the three apparatus driving slowly in search of the crash site. Direct access to the site was not possible, and the three apparatus had to backtrack to an access road and use the airport perimeter road to reach the crash site. Given the unfavorable conditions found during this accident, the crews' familiarity with the airport and its surroundings played a crucial role in their emergency response.

When responding to an aircraft emergency, airport familiarity allows responders to go anywhere on an airfield, during any kind of conditions, in the safest and quickest manner. Because fires involving aircraft may penetrate and/or spread through the fuselage quickly, the life-hazard potential in aircraft fires is tremendous. Nearby aircraft, equipment, and structures also may be exposed to the fire. Aircraft rescue and fire fighting (ARFF) units must be intimately familiar with airport layout and likely environmental conditions to be able to respond to the scene quickly.

While large airports may have one or more fire stations at the airport itself, many airports rely on both airport fire services and on local fire departments that surround the airport property through mutual aid/automatic agreements. Smaller airports may not have any on-airport fire service and may be served by surrounding fire departments or by multiple departments through mutual aid/automatic agreements.

Regardless of the responding department or size of the airport, emergency response personnel must be able to find their way quickly to any point on the airport — even at night or when visibility is reduced by inclement weather.

This includes using alternate response routes when the primary response routes are not available. ARFF personnel must be thoroughly familiar with the airport layout – particularly the runways and their numbering system, along with taxiways, roads, gates, fences, and geographical features peculiar to the airport. Understanding how runways are used will dictate to responders where aircraft will be taking-off, landing, or taxiing.

Familiarity with airport layout, driving regulations, and communications procedures is important not only to ARFF personnel but also to those firefighters assigned to nearby structural stations. At times, additional resources must be called to support the airport fire department. These responding units also must know how to reach the scene quickly and safely. Mutual aid training must address airport familiarization while making arrangements with the air traffic control (ATC) or airport operations for mutual/automatic aid personnel to drive vehicles on and around the airfield.

Fires in aircraft or associated equipment and facilities can be costly in both human and economic terms. Even if no injuries result, fire can destroy expensive property, impact airport employees' job security, affect airport suppliers, and seriously inconvenience the public. In addition to cultivating strong ARFF skills, it is important to practice good fire prevention techniques throughout all areas of the airport.

Types and Classifications of Airports

There are two basic types of airports: controlled and uncontrolled. Controlled airports have operating towers with air traffic controllers who manage aircraft movement both in the air and on the ground. Uncontrolled airports are those that do not have a staffed and operating control tower. Some airports may staff and operate their control tower only during specific times, such as during daylight hours, and be uncontrolled at night.

Airports are classified by various agencies such as the National Fire Protection Association (NFPA®), Federal Aviation Administration (FAA), International Civil Aviation Organization (ICAO), and Transport Canada (TC) in order to determine the level or index of fire protection needed **(Table 2.1)**. For example, the FAA classifies airports that are used by air carrier aircraft with seating for more than 10 passengers into different index categories. FAR Part 139.315, *Aircraft rescue and fire fighting: Index Determination,* states that the index is determined by a combination the length of air carrier aircraft (expressed in groups) and the average number of daily departures by air carrier aircraft. If there are five or more average daily departures of air carrier aircraft in a single Index group servicing that airport, then the Index of the group having the longest aircraft and an average of five or more daily departures is the Index required for the airport. If there are less than five average daily departures of air carrier aircraft in a single Index group servicing that airport, the next lower Index from the Index group with air carrier aircraft is the Index required for the airport. The minimum designated Index is Index A.

Additional guidance for determining FAA airport index requirements can be found in FAR Part 139.319, *Aircraft rescue and fire fighting: Operational Requirements.*

NFPA® and ICAO base their airport categories on the longest airplanes using the airport as well as on the fuselage width of these aircraft. ARFF per-

Table 2.1
Airport Categories and Indexes

FAA	ICAO	NFPA	TC	Length in ft (m)*	Width in ft (m)*
GA-1	1	1	1	30 (9)	6.6 (2)
GA-1	2	2	2	39 (12)	6.6 (2)
GA-2	3	3	3	59 (18)	9.8 (3)
A	4	4	4	78 (24)	13.0 (4)
A	5	5	5	90 (28)	13.0 (4)
B	6	6	6	126 (39)	16.4 (5)
C	7	7	7	160 (49)	16.4 (5)
D	8	8	8	200 (61)	23.0 (7)
E	9	9	9	250 (76)	23.0 (7)
--	--	--	10	At least 250 (76)	25.0 (8)
--	10	10	--	295 (90)	25.0 (8)

* Up to but not including...

NOTE: Information compiled from NFPA 414, Standard for Aircraft Rescue and Fire-Fighting Services at Airports; FAA 14 CFR 139.315, Certification Of Airports; ICAO Airport Services Manual, Part 1, Rescue and Fire Fighting; and Canadian Air Regulations (CAR) 303.05, Aircraft Category for Fire Fighting.

sonnel should work with the authority having jurisdiction (AHJ) to ensure the requirements affecting fire protection for the index system used at their airport are met.

Airport Traffic Patterns

Airport firefighters must understand the air traffic patterns within the vicinity of the airport. Unless otherwise directed by an air traffic controller, all aircraft entering the airport area must do so by flying a traffic pattern. When an aircraft declares an emergency, that aircraft is given priority and may not fly a traffic pattern but rather a straight-in or modified approach.

Airport firefighters who understand how aircraft enter the traffic pattern will know the aircraft's position in relation to the airport runway during inbound emergencies. The components of a typical traffic pattern include the following legs **(Figure 2.1, p. 32)**:

- *Crosswind leg* — flight path at right angles to the landing runway off its upwind leg

- *Downwind leg* — flight path parallel to the landing runway in the direction opposite to landing; normally extends between the crosswind leg and the base leg

- *Base leg* — flight path at a right angle to the landing runway off the approach end. The base leg normally extends from the downwind leg to the intersection of the extended runway line. The aircraft must make a 90-degree turn from the base leg before it can begin its final approach.

- *Final approach* — portion of the landing pattern in which the aircraft is lined up with the runway and is heading straight in to land

Traffic pattern — Traffic flow that is prescribed for aircraft landing or taking off from an airport.

Straight-in approach — Entry into the traffic pattern by interception of the extended runway centerline (final approach course) without executing any other portion of the traffic pattern.

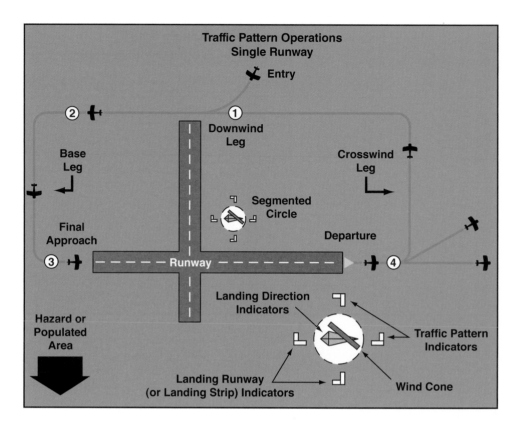

Figure 2.1 Typical aircraft traffic patterns.

Runway — Defined rectangular area on airports prepared for the takeoff or landing of aircraft along its length.

Vector — Compass heading or course followed by or to be followed by an aircraft.

Some airports operate on a straight-in approach pattern. Aircraft fly to a predetermined vector conduct a 90 degree turn which lines them up on for a straight-in landing. The direction that the wind is blowing should determine the vector and landing runway. Once an aircraft lands at the airport, it must move along designated routes to the passenger gate, cargo hangar, or maintenance areas. ARFF vehicles may use the same access routes as aircraft, so it is important that an airport firefighter know the meanings of runway and taxiway designation systems.

Runway and Taxiway Designation Systems

Aircraft take off and land facing into the wind. Therefore, runways are laid out to take advantage of the prevailing winds at that airport. Aircraft awaiting clearance for take-off may lineup on the taxiways near the downwind end of the runway. When the wind is light and not a critical factor, air traffic controllers may use several runways simultaneously to expedite the flow of traffic.

Runway numbers are taken from the nearest compass bearing (relative to magnetic north) rounded off to the nearest 10 degrees. Compass bearings start at north and run clockwise from 0 to 360 degrees. A runway with a compass heading of 340 degrees is numbered 34 for aircraft approaching from the south. The same runway is numbered 16 for aircraft approaching from the north because from that direction it has a compass bearing of 160 degrees. There is always a difference of 180 degrees between opposite ends of the same runway. When the number of the runway is 06 or 09, the number may have a bar placed underneath (06 or 09) to avoid confusion.

Letters, where required, distinguish among parallel runways. At most airports, parallel runways are designated by a number followed by L (left) and the same number followed by R (right) **(Figure 2.2).** For example, one set of parallel runways might be identified as 36L and 36R from the north and as 18L and 18R from the opposite end. If there are three parallel runways, they are identified in a similar fashion. In this case, however, the letter "C" is used to denote the "center" runway. Therefore, three parallel runways with a heading of 180 degrees would be labeled 18L, 18C, and 18R (for 18 Left, 18 Center, and 18 Right).

A runway will also have a "safety area" around it. The typical runway serving large jet aircraft is 150 feet wide. The safety area for this sized runway will usually extend 250 feet to each side of the runway centerline (500 feet wide) and 1,000 to 2,000 feet outward of the approach and departure ends. The ground in the safety area should support an aircraft should it veer off or overrun the runway.

Taxiways are specially designated and prepared surfaces on an airport for aircraft to taxi (travel) to and from runways, hangars, ramps, gates, etc. In simpler terms, they are the roadways for aircraft surface movement. Taxiways are required to be given an alphanumeric designation starting typically with A (Alpha), then taxiway Bravo, taxiway Charlie, and so on. The convention is to name principal taxiways first, such as those parallel to a runway, then to name the "stubs" and "feeders" with the taxiway they attach to. Principal taxiways are named first, then the "stubs" or "feeders" connected to that taxiway are named after it. For example, taxiway Alpha 1 attaches perpendicularly to taxiway Alpha, and the next similar taxiway is called Alpha 2. Taxiway designations are not standardized and are generally determined locally with assistance from the FAA Taxiways may be referred to as a "parallel taxiway" (parallel to a runway) or a "cross taxiway" (crosses a runway).

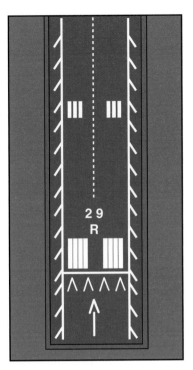

Figure 2.2 An example of runway identification markings.

Airport Lighting, Marking, and Signage Systems

In addition to runway numbers and taxiway identification systems, colored lights, markings, and signs are used to identify various areas, buildings, and obstructions at airports. ARFF personnel should understand the lights, markings, and signage systems used on their particular airport.

FAA Standards for Lighting, Marking, and Signage

The following FAA Advisory Circulars describe the minimum standards for airport lighting, marking, and signage systems:

— AC 150/5340-1J Standards for Airport Markings

— AC 150/5340-18D Standards for Airport Sign Systems

— AC 150/5340-30C Design and Installation Details for Airport Visual Aids

Surface Lighting

While taxiway designations may vary from airport to airport, runway and taxiway surface lighting is standard at all airports. Since these lights are controlled by ATC personnel, ARFF responders can request the intensity or brightness be adjusted depending on weather conditions. **Figure 2.3, p. 34** shows the various types of airport lights which are located as follows:

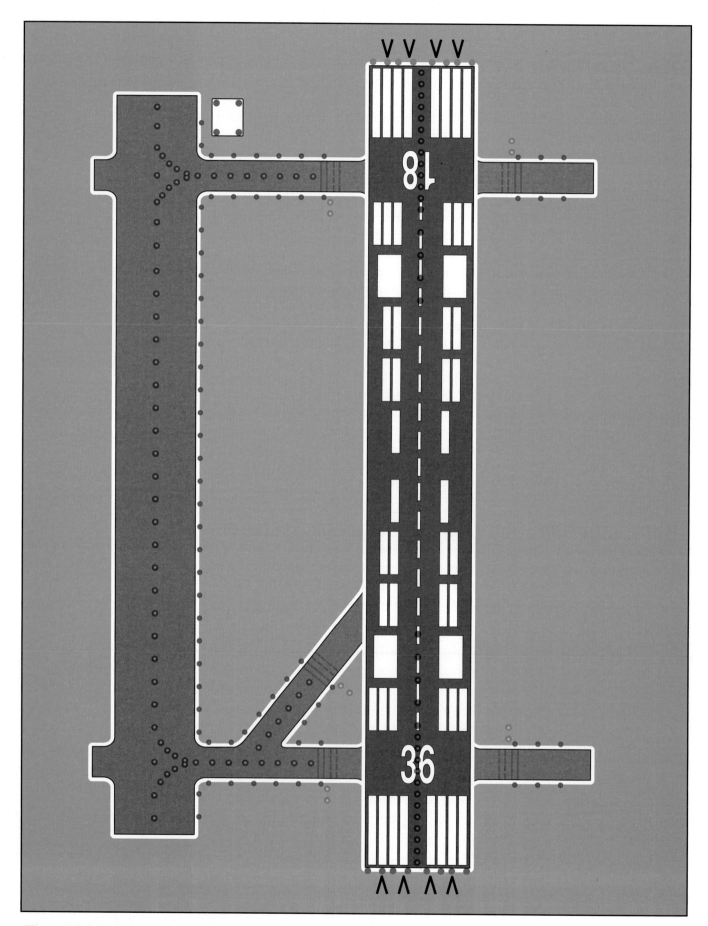

Figure 2.3 Colored lights are used to identify different areas of the runways and taxiways.

- *Blue lights* or reflective markers are used to outline taxiways, are usually located along the edges, and are spaced 100 feet (30 m) apart.

- *White lights* are used to outline the edges of runways and to identify runway centerlines. Outline lights are spaced every 200 feet (60 m); centerline lights are spaced every 50 feet (15 m). White lights are also used to denote vehicular traffic areas on ramps.

- *Green lights* are used to identify the approach end of runways and some taxiway centerlines.

> NOTE: Not all taxiways are required to have centerline lighting.

- *Red lights* are used to mark obstructions such as building structures, parked aircraft, unserviceable areas, construction work, and the departure end of the runway. Runway centerline lighting alternates red and white the last 3000 feet (914.4 m) and becomes all red the last 1000 feet (304.8 m).

- *Yellow or amber lights* are used to identify locations of hold bars, areas that can be crossed only with permission from the control tower. These lights are called "guard lights" that are placed on both sides of the hold lines. They are two sets of two flashing lights. Yellow and Amber lights also serve as runway edge lights for the last 2000 feet (609.6 m) at the departure end of the runway.

Markings

Colored markings are used at airports also. The three colors commonly used for airport markings are white, red, and yellow indicating the following:

- *White* is used for runway identification numbers/letters, landing zone bars, and striping.

- *Red* is used to designate restricted areas such as fire lanes and no-entry areas. Permission must be granted prior to crossing a red line into a restricted area.

- *Yellow* is used for hold bars, taxiways, and Instrument Landing System (ILS) critical areas. Yellow may also mark non-load-bearing surfaces.

Hold position markings (often called hold lines or hold bars) act like stop signs for all vehicles or aircraft using taxiways **(Figure 2.4)**. Hold position markings consist of four yellow lines — two solid and two dashed — which extend across the entire width of the taxiway. When approaching a hold position marking from the solid-line side, the vehicle or aircraft is required to stop until either visual clearance is confirmed (uncontrolled airports) or air traffic control (ATC) has approved further movement (controlled airports). When approached from the dashed-line side, the hold position marking is not applicable, and vehicles can cross immediately to the other side without obtaining clearance. Hold position markings are usually located on the edge of the runway safety area. Some airports require that dashed yellow taxiway lines be used to keep aircraft/vehicles out of these areas during inclement weather conditions. Unauthorized entry into a runway safety area can be considered the same as actually entering the runway.

Specialized hold position markings can be found in ILS critical areas usually located on taxiways that are near the end of the runway **(Figure 2.5, p. 36)**. The ILS sends signals to landing aircraft which indicate exact speed and location in relation to the runway. Vehicles parked in the ILS area may cause these signals

Ramp — area at airports intended to accommodate aircraft for purposes of loading or unloading passengers or cargo, refueling, parking, or maintenance.

Hold bar — Airport marker for areas on the airport ramp, taxiways, and runways that can be crossed only with permission from the control tower.

Figure 2.4 An example of Hold Position markings (also called hold lines or hold bars). *Courtesy of James Nilo.*

Figure 2.5 An example of ILS Area markings.
Courtesy of James Nilo.

to be obstructed, which may cause the landing aircraft to receive inaccurate information from the ground.

A taxiway has a single, continuous yellow centerline along its length. A dashed taxiway line will be used showing the pilot that they are approaching a runway when operating in inclement weather or foggy conditions. A double continuous yellow line may be used to show the location of the taxiway edge.

Runways sometimes have areas that are not suitable or legal for takeoff and landing. Often referred to as "special-purpose areas," their markings indicate their purpose and associated restrictions. The most common of these areas is the displaced threshold, which is indicated by a solid white line across the runway. This line is where the runway officially begins and is followed by either the runway number or eight threshold markers. If there are white arrows pointing at the displaced threshold line, the preceding paved area can be used for taxi, takeoff, and rollout. If the area is not suitable for aircraft operations, it is marked with yellow chevrons. Extra pavement areas are often provided to

Threshold — Beginning or end of a runway that is usable for landing or takeoff.

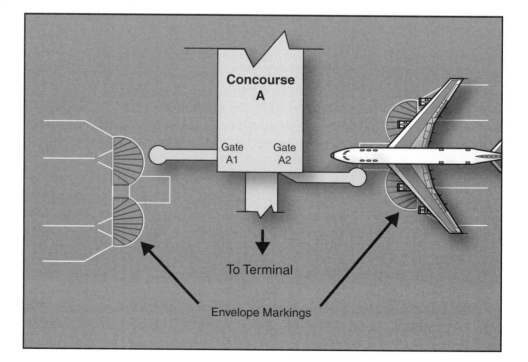

Figure 2.6 Examples of Envelope Area markings.

allow jet blast to dissipate and for overruns during aborted takeoffs. A painted or lighted "X" on a runway or taxiway means that runway or taxiway is closed to aircraft and vehicle operations.

Red and white lines are used to designate an "envelope" **(Figure 2.6)**. This is an area on a ramp or at a gate or jetway, indicating the area that will be occupied by a parked aircraft. Avoid blocking, parking inside, or too close to an envelope with an ARFF vehicle.

Vehicle roadway zipper markings are used to delineate the edge or edges of certain roadways that are located on or cross areas that are also used by aircraft. Zipper markings use two side-by-side alternating dashed white lines to define the edge of the vehicle roadway. Since zipper markings indicate that you are driving on an aircraft maneuvering area, no driver may proceed through a zipper marked roadway without first stopping their vehicle at the mandatory stop sign and yielding to all moving aircraft **(Figure 2.7)**.

Figure 2.7 An example of Vehicle Roadway Zipper markings.

Signs

Airport firefighters must be able to identify and understand the various signs that are unique to airport operations. Descriptions of the signs used at airports include the following **(Figure 2.8, p. 38)**:

- *Mandatory instruction signs* provide instructions that must be obeyed They include identification of holding positions, runway intersections, ILS critical areas, runway approach, and entry signs.

- *Runway hold position signs* have white inscriptions on a red background. **(White on red - stop ahead.)**

- *Location signs* identify runways or taxiways and other specific locations on the airport. A location sign has a yellow inscription on a black back ground. **(Yellow on black - tell where you're at!)**

- *Direction signs* identify the direction of taxiways leading out from an intersection. They have black inscriptions on yellow backgrounds. **(Black on yellow - tell a fellow.)**

- *Destination signs* indicate destinations such as runways, terminals, and cargo areas on the airport. Like direction signs, destination signs have black inscriptions on a yellow background. **(Black on yellow - tell a fellow.)**

Figure 2.8 Examples of various airport signs and their meanings.

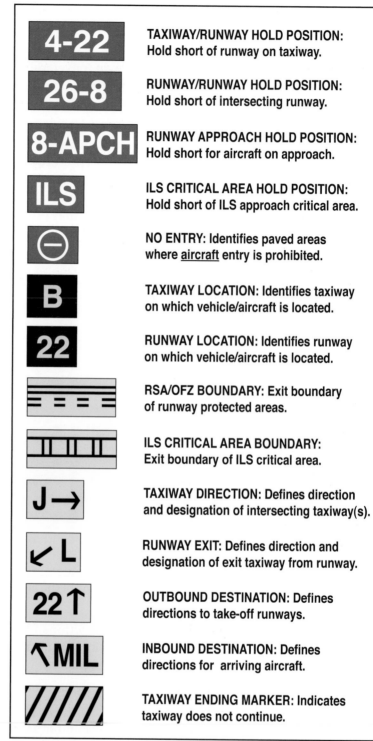

4-22	**TAXIWAY/RUNWAY HOLD POSITION:** Hold short of runway on taxiway.
26-8	**RUNWAY/RUNWAY HOLD POSITION:** Hold short of intersecting runway.
8-APCH	**RUNWAY APPROACH HOLD POSITION:** Hold short for aircraft on approach.
ILS	**ILS CRITICAL AREA HOLD POSITION:** Hold short of ILS approach critical area.
⊖	**NO ENTRY:** Identifies paved areas where <u>aircraft</u> entry is prohibited.
B	**TAXIWAY LOCATION:** Identifies taxiway on which vehicle/aircraft is located.
22	**RUNWAY LOCATION:** Identifies runway on which vehicle/aircraft is located.
≡≡≡≡	**RSA/OFZ BOUNDARY:** Exit boundary of runway protected areas.
⫿⫿⫿	**ILS CRITICAL AREA BOUNDARY:** Exit boundary of ILS critical area.
J→	**TAXIWAY DIRECTION:** Defines direction and designation of intersecting taxiway(s).
↙L	**RUNWAY EXIT:** Defines direction and designation of exit taxiway from runway.
22↑	**OUTBOUND DESTINATION:** Defines directions to take-off runways.
↖MIL	**INBOUND DESTINATION:** Defines directions for arriving aircraft.
///////	**TAXIWAY ENDING MARKER:** Indicates taxiway does not continue.

- *Information signs* provide pilots with information such as applicable radio frequencies or noise-abatement procedures. These signs have yellow backgrounds with black inscriptions.

- *Runway distance remaining signs* indicate the distance of runway remaining. The number displayed, in thousand-foot increments (304.8 meter increments) represents how many feet (meters) of runway is left before the threshold. A white number — for example, a "4" — on a black background indicates that there is 4000 feet (1 219.2 meters) of remaining runway.

Other signs seen around the runway include communication frequency signs, which indicate the frequency for pilots to talk to ground control, and noise restriction signs, which indicate the times when aircraft must operate in reduced power settings to assist in eliminating noise. Airports also have typical roadway signs seen on highways and roads. They are used on the airport where roads may intersect taxiways or runway approach areas.

Airport Design

The airport layout is the key factor in determining the most appropriate response route for ARFF vehicles. To become familiar with airport design and layout, firefighters must become familiar with the following systems, resources, and locations:

- Segmented circle
- Grid maps
- Airport topography
- Structures
- On-airport navigation aids
- Roads and bridges
- Runways
- Airport ramps
- Controlled access points
- Fences and gates
- Designated isolation areas
- Water supply
- Fuel storage and distribution
- Airport drainage systems

Segmented Circle

The segmented circle is an airport marker system that is often located in the center of the airport. It is illuminated by lights at night and usually contains a windsock. Traffic pattern indicators extend outward from the circle and identify the appropriate landing pattern for that airport.

Grid Maps

Grid maps are important when planning emergency response routes. ARFF and airport support personnel use these maps to identify ground locations. It is important that mutual aid departments understand how to read grid maps and be familiar with the grid maps of the airports they respond to.

Grid maps are marked either using rectangular coordinates or by referring to azimuth bearings. They may be standard maps, large-scale commercial maps, or modified outline maps. Whatever the type of map used, the grid map should include an area encompassing the emergency response area outside the airport.

In addition to the marked coordinates used with the grid system, these maps should include traffic patterns and control zones. NFPA® 403, *Standard*

> **WARNING!**
> Understand that aircraft ALWAYS have the right-of-way, unless directed otherwise by Air Traffic Control Tower personnel. ARFF apparatus drivers failing to understand or obey airport ground lighting, markings, and signs can lead to accidents on the airport as well as runway incursions.

Incursion — any occurrence in the airport runway environment involving an aircraft, vehicle, person, or object on the ground that creates a collision hazard or results in a loss of required separation with an aircraft taking off, intending to take off, landing, or intending to land.

Grid Map — Plan view of an area subdivided into a system of squares (numbered and lettered) to provide quick reference to any point.

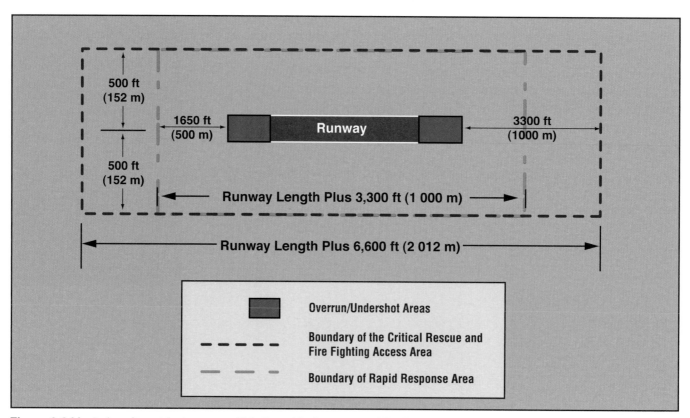

500 ft (152 m)

500 ft (152 m)

1650 ft (500 m)

Runway

3300 ft (1000 m)

Runway Length Plus 3,300 ft (1 000 m)

Runway Length Plus 6,600 ft (2 012 m)

Overrun/Undershot Areas

Boundary of the Critical Rescue and Fire Fighting Access Area

Boundary of Rapid Response Area

Figure 2.9 Most aircraft accidents occur within the critical rescue and fire fighting access area of a runway.

for Aircraft Rescue and Fire Fighting, defines two areas for emergency response that should be identified on the grid map; the Rapid Response Area (RRA) and the Critical Rescue and Fire Fighting Access Area (CRFFAA) **(Figure 2.9)**. The RRA is a rectangle that incorporates a runway and area surrounding it that extends up to but not beyond the airport's property line. It extends 500 feet from each side of the centerline of the runway and 1,650 feet beyond each end of the runway. NFPA® 403 states that the first responding ARFF vehicle must arrive within 2½ minutes to any point within the RRA that is located on the airport property. The CRFFAA is the rectangular area surrounding any runway. Its width extends 500 ft (150m) from each side of the runway centerline, and its length is 3,300 ft (1 000 m) beyond each runway end. According to NFPA® 402, *Guide for Aircraft Rescue and Fire Fighting Operations*, the majority of major commercial aircraft accidents occur within the critical rescue and fire fighting access area.

By inspecting the mapped area, ARFF personnel can determine pertinent terrain features that should be included on the map. Standard map symbols indicating landmarks, bodies of water, roads, bridges, drainage systems, and other features not ordinarily shown on maps are necessary so that a complete description of the accident/incident scene can be given to responding emergency personnel. A map locator system using a grid map is the link that ties together the operations of all groups having some responsibility in the event of aircraft accidents/incidents. Complete, up-to-date copies of such maps must be furnished to the following:

- Control tower personnel
- Local fire departments
- Local law enforcement agencies
- Ambulance and emergency medical personnel
- Local government agencies
- All others with legitimate interests.

In an emergency situation, the location of the emergency scene should be described in terms of the grid system. The incident location can be quickly identified by using the numbered and lettered grid coordinates. At some locations, grid map coordinates are read "number" point "number" then "letter" point "number." For example 5.7, L.3., would be read "5 point 7, Lima point 3." At other locations, they are read letter" point "number" then "number" point "number." For example L.3., 5.7, would be read "Lima point 3, 5 point 7." At locations where the entire alphabet has been used, the next grid becomes AA, the following BB, and so on. ARFF personnel must learn the system used at their location. It is also helpful for the description to include identifying landmarks. All information possible should be included in the description of the accident/incident location so that ARFF personnel may correctly identify and quickly reach the location.

Other Useful Airport Maps

Other maps that may be available to the airport firefighter include utility maps (water distribution, electric service, and gas line distributions), structural locator maps, fuel spill control, and topographic maps. The safest response route obviously saves time in responding to accidents. Using all available maps to fully understand the environment you are entering may help save lives.

Airport Topography

An airport firefighter must be knowledgeable about the topographic layout of both the airport and its immediate surrounding area. Airport topography is important when determining response routes for apparatus and fuel drainage direction when a spill occurs. Terrain may be impassable during inclement weather. For example, normally dry areas may be converted to mud by heavy rains; snow may pile beyond the capabilities of snow-removal crews; or water may collect in low-lying areas blocking access to some points on the airport.

Knowledge of topography also helps predict fire spread if an aircraft crashes and catches fire in an area that has varying elevations. The topography in the immediate area of a fire affects both its intensity and its rate and direction of spread. Wind channeling through various topographical features also affects the fire spread. The effects of terrain and wind are discussed further in Chapter 11, "Strategic and Tactical Operations." For more information on how fire is affected by weather and topography, see IFSTA's **Fundamentals of Wildland Fire Fighting** manual.

Topography — Features of the earth's surface, both natural and constructed, and the relationships among them.

Airport Structures

Because ARFF personnel may be required to respond to alarms within airport structures as well as aircraft emergencies, they must be familiar with the hazards associated with the structures at an airport. Regardless of the facilities found on the airport, an airport firefighter's ability to respond and react relates directly to familiarity with the facility and time spent with preparing preplans, and conducting inspections. This section will address two areas — terminals and maintenances facilities — in particular, though firefighters should also be familiar with other airport structures such as airfreight facilities, the air traffic control tower, multi-story parking facilities, and passenger transport systems.

Terminals

The occupant load and fuel load within a terminal varies depending on the volume of air traffic at the time. Some of the major concerns for ARFF personnel responding to an emergency at an airport terminal include the following:

- *Life safety* — Large crowds of people unfamiliar with exit locations may occupy terminal buildings. The exits may egress onto restricted airport operations areas, which pose additional hazards. Airports should have a plan to deal with an evacuation of occupants out onto the ramp area.

- *Jetways* — Because jetways connect aircraft to the terminal, they can provide a means for smoke and flame to spread from one area to the other. When responding to an aircraft fire at gate areas responders should remember to retract the jetway eyebrow or awning to allow smoke and/or gases to escape the aircraft and not enter the terminal **(Figure 2.10)**.

- *Baggage handling and storage areas* — These areas, usually located on lower levels, may contain hazardous materials, and often have narrow passageways, conveyor belts, and may be loaded with baggage and cargo, which could make it difficult to extend handlines and conduct other fire suppression operations.

Jetway Eyebrow — Accordion-like canopy that permits the jetway to dock with aircraft that have differing contours in order to protect passengers and crew from the weather during aircraft boarding and de-boarding.

Figure 2.10 A jetway eyebrow covering the front entrance into an aircraft.

Aircraft Maintenance Facilities

Aircraft maintenance facilities conduct a variety of operations that are a concern to fire safety personnel **(Figure 2.11)**. These include the following:

● Maintenance and repair of aircraft fuel tanks and systems

● Use of flammable and hazardous chemicals for painting and striping operations

● Repair of aircraft electrical, avionics, and radar systems

● Heavy aircraft maintenance that includes disassembling large parts of the aircraft and its interior, using cleaning fluids, and reassembling the aircraft with various sealant, glues, and paints

● Welding, cutting, and grinding operations used to fabricate or repair aircraft parts or assemblies

● Storage of hazardous materials to be used in aircraft maintenance operations

Figure 2.11 A variety of aircraft maintenance operations can be conducted inside hangars.

Figure 2.12 An example of an aircraft safely halted by an Engineered Material Arresting System (EMAS). *Courtesy of Greenville Airport Commission.*

Runways

Airport runways provide the appropriate surface for aircraft takeoffs and landings. As described previously, runways are marked and lighted to provide guidance for flight deck crews and those airport personnel and equipment operating on the airport.

A recent addition to a growing number of runways is the soft-concrete arresting bed such as the Engineered Material Arresting System (EMAS). These systems are designed to prevent aircraft from overrunning runways that end close to busy roads or densely populated areas. The arresting beds are positioned at the ends of runways and are made out of soft, aerated cement that cannot support the weight of an aircraft. The aircraft will sink into the soft arresting bed and come to a safe, slow halt. The various systems of this type are designed to allow ARFF vehicles to drive safely on top of the surface of the soft-concrete arresting bed **(Figure 2.12)**.

On-Airport Navigation Aids

Navigational aids (NAVAIDs) are visual or electronic devices, either airborne or on the ground, which provide point-to-point guidance information or position data to aircraft in flight. Airport firefighters do not need to know the details of how navigational aids work. They should, however, be able to identify navigation

Engineered Material Arresting System (EMAS) — Bed of aerated cement material that is designed to crush under an aircraft's weight to provide a predictable and controlled deceleration.

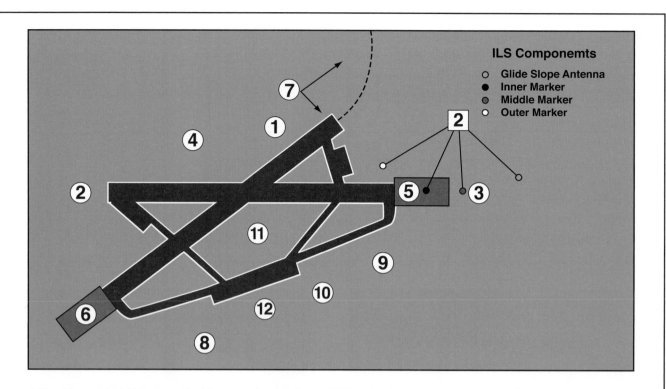

ILS Componemts

○ Glide Slope Antenna
● Inner Marker
◓ Middle Marker
○ Outer Marker

1. **Visual Approach Light Systems**. Precision approach path indicators (PAPI) or visual approach slope indicators (VASI) consist of red and white lights located adjacent to the runway to provide the pilot with a visual descent path.

2. **Instrument Landing System (ILS)**. The instrument landing system provides pilots with electronic guidance for aircraft alignment, descent grade, and position until visual contact confirms the runway alignment and location.

3. **Non-Directional Beacon (NDB)**. The non-directional beacon transmits radio signals by which a pilot, using aircraft instruments, can determine his or her location from the signaling station. An NDB is usually mounted on a 35 foot (11m) pole.

4. **Very High Frequency Omnirange (VOR)**. The standard very high frequency omnirange located on an airport is known as a TVOR. TVORs radiate azimuth information for nonprecision instrument approach procedures.

5. **Approach Lighting Systems (ALS)**. Approach lighting systems are configurations of lights positioned symmetrically along the extended runway centerline. They provide visual guidance to landing aircraft by radiating light beams in a directional pattern by which the pilot aligns the aircraft with the extended centerline of the runway on the final approach for a precision landing.

6. **Omnidirectional Approach Lighting Systems (ODALS)**. Omnidirectional approach lighting systems are configured so as to radiate flashing light beams in all directions. These systems are positioned at the approach end of runways where aircraft conduct non-precision landings.

7. **Lead-In Lighting Systems (LDIN)**. Lead-in lights are flashing lights installed at or near ground level to designate the desired course an aircraft should fly to an ALS or to a runway threshold.

8. **Airport Rotating Beacon**. Airport rotating beacons indicate the location of an airport by projecting beams of light spaced 180 degrees apart. Alternating white/green flashes identify a lighted civil airport; white/white flashes an unlighted civil airport.

9. **Airport Surveillance Radar (ASR)**. Airport surveillance radar scans 360 degrees of the airport to provide air traffic controllers with the location of all aircraft within 60 nautical miles of the airport.

10. **Airport Surface Detection Equipment (ASDE)**. Airport surface detection equipment is used to compensate for the loss of line of sight to surface traffic during periods of reduced visibility.

11. **Automatic Weather Observation Stations (AWOS)**. Automatic recording instruments measure cloud height, visibility, wind speed and direction, temperature, dew point, etc.

12. **Airport Traffic Control Tower (ATCT)**. Air traffic controllers control flight operations within the airport's designated airspace and the operation of aircraft and vehicles on the movement area.

Figure 2.13 ARFF personnel should be familiar with the types and locations of navigational aids (NAVAIDS) found on their airport.

aids and know their locations on the airport. The presence of ARFF vehicles within the operating locations of some navigational aids may interfere with their signals; therefore, ARFF vehicles should respond via routes that do not hamper the operation of these devices (ILS systems). Also, firefighters within some of these operational areas may be harmed by the radio waves produced by this equipment. **Figure 2.13** describes some of the navigational aids that may be found on an airport and shows their typical placement on the airport.

Roads and Bridges

Roads on the airport are used for normal vehicle transportation on and around the airport. Service roads are used to reach the ends of runways and other remote parts of the airport. Some roads may not be suitable for ARFF vehicle use, because of narrow access or low overhead obstructions. Emergency response personnel should plan alternate routes for those roads that may become impassable in adverse weather. ARFF crews should know the load limits of all bridges on the airport and in the local vicinity and plan alternative routes to areas serviced by bridges with low load limits.

Airport Ramps

Ramps/aprons tend to be the most congested areas on the airport. The following list includes functions, equipment, and vehicles that make up the bulk of the activity in these areas (**Figure 2.14**):

- Pedestrian traffic
- Fueling operations
- Baggage handling
- Service-vehicle movements
- High-voltage electrical feed to aircraft from mobile ground power units (GPUs)
- Aircraft maintenance operations
- Hazardous materials/dangerous goods being shipped and/or transferred

Firefighters should stay clear of aircraft on ramp and apron areas. Do not park behind an aircraft at a terminal gate. Try to check with ramp personnel to confirm where the best and safest place to park is. Try to leave someone with the fire department vehicle when parked in questionable areas. Yield to aircraft pushing back from gates, unless waved on by one of the ground crew.

WARNING!

Several navigational aids pose an electrical hazard to firefighters. The airfield lighting system and navigational aids operate on high-voltage electrical systems. Firefighters should avoid contact with these devices.

Figure 2.14 An example of a congested ramp area with a wide variety of personnel, ground vehicles, and aircraft in motion.

Tug — Specialty vehicle used to move aircraft on the ramp.

Movement Area — Runways, taxiways, and other areas of an airport that are used for taxiing or hover taxiing, air taxiing, and takeoff and landing of aircraft exclusive of loading ramps and aircraft parking areas.

Foreign Object Debris (FOD) — Substance, debris or article alien to the vehicle or system which would potentially cause damage.

Foreign Object Damage — Damage attributed to a foreign object that can be expressed in physical or economic terms that may or may not degrade the product's required safety and/or performance characteristics.

Pushback

A pushback is when a passenger aircraft backs away from the jetway or terminal area to taxi to the departure runway. At some airports, aircraft may use engine thrust reversers to move in reverse, but normally the aircraft will be pushed back by a tug. Aircraft pushing back will have their red anti-collision lights illuminated, which are located on the top and bottom of the aircraft fuselage.

In preparation for pushback, air stairs, jetways, and wheel chocks must be moved prior to moving an aircraft. Aircraft doors, hatches, cargo doors should be closed. Baggage-handling equipment, fueling vehicle, and other ground support equipment should have completed loading operations and moved away from the aircraft. A tug and tow-bar should be attached to the aircraft nose wheel, and the tug driver should be seated, with inter-phone connected. One or more wing-walkers with wands or lights may be in place. When these precautions and conditions have been met, an aircraft can safely be pushed back and may proceed to taxiing.

Firefighters need to be aware of foreign object debris (FOD) on airport ramps and other driving surfaces. Loose debris, trash, and other objects on the airport can be sucked up and into the intakes of jet engines, causing considerable damage also called Foreign Object Damage. Firefighters should always be vigilant for FOD and take the time to pick up any and dispose of it properly. When driving from unpaved areas onto aircraft movement areas, personnel should always stop and check vehicle tires for rocks, mud, and other objects stuck in the tire tread.

Airport Security and Controlled Access Points

Following several terrorist events, airports around the world have implemented greater security procedures on and around their locations. Special guidelines for the parking of vehicles near terminals and other airport structures have been developed. Additionally, special guidelines for the parking of emergency vehicles near or in front of airport terminals during periods of elevated threat levels include maintaining a minimum distance of 10 ft (3 m) between the vehicles to makes it more difficult for potential criminals or terrorists to sneak between vehicles unobserved.

ARFF personnel should also secure any identification badges, uniform pieces, turnout gear, vehicles, and fire stations when they are not in use or occupied. If would-be hijackers or terrorists gained control of a fire station or stole any secure items, they could destroy the airport's ARFF capability or use the stolen items to circumvent airport security. Because of their access to controlled areas of airports, ARFF personnel can also be useful in spotting potential security lapses and breaches. Such lapses or breaches should be brought to the attention of airport security or airport operations immediately so that remediation can occur. FAA personnel may enter controlled areas, without wearing the proper identification, in order to test the security procedure awareness of airport employees.

Controlled access points are areas where access is limited in order to eliminate unnecessary or unauthorized traffic **(Figure 2.15)**. A solid red hold line, a red and white dashed line, or a mandatory sign may identify these points. These areas may be staffed by a security guard at the designated entry-control point as part of the Security Identification Display Area (SIDA). Airport ramps

Figure 2.15 An ARFF vehicle entering a controlled area of an airport.

serving passenger air carrier aircraft will be in a SIDA. Every person working in that area must visibly display the proper identification on their outer clothing. The entry control point may be the only way to enter a controlled area. Controlled access points are also used for controlling entry into areas designated as isolation areas, ILS areas, munitions areas, and fuel storage areas.

Fences and Gates

Airport facilities require protection from vandals and any unauthorized individuals. For security purposes, airports provide perimeter fences to keep people and animals from inadvertently entering the airport as well as keeping them from entering restricted areas of the airport.

While serving their intended purposes, these fences also pose a barrier to ARFF vehicles trying to leave the airport using other-than-normal exit points. Historically, frangible (breakaway) fences and gates were strategically located along airport fence lines to allow rapid access for ARFF vehicles to areas outside the airport boundaries. By knowing the exact locations of frangible fences and gates, ARFF crews could reduce vehicle response times to areas outside the airport boundaries. If it was not possible to unlock such devices in a timely manner, ARFF vehicles could strike the section(s) of the fence or a gate designed to break away or collapse.

Some airports have removed frangible (breakaway) fences and reduced the number of gates along their fence lines because of the security risk they pose. If such access points have been removed, the ARFF agency must identify alternate routes of travel for ARFF vehicles to respond off the airport. Some airports have started installing High Tension Cable Barriers to strengthen their existing fences rendering the frangible fences unusable.

Some older style gates have been replaced with more secure gates. If the airport fire department does not keep keys to these gates, security personnel should carry them. If time permits, security may be notified to unlock and open the gates. Firefighters must also know whether these areas are accessible year-round and during inclement weather.

Security Identification Display Area (SIDA) — Portions of an airport, specified in the airport security program, in which security measures required by regulation must be carried out; includes the security area and may include other areas of the airport.

Breakaway/Frangible Fences and Gates — Fences and gates designed and constructed to collapse when impacted by large vehicles to allow rapid access to accident sites. A firefighter's knowledge of their locations is vital in the event of a response off the airport.

Designated Isolation Areas

The isolation area is a predetermined area designed for temporary parking of aircraft experiencing problems with hazardous cargo, hot brakes, or weapons malfunctions among other problems. It can also be used for handling dangerous circumstances such as a hijacked aircraft, bomb threat, or terrorist attack. The location is selected because of its distance from the major facilities and other aircraft traffic. ARFF personnel should be aware of designated isolation areas at their airports and the status of aircraft parked within those areas because of the specific hazards they represent.

Water Supply

There are generally two sources of water for airport fire protection: fixed systems and mobile supplies. Common fixed system components include wells, drafting pits, pumps, storage tanks (surface level and elevated), water distribution mains, and fire hydrants. Dedicated fire mains or domestic water supply mains distribute water through fixed systems. Some airports have hydrants located along aircraft operational areas. These hydrants may be located underground in containment vaults. Most airports will only have hydrants near structures or perimeter roads. Common mobile water supply systems include fire apparatus and water tankers/tenders. For airport locations known to be deficient in water supply, arrangements for the automatic dispatch of water tankers/tenders need to be made in advance.

Fuel Storage and Distribution

Having a working knowledge of the airport fuel storage and distribution facilities is important for ARFF personnel. These facilities include the following:

- Fuel storage tanks or supply pipeline
- Fuel distribution systems or loading areas
- Ramp areas where aircraft are fueled

Firefighters should study the location of these facilities on a map of the airport and learn the function and operation of shutoff valves and switches from a technical manual. All firefighters assigned to the airport should periodically visit each of these sites and become thoroughly familiar with their location, functions, and operation.

ARFF personnel may perform the FAA Part 139 required quarterly inspections of fuel storage and distribution points. These inspections are useful in identifying fire hazards and safety concerns. Firefighters should also become familiar with the various types of refueling vehicles assigned to their airports and the safety components of each. The ARFF agency may also be responsible for providing fire safety training to fueling supervisors and personnel. FAR Part 139 requires that the airport emergency plan contain response procedures for fuel storage facility fires. The airport fire department will be the first responders and will be tasked with planning and preparing for these types of incidents.

The following sections discuss fueling operations, the associated hazards that ARFF personnel may experience on a regular basis, and required fire extinguishment equipment required during fueling operations.

Fueling Operations

Fueling operations are a constant hazard and represent the number one fire prevention consideration at airports. Tank trucks, railcars or pipelines are used to deliver fuel to airports. Fuel is also stored in aboveground or belowground bulk storage tanks. For more information on emergencies involving fuel storage tank, see *Storage Tank Emergencies* by Hildebrand, Noll and Donahue. At larger airport facilities, the fuel is transferred by underground piping, which terminates at a sub-surface fuel hydrant located at each gate. A fuel service truck or cart connects to the underground system and transfers the fuel into the aircraft **(Figure 2.16)**.

Figure 2.16 A fuel transfer cart pumping fuel from underground fuel lines into an aircraft's fuel tanks. *Courtesy of William D. Stewart.*

Figure 2.17 An aircraft being refueled by fuel tank truck. *Courtesy of Edwin A. Jones, USAFR.*

Tank truck is the most common method of aircraft fuel delivery **(Figure 2.17)**. These tankers transport fuel from a storage location and pump their contents into the aircraft. Common capacities of these tankers can range from 500 to 10,000 gallons (2 000 to 40 000 liters). In order to load the tank truck or transfer fuel into the aircraft, fueling personnel must hold open a "dead man device" or hold tension on a "dead man rope" that holds open a spring-loaded valve. The term *dead man* is used to denote the release mechanism of the valve during an emergency or the incapacitation of fueling personnel. This release shuts down the fueling operation. Fuel trucks are also required to have emergency shutoff switches at both ends of the vehicle.

A third method of fueling an aircraft is referred to as a fueling island. This operation is similar to an automobile gas station, where small aircraft can taxi up and get fuel.

During aircraft fueling operations, metal cables are used to equalize static electrical charges between the fueling operation (such as a vehicle or loading rack) and the aircraft. Grounding to a static ground electrode in the pavement is not required by NFPA® standards. However, the carrier, other standards, airport regulations, or military regulations may still request a static ground electrode.

Fuel is loaded onto aircraft in two methods: single point fueling connections and over-the-wing connections. Single point fueling connections are located in the fuselage sides or under the wings of larger aircrafts. These connections are used to fill onboard tanks from a single location. Larger aircraft may also have over-the-wing fueling connections for servicing individual tanks. Flight or maintenance crews can use onboard pumps to transfer fuel between the various onboard tanks once fuel has been loaded. The over-the-wing method is used on most smaller aircraft with a handheld fuel nozzle being used to transfer the fuel.

Because of the demand for "on-time" performance and the necessity for all-weather flying, servicing crews must perform their duties quickly and at all hours of the day and night. This increases the risk of fuel handlers cutting corners on safety procedures. Some examples of poor fueling practices include circumventing safety shut-off devices, operating poorly maintained vehicles and equipment, and overfilling aircraft or truck tanks.

In addition to poor safety practices, fuel vapor poses another hazard during fueling operations. When fuel is transferred into an aircraft tank, the incoming fuel forces vapors out through tank vents that are usually found at the wingtips. So, an explosive vapor-air mixture can be formed in the vicinity of any fueling operation. As the ambient temperature increases, so does the amount of vapor generated by the fuel. Fuel vapors are not only invisible but also heavier than air and may be moved by the wind or may settle onto the ground and into depressions.

Ignition Sources

In any aircraft area, there are numerous ignition sources that may ignite fuel vapors. These sources include static electricity (such as that caused by low-conductivity liquids, refueling vehicles, and clothing), adverse weather conditions (lightning), electromagnetic energy (radar), portable communication equipment, and open flames.

Static electricity. Controlling static electricity is extremely important during fueling operations. Aircraft, similar to any vehicle with rubber tires, have the ability to build up a static charge when moving or at rest. Static charges also build up when air flows over aircraft surfaces. The generation of static charges is greater when the humidity is low (dry air) or when the air carries particles such as dust, dry snow, or ice crystals. Certain aircraft service operations such as fueling and fuel filtering also produce static charges. The degree of static buildup depends on the fuel type; the amount of fuel; the velocity of the fuel moving through piping, hoses, and filters; and the presence of impurities in the fuel. Bonding equalizes the electrostatic potential between the fueling vehicle and the aircraft or loading facility. Bonding should only be done with properly maintained equipment connected to unpainted metallic surfaces.

Adverse weather conditions. Adverse weather conditions can generate lightning which can pose a serious hazard in conjunction with fueling operations. The local authority having jurisdiction (AHJ) normally provides guidelines regarding fueling operations in adverse weather. ARFF personnel need to monitor weather conditions and fueling operations to ensure ignition hazards are reduced.

Electromagnetic energy. Transferring fuel is hazardous in close proximity to the electromagnetic energy created by operating radar sources. The aircraft's onboard weather radar, portable and mobile radio equipment, and cellular telephones should not be used around aircraft when fueling operations are being conducted.

Open flames. Open flames should be strictly controlled or prohibited in aircraft operation areas or within 50 feet (15 m) of any aircraft fueling operation. The most commonly encountered open-flame hazard is smoking near aircraft or aircraft fueling operations. Other hazards include welding or other hot-work maintenance operation. For more information about fueling operations, see NFPA® 407, *Standard for Aircraft Fuel Servicing.*

Other Fueling Considerations

In addition, aircraft batteries, battery chargers, or other electrical equipment should not be connected, disconnected, or operated during fuel servicing. Defueling operations can be just as hazardous as fueling. Radios and electronic flash equipment should not be operated within 10 feet (3 m) of fueling equipment or of the fueling points or vents of the aircraft. Ground power units (GPU) should be located as far as practical from aircraft fueling points and tank vents in order to reduce the danger of igniting any flammable vapors released during fueling operations.

Fire Extinguishers Required for Fueling Operations

Fire extinguishers of appropriate size and type (with a minimum rating of 20-B) should be readily accessible within the area of fueling operations. However, NFPA® 407, *Standard for Aircraft Fuel Servicing,* requires a minimum 80-B, 125 pound (55 kg) fire extinguisher where fuel flows exceed 200 gpm (750 L/min). They must also be installed at emergency remote-control stations of airport fixed fuel systems. If extinguishers are not permanently located in the area but are brought to the servicing area prior to the refueling operation, they should be stationed upwind within 100 feet (30 m) of the aircraft being serviced.

For normal ramp area protection, extinguishers may be located approximately midway between gate positions. In these situations, the distance between extinguishers should be less than 100 feet (30 m), and the extinguishers should have at least a 20-B rating **(Figure 2.18)**. Additional information concerning portable extinguishers for aircraft servicing ramps and aprons may be found in local publications or NFPA® 10, *Standard for Portable Fire Extinguishers.*

Figure 2.18 A flightline extinguisher located near a jetway.

Airport Drainage Systems

The airport's drainage system is designed to control the flow of fuel that may be spilled on a ramp and to minimize resulting possible damage. The system may be equipped with drain inlets with connecting piping or open-grate trenches. The aircraft fueling ramps must slope away from terminal buildings, hangars, loading walkways, or other structures. Fuel is not permitted to go directly into the storm water system and must flow through an approved fuel/water separator. The final separator/interceptor for the entire airport drainage system should be designed to allow disposal of combustible or flammable liquids into a safely located, approved containment facility. Airport firefighters must know the type of drainage system design at their airport. This information is critical when planning, confining, and containing fuel spills.

ARFF Fire Stations

Strategically locating fire stations on the airport allows ARFF apparatus and personnel to meet emergency response times. For this reason, airport fire stations should be in a central location where there is a good view of the flight line, taxiways, apron/ramp, and hangar areas to allow ARFF personnel to monitor airfield activities. To facilitate surveillance, some airport fire stations incorporate an observation tower for monitoring ground activities. If properly constructed, a fire station observation tower may be an ideal location for the fire department communications/dispatch center.

Although it is not always practical for ARFF personnel to constantly observe ground operations from the airport fire station, when feasible, they should visually monitor the following:

- Taxiing operations, integrity of aircraft landing gear, ground operation of engines, and aircraft maintenance on the flight line
- Fueling/defueling operations
- Roads, taxiways, and fire lanes that may be blocked by aircraft or other vehicles
- Current weather conditions that might affect the movement of emergency vehicles and the takeoff/landing patterns of aircraft.
- Population v/s Time of day

Observing these activities allows firefighters to gain an awareness of what is happening on their airport and also assists in the development and implementation of a fire prevention program.

Summary

In order to perform their jobs safely and efficiently, airport firefighters must be thoroughly familiar with the airport itself. They must understand what type and classification of airport they work at to better understand the aircraft rescue and fire fighting requirements needed by that airport. Familiarity saves in response time. Reduced response time may save lives while protecting the safety of the responders.

Review Questions

1. What are the two basic types of airports?

2. Unless directed otherwise by an air traffic controller, how must all aircraft enter the airport area?

3. How are runway numbers created?

4. What does a red colored marking denote?

5. What does a runway hold position sign look like?

6. How are grid maps marked?

7. What is a jetway eyebrow?

8. What identifiers designate a controlled access point?

9. What are the two general sources of water for airport fire protection?

10. What is the purpose of an airport drainage system?

Aircraft Familarization

Chapter Contents

chapter **3**

Key Terms

NFPA® references for Chapter 3:

Aircraft Familiarization

Learning Objectives

After reading this chapter, students shall be able to:

1. Discuss various types of aircraft. (NFPA® 1003, 5.2.2, 5.4.1)

2. Explain major aircraft components. (NFPA® 1003, 5.2.2, 5.4.1)

3. Describe the various aircraft engine types and applications. (NFPA® 1003, 5.2.2, 5.4.1)

4. Describe aircraft construction and structural materials. (NFPA® 1003, 5.2.2, 5.4.1)

5. Discuss aircraft systems. (NFPA® 1003, 5.2.2, 5.4.1)

Chapter 3
Aircraft Familiarization

Case History

United States Air Force Fire Protection Specialists at bases with flying missions conduct frequent aircraft familiarization training sessions and drills on the aircraft assigned to their installations and on those aircraft that frequently stop at those installations. Each of these sessions and drills reinforce the firefighters' knowledge of the aircraft's major systems and components, safety systems, weapons (if applicable), and cockpit/fuselage access and crew egress procedures.

The importance of this training can be illustrated by an accident that occurred at Williams AFB, near Chandler, Arizona in 1984. A trainee pilot was taking his solo flight in a T-38 Talon jet trainer when the aircraft failed to lift off. The aircraft crossed the runway overrun and crashed into a rock covered embankment below the perimeter fence. ARFF apparatus and crews arrived within minutes and extinguished two small fires on the aircraft wreckage. The three member rescue crew promptly opened the aircraft canopy, shutdown the aircraft systems, safetied the ejection seat, and pulled the dazed pilot from the aircraft. During the post incident debriefing, the rescue crew members stated that they didn't have to stop and think of what sequence to perform the rescue in; they "knew" it from their aircraft familiarization training sessions.

The 2007 United States Department of statistics indicates that air travel continues to be the safest method of transportation. Every day, thousands of people take to the skies relying on the airline industry to get them to their destinations safely. But what happens when things go wrong? As an airport firefighter every second counts when things go wrong. Critical time is lost if AARF personnel are unfamiliar with the methods from which to gain access and rescue those trapped inside an aircraft. Airport firefighters must be familiar with the different types and classifications of aircraft on which they may have to perform rescue and fire fighting operations. It is also important to be familiar with the operation of cockpit windows and hatches that can be opened to aid in ventilation, extrication, and egress if necessary. ARFF personnel should gather and have available as much aircraft familiarization reference material as possible and develop emergency preplans for the commonly encountered aircraft. Critical aircraft response information manuals and computer programs are available for civilian and military aircraft. ARFF personnel must also be trained to recognize the many and varied aircraft systems found on each type of aircraft.

To enhance personal safety, ARFF crewmembers must exercise extreme caution when working in and around aircraft. One of the most important aspects of ARFF operations is aircraft familiarization training because the safety of the occupants is the number one priority. Enhanced knowledge of aircraft helps ensure that ARFF operations can be performed in the quickest, safest manner. In-depth knowledge of egress systems allows rescue crews to assist or perform the evacuation process and increase the chance of passenger and crew survival.

This chapter describes the different types of aircraft used in civilian and military aviation. It identifies components for both fixed-wing and rotary-wing aircraft. This chapter also describes the types of engines used on aircraft and their applications. Aircraft construction and structural materials are discussed. Finally, this chapter outlines the various systems found on aircraft.

Types of Aircraft

Generally, aircraft are categorized according to their intended purpose. Depending on their uses, some aircraft may be included in more than one category. Aircraft such as the DC-10, for example, may be configured as a commercial transport (passenger aircraft), as a cargo aircraft, or as a refueling tanker by the military. Naturally, the hazards around the aircraft stay the same, but the hazards found inside the aircraft can vary dramatically. Classifications of aircraft generally include the following:

- Commercial transport
- Commuter/regional
- Cargo, including combination aircraft (combi-aircraft)
- General aviation
- Business/corporate aviation
- Military aviation
- Rotary-wing (helicopters)
- Fire-fighting aircraft
- Other

Commercial Transport

Those aircraft used for commercial transport of passengers are generally of large-frame construction and can be categorized as either narrow- or wide-bodied. However, newer designs of aircraft known as *new large aircraft* are in use. The sections that follow discuss the various commercial transport designs.

Figure 3.1a An example of a narrow body aircraft. *Courtesy of Edwin A. Jones, USAFR.*

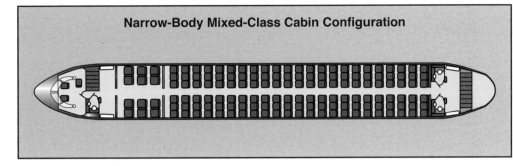

Narrow-Body Mixed-Class Cabin Configuration

Figure 3.1b An example of the interior configuration of a narrow body aircraft.

Narrow Body

Narrow body aircraft cabins are designed with a single aisle usually 18 to 20 (46 to 51 cm) inches wide and may seat up to 235 persons if arranged in a single (coach) class configuration **(Figure 3.1 a and b)**. These aircraft are equipped with two to three jet engines and carry as much as 13,000 gallons (52 000 L) of jet fuel. Older narrow body aircraft are designed with plug-type cabin doors while some newer aircraft use "vault type" doors. Narrow body aircraft doors swing out and forward. Some aircraft doors incorporate pneumatic emergency opening systems that assist in opening the door if jammed during a low-impact crash. In accordance with Federal Aviation Regulation (FAR) 121.310, *Additional Emergency Equipment,* any aircraft with a doorsill height of 6 feet (2 m) or more off the ground when the aircraft's wheels are extended must be equipped with an emergency escape slide. Some narrow-body aircraft escape slides cannot be disarmed from the outside and will automatically deploy when the doors are opened from the outside. Over-the-wing escape hatches are provided and may contain an escape slide, which activates when the hatch is opened from the inside. Cargo and luggage is usually bulk-loaded into two to three cargo compartments that are found along the bottom of the fuselage with access being provided on the right side of the aircraft.

Wide Body

These aircraft have two, three, or four jet engines and may carry over 58,000 gallons (220 000 L) of jet fuel. Wide-body aircraft cabins have dual aisles creating a center section of seats, allowing the aircraft to carry over 500 passengers **(Figure 3.2 a and b).** Doors are generally power-assisted and may contain a pneumatic or spring-tension emergency operation system. Some wide-body aircraft doors open up into the overhead area, while others swing out and forward. Older aircraft tend to use plug type doors, while newer aircraft use vault type doors. Almost all escape slides can be de-armed from the outside.

Figure 3.2a An example of a wide body aircraft. *Courtesy of Edwin A. Jones, USAFR.*

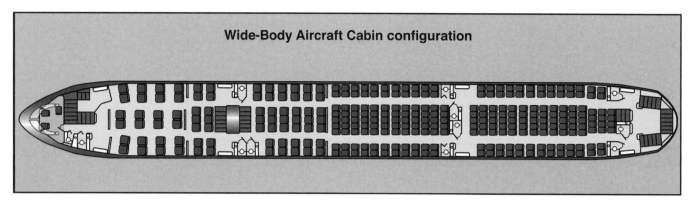

Wide-Body Aircraft Cabin configuration

Figure 3.2b An illustration of the interior configuration of a common wide body aircraft.

Most slides are doublewide in design and expand beyond the outside door opening when inflated. In wide-body aircraft, over-the-wing escape doors are more common than hatches. Most of the luggage and cargo is preloaded into containers or onto pallets before being unit-loaded into lower cargo compartments. Both fire detection and fire-extinguishing systems can be found in wide-body aircraft cargo compartments.

New Large Aircraft (NLA)

With the growing use and availability of lightweight, strong composite material components, aircraft manufacturers have developed a new breed of large aircraft **(Figure 3.3a).** Referred to as NLA, or *very large aircraft* (VLA), these aircraft may incorporate a passenger capacity of up to 900 passengers **(Figure 3.3b).**

Airports are currently being redesigned to accommodate aircraft of this size. ARFF agencies may need to reassess the type and number of apparatus as well as staffing needs to meet the potential rescue and firefighting needs of these new large aircraft. Because the NLA will feature passenger cabins that incorporate double-deck seating configurations, they pose numerous rescue concerns for responding ARFF personnel. In particular, ARFF personnel will

Figure 3.3a An example of a new large aircraft.
Courtesy of Edwin A. Jones, USAFR.

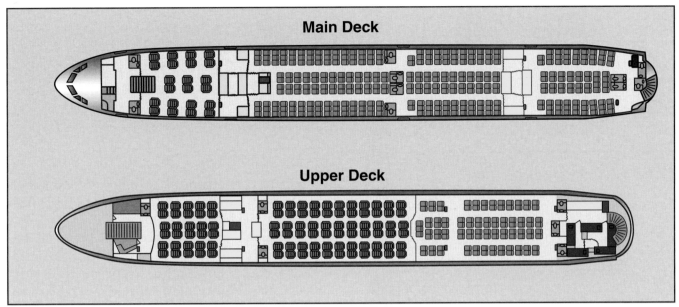

Main Deck

Upper Deck

need to plan how to gain access to the upper deck in order to remove passengers. Another concern that ARFF personnel need to take into consideration is the collapse or potential collapse of the upper deck. Such a collapse could endanger passengers and ARFF personnel. ARFF personnel will need to be proficient in confined space rescue and advanced extrication.

Commuter/Regional Aircraft

Aircraft used for the commercial transport of passengers on short routes, typically to and from hub airports to smaller airports, are referred to as *commuter/ regional aircraft*. Twin engine turboprop aircraft are becoming a thing of the past with current trends moving towards the use of jet-powered aircraft in this role **(Figure 3.4 a and b)**. These pressurized aircraft can carry from 19 to 60 passengers and fly as fast and far as their larger counterparts. The interiors can be somewhat cramped and congested and can present a difficult work environment under emergency conditions **(Figure 3.5)**. These aircraft tend to have a limited number of egress locations and often have only one cabin entry door. They are also equipped with a forward service door for catering and cleaning services. Depending on the model/type, the passenger cabin may be accessed through the rear cargo area.

Figure 3.4a A commuter/regional aircraft equipped with turboprop engines.

Figure 3.4b A jet-powered commuter/regional aircraft.

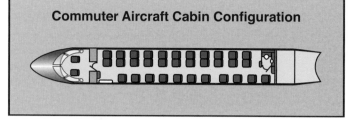

Figure 3.6a A larger type of commuter/regional aircraft. *Courtesy of Edwin A. Jone, USAFR.*

With increases in air travel, commuter/regional aircraft are busier than ever. With increased passenger loads, some airlines have moved to larger aircraft to serve commuter/regional travel **(Figure 3.6a)**. These models are stretched versions of their predecessors, with one or two additional doors and seating arrangements to carry up to 100 persons **(Figure 3.6b)**. Most of the systems and their shutdowns remain in the same locations. The largest hazard involves the entry stairs, which are often built into the main cabin door. When involved in a low impact crash the stairs may impede evacuation by becoming lodged in the door opening.

Cargo Aircraft

These aircraft are used primarily for the transport of cargo and can include any of the previously discussed aircraft. They are commonly referred to as *freighters* **(Figure 3.7)**. Many freighters are former passenger aircraft modified to carry cargo pallets or containers and can contain significant amounts of dangerous goods. *Combi-aircraft* (combination aircraft) are those aircraft carrying passengers and cargo on the main deck and additional cargo below the deck. Some

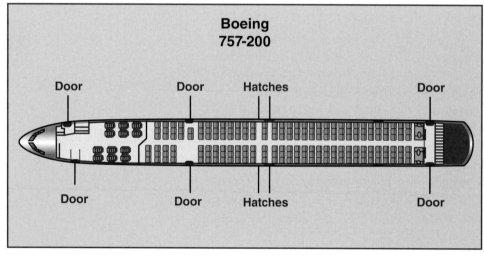

Figure 3.6b An example of the interior configuration of a larger commuter/regional aircraft.

cargo aircraft are used as freighters during the week and converted to passenger aircraft for weekend excursions.

Except for the two forward entry doors, all other doors and exit hatches may be disabled or blocked off as part of the modifications to an all-cargo configuration. Large-frame aircraft have large, hydraulically operated cargo doors located forward or aft of the wing on the left side of the aircraft.

NOTE: The sides of an aircraft are designated according to the pilot's left or right.

Although most have cargo doors that can be operated manually in an emergency, electrical power is needed to open these doors under normal conditions. Containers and pallets are loaded sequentially into numbered or

Figure 3.7 A modern cargo/freighter aircraft. *Courtesy of Edwin A. Jones, USAFR.*

lettered positions from the front of the aircraft back. On narrow-body cargo freighters, the lower compartments are usually bulk-loaded with packages no heavier than 70 pounds each. The sections that follow discuss the various types of cargo compartments in detail and how the various cargo compartments are accessed.

Classes of Cargo Compartments

There are five classes of cargo compartments aboard aircraft. They are designated as Classes A, B, C, and E. Class D compartments have been discontinued on new aircraft, and Class D compartments on older aircraft must be upgraded to Class C. Each compartment has specific properties in terms of its location on the aircraft, installed fire detection and protection systems, and access.

ARFF firefighters should know the various classes of cargo compartments on aircraft at their airports. Cargo compartments are different from stowage areas on aircraft. This section discusses cargo areas other than those considered stowage compartments by Federal Aviation Administration (FAA) requirements as stipulated in CFR 14 Part 25.857, *Cargo compartment classification*. Stowage compartments such as overhead storage areas used for the storage of carry-on articles and baggage are not considered as cargo compartments.

Each class of cargo compartment is usually larger than the preceding class with Class A being the smallest cargo compartment and Class E comprising the entire main deck of a cargo aircraft. Following are the classes of compartments as defined by FAA requirements:

- *Class A* — a compartment in which the presence of a fire would be easily discovered by a crewmember while at his or her station, and where all compartments are easily accessible in flight. These compartments can be located between the flight deck and the passenger cabins. They can also be found adjacent to the galley or at the back of the aircraft.

- *Class B* — compartment with a separate, approved smoke or fire detection system to give warning to the pilot or flight engineer; has sufficient access in flight to enable a crewmember to effectively reach any part of the compartment with a hand-held fire extinguisher. When accessing these compartments, hazardous quantities of smoke, flames, or extinguishing agent will not enter any compartment occupied by crew or passengers.

- *Class C* — differ from Class B compartments primarily in that built-in extinguishing systems are required for control of fires in lieu of crew member accessibility. Smoke or fire detection systems must be provided. There are means to prevent hazardous quantities of smoke, flames, or extinguishing agent from entering any compartment occupied by crew or passengers. Ventilation controls are provided within the compartment to maintain a proper concentration of extinguishing agent. Class C compartments are usually found under the passenger cabin floor in wide-bodied aircraft. Class C and upgraded Class D compartments are the types of cargo compartments usually found on modern passenger aircraft. Class C and upgraded Class D compartments are also found under the main deck floor on cargo-only aircraft.

- *Class D* — prior to industry changes, Class D compartments were originally designed without fire detection or fire extinguishing systems. Very low airflow within the compartment was intended to inhibit any occurrence of fire. Class D compartments are no longer an option for new aircraft. Current aircraft that have Class D compartments under previous definitions must be upgraded to comply with the requirements of Class C compartments if the aircraft is used for passenger transport or Class E compartments if the aircraft is used only for cargo transport.

- *Class E* — used only for the carriage of cargo. Typically, a Class E compartment is the entire cabin of an all-cargo airplane. A smoke or fire detection system is required. In lieu of providing extinguishment, means must be provided to shut off the flow of ventilating air to or within a Class E compartment. In addition, procedures such as depressurizing a pressurized airplane are stipulated in the event that a fire occurs. There are means to prevent hazardous quantities of smoke, flames, or extinguishing agent from entering any compartment occupied by crew or passengers. The required crew emergency exits must be accessible regardless of configuration or cargo loading conditions.

Gaining Access to Cargo Compartments

Most cargo doors are hinged at the top of their opening and swing out and up. A few open up and into the compartment. Most older narrow-body aircraft cargo doors open manually. Newer narrow-body and almost all wide-body aircraft cargo doors open electrically and hydraulically.

Mechanically operated cargo doors can usually be opened manually by releasing a latching handle that releases the door locks and inserting a ¼-inch, ⅜-inch, or ½-inch ratchet drive into the appropriate size socket hole and rotating the drive. Pneumatic drivers cannot be used because they turn too fast and jam up the mechanism. The socket hole is usually found in the vicinity of the cargo door. Large cargo doors may also have mechanical locking devices which when opened, relieve the pressure in the compartment. Many different door opening procedures may be encountered, so ARFF personnel should request the assistance of air carrier mechanics and/or maintenance personnel, if available.

Figure 3.8a A medium general aviation aircraft.

Figure 3.8b A larger general aviation aircraft with multiple engines. *Courtesy of Edwin A. Jones, USAFR.*

General Aviation

General aviation aircraft are used primarily for pleasure or training and are typically small, light, and nonpressurized **(Figure 3.8 a and b)**. They are typically powered by single or twin internal-combustion engines and present fire fighting and rescue challenges similar to those in highway vehicle accidents. General aviation aircraft usually carry one to ten passengers and up to 90 gallons (360 L) of aviation gasoline (AVGAS). Some general aviation aircraft may be larger and carry up to 500 gallons [2 000 L] of fuel. According to National Transportation Safety Board (NTSB) statistics, a majority of aviation accidents involve this type of aircraft and account for most aircraft-related fatalities.

Business/Corporate Aviation

Aircraft primarily used for business-related transport range from smaller, light, non-pressurized aircraft to large "commercial-type" jets (such as a Boeing 737 or Boeing Business Jet) and include many different models and manufacturers. Some very large models of corporate aircraft may be encountered, carrying enough fuel to fly to Europe or Asia.

Business aircraft are often powered by twin jet engines that operate on jet fuel **(Figure 3.9a)**. Typically, business/corporate aircraft are pressurized and generally accommodate six to nineteen passengers **(Figure 3.9b)**. Many have custom-designed interiors that differ greatly from normal configurations. This type combined with general aviation aircraft account for the largest

Figure 3.9a An exterior view of a business/corporate aircraft. *Courtesy of Edwin A. Jones, USAFR.*

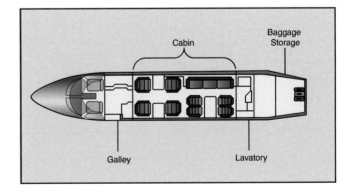

Figure 3.9b An example of the interior layout of a business/corporate aircraft.

variety of aircraft styles and configurations. Most will have one entry door, usually located forward of the wing on the left side of the aircraft. Some have one over-wing escape hatch on the right side, while others will have an escape hatch on both sides. Many of the over-wing escape hatches cannot be opened from the outside. Doors, hatches, cargo compartments, and other spaces can often be locked. These aircraft will usually not have cockpit windows that can be opened.

Military Aviation

Military organizations operate a wide variety of aircraft to support military objectives. Military aircraft can fly anywhere in the world and often use or are based at civilian airports. Many military aircraft may include civilian models that have been converted to support some military function. Therefore, all firefighters should be familiar with the potential hazards associated with military aircraft.

Military aircraft range from single-engine fighters to large, multiengine transports and bombers. Because of the high altitude, high speed, complex instrumentation, and armament required by the military, this type of aircraft presents additional hazards for emergency responders. Although the crew is often limited to a few people, the aircraft may have armament, liquid oxygen, high-powered radar, extensive composite material construction, and explosive ejection devices.

This section describes the various types of military aircraft in use, the emergency systems incorporated with these aircraft, and the procedures to follow if involved in a response to a military aircraft accident. Also covered are the various aircrew survival systems, actuating devices, aircraft emergency shutdown procedures, weapons and weapons systems, as well as appropriate fire fighting procedures.

Military Aircraft Types

Terminology unique to military aircraft is used to describe the particular aircraft types and to identify where weapons and ordnance may be found. Familiarity with these terms and with aircraft design variations allows ARFF personnel to better prepare for an emergency involving these military aircraft. It is important to remember that military operations are not limited to the areas around military bases but can extend to anywhere within the country. Military aircraft are often used to assist in civilian rescue operations, disaster relief, and other types of emergencies.

Military aircraft are assigned a designator letter, which can be used by response workers to identify the aircraft type. These letters correspond to an aircraft and its assigned mission. These designator letters are the following:

A — Attack

B — Bomber

C — Cargo/passenger

E — Special electronic installation

F — Fighter

H — Helicopter

K — Tanker

O — Observation

P — Patrol

Q — Unmanned Aerial Vehicle (UAV)

R — Reconnaissance

S — Antisubmarine

T — Trainer

U — Utility

V— Vertical Take-Off and Landing / Short Take-Off
and Landing (VTOL/STOL)

X — Research

Fighter and Attack Aircraft

Fighter and attack aircraft are designed to engage in air-to-air and/or air-to-ground combat **(Figures 3.10 a and b)**. Some attack aircraft may be as large as the four-engine AC-130 gunship, but most incorporate a one- or two-seat configuration **(Figure 3.11)**. Weapons such as internally mounted cannons, missiles, and bombs are carried beneath the wings and/or in the fuselage. Except for the AC-130 and similar large gun-ships, fighter and most attack

Figure 3.10a An A-10 Thunderbolt II (Warthog) attack aircraft. *Photo by SrA Joshua Strang (USAF), Defense Visual Information Center (DVIC).*

Figure 3.10b The F-22 Raptor is an example of a fighter aircraft. *Photo by SMSgt Thomas Meneguin, (USAF), Defense Visual Information Center (DVIC).*

Figure 3.11 The AC-130 Spectre Gunship is an example a large attack aircraft. *Photo by TSgt Bob Simons (USAF), Defense Visual Information Center (DVIC).*

Figure 3.12 The B-2 Spirit bomber aircraft. *Photo by PH2 Jorge L. Mendez (USN), Defense Visual Information Center (DVIC).*

Figure 3.13 Cargo aircraft include the C-17 Globemaster III. *Photo by TSgt Richard T. Kaminsky (USAF), Defense Visual Information Center (DVIC).*

Figure 3.14 The KC-10 Extender is an example of a tanker aircraft. *Photo by MSgt Lance Cheung (USAF), Defense Visual Information Center (DVIC).*

aircraft are equipped with canopy-removal systems and ejection seats. Small explosive bolts are found on weapon racks and external fuel tank attachment points to eject or jettison the weapons and tanks. The cargo-type aircraft that have been converted to attack aircraft are equipped with conventional weapons and carry a substantial amount of ammunition.

Bomber Aircraft

Aircraft designed to carry and drop a large quantity of air-to-ground weapons are referred to as bombers **(Figure 3.12)**. They can be four- to eight-engine aircraft and hold a crew of two to eight. They have explosive ejection seats and can carry weapons internally, externally, or both. A large fuel load and a significant quantity of high explosives are to be expected on a fully loaded aircraft of this type.

Cargo Aircraft

ARFF personnel may be most familiar with the C-5, C-17, and C-130 which are used to carry cargo. Military cargo aircraft may range from relatively small to quite large **(Figure 3.13)**. Most military cargo aircraft are designed to carry both cargo and/or personnel at the same time. These aircraft do not have ejection seats or canopy-removal systems; however, they may have jet-assisted takeoff (JATO) units attached to the sides of the fuselage. Cargo aircraft may carry a wide variety of cargo, which may include armored personnel vehicles, tanks, munitions, food, personnel, and supplies.

Tanker Aircraft

Tanker aircraft are cargo aircraft modified for in-flight refueling of other aircraft. Some examples include the KC-10 and the KC-135. They may be configured to perform the dual functions of cargo transport and fuel tanker at the same time **(Figure 3.14)**. Their exceptionally large fuel load sets them apart from other cargo-type aircraft. Fuel load for this style of aircraft can be over 50,000 gallons (200 000 L), so responders may be faced with a very large volume of fire in the event of an accident.

Utility Aircraft

Identified with a U, utility aircraft are usually relatively small aircraft that perform a variety of support functions. They normally do not carry weapons or have ejection systems, and they are quite similar to general aviation aircraft **(Figure 3.15)**. The passenger load varies with the size and mission of the aircraft. A noteworthy exception is the U-2 high-altitude reconnaissance aircraft. Although

Figure 3.15 Utility aircraft include the UC-35 Citation. *Photo by LCPL Antonio (USMC), Defense Visual Information Center (DVIC).*

Figure 3.16 One special purpose aircraft is the E-3C Airborne Warnings and Control System (AWACS) aircraft. *Photo by SSgt Jason W. Gamble (USAF), Defense Visual Information Center (DVIC).*

designated with a U, this is a specialized jet equipped with an ejection seat and sophisticated surveillance equipment.

Special-Purpose Aircraft

Special-purpose aircraft serve many functions for the military such as reconnaissance, command and control, testing, or electronic surveillance. Their designator letter varies depending on the mission of the aircraft. The term *special-purpose aircraft* also describes the various uses of a common military aircraft. For example, the military version of the Boeing 707 is used as a C-135 cargo aircraft, KC-135 tanker, EC-135 electronics platform, E-3C AWACS (airborne warning and control system) aircraft, and other advanced range instrumentation aircraft (ARIA) **(Figure 3.16)**.

Helicopters

DOD makes extensive use of helicopters for military assaults and transportation. Helicopters play a major role in military operations and account for a large part of the aviation fleet **(Figures 3.17a and b)**. When ammunition and weapons are attached, they are usually carried inside the cabin or on pods

Figure 3.17a The AH-64 Apache is an example of an attack helicopter. *Photo by SSgt Michael R. Holzworth (USAF), Defense Visual Information Center (DVIC).*

Figure 3.17b Military cargo helicopters include the CH-46 Sea Knight. *Photo by LCPL Andrew Williams (USMC), Defense Visual Information Center (DVIC).*

attached to the fuselage. Auxiliary fuel tanks also may be carried internally or externally. Helicopters normally carry a crew of two to five but also may carry passengers and equipment. The AH-1 and AH-64 have hatches that can be jettisoned explosively.

Military Aircraft Information

Technical Order (T.O.) 00-105E-9, Aerospace Emergency Rescue and Mishap Response Information, contains specific information regarding numerous U.S. military and North Atlantic Treaty Organization (NATO) ally aircraft. Due to security concerns, personnel must now register online to gain access to this technical order. Technical Order 00-105E-9 access and registration can be found at http://www.robins.af.mil/library/technicalorders. asp. An easier way to preplan for airport specific transient aircraft may be to contact the local military installation and ask for the Air Force Technical Order (AFTO) Form 88 for those aircraft. These are the base plans on fire attack and are very base specific.

Rotary Wing (Helicopters)

Rotary-wing aircraft or helicopters can range in size from small, single-seat models to large transports capable of carrying up to 50 passengers. Some helicopters like the Sikorsky Skycrane may be equipped to carry loads weighing more than 10 tons (9 100 kg) **(Figure 3.18)**. Because most helicopters are not as rigidly constructed as "fixed-wing" aircraft, they tend to collapse when involved in accidents, often trapping the occupants. Rotary-wing aircraft also do not have much of a glide slope, creating a tendency to fall vertically from the sky during flight control problems rather than gliding as a fixed-wing aircraft would.

Helicopters may have piston engines or gas turbine engines with fuel capacities ranging from 70 to 1,000 gallons (280 L to 4 000 L). The internal fuel tanks are usually located under the cargo floor and may have rubber bladders, while auxiliary fuel tanks may be either located inside the main cabin in the aft section or attached to the outside of the aircraft. The main rotor(s) serves the same purpose as the wings and propeller on a fixed-wing aircraft — that is, to provide lift and directional motion. The helicopter tail rotor, if the helicopter is so equipped, provides directional control **(Figure 3.19)**. Helicopters are constructed of materials similar to those used for fixed-wing aircraft such as aluminum, titanium, magnesium, and a variety of composite materials.

Figure 3.18 A Sikorsky□ Skycrane□.
Courtesy of William D. Stewart.

Figure 3.19 The main and tail rotors of a modern helicopter.

Fire Fighting Aircraft

In addition to medevac and high-angle rescue roles, aircraft can be used in a variety of roles in the support of fire fighting operations. These roles include the use of fixed-wing aircraft for transporting smokejumpers relatively short distances. Fixed-wing air tankers can carry 800 to 3,000 gallons (3 200 L to 12 000 L) of fire fighting agent that can be dropped on a fire **(Figures 3.20 and 3.21)**. Evergreen International Aviation, Incorporated's 747 Supertanker is designed to carry approximately 20,500 gallons (66 600 L) of fire retardant.

Rotary-wing aircraft can carry 100 to 1,000 gallons (400 L to 4 000 L) of agent in slung buckets suspended from the aircraft or up to 3,000 gallons (12 000 L) of agent in tanks mounted on the underside of the aircraft. Rotary-wing aircraft can also be used to transport firefighters and cargo, to serve as infrared imaging platforms, and as a tool for conducting backfiring operations. ARFF personnel need to be aware that helicopters supporting backfiring operations carry flammable "ping pong balls" in the cargo area or may have a torch carrying jellied gas slung under the helicopter. Various light aircraft, like the Aero Commander□, are used by the Air Tactical Group Supervisor to coordinate all aircraft operations over a fire.

Figure 3.20 A Canadair 215 making a water drop during wildland fire operations. *Courtesy of Ron Stoffel, Minnesota Department of Natural Resources Forestry Division.*

Figure 3.21 Tanker 910 (a DC-10) taxiing. *Courtesy of 10 Tanker Air Carrier.*

Other Types of Aircraft

Airports are home to many different types of aircraft or aviation-type activities not included in the categories previously listed. It is extremely important for ARFF personnel to be familiar with the aircraft that operate in and around their airport. This helps to ensure a safer working environment when rescue operations become necessary. The following list includes some types of aircraft that might be part of any airport:

- Vintage/antique aircraft
- Lighter-than-air craft (blimps, hot-air balloons)
- Tilt-rotor aircraft **(Figure 3.22)**
- Ultralight aircraft
- Experimental/amateur aircraft
- Agricultural spraying (crop-dusting) aircraft **(Figure 3.23)**
- Skydiver transport aircraft
- Aerobatics aircraft
- Medical evacuation/transport aircraft

Major Components of Aircraft

For airport firefighters to understand aircraft and the possible emergencies they may encounter, they must be familiar with the terminology of the major components involved in aircraft construction. This information will assist the firefighter in completely understanding the situation when performing aircraft rescue and fire fighting operations. The following sections discuss the major components of both fixed-wing and rotary-wing aircraft.

Fixed-Wing Aircraft Components

Features and components of a fixed-wing aircraft include the fuselage, wings, and tail section **(Figure 3.24)**.

Fuselage

The main body of an aircraft to which the wings and tail are attached is referred to as the *fuselage*. Currently, aluminum makes up the majority of material used to construct fuselages. However, trends are moving toward using more

Figure 3.22 A MV-22 Osprey is an example of a tilt-rotor aircraft. *Photo by PH3 Timothy Bensken (USN), Defense Visual Information Center (DVIC).*

Figure 3.23 An example of a crop duster aircraft. *Courtesy of Paul Pestel.*

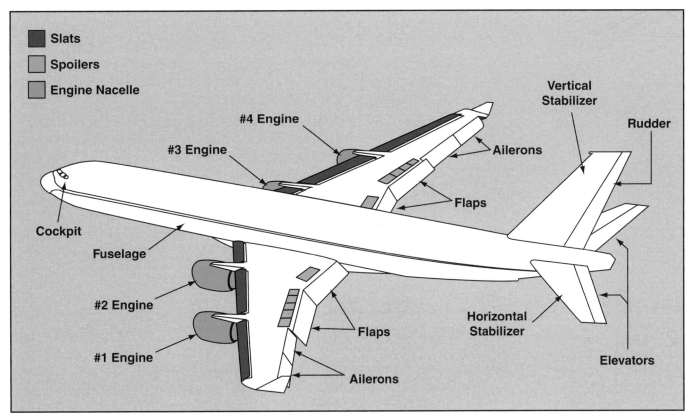

Figure 3.24 Components of fixed-wing aircraft.

composite materials, and in fact, some new generation aircraft are constructed primarily of composite materials. Depending on the type of aircraft, the aircraft skin varies in thickness as it forms and covers the various sections along the structure. The fuselage houses the crew, passengers, cargo, and additional fuel storage. Most of the aircraft systems are found within of the fuselage. The following compartments and equipment are associated with or can be found in or on the fuselage:

- *Landing gear* — provides a mechanism for supporting the aircraft while on the ground and is commonly either tricycle or conventional design. Tricycle gear consists of a single strut under the nose and two main struts extending from under the wings or out of the fuselage. Conventional gear consists of a tail wheel and two main struts under each wing. The nose gear or tail wheel is used for steering while the main gear is equipped with brake systems.

- *Cockpit* — also referred to as the *flight deck* on airliners; fuselage compartment occupied by the pilots or flight crew. The cockpit in certain military (fighter, attack, bomber, and training) aircraft may be equipped with ejection seats. The canopy is a transparent enclosure over the cockpit of various types of aircraft. It is usually constructed of special plastics for durability during flight. Circuit breaker panels are also located in the flight deck area.

- *Passenger Compartment* — the fuselage compartment located behind the flight deck and occupied by the passengers and flight attendants, who are sometimes referred to as the "cabin crew." The following locations and systems can also be found in and around the passenger compartment:

— **Galleys:** compact food storage and preparation areas found on medium, large, and very large aircraft. Galleys may be located at the front, center, or rear areas of the aircraft.

— **Lavatories:** restrooms onboard aircraft that passengers and crew may use to refresh themselves. Lavatories generally include a toilet and sink. They may be located in the front, center, or rear areas of the aircraft. Both galleys and lavatories are modular units that can break loose during crash impacts.

— **Storage bins:** located at numerous points throughout aircraft. Storage space is designated for carry-on luggage, flight attendant equipment and supplies, and so forth. Overhead luggage compartments, along with seats, can also break lose during crash impacts.

— **Emergency exits:** include the normal ingress and egress doors as well as special hatches located along the fuselage, rear air-stairs, and tail cones capable of being jettisoned.

— **Exit rows:** seat rows where emergency exits are located are designated as exit rows. These rows are generally located near the front doors, over the wings, and near the rear doors of the aircraft. The passengers seated in those rows must meet certain minimum requirements that would allow them to be able to open the emergency exit.

— **Emergency lighting:** provide interior light during an emergency and assist passengers in locating emergency exits. Emergency exit lights are found along the floor or sides of the seats, on one side of an aisle. They do not indicate the direction of travel. Lights at an exit location are a red color, while the remainder of the lights are white.

— **Light ballasts:** boost voltage and control current to fluorescent interior lights. ARFF personnel should be familiar with the locations of these ballasts because they may overheat and create a burning odor in the aircraft. Most newer light ballasts have a thermal limiter that prevents overheating.

— **Supplemental oxygen cylinders:** supply emergency oxygen for the flight deck crew, flight attendants, and passengers.

● **Static eliminators** — also called static wicks; spiked metal pieces that are electronically bonded to the aircraft frame. Each static eliminator is insulated from the aircraft by being sealed within a fiberglass rod. Any buildup of static electricity around the aircraft is collected by the spikes, passed through the aircraft frame, and dissipated back into the air.

● **Pitot tubes** — tubular devices mounted on the exterior of an aircraft. During flight, the flow of air into the tubes is measured to determine the airspeed of the aircraft.

Wings

The wings are designed to develop the major portion of the lift required for flight. They, too, are generally constructed of aluminum and carry a majority of fuel. However, as with the fuselage, some wings are constructed entirely out of composite materials. Some military aircraft may have weapons and additional fuel tanks attached to the wings. Along with the tail section, the wings house the *flight control surface* devices. The following components are located on or associated with the wings:

- *Engines* — produce thrust that propels the aircraft. They can be either internal combustion reciprocating or gas turbine. Turbine engines vary in size and thrust-producing capability depending on the type and use of the aircraft.

- *Nacelle* — housing around an externally mounted aircraft engine. It can be constructed of aluminum or composite materials. In the event of an engine fire, fuel often pools in the bottom of the nacelle. This pooling can create a hazardous situation if the nacelle is opened during the extinguishment phase of fire fighting operations.

- *Ailerons* — attached to the trailing edge of the wings. They are the movable, hinged, rear portion of the aircraft wing that controls the rolling (banking) motion of the aircraft.

- *Flaps and slats* — airfoils that extend from the leading edge and/or trailing edge of a wing. Slats are airfoils that extend only from the leading edge of a wing. These devices are used to improve the aerodynamic performance of the aircraft during takeoff and landing.

- *Spoilers and speed brakes* — spoilers are movable panels located on the upper surface of a wing and raise up into the airflow to increase drag and decrease lift. Speed brakes are aerodynamic devices located on the wing or along the rear or underside of the fuselage that can be extended to help slow the aircraft.

- *Vortex generators* — vane-type devices attached to the wings or vertical stabilizers of an aircraft. They are designed to maintain a steady flow of air over the control surfaces located on the wing's trailing edge.

Tail (Empennage)

The aircraft tail section includes the vertical and horizontal stabilizers, rudders, and elevators. Generally, the tail section houses the auxiliary power unit (APU), which provides electrical power to operate the essential systems when the aircraft engines are not running. Some aircraft are equipped with rear stairs or a tail-cone jettison system that is designed to provide additional means of egress. The following flight surface controls are located on the tail section:

- *Elevator* — hinged, movable control surface found along the rear of the horizontal stabilizer; attached to the control wheel or stick and is used to control the up-and-down pitch motion of the aircraft

- *Rudder* — hinged, movable control surface attached to the rear part of the vertical stabilizer and is used to control the yaw or turning motion of the aircraft.

Flight control surface — Devices that enable the pilot to control the direction of flight, altitude, and attitude of the aircraft; includes ailerons, elevator, rudder, flaps and slats, spoilers, and speed brakes.

Airfoils — Relates to the shape of a wing, propeller blade, or horizontal or vertical stabilizer as it is viewed in cross-section; generate the lift needed for the aircraft to fly.

Leading edge — Front or forward edge of an aircraft's wings or stabilizers.

Trailing edge — Rearmost edge of an aircraft's wings or stabilizers.

Stabilizer — Airfoil on an airplane used to provide stability; that is, the aft horizontal surface to which the elevators are hinged (horizontal stabilizer) and the fixed vertical surface to which the rudder is hinged (vertical stabilizer).

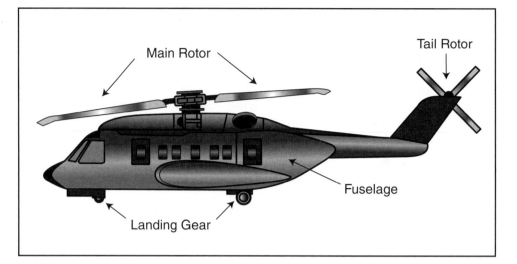

Figure 3.25 Components of rotary-wing aircraft.

Rotary-Wing Aircraft Components

The main sections of a rotary-wing aircraft include the following **(Figure 3.25)**:

- *Fuselage* — houses the same components as a fixed-wing aircraft fuselage. It is not built for high altitude pressurization and is not as ruggedly constructed as larger fixed wing aircraft, causing helicopters to fragment more during crash impacts.

- *Main rotor*(s) — provide lift and propulsion for the helicopter to fly. Some helicopters are designed with two main rotors, and others have one main rotor and one tail rotor. Depending on the helicopter type and use, the main rotor may consist of two to seven rotor blades.

- *Tail rotor* — provides the helicopter with directional control. It counteracts the torque produced by the main rotor. Some newly designed helicopters can operate by using engine exhaust to provide control of the aircraft, thus eliminating the need for a tail rotor.

- *Landing gear* — used to support the aircraft when it is not in flight. The two types of landing gear assemblies are conventional and skid support.
  - *Conventional gear* consists of main gear and either a nose or tail gear. This gear may or may not retract depending on the type of helicopter. Retractable landing gear is housed in pontoons that provide flotation support for helicopters that land in water.
  - *Skids* are used on smaller helicopters in the place of conventional landing gear. The skids are permanently mounted to the exterior and resemble platforms. Because they are without wheels, helicopters with skids often "hover taxi" to move along taxiways or the parking ramp.

Engine Types and Applications

The two different types of engines used to power aircraft are the internal-combustion reciprocating engine and the gas turbine, or jet engine. This section examines these types of engines and the hazards they may pose to responding firefighters.

Figure 3.26 A radial-style internal combustion engine. *Courtesy of Jeff Reichmann, Reichmann Safety Services.*

Figure 3.27 An internal combustion engine with the cylinders arranged in the horizontally-opposed configuration. *Courtesy of Doddy Photography.*

Internal-Combustion Reciprocating Engines

Many aircraft are powered by internal-combustion reciprocating engines. These engines operate through the combustion of fuel and air vapors within combustion cylinders causing pressure to move pistons back and forth within these cylinders. The movement of the pistons causes a crankshaft to turn thus turning the aircraft's propeller(s). The cylinders may be configured around a central crankshaft (radial engine) **(Figure 3.26)** or in a horizontally-opposed arrangement much like the engine found in an automobile. Power from the engine is transmitted through the crankshaft to the propeller.

Reciprocating engines use aviation gasoline (AVGAS) as their fuel. Unlike most automotive engines, they are air-cooled to eliminate the weight of the heavy engine blocks typical of liquid-cooled engines. These aircraft engines use relatively large amounts of oil and often carry a large oil tank adjacent to the engine. An accessory section drives the pumps for the fuel, oil, and hydraulic systems and the generators for the electrical system.

Most aircraft with this type of engine are used primarily for general aviation. The fuselage is usually made entirely of lightweight metal or of a metal frame with a fabric covering. An aircraft powered by reciprocating engines can be rated up to 400 horsepower, weigh up to 3,500 pounds (1 588 kg), and may carry from one to six passengers **(Figure 3.27)**.

Twin-engine and four-engine larger aircraft used for general, commercial, and military aviation may also utilize reciprocating engines. This design often limits the number of passengers, but the aircraft may still be configured to carry as many as 90 people.

Spinning propellers and hot engine parts produce hazards from these engines. A magneto is another hazard that poses an immediate risk during extrication. At least two magnetos are found on all internal combustion engines and are designed to produce sparks that keep the engine operating. If while performing extrication, rescuers were to bump or rotate the propeller, the magneto could ignite any unspent fuel remaining in the engine cylinders and cause the engine to restart and the propeller to rotate.

Magneto — Device used in gasoline engines that produces a periodic spark in order to maintain fuel combustion.

WARNING!
Disconnecting the battery does not prevent the magneto from functioning, so personnel must exercise caution when working in the area of the propeller. A safety zone should be established around the engine, keeping all personnel clear of the engine.

Gas Turbine Engines

There are four main types of gas turbine engines: turbojet, turbofan, turboprop, and turboshaft. In all types of gas turbine engines, air is drawn in through the front, compressed, mixed with fuel and ignited, and then exhausted out the back. The rapid expansion of the fuel/air mixture, when ignited, generates engine power which is used for one of two purposes:

- To drive the aircraft by expelling high-speed exhaust gases
- To drive a fan, propeller, or rotor

Gas turbine engines use jet fuel to operate and can be damaged if AVGAS is mistakenly added.

The four major components of all gas turbine engines are the compressor section, combustion section, turbine and exhaust section, and accessory section. Air is drawn into the compressor section at the front of the engine where it is compressed and accelerated by rotating blades.

The compressed air enters the combustion section, which is divided into a number of chambers, where it is mixed with atomized fuel and ignited. This action results in the expansion of heated gases and the production of high-pressure, high-velocity exhaust gas. At this point, the superheated gas is directed through turbine blades at the rear of the engine. The turbines are attached to a common shaft with the compressor blades. In this arrangement, the high-speed gases cause the turbines to rotate which in turn drives the compressor section. Components of other aircraft systems that support the engine or are powered by it are contained in the accessory section. These accessories include the fuel control unit and fuel pump, hydraulic pump, oil pump and cooler, and electrical generator.

Other Gas Turbine Functions

Gas turbine engines also support the aircraft cabin air-conditioning system and the wing de-icing system. Air is bled from the compressor section and used to pressurize and power the air-conditioning fan for the cabin. Hot air is also bled from the exhaust side of the engine and ducted to the leading edge of the wing and engines to keep them from accumulating ice.

Figure 3.28 An A-6E Intruder (back ground) is powered by two turbojet engines like the one shown in the foreground. *Courtesy of PH2 Dale W. Novotasky (USN), Defense Visual Information Center (DVIC).*

Figure 3.29 The fan blades of a turbo-fan engine. *Courtesy of Edwin A. Jones, USAFR.*

Figure 3.30 An example of a turboprop engine.

Figure 3.31 An example of a turboshaft engine on a military helicopter. *Courtesy of Edwin A. Jones, USAFR.*

The following are more detailed descriptions of the four, standard designs for gas-turbine engines:

- *Turbojet* — the simplest of the gas turbine engines **(Figure 3.28)** and is also referred to as a jet engine; used primarily to propel aircraft by using a high velocity exhaust stream. When the exhaust stream momentum exceeds the momentum of the intake air stream forward thrust is produced.

- *Turbofan* — most commonly found on aircraft today, especially on large jetliners; contains an additional component that the turbojet does not have — a large fan at the front of the engine **(Figure 3.29)**. This fan helps increase the engine's thrust by increasing the total airflow of the engine. Turbofans are also referred to as high bypass jet engines.

- *Turboprop* — widely used for small- and medium-sized commuter and cargo aircraft; consists of a propeller that is driven by a small turbojet engine. Turboprop engines are easily distinguished from piston engines by the turboprop's streamlined engine nacelle and a single or dual exhaust port that is much larger in diameter than those on piston engines **(Figure 3.30);** used on a variety of aircraft having one, two, or four engines.

- *Turboshaft* — most commonly found in helicopters; basically the same as a turboprop; however the output shaft is not connected to a propeller. Instead, the power turbine is connected, either directly or through a gearbox, to a shaft that drives the helicopter's main and tail rotors **(Figure 3.31)**.

Engine Additions and Variations

Additional components may be added to the basic gas turbine engine to redirect engine exhaust gas streams, to increase engine thrust, and to slow aircraft speed when landing. These additional components include the following:

- Exhaust nozzles that rotate to redirect the exhaust gas stream downward to enable vertical takeoff and landing. The Harrier attack jet uses this type of engine exhaust system **(Figure 3.32, p.80)**. A unique variation of this principle is found incorporated in the design of tilt-rotor aircraft. These have turboprop engines driving very-large-diameter propellers.

Figure 3.32 The AV-8B Harrier uses rotating exhaust nozzles to give the aircraft vertical takeoff and landing capabilities. *Photo by SGT Ezekiel R. Kitandwe (USMC), Defense Visual Information Center (DVIC).*

Figure 3.33 A thrust-reversal system in use during an aircraft landing. *Courtesy of Edwin A. Jones, USAFR.*

The entire engine nacelle pivots from vertical, for helicopter-like takeoff and landing, to horizontal, for aircraft-like high-speed flight.

- An afterburner (augmentor) provides additional thrust for short periods, improving takeoff and climb capability, and enhancing the performance of military fighter aircraft. This is accomplished by injecting and burning raw fuel in the superheated exhaust stream behind the turbine section.

- Thrust-reversal systems consist of internal or external doors and vanes that operate to deflect jet exhaust forward to assist in slowing the air craft during its landing rollout. These devices can be hydraulically powered, or on some aircraft, pneumatically actuated **(Figure 3.33)**.

Landing Roll Out— Distance from the point of touchdown to the point where the aircraft is brought to a stop or exits the runway.

Aircraft Construction and Structural Materials

In an effort to help ensure personnel safety, airport firefighters should have a thorough knowledge of aircraft construction, the materials used, and the hazards they may pose during and after fire fighting operations. The inherent properties of the materials and the manner in which these components are assembled may affect fire fighting operations. Materials commonly used in late-model aircraft construction include metals such as aluminum, steel, magnesium, and titanium; composite materials and metal alloys; plastics; and wood. These materials are often used in any number of combinations. ARFF personnel should be aware that when the surfaces of different materials are uniformly painted, the variation in construction may not be apparent without close investigation.

Metals

A number of metals are utilized in the construction of aircraft. The most common metals used in aircraft include aluminum and aluminum alloys, steel, magnesium and magnesium alloys, and titanium. The sections that follow discuss how these metals are employed in aircraft construction.

Aluminum and Aluminum Alloys

Due to its lightweight characteristics, along with the ability to be molded into a variety of shapes, aluminum has been an ideal material for aircraft construction. This lightweight material also can be molded and used in sheets for skin surfaces, or it can be formed into honeycomb sheets, which are often used to form walls and floor sections. One disadvantage to using aluminum for aircraft construction is that it does not withstand heat well; it melts at relatively low temperatures (approximately 1,200°°F [649°°C]).

Aluminum alloys are created by mixing components of different types together in a molding process that produces stronger, yet lighter construction materials. These alloys can be found molded into landing gear parts, structural and load-bearing members, as well as parts of the door operating assemblies. The most common alloys currently used in the construction of aircraft include aluminum-beryllium and aluminum-lithium. The percentage of aluminum used in aircraft construction continues to decrease as new, composite materials are developed to replace it.

Steel
In certain parts of the aircraft, such as in the engine and landing gear, high strength is required and/or high heat tolerance is critical. Steel is used in these components, even though the weight of steel per volume is much higher than other structural materials.

Magnesium and Magnesium Alloys
Because they are both strong and lightweight, magnesium and magnesium alloys are used for the landing gear, wheels of some older aircraft, engine-mounting brackets, crankcase sections, cover plates, and other engine parts. Magnesium and its alloys are generally used in areas where forcible entry will not be required. Unless ground into a dust or into small particles, magnesium is difficult to ignite; however, once ignited, it burns intensely and is very difficult to extinguish.

Titanium
Titanium is a metallic element used to reinforce skin surfaces against impinging exhaust flames or heat. Titanium is used for internal engine parts such as turbine blades, auxiliary power unit enclosures, and landing gear parts. Like magnesium, titanium is a combustible metal that burns with intensity and makes extinguishment difficult.

Composites, Advanced Composites, and Advanced Aerospace Materials
A growing number of lightweight composite, advanced composite, or advanced aerospace materials are currently being used in modern aircraft construction. The percentage of composite materials will only increase as manufacturers develop more and more ways to incorporate their use **(Figure 3.34 page 82)**. Much of the success of NLA's is because of composite, advanced composite, or advanced aerospace materials.

Composite materials are composed of two or more organic or inorganic components. One serves as the matrix that holds everything together while the other (usually a fiber or linear structure) serves as a reinforcement to add strength and stiffness to the combined material. Fiberglass is a common example of a composite material.

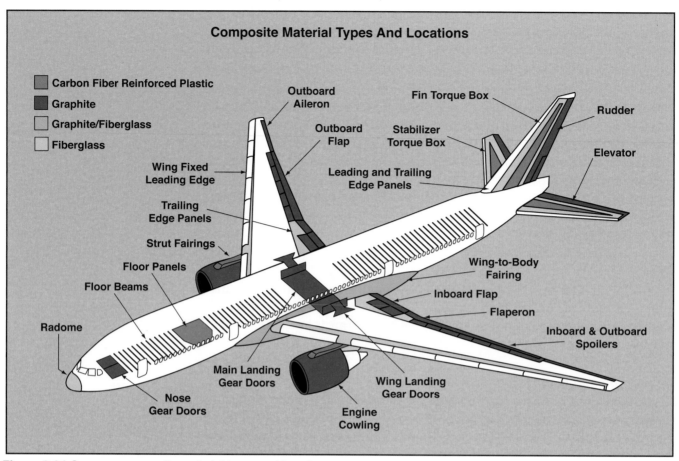

Composite Material Types And Locations

Carbon Fiber Reinforced Plastic
Graphite
Graphite/Fiberglass
Fiberglass

Outboard Aileron
Fin Torque Box
Rudder
Outboard Flap
Stabilizer Torque Box
Elevator
Wing Fixed Leading Edge
Leading and Trailing Edge Panels
Trailing Edge Panels
Strut Fairings
Wing-to-Body Fairing
Floor Panels
Floor Beams
Inboard Flap
Flaperon
Radome
Inboard & Outboard Spoilers
Main Landing Gear Doors
Wing Landing Gear Doors
Nose Gear Doors
Engine Cowling

Figure 3.34 Common composite material types and locations.

Advanced composites also possess high strength and stiffness but also have other properties such as resistance to corrosion, low weight, or special electrical or thermal properties. Aramid (Kevlar)/Epoxy, Boron/Epoxy, and Graphite/Epoxy are examples of advanced composite materials.

Advanced aerospace materials are specialized to meet specific aerospace environment, construction, or performance needs. An example of advanced aerospace materials is radar absorbent material (RAM).

An article on advanced composites and advanced aerospace materials, "Advanced Composites/Advanced Aerospace Materials [AC/AAM]: Mishap Risk Control and Mishap Response," by Dr. John M. Olson, is included in Appendix C of this manual. It contains guidelines that departments may want to incorporate into their standard operating procedures in an effort to enhance ARFF personnel safety. Personnel should become familiar with this study and take the necessary precautions when faced with aircraft emergencies involving advanced composites and aerospace materials.

Plastics

As aircraft construction methods changed through the decades, so did the materials used to build them. As plastics became more readily available, numerous uses for plastics in aircraft construction were found, often to replace wooden components. Wood interior paneling, passenger cabin dividers, and seat components were replaced with pre-formed plastic components. Plastic is also used in a variety of tubing, conduit, and other aircraft cabin components.

Wood

Some older aircraft have a considerable amount of wood in structural areas such as wing spars and bulkheads; bulkheads of some aircraft are made almost entirely of wood. However, the most common construction technique is to combine tubular steel framing with wooden components. Because there is a high probability that an aviation-type fuel is present, aqueous film forming foam (AFFF) should be used in fire fighting operations even though these are Class "A" materials.

In addition, corporate-style aircraft incorporate elaborate wood fixtures for interior furnishings. These furnishings are often structural framework, fabrics, and laminated wood products with epoxy-type finishes that when exposed to fire produce a wide variety of toxic vapors.

Aircraft Systems

Fuel, hydraulic, electrical, oxygen, flight-control, landing-gear, and egress or escape aircraft systems all create potential hazards. When planning strategies for aircraft accidents/incidents, rescue personnel should carefully consider each of these potential hazard areas and develop tactics, SOPs, etc. that address and attempt to eliminate and control the hazards while performing a rescue.

Standardized Coding

In an effort to assist aircraft mechanics, aircraft manufacturers have developed a color-coded labeling system that addresses all tubing, piping, and cabling found in an aircraft. ARFF personnel can use this system to assist them when performing extrication operations. Aircraft of all types contain varying amounts of tubing, hose, and other conduits that may be of the same size and appearance, so it is often difficult to distinguish among them. Therefore, a standardized coding system has been designed to simplify their identification and reduce the risk of misidentification.

The coding is presented in three different forms: colors, labels, and symbols to make it easier to accurately identify tubing, hose, and piping **(Figure 3.35, p. 84)**. Color is used because it may be identified from a distance. Labels are necessary for the color-blind and for situations in which fire, heat, and smoke may obscure or alter the color. Finally, symbols not only aid in helping confirm the colors and labels, but also they are more readily recognized by those who do not read English. Being aware of these codes allows ARFF personnel to proceed quickly but cautiously when encountering these conduits during aircraft extrication procedures.

Fuel Systems

The largest system in the aircraft is the fuel system. The components of the fuel system — tanks, lines, control valves, and pumps — are located throughout the aircraft. Therefore, the fuel system presents the greatest hazard in an aircraft accident. The fuel system consists of two major parts: the tanks and the distribution system.

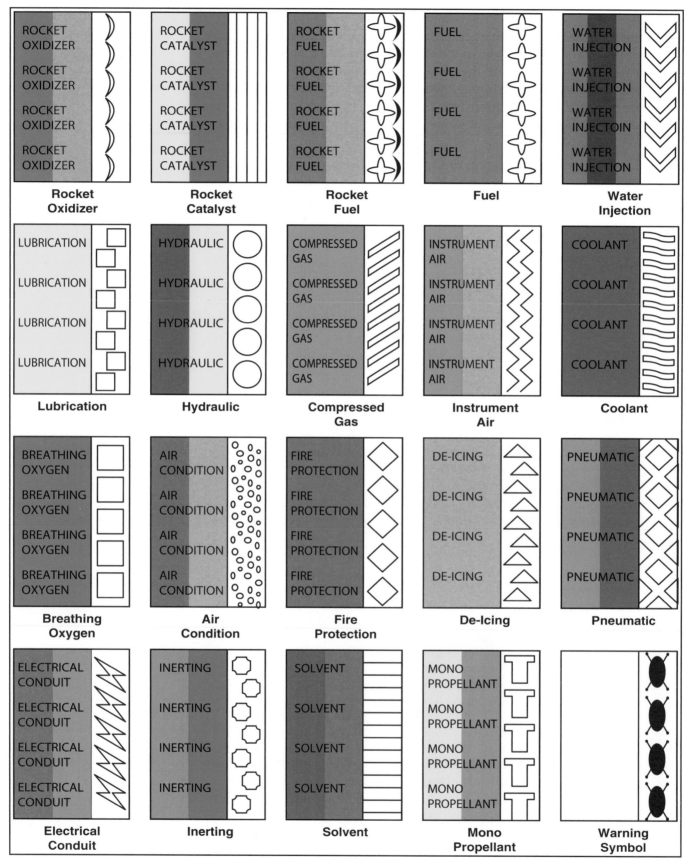

Figure 3.35 A color/label/symbol system is used to identify the functions of various tubing, hoses, and piping in aircraft.

Range of Fuel Capacity

Commercial aircraft fuel capacity can range from 3,000 gallons to over 58,000 gallons (12 000 L to 220 000 L) as found on a Boeing 747-400. New large aircraft such as the Airbus A-380 are being designed to carry a fuel load of more than 100,000 gallons (378 541 L).

Fuel Tanks

Depending on the type and use of aircraft, fuel tanks may be found and constructed as separate units or as an integral part of the aircraft. Small general aviation aircraft have tanks that are generally found in the wings and that are constructed of aluminum, composite, or rubber bladders. Business-style, commuter, and commercial aircraft also use the wings to store fuel by incorporating integral tanks. Integral tanks are formed by sealing the inside structure of the wing with specialized epoxy.

In addition to the wing area, business, commuter, and commercial aircraft use the center fuselage section between the wings to store fuel **(Figure 3.36)**. Additional tanks are sometimes installed forward or aft of the center fuselage tank.

Some aircraft that are designed to fly great distances use double-walled fuselage tanks. Because these tanks are outside the box structure of the wing center section, they do not have any substantial structural protection. Other areas for additional tanks include center fuselage pods, wingtips, tail (horizontal or vertical stabilizers), or tailcones. Military aircraft also use auxiliary tanks or fuel pods, which are mounted externally, to extend their flying range **(Figure 3.37, p. 86)**.

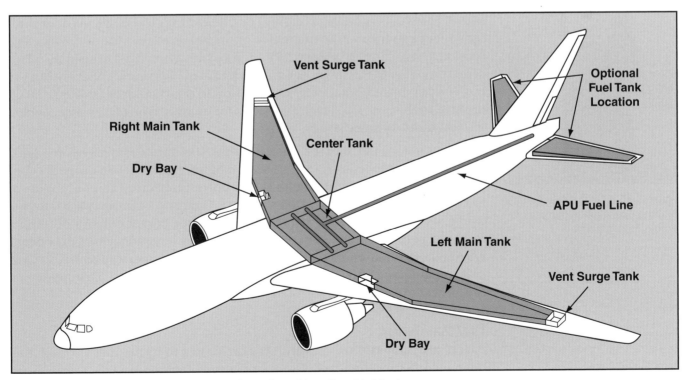

Figure 3.36 A typical aircraft fuel tank configuration with optional tail tanks.

Figure 3.37 This F-16 Fighting Falcon has two external fuel tanks mounted temporarily under the wings. *Photo by TSgt Michael Ammons (USAF), Defense Visual Information Center (DUIC).*

Regardless of the fuel-tank construction, fuel may be released if the aircraft is damaged. Although the damage may seem insignificant and remote from the aircraft cabin, ARFF personnel should thoroughly examine both the interior and exterior of the aircraft for fuel leaks. Even minor damage can be critical because leaking or seeping fuel may pool in low-lying sections of the fuselage.

Civilian and military aircraft, both fixed-wing types and helicopters, utilize auxiliary fuel tanks. On military aircraft, tanks may be jettisoned in flight to improve speed and maneuverability. The fuel capacity of auxiliary tanks can vary from 30 gallons (120 L) in a small civilian aircraft to 2,000 gallons (8 000 L) per tank in large military aircraft. Helicopter auxiliary tanks can be located inside or outside the cabin. During flight operations, the fuel within auxiliary tanks is usually consumed first.

Crash-resistant fuel tanks with self-sealing fittings and automatic shutoffs are in limited use. Although the technology for fuel tanks has continued to advance, these improvements have not been widely adopted. Some military aircraft have open-celled foam blocks that are cut to fit and placed in the tanks. While these vapor-suppressing blocks are primarily to protect against explosion after projectiles, such as incendiary bullets, have penetrated the vapor space, they are also effective in suppressing fire after a crash.

Fuel tanks may be filled individually through service openings on the top side of the wings (gravity refueling) or filled through a single point or multiple fueling points on the underside of the wings or the side of the fuselage (pressure refueling) **(Figure 3.38)**. In pressure refueling, a system of valves directs the fuel to the tanks needing to be filled. Sensing devices within the individual tanks automatically stop the flow to a particular tank when it is full or filled to the required level. Dipstick fuel-quantity gauges are also located on the bottom of some wings.

Figure 3.38 A typical pressure refueling operation. *Courtesy of Doddy Photography.*

Over a period of time, the epoxy sealing fuel tanks may develop a leak. Normal repair procedures involve maintenance personnel entering the confined spaces of fuel tanks through access ports found on either the top side or the bottom side of the wing. Due to the confinement of these spaces, rescue workers should meet with aircraft maintenance personnel and develop a response plan in which to effectively handle any emergency that may occur during these maintenance operations. As a precautionary measure, the aircraft maintenance division should notify the airport fire department when this procedure is being performed.

Fuel Distribution

Fuel is distributed from the aircraft's fuel tanks to its engines through fuel lines, control valves, and pumps located throughout the aircraft. Aircraft with engines or auxiliary power units (APU) located in the tail section may have fuel lines routed through interior walls, through the roof, or between the main cabin floor and the cargo area of the aircraft.

Fuel lines vary in sizes from ⅛ inch (3 mm) to 4 inches (100 mm) in diameter. They are constructed of metal, rubber, or combinations of materials and are often shrouded to control developing leaks. Pumps that are capable of producing pressures from 4 to 40 psi (28 kPa to 280 kPa) control the fuel flow within fuel lines. Deactivating fuel pumps can control fuel system leaks. Deactivation is best accomplished by securing aircraft power and fuel controls in the flight deck area.

Temperature changes cause fuel in the tanks to expand and contract. In order to reduce pressure buildup caused by expansion, fuels tanks are equipped with vents and vent tanks which hold residual and released fuel vapors. Under normal conditions, the small amounts of fuel that escape, evaporate quickly, so such venting is usually not hazardous. Quite often, however, fueling personnel overfill the main tanks so that when expansion does occur, the fuel vents into the vent tanks, continuing through the overflow tube and onto the aircraft parking area.

Heating of fuel cells exposed to direct fire or radiant heat can also cause expansion of fuel which may release fuel vapors from vents. There are also other causes for fuel spills under aircraft that are not hazardous under normal conditions. For example, minor spillage may occur when aircraft engines are shut down or when petcocks are opened to drain water and sediment from fuel tanks. These small amounts of fuel usually do not represent a significant fire hazard.

Petcock — Small faucet or valve for releasing or draining a gas (such as air).

Two basic types of fuel that rescue workers encounter include AVGAS and jet fuel. These fuels can be mixed in a variety of ways depending on the use of aircraft, and are covered in greater detail in Chapter 4, "Safety and Aircraft Hazards." The level of hazard also varies depending on the fuel, how it is mixed, and the scenario in which it has been released.

Hydraulic Systems

An aircraft's hydraulic system generates the immense power necessary to operate the control surfaces on an aircraft and to extend and retract the landing gear. This system consists of a hydraulic fluid reservoir, electric or engine-driven pumps, appliances, various hydraulic accumulators, and tubing that interconnects the system. The hydraulic fluid is supplied to a pressure pump that moves the fluid throughout the hydraulic system and to accumulators where some of the fluid is stored under pressure. This stored fluid may then be used to supply hydraulic pressure to critical aircraft systems such as landing gear, nose-gear, steering, brakes, and wing flaps **(Figure 3.39, p. 88)**. An accumulator may store this fluid under pressure for a considerable period of time even after the engines have been stopped. Most modern aircraft hydraulic systems operate at a pressure of 3,000 psi (21,000 kPa) or higher and may carry as much as 185 gallons (740 L) of hydraulic fluid.

Of the three types of hydraulic fluid produced, synthetic hydraulic fluids are the most widely used. Old, vintage aircraft relied on either a hydrocarbon-based fluid or a vegetable-based fluid. A red mineral oil based hydraulic fluid may also be encountered. Synthetic fluid is most popular because it presents a significantly reduced flammability hazard. Its flash point is twice that of non-synthetic fluid, and once on fire, the flame-spread rate is slower. The most common synthetic hydraulic fluid is a phosphate-ester-based material.

Typical Hydraulic System

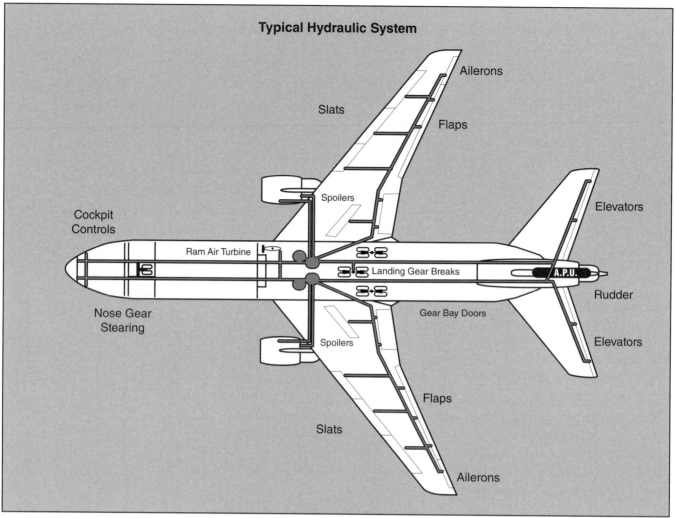

Figure 3.39 Typical configuration of an aircraft's hydraulic system and the various aircraft systems the hydraulic system provides pressure to.

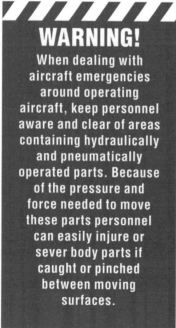

There are drawbacks associated with synthetic fluids. During rescue or fire suppression operations, ARFF personnel must exercise extreme caution to avoid cutting pressurized hydraulic lines. When released in the form of a fine mist, synthetic fluid is extremely flammable. If sprayed on hot brakes or hot engine components, the fluid may ignite. A hydraulic fire produces a "torch effect" or, if confined, may explode. Personnel also must guard against hydraulic fluid contacting skin, eyes, and protective clothing because this type of fluid can cause severe skin and eye irritation as well as erode protective clothing surfaces.

Wheel Assemblies

As stated earlier, the landing gear is designed to support the weight of an aircraft when it is on the ground. The landing gear contains the wheel assembly, which consists of rims, brakes, and tires. Wheel assemblies or *bogies* contain rims that in older style aircraft may be made of magnesium and in newer aircraft, titanium or aluminum alloys. Most aircraft rims are equipped with fusible plugs that are designed to melt, automatically deflating the tires when the rim reaches a predetermined temperature (**Figure 3.40**).

Figure 3.40 Fusible plugs are designed to melt and deflate aircraft tires. *Courtesy of Edwin A. Jones, USAFR.*

Figure 3.41 ARFF personnel looking at an aircraft brake assembly.

Aircraft brakes are designed to slow and stop the aircraft after landing, during an aborted takeoff, or while taxiing. Aircraft brake systems can be very complex with as many as three independent sources of hydraulic power for the brakes on a large jet aircraft as well as two separate anti-skid systems and an auto-brake system. The brake assemblies are made of magnesium, beryllium, or asbestos in older aircraft and carbon composite in newer aircraft. Aircraft brakes frequently become overheated due to the combined effects of the aircraft weight, the landing speed, and the extra braking power required for short runways **(Figure 3.41)**. Brakes and wheels may reach their maximum temperatures 20 to 30 minutes after the aircraft comes to a stop.

Large aircraft tires may have pressures exceeding 200 psi (1 400 kPa). They are usually filled with nitrogen (an inert gas) due to the tremendous amount of heat generated during takeoffs and landings. Procedures for handling aircraft emergencies involving wheel assemblies are covered in Chapter 11, "Strategic and Tactical Operations."

Power, Electrical, and Auxiliary Systems

An aircraft relies on an electrical system to supply current for lights, electronic equipment, hydraulic pumps, fuel pumps, armament systems, warning systems, and other devices **(Figure 3.42 page 90)**. Some aircraft can have up to several miles of wiring to carry electricity throughout the aircraft. Aircraft electrical systems use both AC and DC current to supply electrical power because some equipment operates more efficiently on one type than on the other. Light aircraft operate on 12- or 24-volt DC systems; large aircraft operate on 24/28-volt DC and 110/115-volt AC. However, some aircraft may use electrical systems with voltages as high as 270 volts DC.

Bogie — Tandem arrangement of landing gear wheels with a central strut; swivels up and down so all wheels stay on the ground as the attitude of the aircraft changes or as the slope of the ground surface changes.

WARNING!

When dealing with a landing gear emergency such as a hot brake or gear fire, always approach landing gear either forward or aft of the gear assembly. If heated beyond limits, landing gear assemblies and tires may explode, sending debris and pieces out from the sides of the assembly. These pieces can travel with enough velocity to be fatal or puncture fuel cells located in the wings.

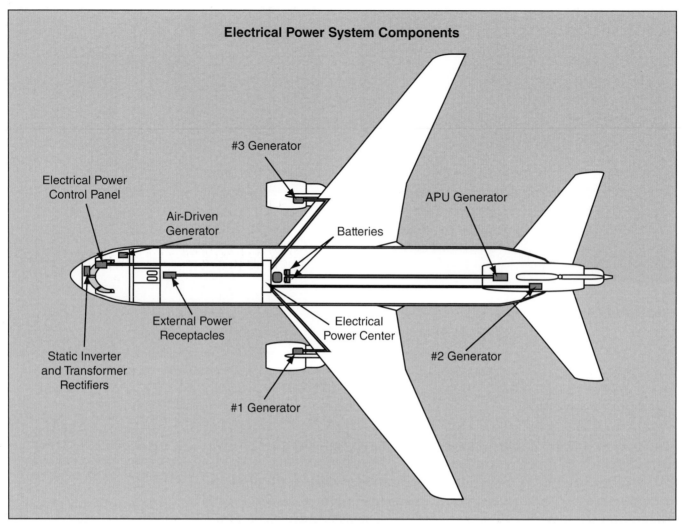

Electrical Power System Components

Figure 3.42 Typical configuration of an aircraft's electrical system.

The sections that follow discuss the various power systems on board an aircraft including the following:

- Batteries
- Auxiliary Power Units (APU)
- Emergency Power Units (EPU)
- Ground Power Units (GPU)

Aircraft Batteries

Aircraft batteries are divided into two general types: lead acid and nickel cadmium. Fundamentally, there is no difference in the operation of aircraft and automobile wet cell batteries. Both have the same type of plates immersed in an electrolyte solution and operate on the same basic principles. The aircraft battery, however, requires a great deal more care because of the unusual conditions under which it operates. Aircraft batteries are built so that they will not leak when an airplane is upside down. Voltage is usually 12 to 30 volts. To save weight, aircraft batteries have an exceedingly small capacity – only one-third that of the average automobile battery.

Figure 3.43 ARFF firefighter using the quarter-turn quick disconnect on an aircraft battery. *Courtesy of Edwin A. Jones, USAFR.*

Most commercial and military aircraft batteries are equipped with quick-disconnect terminals. Usually, a quarter-turn terminal device on the battery cable terminal will connect or disconnect the battery **(Figure 3.43)**. Depending on the type and use of aircraft, the number and location will vary. ARFF personnel assigned to airport duty should familiarize themselves with the locations of the batteries and electrical system shutoffs on the types of aircraft common to that facility. The battery(ies) will usually be near the ground power connection. Sometimes the battery location can be identified by a compartment drain and/or vent on the bottom of the aircraft. Military aircraft will often have the battery compartment marked.

All aircraft shutdown functions must be accomplished prior to deenergizing the electrical system. The emergency lighting systems on passenger aircraft have their own batteries, independent of the rest of the aircraft systems. Functions such as normal cargo-door operation, extinguishing system discharge, cockpit shutdown procedures, and emergency shutdown procedures cannot be completed without electrical power on the devices that perform these functions.

Auxiliary Power Unit (APU)

An auxiliary power unit (APU) is a small jet engine with a generator attached which is used while the aircraft is on the ground and at the gate to operate systems instead of running one of the engines **(Figure 3.44, p. 92)**. Running engines would create hazards to ground maintenance personnel while servicing the aircraft. APU turbine engines provide pneumatic air and AC electrical power to start the aircraft engines, power the cockpit, recharge the batteries, light the cabin, and maintain comfortable cabin temperatures. While the aircraft is airborne, the APU can sometimes be used as a backup electrical power source. Found on most commercial aircraft, some commuter and corporate, the unit is generally located in the tail section of the aircraft. External APU controls on large aircraft usually are found on the nose gear, belly, tail, or main gear compartment.

The APU may often use two air intakes to function. One is used for the operation of the unit while the other is used to cool the compartment. Personnel should be familiar with the intake that cools the compartment. A firefighter

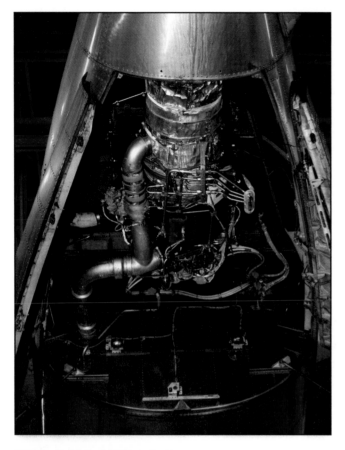

Figure 3.44 An APU located in the tail section of a commercial aircraft.

Monopropellant — Chemical or a mixture of chemicals that is stable under specific storage conditions, but reacts very rapidly under other conditions to produce large amounts of energetic (hot) gasses. Monopropellants, such as hydrazine, are commonly used in aircraft emergency power units.

Hypergolic — Chemical reaction between a fuel and an oxidizer that causes immediate ignition on contact without the presence of air.

might be able to use this intake to discharge extinguishing agent into the APU compartment.

When battling an APU fire, rescuers must exercise extreme caution when accessing the unit because the access doors are often found below the unit. Pooling fuel may be held within the voids of these access doors and could spill out when the doors are opened. ARFF personnel should also check for fire extension in all areas inside the aircraft that are adjacent to the APU compartment. When dealing with any emergency situation involving an aircraft system, ARFF personnel should request the assistance of mechanics or maintenance personnel familiar with the type and model of involved aircraft.

Because the APU is a small jet engine, it can create a noise hazard and an exhaust hazard to anyone who walks past the exhaust port while it is running. Also, because the APU operates on jet fuel, there is always the possibility that it will catch fire. Many newer aircraft incorporate an automatic system that deactivates the unit if a fault, overheat, or fire is detected. Manual controls are located in the cockpit and on an external fire protection panel to deactivate the unit and discharge the APU fire extinguishing bottle. Airport firefighters should be familiar with the APU locations, internal and external shutdowns, and the battery that supplies the APU for the aircraft that operate at their airport.

Emergency Power Unit (EPU)

EPUs fill the need for a highly reliable and quickly responsive means of obtaining emergency electrical power (for restarting engines) and hydraulic power (for flight-control operation) aboard airborne aircraft. There are basically three types of EPUs: ram-air-turbine (RAT), jet-fuel, and monopropellant.

ARFF personnel should be familiar with the general location of the ram-air-turbine because it may deploy when the electrical system is deenergized. Deployment causes a compartment in the lower area of the fuselage to open allowing the RAT to fall out of the aircraft possibly striking rescue personnel **(Figure 3.45)**. A jet-fuel EPU has the same hazards as a jet-fuel APU. On the other hand, monopropellant EPUs, used in aircraft such as the F-16 fighter and the space shuttle, are extremely hazardous because they are powered by a toxic and caustic fuel called *hydrazine*.

Hydrazine is a clear, oily liquid that has a smell similar to ammonia. Some forms of hydrazine may be classified as hypergolic, which means that it ignites spontaneously on contact with an oxidizer. Hydrazine poses a health hazard in both the liquid and vapor forms. Liquid hydrazine can cause severe local damage or burns if it comes in contact with the eyes or skin. It can penetrate the skin to cause systemic effects similar to those produced when swallowed or inhaled. If inhaled, the vapor causes local irritation of the eyes and respiratory tract and the following systemic effects:

Figure 3.45 An example of a deployed ram air turbine (RAT). *Courtesy of Edwin A. Jones, USAFR.*

Figure 3.46 A ground power unit (GPU) connected to an aircraft. *Courtesy of Edwin A. Jones, USAFR.*

- Short-term exposure effects involve the central nervous system with symptoms including tremors
- High concentrations can cause convulsions and possible death
- Repeated or prolonged exposures may cause toxic damage to the liver and kidneys, as well as anemia (blood deficient of red blood cells)

    Check the MSDS for specific hazards associated with each type of hydrazine.

Ground Power Units (GPU)

GPUs can be mobile (on carts, trailers, or trucks), fixed-mounted in buildings, or bridge-mounted on jetways that connect the aircraft to the terminal building, and they are used to provide onboard electrical power while the engines or APU are not operating. GPUs can be used to produce either AC or DC power and come in diesel- or gas-fueled models **(Figure 3.46)**. Airport firefighters should be familiar with the shutdown and disconnection procedures of GPUs at their airport.

Aircraft Lighting

When responding to an aircraft emergency at night, aircraft lighting may be the only means by which personnel can designate their location relative to the aircraft. A red light can be found at the left wingtip while a green light can be found at the right wingtip. A white light(s) is found at the tail section on the end of the fuselage. Lights designed to illuminate the logo found on the sides of the vertical stabilizer are referred to as "logo lights." Landing lights consist of high-intensity spotlights that can be found on the wings and landing gear. Rotating or flashing red anti-collision lights are also used to indicate that aircraft engines are operating. They can be found on the top of the vertical stabilizer or on the top and underside of the fuselage.

WARNING!
Wear full personal protective equipment (PPE) at all times when dealing with hydrazine emergencies as it may be absorbed through the skin. Even short exposures may have serious effects on the nervous and respiratory systems.

WARNING!
Disconnecting the GPU from the aircraft prior to the power being shut off can cause electrocution or arcing. Arcing could provide an ignition source for flammable vapors that have collected in the area.

Figure 3.47 An aircraft oxygen cylinder. *Courtesy of Edwin A. Jones, USAFR.*

Oxygen Systems

All aircraft intended for high-altitude operations use an oxygen-supply system to provide life support for crew members and passengers. Oxygen is normally stored in either a gaseous or liquid state.

Oxygen cylinders can be found in various locations in all varieties of aircraft. The flight deck is supplied by a separate system comprised of a single cylinder, which is usually found in the cockpit, forward cargo hold, or electronic equipment compartment. On many passenger aircraft, the crew and passenger oxygen supply is stored in pressurized cylinders within the fuselage **(Figure 3.47)**. The flight crew on commercial aircraft will always use compressed oxygen systems. Small medical cylinders are located throughout the cabin and their location will vary depending on cabin configuration. Ejection seat systems of military aircraft have a small emergency oxygen cylinder attached to the seat. Some medical transport helicopters and most military fighter, bomber and attack aircraft employ the use of liquid oxygen cylinders; a regulating system converts the liquid oxygen into usable oxygen.

Commercial aircraft are equipped with a system for chemically generating oxygen for passengers. Chemically generated oxygen systems, when activated, produce substantial amounts of heat because of the exothermic chemical reaction. This heat is normally contained within the oxygen-generating unit but may ignite combustibles if in direct contact. Once the reaction is started, it is impossible to stop until the unit has exhausted its chemical. These units are often located in the seat backs or in overhead compartments.

Passenger aircraft operating at 25,000 feet (7 620 m) are equipped with drop-down oxygen systems for passengers and supplemental oxygen systems for flight crews. Passengers are instructed on how to use the drop-down system upon boarding a flight. Flight attendants can rely on personal breathing equipment (PBE) when trying to work in a smoke-filled cabin due to an emergency. PBE devices are aluminized hoods with a small cylinder of oxygen that are placed over the flight attendants head with a clear panel to aid in seeing.

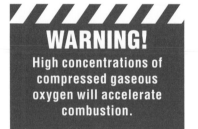

WARNING!

High concentrations of compressed gaseous oxygen will accelerate combustion.

In most cases, oxygen cylinders aboard aircraft are painted green; however, this coloring system is not used universally. ARFF personnel should not depend on the color to identify cylinders following an accident/incident. Oxygen cylinders will have manual shut off on its valve, as well as a rupture disc and vent. If ARFF personnel can access the cylinders, they should be able to shut them down. When exposed to fire, oxygen cylinders will usually vent and not explode. The venting may accelerate the fire and result in damage in the areas surrounding the cylinders. Some aircraft have an indicator on the outside of the fuselage to indicate if the oxygen system has vented.

Liquid oxygen (LOX) is light blue and transparent, with a boiling point of -297°F (-147°C). LOX may produce burns similar to but more severe than frostbite if it is allowed to contact the skin. Like gaseous oxygen, LOX is not flammable by itself, but it will support combustion. Lox readily forms combustible and explosive mixtures when it comes in contact with combustible materials — especially materials such as oil, grease, cloth, wood, paper, acetylene, gasoline, kerosene, powdered metal, and asphalt.

Oxygen systems on aircraft may present severe hazards to firefighters during emergency operations. As long as an oxygen-enriched environment is present, fire will burn with greater intensity. There is danger of an explosion if liquid oxygen mixes with flammable/combustible materials. An explosion or deflagration may also result if an oxygen storage tank or liquid oxygen container ruptures because of heat expansion or impact.

Cylinders that have shifted or have been displaced from their mountings by the impact of a crash should not be disturbed unless doing so is necessary to perform a rescue. The area should be isolated, and the containers should be protected from fire or unnecessary manipulation until they can be disposed of properly. If shutting off the cylinder lessens the intensity of the fire, firefighters should do so if they can accomplish this safely.

In fires involving LOX, the flow of oxygen and/or fuel should be stopped. The smothering and blanketing agents normally used in aircraft fire fighting are ineffective if the fire is being supplied with liquid oxygen. One acceptable method of stopping a liquid oxygen leak is to spray the leak with water fog. The super-cold LOX immediately converts the water to ice, which forms a plug, sealing the leak.

WARNING!
Do not disturb asphalt onto which LOX has been spilled because it is explosively unstable and extremely shock-sensitive. Until the LOX has dissipated, merely walking on the spill or dropping something onto it may cause a violent reaction.

Radar Systems

Radar systems can present both ignition sources and health hazards. Most aircraft radar systems are activated on the ground just before takeoff and deactivated after landing. Because aircraft radar systems are located in the aircraft nose, ARFF personnel should NOT approach an aircraft's nose if they believe the radar system is active. Radar energy can generate heat within nearby materials and act as an ignition source. This energy can also create cellular damage in human tissues and cause other adverse health effects. Once an aircraft's engines and power are shut off, the radar is also turned off. Extra caution should be taken around military surveillance aircraft and command and control aircraft. These aircraft have very powerful radar systems as shown by the large external radar antennas and devices mounted on the aircraft.

Fire Protection Systems

Many modern aircraft are equipped with fire protection systems that may be activated by the flight crew or ground crew to extinguish fires in engines, APUs, and cargo compartments. The quantity of extinguishing agent and configuration of the system is specifically designed for each aircraft type. A typical fire suppression system consists of pressurized containers, tubing to deliver the agent, nozzles, and appliances for actuating and controlling agent discharge **(Figure 3.48, p. 96)**. After a crash, these systems may or may not be usable, but ARFF personnel should be familiar with their location and operation because they may assist in securing aircraft systems. Once the battery has been disconnected, however, and all electrical power removed, the fire suppression system will not operate.

Handheld extinguishers for use on interior fires are located in the cockpit and throughout the cabin. Detection and suppression units are used in lavatories aboard most aircraft. A smoke detector is present that sounds an audible alarm to alert the cabin crew and there is a warning light on the annunciator panel in the cockpit. Also, a small heat-activated extinguisher bottle is installed to protect the lavatory trash bin.

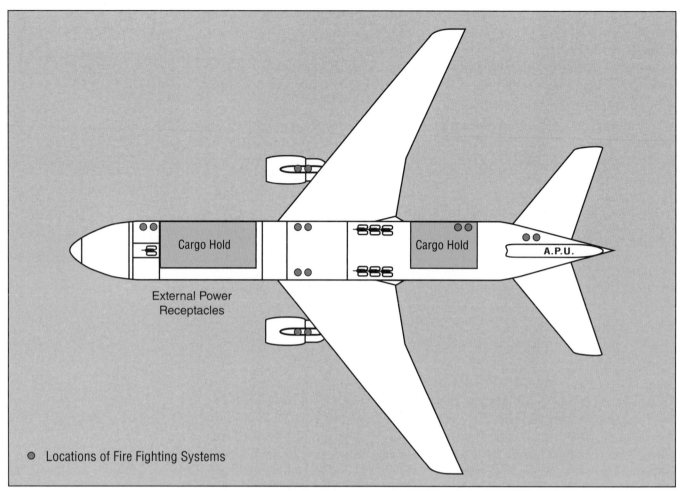

Cargo Hold

External Power
Receptacles

Cargo Hold

A.P.U.

Locations of Fire Fighting Systems

Figure 3.48 Common locations of aircraft fire fighting systems.

Passenger/Crew Air Bags

While air bag safety devices for automobile drivers and passengers have become commonplace, it is only recently that air bag technology has been applied to aircraft. The aviation industry is adopting self-contained aircraft restraint systems with airbags built into the restraint webbing. The FAA has approved of such systems, and they are being installed in various, general aviation and some foreign commercial aviation aircraft.

On one such system, sensor mechanisms activate inflation devices during a crash. The inflation device then uses compressed helium to inflate the air bags to protect the passengers, flight deck crew, and flight attendants. The air bags are designed to deflate in less than 10 seconds to allow personnel to egress the aircraft.

Because some air bags may not deploy during a crash and may pose a hazard to aircraft occupants and ARFF personnel during rescue operations, airport firefighters should become familiar with each of the various types of air bag systems they may encounter so that they may properly safety these devices following.

Flight Deck Emergency Shutdown Systems and Procedures

It may be necessary for ARFF personnel to conduct emergency shutdown procedures on an aircraft. Emergency shutdown procedures vary from a simple,

Figure 3.49 The T-handles for an aircraft's fire fighting system. *Courtesy of Edwin A. Jones, USAFR.*

Figure 3.50 The throttle and fuel control devices of this general aviation aircraft are located between the two steering yokes.

single action to a complicated sequence of procedures depending upon the type of aircraft. A common first step in any aircraft is to move the throttles(s) to the IDLE or OFF position. Accomplishing this may require lifting the throttle(s) past a detented position. The next step may be to activate the fire protection system. Shutting off the battery switch(es) should be the last step in cockpit shutdown procedures.

On almost all commercial transport-type aircraft and some commuter aircraft, the shutoff procedure involves activating T- or L-shaped engine and APU fire shutoff handles. Pulling these handles simultaneously shuts off the engine's fuel, hydraulic, pneumatic, and electrical connections while arming the fire suppression system. An extinguisher bottle discharge button or switch is usually located adjacent to each fire shutoff handle for activating the suppression system. The T- or L-shaped handles are usually located around the throttles or, in some cases, on the cockpit overhead panel **(Figures 3.49)**. Some aircraft also have APU shutdown and bottle discharge buttons on an external fire protection panel located on the nose landing gear or in the main wheel well.

When operating the fire protection systems, the batteries must be on to provide electrical power to the system. Once engine shutdown is complete, battery shutdown and disconnect procedures can be accomplished if access is possible. Smaller general aviation aircraft may require fuel switches or fuel cutoffs to be de-activated in addition to retarding the throttle(s) to shut down the aircraft **(Figure 3.50)**.

Military aircraft often require personnel to follow a highly detailed set of procedures to accomplish aircraft shutdown. If any ARFF personnel are unfamiliar with these procedures, it is recommended that they stay clear of the cockpit to avoid injury. Many of the larger military aircraft resemble commercial aircraft of the same type, so shutdown procedures often are the same.

Ingress/Egress Systems

Aircraft are generally designed to be evacuated in 90 seconds or less in the event of an emergency. A main cabin door is provided for normal enplaning and deplaning operations while service doors are provided for catering and cleaning operations. These cabin doors are the primary means of egress, with secondary means consisting of over-/under-wing hatches, tail-cone jettison systems, rear air-stairs or stairs that lower at the rear of the aircraft, and roof hatches.

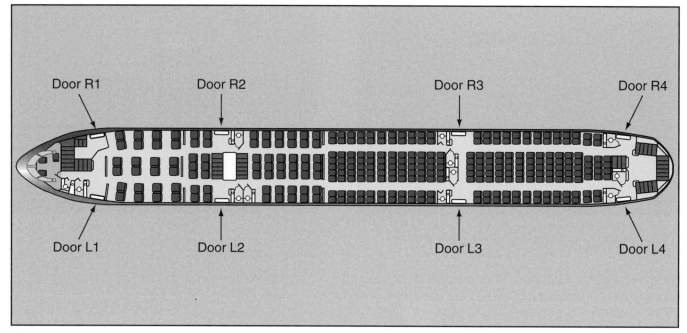

Door R1   Door R2   Door R3   Door R4

Door L1   Door L2   Door L3   Door L4

Figure 3.51 Understanding door numbering is helpful when directing responding ARFF apparatus and personnel.

Airline crew members identify cabin doors on an aircraft by reference to a number and a left or right designator. For example, a door may be referred to as "L1" or "1 Left," meaning left side, first door closest to the front of the aircraft. The left side refers to the pilot's left as he or she is seated in the cockpit. "R2" or "2 Right" would refer to the right side, second door back from the cockpit **(Figure 3.51)**. These designations become very important when communicating with the flight crew or assigning personnel to assist evacuation operations. Because the design of aircraft egress systems varies greatly among different aircraft types, ARFF personnel must make it a point to become familiar with the aircraft that frequent their airport and know how to operate the various emergency egress systems. The sections that follow detail the various means of ingress/egress on a variety of aircraft, especially those carrying passengers.

Aircraft Doors

Primary egress from aircraft is through the doors normally used for servicing or for routine entry or exit. These doors may be located on both sides or on just one side of the fuselage and are usually simple to operate. All doors have an exterior latch release that disconnects the locking device and permits the door to swing open, pivot open, swing down, or fall free from the aircraft **(Figure 3.52)**. Commercial aircraft will have opening instructions on or adjacent to each door and hatch.

There are many different variations of cabin doors depending on the size and type of aircraft encountered. Opening and operating procedures can vary widely on doors found on the same aircraft, so AARF personnel should spend time reviewing the doors on a variety of aircraft. Knowing how to operate the door from inside the aircraft also is vital should quick egress become necessary during interior operations **(Figure 3.53)**. Some major airports will have air carrier crew recurrent training facilities. These facilities will usually have mockups of all the doors, hatches, and other egress systems utilized on their fleet of aircraft. Most will welcome and accommodate visiting firefighters.

Figure 3.52 An ARFF firefighter practicing opening an aircraft door from the exterior.

Figure 3.53 ARFF personnel should also practice opening aircraft doors from the interior.

Such training programs are an excellent opportunity to visualize the operating mechanisms and operate all the common aircraft egress systems, from inside and outside. Firefighters will also learn crew evacuation procedures. Most facilities have a fuselage mockup from which firefighters can actually conduct an evacuation.

Pressurization

Generally, all aircraft that operate above 14,000 feet (4 267 m) have the ability to pressurize the cabin. The pressurization system operates by controlling a motor-driven outflow valve that opens and closes to regulate the amount of cabin air that is exhausted outside the aircraft. The outflow valve may be located on the left or right side of the rear fuselage or on some aircraft, on the left side of the fuselage just forward of the wing **(Figure 3.54)**. During normal operation on the ground, the cabin should be depressurized, which is indicated by the outflow valve being fully open. Pressurization automatically commences just prior to takeoff and is usually maintained until just after landing unless a malfunction prevents the outflow valve from opening properly. Most large aircraft will have a squat valve on the main or nose landing gears that should fully open the outflow valve when the aircraft lands.

It is impossible to open plug type main cabin doors or the over-/under-wing escape hatches if the cabin is pressurized. So, if firefighters are unable to open this type of door or hatch, they should find and force open the outflow valve before attempting to open one of these doors. Some aircraft entry and cargo doors may also have pressure-releasing devices. A vault type door, found on many newer models of large commercial aircraft, can be opened under pressure. Opening this type of door under pressure is dangerous and can cause serious injury or death to anyone near the door, on the inside or outside of the aircraft. Airbus aircraft doors will have a small view window, through which a white or red light will indicate whether the aircraft is still pressurized or not.

Figure 3.54 A typical aircraft cabin outflow valve. *Courtesy of William D. Stewart.*

Some wide-bodied commercial aircraft incorporate doors that open by moving upward into the fuselage. These doors also have an escape slide for egress but are designed to de-arm when opened from the outside. The doors move on tracks and are built with a pneumatic-assist feature that powers the door open when opened in the armed or emergency mode. The exterior operating handle can be found either forward or aft of the door on the side of the fuselage.

ℹ️ Means of Egress Lighting

Commercial airliners are required to have floor lighting installed in the aisles to provide egress assistance for passengers. Track lighting is usually installed directly on the aisle floor or at the base of the seats. White or green lights lead to red lights. In turn, the red lights indicate the location of emergency exits. Additionally, exit signs are required to be installed at floor level (no more than 13 inches [325 mm] off the floor) at each emergency exit. If the need to evacuate arises while conducting an interior search, remember the lighting layout.

Figure 3.55 An exit door that is hinged at the bottom and swings out and down on a commuter aircraft. *Courtesy of William D. Stewart.*

Small general aviation aircraft may have exit doors on both sides of the fuselage; others have them on one side only. Unlike most larger aircraft, commuter aircraft have exit doors that are hinged on the bottom, open downward, and have steps built into them **(Figure 3.55)**. Compressed-air pistons or heavy spring tension mechanically assist the opening of these doors. ARFF personnel should stay clear of the path of these doors to avoid injury.

Some aircraft doors have "speed locks" that deploy after the aircraft reaches a certain speed to insure that the door cannot open in flight. The speed lock releases automatically after the aircraft has landed and is traveling below a certain ground speed. However, it is possible for the speed lock to fail, in which case it will not release. It may be useful for ARFF personnel to be aware of such devises and the bypass mechanisms that accompany them.

Aircraft Slides

If the bottom doorsill on a given aircraft is 6 feet (2m) or more above the ground, then the Federal Aviation Administration requires that the aircraft doorway be equipped with an inflatable emergency escape slide. Slides must be automatically deployed and inflated in 6 seconds. They must be self-supporting on ground regardless of gear collapse and be usable in up to a 25-knot wind, with the assistance of only one person. Before an escape slide is certified, it must pass five consecutive successful deployment and inflation demonstrations. Slides are required to be able to move 70 persons per lane, per minute.

Cabin doors on many narrow body aircraft are considered armed when the "girt bar" for the escape slide is secured to retention clips located at the bottom doorsill or when the interior door lever is moved to "armed mode." The cabin crew arms slides and doors when the aircraft leaves the gate. They remain armed until the aircraft lands and opens its doors at its destination gate.

Figure 3.56 When laddering an aircraft to access a door, the ladder should be placed on the side opposite the door's hinges.

When cabin doors are in the armed mode, opening the door from outside the aircraft may be difficult due to resistance and may be dangerous due to the inflation and deployment of the escape slide. Because the slide deploys in a matter of a few seconds with explosive force, ARFF personnel must be very cautious when opening doors from the outside under emergency conditions. If ground ladders must be used to access these doors, they should be positioned beside the door on the side opposite the hinges (aft of the door on almost all commercial aircraft with hinged doors **[Figure 3.56]**).

As discussed earlier, some models of wide-body aircraft have doors which retract into the overhead area. On these aircraft, the slide can usually be disarmed by normal opening procedures from the outside of the aircraft. In this case, airport firefighters should position the ladder on the side where the door controls are located, which may be found on either side of the door. Doors can be armed or disarmed from inside the aircraft on all wide-body aircraft and some newer narrow-body aircraft. Firefighters should become familiar with the procedures for both arming and disarming a door from inside the cabin. Knowing how to activate the escape slide from inside may prevent serious injuries.

When the flight crew has initiated an evacuation, ARFF personnel should expect to see every usable exit open and slides deployed within seconds after

Figure 3.57 ARFF personnel should be prepared to assist passengers and crew evacuating an aircraft by slides. *Courtesy of William D. Stewart.*

the aircraft comes to a stop. Once deployed, the escape slides must be protected from flame impingement and held steady in high-wind conditions. Flight attendants may have instructed several passengers to stay at the bottom of the slides to help evacuees. Available emergency responders should also assist when possible (**Figure 3.57**). Without assistance, people tend to pile up at the bottom of the slide, often causing additional injuries. Escape slides are extremely slippery due to a Teflon coating. Subsequently, it is typical for a small percentage of aircraft occupants to suffer minor to moderate injuries when using the slides.

A few older, narrow-body aircraft slides have a manual inflation handle. All escape slides have a pull-type, manual inflation handle somewhere at the top of the slide. It is usually marked and red in color. Sometimes escape slides fail to inflate for various reasons. Evacuees and emergency responders may still pull deflated slides taut and use them for escape while deflated.

Slides can also be disconnected from the aircraft and used as rafts. The top of the slide has a lanyard to detach the slide raft from the aircraft after passengers have boarded during a water evacuation.

Aircraft Hatches

Hatches and windows in most aircraft are plug-type design meaning that the exits must be pushed *inward* from the *outside* or pulled *inward* from the *inside*. On commercial and passenger-carrying aircraft, these hatches or doors or located above or below the wings depending upon the height of the wings on the fuselage.

Many newer aircraft incorporate an inflatable escape slide that is activated when overwing exits are opened from inside the aircraft. Most overwing escape slides are designed to de-arm when the exit is opened from the outside. This escape slide is housed in the side of the fuselage and when activated expands outward and off the trailing edge of the wing. Again, aircraft familiarization training is necessary to ensure that all available means of evacuation are utilized during an emergency.

 Automatic Over-wing Exit Door

On Boeing 737 600-, 700-, 800-, and 900-series aircraft, the over-wing, plug-type hatch has been replaced with a spring-loaded over-wing hatch, which is hinged at the top. When activated from either the inside or the outside, this hatch will spring upward and outboard of the fuselage. A firefighter should be aware of the rapid opening hatch and the hand-trapping hazards it may pose. Boeing calls this door an "automatic over-wing exit door."

Most commuter aircraft have over-wing or under-wing exits, which are too small to accommodate a firefighter in full protective clothing with SCBA, but these exits offer a good opening for introducing handlines. Over-wing exits on larger aircraft may be large enough to allow easy access to the interior, even for firefighters in full protective clothing and SCBA. If ground ladders are needed to access over-wing exits, they should be positioned at the leading edge of the wing.

Windows

Most large commercial aircraft will have cockpit or pilot's escape windows on each side of the aircraft. All are big enough for persons to use to evacuate the aircraft. Sometimes one or both of the windows can be opened from the outside by reaching though a small knock-in panel. The access panel is usually just below the window and a ladder will be needed to reach the panel and the escape window when the aircraft is upright on its landing gear. The windshield is glass sandwiched between plexiglass and may be extremely difficult to break with handtools. The cabin windows are of a triple pane construction. Two of the window panes are held together in a rubber band and held in the window frame by clips. The third and most inner pane is part of the interior wall finish. The cabin windows may be knocked *in* with an axe or sledge hammer for ventilation or the introduction of a fire stream.

Other Means of Egress

Rear stairs, emergency exit doors, overhead hatches and tail-cone jettison exits are some of the other devices that may be available to assist in evacuating an aircraft. A few medium-frame aircraft incorporate stairs built into the rear of the aircraft. Although not designed as a true emergency exit, these stairs provide an alternate means of accessing the main cabin if the aircraft is on its wheels. ARFF personnel should ensure that the aircraft is stabilized prior to entering so that if the aircraft shifts, the means of egress is not closed off. The rear air stairs can be lowered from inside and outside the aircraft **(Figure 3.58)**. There is a small access panel on the tail area, to the right of the air stairs. Inside the small compartment, markings will indicate the direction to push the control mechanism to let the stairs free fall open.

Smaller aircraft may be built with an exit specifically designed for emergency use only. These exits are commonly found on commuter aircraft and fall off the aircraft when opened. Due to the weight of the exit, personnel must stand clear and exercise extreme caution when opening. Some aircraft have

Figure 3.58 Some medium-frame commercial aircraft are equipped with stairs at the rear of the aircraft. *Courtesy of Edwin A. Jones, USAFR.*

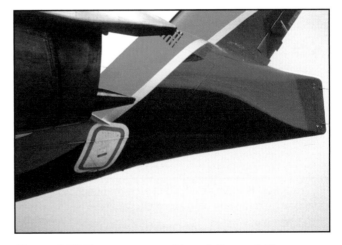

Figure 3.59 The access panel for a tail-cone jettison system. *Courtesy of William D. Stewart.*

overhead hatches that, when installed, provide another means of evacuating and ventilating an aircraft. Most are located over the flight deck and vary in method of operation.

A tail-cone jettison system is activated from inside or outside the aircraft by pulling on the activation handle that is located at the left rear portion of the fuselage. The exterior control is on the left rear area while the interior control is inside the tail. Firefighters will need to stand on something to reach the exterior control **(Figure 3.59, p.103)**. The control may be secured with a breakable seal. Once pulled, the tail cone separates from the aircraft and falls to the ground. From the opening, an escape slide deploys and automatically inflates. Depending on the model, passengers exit the cabin through either a hatch or a standard-size cabin door located on the back wall of the cabin. If the tail cone has not been jettisoned, firefighters need to search that area for trapped occupants before jettisoning the cone.

Emergency Cut-In Areas

Attempts to forcibly enter an aircraft should be made only after all other means of entry have failed. Military aircraft have distinctive identification points for forcible entry that are bordered with contrasting markings and are stenciled with the words "CUT HERE FOR EMERGENCY RESCUE" **(Figure 3.60)**. Some civilian aircraft may have cut-in marks painted on the exterior of the fuselage to indicate those points where access to trapped occupants is possible. These places are identified as emergency cut-in areas because they are free of underlying hazards such as tubing, piping, and wiring. On large aircraft most of the system will be located below the main deck. Generally, the best area to avoid aircraft systems is within 20 inches above and below the cabin windows. Cutting a fuselage is a time-consuming process that taxes the strength and endurance of personnel. Personnel should take time to become familiar with areas on an aircraft that are suitable for cut-in areas, but they should use this method as a last resort because it is one of the most hazardous and time consuming means of forcible entry.

Data Recording Systems

Of critical importance to aircraft accident investigations are the so-called "black boxes." Identified as the flight data recorder (FDR) and the cockpit voice recorder (CVR), they are usually located in a cargo compartment wall or the tail section of the fuselage. Neither unit is black, but they are painted either international orange or bright red with a wide band of reflective material around them. As with any other piece of evidence, these units should be protected in place and should only be removed by ARFF personnel

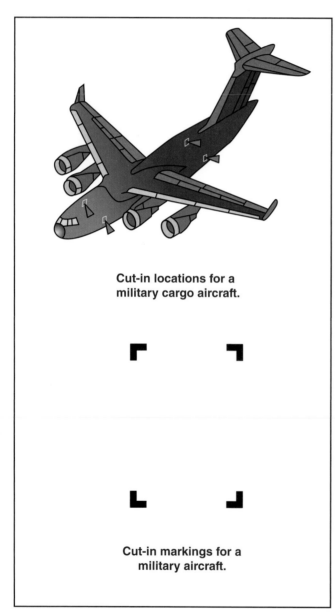

Cut-in locations for a military cargo aircraft.

Cut-in markings for a military aircraft.

Figure 3.60 An example of cut-in area markings and their locations on a military cargo aircraft.

Figure 3.61 ARFF personnel being trained on pitot tube locations.

if the units are in imminent danger of being damaged or destroyed. A chain of custody should be established and maintained until the proper authorities can remove the recorders from the area. If a unit is found submerged in water, it should be left in water because the recording device contains a metal ribbon that is conducive to rusting. If there is a chance of them being lost, they should be removed from the water and stored in fresh water until retrieved by the National Transportation Safety Board (NTSB).

Miscellaneous Systems and Components

Some aircraft contain other miscellaneous systems and components. These include anti-icing systems, pressurized cylinders, pitot tubes, and antennas as follows:

- *Anti-icing systems* — electric components typically used to heat cockpit windows, propellers, and items such as probes, ports, and drain masts along the fuselage; high-temperature bleed air from the engine exhaust is used to heat engine inlets and the leading edge of the wings.

- *Pressurized cylinders* — located throughout any size aircraft; some of these, such as oxygen cylinders, have pressure-relief valves. Other unvented cylinders used for hydraulic fluids, fire extinguishing systems, rain repellent, pneumatic systems may explode during aircraft fire fighting operations if heated due to external heat sources.

- *Pitot tubes* — measure air pressure for use in certain cockpit instrument displays such as the airspeed indicator; two to four L-shaped pitot tubes are usually located on both sides of the forward fuselage, just below the cockpit windows, of transport-type aircraft. Due to the vital functions performed in conjunction with these tubes, personnel should not touch or handle these devices during training **(Figure 3.61)**.

- *Antennas* — protrude from the top and underside of the fuselage; aircraft are equipped with multiple antennas for communications and navigation, VHF, UHF, satellite communications, global positioning, and onboard air-phones.

WARNING!

Pitot tubes are heated to prevent ice from forming on them during flight. As a result, ARFF personnel should not touch pitot tubes because they can get hot enough to cause burns.

Summary

An airport firefighter's safety is linked to the level of training and familiarization the firefighter has with the types of aircraft that may be encountered during ARFF operations. ARFF personnel must be thoroughly familiar with the various civilian and military aircraft. They must be able to recognize the unique features and components of fixed-wing and rotary-wing aircraft. To function safely around aircraft engines under normal and emergency conditions, airport firefighters need to be familiar with the types and applications of the different engines that are used to power aircraft.

ARFF personnel should be trained to recognize the materials used in the manufacture of aircraft and understand how these materials behave during aircraft crashes and fires. Additionally, airport firefighters must be able to identify and deal with the numerous fuel, power, and safety systems used aboard aircraft.

Review Questions

1. What rescue concerns are emerging with the use of new large aircraft (NLA)?

2. Which designator letter is assigned to unmanned aerial vehicles?

3. How do static eliminators work?

4. List the main sections of a rotary-wing aircraft.

5. Which type of gas turbine engine is most commonly found on aircraft today?

6. Why is magnesium commonly used for engine-mounting brackets?

7. Why are labels necessary in the use of standardized coding?

8. What systemic effects can be caused by exposure to hydrazine vapor?

9. How are escape slides disconnected from aircraft to be used as rafts?

10. What color are flight data recorders (FDRs)?

Safety and Aircraft Hazards

Chapter Contents

Key Terms

NFPA® references for Chapter 4:

NFPA® 1003 (2010)
5.1.1.3
5.1.1.4
5.1.2
5.2.4
5.4.1
5.4.2

**NFPA® 1002
(2009 - Chapter 9)**
9.1.2
9.1.3
9.2.1

Federal Aviation Regulations (FAR):

139.319(i)
139.319(j)

Safety and Aircraft Hazards

Learning Objectives

After reading this chapter, students shall be able to:

1. Discuss personal protective equipment. (NFPA® 1003, 5.1.1.3)

2. Recognize the importance of firefighter safety. (NFPA® 1003, 5.1.1.3, 5.2.4)

3. Explain hazards associated with aircraft rescue and fire fighting. (NFPA® 1003, 5.1.1.3, 5.2.4, 5.4.1)

4. Describe hazards associated with aircraft cargo. (NFPA® 1003, 5.1.1.3, 5.2.4, 5.4.2)

5. Discuss military aircraft hazards. (NFPA® 1003, 5.1.1.3, 5.2.4, 5.4.1)

6. Discuss the occurrence of terrorist incidents at airports.

Chapter 4
Safety and
Aircraft Hazards

Case History

A young airport firefighter was tasked with checking an F-16 Falcon's landing gear and brakes following an aborted take off during a heavy rain. The aircraft was parked on a part of the ramp where the rain made footing very slippery. The firefighter was wearing full protective clothing and self contained breathing apparatus in the event of an emergency power unit activation or hydrazine leak from the aircraft. Racing quickly around the nose of the aircraft to avoid the intake of the running engine, the firefighter slipped and began to fall backwards onto the SCBA bottle. The firefighter was able to avoid serious back injury and potentially catastrophic damage to the SCBA air bottle by pivoting to one side. He did, however, injure his right knee which required medical treatment. If the firefighter had focused on moving around the aircraft in a slow, deliberate manner, he could have avoided this injury.

Knowing the obvious safety concerns when responding to aircraft fires and other emergencies will help minimize the danger of being injured or killed. The unexpected combination of aircraft hazards with environmental conditions often finds firefighters off their guard. On average, over 100 fire fighters die in the line of duty in the United States each year. Firefighters must stay alert and focused throughout an entire incident to protect their own lives and the lives of team members.

Every fire department should have standard operating procedures (SOPs) which cover health and safety programs. These procedures may be divided into a variety of categories focusing on different areas of fire department operations. Each member of the department is responsible for reading and understanding the SOPs. Failure to understand health and safety SOPs could result in accident and/or injury. NFPA® 1500, *Standard on Fire Department Occupational Safety and Health Program*, is an excellent source for finding information on the aspects of health and safety for firefighters.

Part of a department's SOPs should be a risk/benefit matrix that identifies the level of acceptable risk for ARFF operations. While ARFF personnel may be placed at some degree of risk during aircraft emergency responses fighting fires and effecting rescues, their being put in jeopardy to recover bodies is inappropriate. The use of a risk/benefit model should help in determining to what extent responders should be exposed. If the benefit is low and the risk is high, it would not be a good decision to take action at that point. However, if the risk is low and the benefit is high, the operation would be considered a reasonable risk. The risk model used by Phoenix (Arizona) Fire Department and other agencies is "We will assume reasonable risk to protect savable lives; we will assume inherent risk to protect savable property; we will assume no risk to protect lives or property that are already lost."

> ## IFSTA Principles of Risk Management
> 1. Activities that present a significant risk to the safety of members shall be limited to situations where there is a potential to save en dangered lives.
> 2. Activities that are routinely employed to protect property shall be recognized as inherent risks to the safety of members, and actions shall be taken to reduce or avoid these risks.
> 3. No risk to the safety of members shall be acceptable when there is no possibility to save lives or property.

This chapter provides an overview of general safety issues found in the various aspects of ARFF operations. The topics covered include personal protective equipment including self-contained breathing apparatus, personal alert safety systems (PASS), hearing protection, eye protection, and different types of personal protective clothing. Chapter 4 also addresses firefighter safety while at the fire station, during emergency responses, and at an emergency scene. General hazards associated with ARFF and specific aircraft hazards for both commercial and military aircraft are also covered. It is important to note injuries can and do occur every day in the field of fire protection.

Personal Protective Equipment

ARFF personnel are equipped with a variety of personal protective equipment (PPE) to protect them while they perform their duties. Personal protective clothing includes station/work uniforms, structural fire fighting protective clothing, chemical protective clothing, and proximity suits. Other items include but are not limited to self-contained breathing apparatus (SCBA), personal alert safety systems (PASS), hearing protection, and eye protection. Having the best equipment available doesn't benefit personnel if they don't use it or use it improperly. It is also important that protective clothing fit properly. Clothing that is too tight may tear, restrict movement, or lose its thermal insulating capabilities.

Personal Protective Clothing

Firefighters must utilize adequate personal protection and wear the full protective clothing ensemble and SCBA during initial approach and attack, while performing rescue, and during overhaul. Each phase of the operation is just as critical as the next, so all phases of an operation should be treated with an equal amount of respect.

Firefighters assigned to ARFF response may need to utilize proximity suits, depending on fire conditions such as fuel load, radiant heat exposure, and rescue considerations. Proximity gear consists of aluminized ensembles that provide superior radiant and thermal heat protection. The flame resistance, strength, and weight of the material are critical to the clothing's usefulness at aircraft incidents; however, firefighters must understand the shielding capabilities and limitations of their personal protective clothing. Participating in live fire training exercises is an effective way to achieve full understanding of the limitations of protective gear.

Self Contained Breathing Apparatus (SCBA) — Respirator worn by the user that supplies a breathable atmosphere that is either carried in or generated by the apparatus and is independent of the ambient atmosphere; worn in all atmospheres that are considered to be Immediately Dangerous to Life and Health (IDLH); also called Air Mask or Air Pack.

Proximity Clothing — Special personal protective equipment with a reflective exterior that is designed to protect the firefighter from conductive, convective, and radiant heat while working in close proximity to the fire; also called Proximity Suit.

Station/Work Uniform

Normal work uniforms should be made of flame-resistant material and should adequately identify ARFF as being authorized to be in the emergency scene area. NFPA® 1500 *Standard on Fire Department Occupational Safety and Health Program* states that station/work uniforms shall meet the requirements of NFPA® 1975, *Standard on Station/Work Uniforms for Fire and Emergency Services*. However, work uniforms are intended for use under full protective equipment and are not intended to be used by themselves as protective clothing **(Figure 4.1)**.

Structural Fire Fighting Protective Clothing

Firefighters must sometimes respond to aircraft emergencies with structural fire fighting protective clothing. They may also respond to nonaviation related calls on airport property. A firefighter in structural personal protective clothing equipment (PPE), which consists of a turnout coat (with collar up), turnout pants, safety boots, leather gloves, flame-resistant hood, helmet (with earflaps down), and SCBA, is adequately protected from all but the most extreme conditions **(Figure 4.2)**. Although limited in some applications, this type of protective equipment may still offer firefighters sufficient protection if they are aware of the hazard being both the nature of the hazard and the limitations of the protective clothing. For example, the radiant heat produced by burning aircraft fuels can be extreme; therefore, it is recommended that proximity suits be used instead of structural clothing for aircraft fire fighting whenever there is a choice, as recommended by NFPA® 1500.

Structural turnout gear is very resistant to cuts and abrasions that can result from contact with jagged metal edges common in damaged aircraft. Structural

Figure 4.1 An example of a standard station uniform for ARFF personnel.

Figure 4.2 A firefighter in structural protective clothing and SCBA assisting a firefighter wearing proximity gear and SCBA.

turnout gear has a moisture barrier to protect firefighters from steam burns and a thermal barrier to provide some heat protection. However, structural clothing is susceptible to "wicking" hydrocarbon fuels, and it does not provide the reflective capabilities of proximity suits. Wicking occurs when the material which the protective clothing is made of absorbs a fuel at the point of contact. The material continues to transfer the fuel absorbed further along the material in the same manner that a wick moves kerosene in a lamp.

The leather footwear often worn with structural PPE can also absorb hazardous liquids. If personnel walk through fuel or any other hazardous liquids found at crash sites, these fluids can be absorbed into the leather components of the boots causing them to become contaminated. For more information regarding structural fire-fighting protective clothing and proximity suits, refer to NFPA® 1971, *Standard on Protective Ensembles for Structural Fire Fighting and Proximity Fire Fighting.*

Chemical Protective Clothing

While most aircraft accidents may contain hazardous materials, not all ARFF firefighters specialize in advanced haz-mat operations. Refer to NFPA® 472, *Standard for Competence of Responders to Hazardous Materials/Weapons of Mass Destruction Incidents*, for information on proper haz mat protective clothing levels. It is the responsibility of every firefighter to understand what substances require them to wear specialized chemical protective clothing.

Proximity Fire Fighting Protective Clothing

There are several terms for proximity fire fighting protective clothing including proximity gear and proximity suits. Proximity gear is similar to bunker or turnout gear except that it has an aluminized outer shell that includes pants, coat, helmet, shroud, gloves, and ARFF Boots. Another type of proximity clothing is referred to as a proximity suit. Proximity suits can be one piece or multiple pieces similar to proximity gear.

Proximity protective clothing is designed for close proximity exposures to high radiant heat **(Figure 4.3)**. Proximity clothing has a reflective outer covering designed to reflect approximately 90% of radiant heat and protects

Hazardous Material — Any material that possesses an unreasonable risk to the health and safety of persons and/or the environment if it is not properly controlled during handling, storage, manufacture, processing, packaging, use, disposal, or transportation.

Figure 4.3 ARFF personnel in proximity clothing during a training evolution.

the wearer from ambient temperatures up to 200°F (93°C) or radiant heat to 2000°F (1 090°C). With the addition of one or more layers of thermal barrier, proximity clothing can also withstand exposure to steam, liquids, and some weaker chemicals.

Proximity protective clothing should not be confused with fire entry suits. Fire entry suits are designed to protect the wearer from total flame engulfment for a brief time, short periods of exposure to ambient temperatures of 1500°F (815°C), and prolonged exposure to radiant heat up to 2000°F (1 090°C). A fire entry suit is not effective or meant to be used for rescue operations. Self contained breathing apparatus must be worn with both proximity protective clothing and fire entry suits. Refer to NFPA® 1971, *Standard on Protective Ensembles for Structural Fire Fighting and Proximity Fire Fighting,* for more information regarding proximity protective clothing.

Self-Contained Breathing Apparatus (SCBA)

Both OSHA 1910.134, *Respiratory Protection,* and NFPA® 1500, *Standard on Fire Department Occupational Safety and Health Program,* have respiratory protection standards that require all persons who may be exposed to respiratory hazards in the performance of their duties to use respiratory protection such as SCBA. Fire departments must adopt and maintain a respiratory protection program that addresses the selection, inspection, safe use, and maintenance of breathing apparatus, training in its use, and air quality testing. NFPA® 1404, *Standard for Fire Service Respiratory Protection Training* explains this in greater detail. A more detailed study of SCBA can be found in the IFSTA **Essentials of Fire Fighting** manual and NFPA® 1981, *Standard on Open-Circuit Self Contained Breathing Apparatus (SCBA) for Emergency Services.*

Due to the potential for respiratory injuries, SCBA must be worn at all aircraft fires. ARFF personnel operating in and around aircraft fires face the same toxic atmospheres they would encounter in typical structural fires **(Figure 4.4)**. Combustion in any aircraft fire can produce carbon monoxide, hydrogen sulfide, hydrogen cyanide, hydrogen chloride, and phosgene. In

Figure 4.4 ARFF personnel should wear SCBA during live fire training evolutions and aircraft fires.

addition to these dangerous gases, there may be other toxic and hazardous materials in aircraft cargo. Many civilian, commercial, and military aircraft use carbon and graphite fibers along with a host of other composite materials in construction, creating a hazard similar to asbestos exposure. Other hazards include superheated air, oxygen deficiency, extinguishing agents, and combustible metals.

Breathing apparatus must be maintained and worn according to manufacturer's requirements. Personnel that may wear respiratory protection must be medically certified by a physician once a year. Personnel must be fit tested annually and achieve a satisfactory face-piece-to-face seal with the mask they are required to wear. Facial hair that interferes with the face piece seal is prohibited. Eyeglass frames must not pass through the seal area of the face piece. Personnel must be trained in the use of respiratory protection and have their ability to properly utilize the equipment tested annually.

Personal Alert Safety Systems

NFPA® 1982, *Standard on Personal Alert Safety Systems (PASS),* established the standards for personal alert safety systems. The PASS device, which all ARFF personnel must wear when entering a hazardous atmosphere, sounds an alarm when a firefighter becomes incapacitated.

Personal Alert Safety System (PASS) — Electronic lack-of-motion sensor that sounds a loud tone when a firefighter becomes motionless; can also be manually triggered to operate.

A PASS unit sounds automatically when the wearer is motionless for approximately 30 seconds, or it can be activated manually. It should be capable of emitting an alarm of 95 decibels (dB) at a distance of 9.9 feet (3 m) for an uninterrupted period of at least one hour. Some PASS devices detect heat, some are integrated into the self-contained breathing apparatus (SCBA), and some even send a signal to a remote transmitter alerting the Incident Commander (IC) that a firefighter is in trouble. Regardless of the unit's features, wearing a PASS device increases the chances of a firefighter being found in an emergency – but only if it is turned on and working properly.

As with any electronic device, a PASS device can develop problems, with the most common problem being dead batteries. It is a good idea to change the batteries of a PASS device at some regular interval. PASS device batteries should be changed on a regular schedule, for example, whenever daylight savings time begins and ends in the spring and fall.

The most likely operational problem with a PASS device is a firefighter not remembering to activate the PASS before entering the hazardous environment. Some manufactures have removed this problem by integrating the PASS into the SCBA **(Figure 4.5)**. This PASS activates when the breathing-air system is activated. The only way an integrated PASS can be deactivated is by deactivating the breathing air. This automation serves two purposes: a reminder to turn on the PASS, and a reminder to turn off the air to the SCBA.

Hearing Protection

ARFF personnel involved in operations around aircraft and aircraft fire fighting vehicles are exposed to noise that may exceed the accepted level of exposure. The use of hearing protection is also important in and around the fire station where noise-producing equipment is operating. Generators, power saws, air compressors, and other equipment may produce noise levels from which a firefighter should be protected. NFPA® 1500, *Standard on Fire Department Occupational Safety and Health Program*, defines the maximum level of noise to which fire protection personnel are allowed to be exposed under various work conditions.

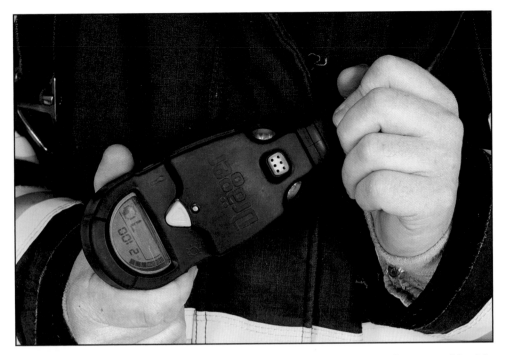

Figure 4.5 A PASS device that has been integrated into a SCBA unit. *Courtesy of Doddy Photography*

Figure 4.6a An ARFF firefighter wearing an integrated radio system/hearing protection headset.

Hearing protection should be made available for firefighters on all ARFF equipment. Earmuff-type protection provides excellent sound reduction for the wearer. Earplugs, which should be fitted for the individual, should be provided to each member of the department. Some radio system headsets provide some degree of hearing protection. Headset manufacturers can provide information about the level of protection each individual device provides **(Figure 4.6 a, b, and c)**.

A hearing awareness program, supported by appropriate SOPs and hearing loss awareness literature including posters, should be implemented to establish and maintain an awareness of hearing protection. Periodic hearing tests should also be available to ARFF personnel. The main point of a hearing awareness program is to motivate personnel to wear hearing protection. Airport firefighters are around more noise than most other types of firefighters. Hearing loss can affect firefighters for their entire lives, so they should take the necessary time to select and use appropriate hearing protection.

Figure 4.6b An ARFF firefighter wearing earmuff style hearing protection.

Eye Protection

ARFF personnel risk eye injury from many different sources during operations around aircraft or fire fighting apparatus and equipment. Numerous projections, such as pitot tubes on aircraft, outside mirrors, and other appendages on fire fighting apparatus, are all potential sources of eye injury if personnel are not alert and are not wearing eye protection. Aircraft engines may render debris harmful to eyes airborne. During aircraft rescue and fire fighting operations, ARFF personnel will normally be wearing SCBA facepieces and helmet mounted face shields which will afford some eye protection.

Other activities, such as operating power tools that generate sparks or clouds of dust and debris, may require that a firefighter also wear goggles or safety glasses. Personal safety glasses combined with other means of eye protection

Figure 4.6c An ARFF firefighter wearing earplugs for hearing protection.

Figure 4.7a The helmet faceshield and SCBA facepiece provide ARFF personnel eye protection during emergency operations.

Figure 4.7b Personal safety glasses should be worn while inspecting and maintaining equipment.

offer the wearer an excellent level of protection. However, eye protection should be selected based on the specific hazard and should meet the requirements of OSHA 1910.133, *Eye and Face Protection*; NFPA® 1500, *Standard on Fire Department Occupational Safety and Health Program*; and ANSI Z87.1, *American National Standard Practice for Occupational and Educational Eye and Face Protection*. **(Figure 4.7 a and b)**.

Firefighter Safety

Accidents are the number one cause of injuries. ARFF personnel should practice safety while on duty in the fire station and during emergency responses and operations. The sections that follow describe firefighter safety in the fire station and during emergencies.

Fire Station Safety

Firefighter safety begins at the fire station. A firefighter's everyday work environment should be as safe as possible. It is the responsibility of all firefighters to maintain this safe working environment. Personnel should take the following common-sense actions to ensure firefighter safety at the fire station:

- Practice good housekeeping.
- Keep floors and all walking surfaces clean, dry, and clear of clutter.
- Ensure that exit areas are lighted and free of obstructions.
- Store all hazardous materials, including flammable liquids, in their proper location.

- Keep material safety data sheets (MSDS) for all hazardous materials (this includes aqueous film forming foam [AFFF] concentrate) and keep them where they can be easily retrieved.

- Use proper lifting and carrying techniques when moving equipment or heavy objects, and don't be afraid to ask for help (**Figure 4.8**).

- Follow and post tool and equipment safety rules.

- Place portable heaters used in stations so that they are out of travel routes and away from combustibles.

- Use only portable heaters that will deactivate if knocked over.

Material Safety Data Sheets (MSDS) — Form provided by the manufacturer and blender of chemicals that contains information about chemical composition, physical and chemical properties, health and safety hazards, emergency response procedures, and waste disposal procedures of the specified material.

Figure 4.8 It is safer (and easier) to lift heavy objects with two personnel than it is with one.

Personnel that observe any situations that warrant a safety concern should bring them to the attention of the health and safety officer. For further information, please refer to the IFSTA **Fire Department Safety Officer** and **Occupational Safety, Health, and Wellness** manuals.

Emergency Response and Scene Management

Because of the inherent dangers involved with emergency responses, ARFF vehicle driver/ operators, supervisors, and ARFF crewmembers should be properly dressed and buckled into their seats prior to departing the fire station. Personnel should not attempt to don their protective clothing while enroute. All loose items must be secure in the cab of the apparatus prior to its movement. Loose items can become projectiles and cause injury or death if the vehicle becomes involved in a roll-over accident. Map books, flashlights, tools and equipment should all be secured prior to responding.

Figure 4.9 ARFF vehicle driver/operators must carefully gauge their speed, weather conditions, and other factors while responding to an airfield emergency.

ARFF vehicle driver/operators and supervisors must select and use the safest possible routes to the incident scene. Vehicle speed must be balanced with appropriate caution based upon the situation, location, weather conditions, and vehicle and driver operator capabilities to prevent vehicle roll over and/or avoiding an accident **(Figure 4.9)**. Awareness of areas on the airfield that are under construction is important since construction zones require deviation from normal response routes and set-up positions.

After safely accomplishing emergency response, creating proper scene management reduces congestion and confusion around aircraft incidents both on the airfield and off. The perimeter of the scene should be secured and entry should be denied to those who are not part of the response. The most common method of organizing an ARFF incident scene is to establish three operating zones, commonly labeled "hot," "warm," and "cold" **(Figure 4.10)**.

- *Hot (Restricted) Zone* — area where aircraft rescue and fire fighting operations are being conducted; includes the area identified as Immediately Dangerous to Life and Health (IDLH). Only personnel who are performing ARFF related tasks and wearing proper PPE are allowed in the hot zone. The size of this zone may vary greatly depending upon the nature and extent of the aircraft and the incident itself. This zone should stay active throughout the entire incident. If the aircraft has broken apart, there may be more than one hot zone.

Figure 4.10 Hazardous area control zones.

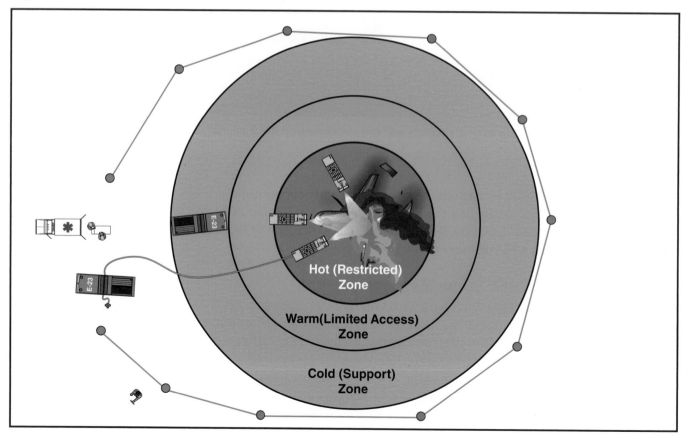

Hot (Restricted) Zone

Warm(Limited Access) Zone

Cold (Support) Zone

- *Warm (Limited Access) Zone* — area immediately outside of the hot zone; access to this zone should be limited to personnel who are not needed in the hot zone but who are directly aiding ARFF personnel and wearing proper PPE in the hot zone.

- *Cold (Support) Zone* — area surrounding warm and hot zones; upwind areas may include the ICP, the public information officer (PIO), and staging areas for personnel and portable equipment; staging area for additional ARFF personnel, rescuers, apparatus and other resources; outer boundary of this area should be cordoned off from the public. An entry/egress corridor should be established to control the movement of vehicles and personnel into and out of the controlled areas.

Cordoned Area

In smaller incidents where no evacuation is necessary, cordoning off the area keeps bystanders a safe distance from the scene and out of the way of emergency personnel. There is no specific distance or area that should be cordoned off. The zone boundaries should be established taking into account the amount of area needed by emergency personnel to work, the degree of hazard presented by elements involved in the incident, wind speed and direction, and the general topography of the area. Cordoning can be done with rope or warning tape tied to signs, utility poles, parking meters, or any other fixed objects readily available **(Figure 4.11)**. However, the material used to cordon off the scene should not be tied to vehicles that may need to be moved during the incident. Once the area has been cordoned off, the boundary should be monitored by law enforcement personnel to make sure that unauthorized people do not cross the line.

Figure 4.11 A firefighter setting up a cordon with warning tape.

Personnel Accountability System — Method for identifying which emergency responders are working on an incident scene.

Personnel Accountability

Each ARFF organization must develop its own system of accountability that identifies and tracks all personnel working at an incident. The system should be standardized so that it is used at every incident. All ARFF personnel must be familiar with the system and participate in it when operating at an emergency incident. The system must also account for those individuals who respond to the scene in vehicles other than ARFF apparatus including airport and privately owned vehicles.

Accountability is vital in the event of a secondary accident or aircraft collapse. If the Incident Commander (IC) does not know who is at the emergency scene and where they are located and when they entered the hazardous area, it is impossible to determine who and how many may be trapped inside or injured. Firefighters can die when they become trapped or disoriented, run out of breathable air, and are not discovered missing. Staying in teams of at least two and maintaining regular contact with the IC are important parts of ensuring that all personnel terminate the emergency together.

To help ensure accountability and safety, both OSHA and NFPA® require the two-in/two-out policy for all *interior* fire fighting operations. In general, there must be at least four fully equipped and trained firefighters at the scene of an emergency before a team of two firefighters may begin interior fire fighting. One of the two outside standby firefighters can be the driver/operator or the incident commander. The only exceptions to the two-in/two-out rule are where a known life hazard situation exists and only immediate action could prevent the loss of life and where a fire is in its incipient stage. If a victim is known to be accessible to rescuers, the two-in/two-out rule may be waived; however, firefighter personal safety must be considered first. If two-in/two-out is waived, a department could not use the accessibility of a victim as an excuse if a firefighter were injured or killed (Canadian regulations call for fire service personnel to follow the two-in/two-out rule *with no exceptions*).

As with any interior fire fighting operation, two-in/two-out is very important to ARFF firefighters. Fighting interior aircraft fires is a dangerous task. A burning aircraft interior can be described as an aluminum inferno filled with burning, dripping plastics and toxic-gas-producing upholstery, having tight enclosed quarters, and filled with 100 or more occupants at times. In some regional aircraft, the size of over-wing/under-wing exits (or, more specifically, the limited space around them INSIDE the plane), may render "Two In/Two-Out" impossible. In situations such as these ARFF personnel should make every attempt to stay in contact with each other through hand signals, verbal exchange, or other means to maintain contact. ARFF personnel should learn their department's two-in/two-out policy and practice often enough to have the procedure become second nature.

Rapid Intervention Team (RIT) — Two or more fully equipped and immediately available firefighters designated to stand by outside the hazard zone to enter and effect rescue of firefighters inside, if necessary; also known as Rapid Intervention Crew (RIC).

The concept of two-in/two-out requires communication with firefighters on the exterior of an aircraft just as it does in structural fires. A Rapid Intervention Team (RIT) team on the outside has to maintain contact with the interior crew and be ready to respond to assist a trapped or injured firefighter. Additionally, NFPA® 403, *Standard for Aircraft Rescue and Fire-Fighting Services at Airports,* requires a dedicated RIT for NFPA® categorized airports 6 through 10 (FAA B through E).

Crews who are operating inside an aircraft must maintain visual or physical contact so that they can help each other if something does go wrong. PASS

Figure 4.12 An ARFF firefighter being decontaminated. *Courtesy of Brian Canady, DFWIA Department of Public Safety.*

devices can be manually activated in case of an emergency to help assist the exterior firefighters in locating downed personnel. One of a firefighter's best defenses in finding his or her way around the cabin is becoming familiar with the aircraft before they actually ever encounter a burning aircraft. Learning how cabin doors, escape slides, and over-/under-wing hatches operate is critical to ensuring a firefighter's safety while inside an aircraft. Aircraft familiarization is a life-saving tool for any firefighter.

Personnel Decontamination

An aircraft accident site is full of hazardous materials and biohazards. Every crash site must be evaluated for hazards and responding crews properly protected. There will always be the need for personnel decontamination at a crash site. Each firefighter, EMS responder, or victim may need decontamination after departing the hot zone **(Figure 4.12)**. A decontamination corridor may need to be established, in the upwind side of the warm zone, so that personnel, personal protection equipment, tools, and other equipment can be decontaminated. Depending on the extent and duration of the operation it may be advisable to leave tools and equipment on site until the incident is terminated, reducing the number of times the equipment is decontaminated.

The procedure for decontamination should be established according to the contaminant that is present. Refer to NFPA® 472, *Standard for Competence of Responders to Hazardous Materials/Weapons of Mass Destruction Incidents*, for guidance in determining what type of decontamination procedure is appropriate for a specific contamination.

Decontamination — Removal of a foreign substance that could cause harm; frequently used to describe removal of a hazardous material from the person, clothing, or area.

Critical Incident Stress Management (CISM)

One of the greatest, silent killers in any emergency responder's life is stress. Aircraft incidents can be more stressful than many other emergencies due to the extremely hazardous conditions and potentially large number of injuries or fatalities. ARFF personnel who have participated in an incident may, in turn, become victims of critical incident stress. Individuals may be able to cope with some amount of stress on their own, but many may need professional help. The AHJ should have teams established and on call to assist in conducting a critical incident debriefing at the conclusion of an incident. It may be necessary

Critical Incident Stress Management (CISM) — counseling designed to minimize the effects of psychological/ emotional post-incident trauma on those at fire and rescue incidents who were directly involved with victims suffering from particularly gruesome or horrific injuries.

to have counselors respond to the accident scene to assist response personnel who are unable to cope with the psychological trauma they have experienced. Counselors should schedule periodic meetings with ARFF personnel to make themselves available if the need arises.

However, not everyone needs to seek professional help for everyday events, but everyone does need to know when to ask for help. Each person has a way of coping with stress. Some ways of coping with stress are good and some are bad. An example of a bad way of coping would be to start consuming alcohol to "ease the pain." This will affect a person not only physically but also mentally. Because alcohol is a depressant, consuming it causes depression to worsen.

An example of coping with stress in a good way would be to take some time to run, jog, or walk. Physical exertion creates a stimulus reaction that reduces negative stressors and makes us feel better. Taking the time to talk to coworkers about a troubling incident also can help. However, if the stresses of fire and rescue become overwhelming, firefighters should seek out professionals to help them handle stress like the counselors provided in critical incident stress debriefings.

Critical incident stress debriefing (CISD) is peer-group or professional interaction immediately after a major incident. The recommended incidents to debrief include mass-casualty situations, loss of a child, and serious injury or loss of a coworker. When personnel should seek CISD ultimately depends upon the situation.

If there has been a large passenger aircraft crash at an airport and there are no survivors, personnel should begin CISD as soon as the fires have been extinguished and while waiting for the investigative teams to arrive. Responders sometimes blame themselves for not being able to do more for someone in need, even though they know that they have, in fact, done all they can do to prevent death and/or a serious outcome. It is not by any means the fault of the rescuer; it lies in the events that caused the crash.

Because the injuries suffered by victims sometimes can be extremely gruesome and horrific, firefighters and any others who had to deal directly with the victims should participate in a CISD process. Because individuals react to and deal with extreme stress in different ways — some more successfully than others — and because the effects of unresolved stresses tend to accumulate, participation in this type of process should not be optional. The process should actually start *before* firefighters enter the scene, if it is known that conditions exist that are likely to produce psychological or emotional stress for the firefighters involved. Firefighters who are about to enter a scene should be briefed about what to expect so that they can mentally prepare themselves.

If firefighters are required to work more than one shift in these conditions, they should go through a minor debriefing, sometimes called *defusing*, at the end of each shift. They should also participate in the full debriefing process within 72 hours of completing their work at an incident. Critical incident stress familiarization and management techniques are also helpful as part of ARFF personnel initial and recurrent training programs.

Aircraft Fire Fighting Hazards

Aircraft accidents can pose many serious hazards. It is important for firefighters to understand the different types of hazards associated when responding to all aircraft emergencies. Each situation brings different hazards and requires firefighters to stay alert at all times while protecting their fellow firefighters.

All aircraft accidents should be considered and treated as potential hazardous material incidents. They usually involve large amounts of fuel and quantities of toxic hydraulic fluids. The incident scene and wreckage may be contaminated with body fluids, lavatory waste, and other blood borne pathogens or biohazard materials as well. Burning rubber tires and combustible metal aircraft components produce some very hazardous products of combustion. Plastic, foam rubber, and leather used in aircraft interior finishes and personal items will give off a wide assortment of toxic gases under fire conditions.

Composite aircraft structural materials can cause asbestos-like respiratory damage and skin irritation. Military aircraft incidents can involve weapons, high explosives, radioactive materials, and exotic fuels, such as hydrazine. Enormous quantities of aircraft fuels are stored and transferred on the airport. These fuels are not only combustible, they also are toxic, irritants, and damaging to the environment. ARFF personnel entering and working in an aircraft incident scene or impact area should be utilizing the proper personal protective equipment and be properly decontaminated immediately after their duties are completed.

Some airports are bases for agricultural spraying operations. Others have aircraft maintenance facilities that utilize paints, solvents, and other toxic chemicals. The presence of hazardous cargo only complicates this already extremely dangerous situation. Almost anything can be transported by aircraft such as those operated by the US Postal Service and numerous shipping and air freight companies.

The sections that follow address general hazards associated with aircraft accidents such as conditions at the scene, aircraft components and hazardous materials, and the hazards associated with engines. Also discussed are more specific hazards associated with helicopters, ballistic recovery systems, and aircraft cargo.

Hazardous Conditions at the Emergency Scene

Safety Officers and supervisors should continually monitor the scene for hazards and take steps to protect emergency personnel. Quite often, more than one safety officer may need to be assigned to work a crash site. Many conditions such as heat stress at an aircraft accident scene are similar to those found in structural fires; however, aircraft scenes offer greater and more specific challenges. The sections that follow discuss conditions all ARFF personnel should keep in mind when responding to any aircraft energency.

Wreckage

Wreckage is the large debris of a broken aircraft and will be in a greater or lesser degree intact. Some systems in the wreckage may continue to function while some may not. The state of stability in wreckage is not always clear, so wreckage should be treated with respect.

Sharp, jagged edges in wreckage can tear personal protective clothing and cause injuries. Wreckage can present obstructions to incident scene access and ARFF vehicle positioning. Large, unstable fuselage sections may collapse, roll, shift, or slide.

The instability of wreckage may create hazards when performing normally ordinary tasks. Some exits (even plug-types) may actually fall from the plane when they are unlatched. For example, the R2 entrance on some DeHaviland Dash 8 aircraft falls outward when opened and weighs 160 lbs. Airport firefighters should exercise caution around aircraft hatches to avoid being struck by falling (or thrown) hatches.

Confined Space Hazards

Aircraft have confined spaces that can prove hazardous to ARFF personnel. Landing gear bays, electronics and avionics bays, and fuel cells are all examples of confined spaces that airport firefighters may encounter. Aircraft maintenance workers may need to enter these spaces to make repairs, upgrade electronics, or repair leaking seams. Quite often the process involves the use of hazardous materials which could slow or delay rescue operations if rescuers are unaware of their presence. ARFF departments should be made aware when these types of operations are being conducted so that precautions can be made to assist in a rescue in the event an emergency occurs while work is being done in one of these spaces. A proactive approach would be to arrange training with maintenance personnel prior to work being done to obtain a better idea of the process and materials' being used before the work is to start. ARFF personnel should always wear full PPE with SCBA and have an air monitor when entering a confined space. Further information on confined space rescue can be found in IFSTA's **Fire Service Search and Rescue** manual.

Heat Stress

Heat stress can be a serious problem when working in full PPE in warm and humid climates. Incident Commanders should make sure that a rehabilitation area is established, that personnel are rotated out of the incident scene in a timely manner, and that their personal needs are attended. The Rehab Area should be away from the sights and sounds of the incident scene, as well as protected from weather extremes. Appropriate food and liquid refreshment should be provided. Seating should be provided to allow firefighters to rest. Personnel that have been working in full PPE and SCBA or in extremely hot and humid conditions should be medically monitored.

Other Important on Scene Conditions

The following, additional difficulties may be encountered at aircraft emergencies:

- Dense vegetation and uneven, soft, or wet terrain can make an emergency scene a difficult and dangerous place to work.

- Adverse weather may pose further complications.

- Extinguishing agent foam blankets can make aircraft surfaces slippery and can hide trip hazards.

- Fall hazards exist from the significant heights encountered with large-frame aircraft.

- Depleted uranium used for counterweights and energized radar systems can be threats to emergency responders. Firefighters should stay away from the aircraft nose, where most radar systems are located, until it is confirmed that the power has been shut down on the aircraft. Military, and some civilian, aircraft may have radar systems on the top or bottom of the fuselage, as well as on the wings.

Fuel Hazards

Because the fuels carried on aircraft represent the primary hazard to both occupants and ARFF firefighters, it is necessary to fully understand aircraft fuels and their characteristics.

Typically, aircraft fuel can be separated into aviation gasoline (AVGAS), kerosene, and gasoline-kerosene blends. AVGAS is used in internal combustion powered engines. Advances in aviation fuel, however, such as those being explored by the United States Air Force Research Laboratories, include the development of alternatives such as "bio-fuels." These bio-fuels are still in development and are derived from biological matter such as corn, soybeans, and sugarcane. **Table 4.1** includes these newly emerging fuel options.

AVGAS is similar to the gasoline used in automobiles except that AVGAS has a higher octane rating than automotive fuel (87 to 92 in automobile gasoline versus 100 to 145 in AVGAS). The ignition temperature, flash point, flammable limits, and flame spread characteristics are also very similar to that of automotive fuel. The variance in the octane rating does not affect the fire fighting characteristics. Spills of AVGAS and low flash point turbine fuels such as Jet B and JP-4 should be blanketed with foam to contain the release of flammable vapors.

Table 4.1
Aviation Fuels

Fuel Type	LEL/UEL	Flash Point	Auto Ignition Temperature	Flame Spread Temperature	Weight	DOT Hazard Class/Packing Group	UN Number
AVGAS	1.4% to 7.6%	-49° F (-45° C)	Comparable to Jet A Blends	700-800 ft/min (213-243 m/min)	6.01 lbs (2.73 kg)	3/II	UN1203
*Jet A *JP A-1 *JP-8	0.6% to 4.7% 0.6% to 4.7% 0.7% to 4.7%	100-106° F (38-41° C)	410° to 500° F (210° to 500° C)	100 ft/min or less (30 m/min or less)	6.5 to 7.0 lbs (2.9-3.2 kg)	3/III	UN1863
**Jet B **JP-4	1.4% to 7.6%	-10° F (-23° C)	470° F (243° C)	700-800 ft/min (213-243 m/min)	6.68 lbs (3.1 kg)	3/II	UN1863
Jet A-2	0.7% to 5.0%	115° F (46° C)	442° F (228° C)	Variable	7.0 lbs (3.2 kg)	3/III	UN1863
Arctic Diesel	0.7% to 5.0%	100° F (38° C)	Variable	Variable	7.0 lbs (3.2 kg)	3/III	UN1993
Below are fuels currently being proposed and tested for future use in either aircraft or flightline vehicles.							
Bio-Fuel		425° F (218° C)					
S-5	Unavailable	141° F (60° C)	This is a Department of Defense developmental fuel. It is not yet in use. It is expected to be in use in 3-7 years. Some information is incomplete.				
S-8	0.7% to 5.0%	100°-125° F (38°-52° C)	410° F (210° C)	S-5 & S-8 are coal derived. Others in development are CNG based.	3/III		UN1993

* These fuels are the same with few additives. **These fuels are the same with few additives.
NOTE: This table is meant for comparison purposes only. All information above is approximate and incomplete. Use material safety data sheets for locally used fuels for exact and complete information.

Jet fuels are divided into two grades: *kerosene grades* and *blends*. The kerosene grades, such as Jet-A and Jet A-1 (JP-5, JP-6, JP-8), are the most common. The important characteristics of these types of fuels are listed in Table 4.1. In general, these types of fuels have higher flash points and slower flame spread ratings than does AVGAS.

Foam application should be considered for spills of kerosene grade fuels. Even though the ambient air temperature may be well below the flash point of the fuel, the ramp/ground surface temperature can be 25°F to 45°F (14°C to 25°C) higher, thus placing emergency responders in a dangerous situation.

> **NOTE:** For more information, see NFPA® 407, *Standard for Aircraft Fuel Servicing*, or the United States Department of Transportation which classifies fuels with a flash point of 140° F (60° C) or less as flammable liquids.

Blended fuels, such as Jet-B (JP-4) fuel, blend gasoline and kerosene. They have a lower flash point (LO) than Jet-A fuels, which makes blended fuels potentially more dangerous when spilled. ARFF personnel should consider immediately applying foam to any spill.

Fuels are delivered from bulk storage to aircraft on the ground in one of two ways. The first method is by conventional fuel tank truck used for overwing gravity refueling and single-point (pressure). The second method is by underground fuel piping systems that use a fuel service vehicle that does not carry fuel, but rather pumps the fuel from subsurface connection points.

> ### Conditions of Flammability
>
> When an aircraft crashes, the force of impact often compromises the fuel system. These ruptures are extremely hazardous because of the presence of many ignition sources such as sparks caused by friction, electrical short circuits, hot engine components, static electricity, and other ignition sources on the ground. Even if a fire has not occurred, the incident should be approached and considered as if fire is present. Precautions must be carried out in all phases of the incident, from the initial response to the recovery of the wreckage.
>
> After an accident in which major structural damage has occurred, aircraft fuel may disperse rapidly and mix with the air to form a mist or vapor. Regardless of the type of fuel involved, this mist is easily ignited, and the resulting fireball acts as an ignition source for other combustibles.
>
> In accidents/incidents involving large amounts of aviation gasoline or jet fuels, reignition (flashback) is a constant threat. ARFF personnel must be aware of the danger of flashback and must completely cover the fuel-saturated areas with foam, reapplying as necessary to maintain the integrity of the foam blanket.

Hazardous Aircraft Components and Materials

Some materials and systems in aircraft present unique hazards. The following materials and aircraft components require special respect due to the hazards they present:

- *Jet Fuel* — a known carcinogen: vapors and smoke can cause chemical pneumonia (in addition to the problems associated with the fires caused by jet fuel)

Flash Point — Minimum temperature at which a liquid gives off enough vapors to form an ignitable mixture with air near the liquid's surface.

Flashback — Spontaneous reignition of fuel when the blanket of extinguishing agent breaks down or is compromised through physical disturbance.

- *Landing gear* — because of the metals used in its construction, landing gear can ignite and burn at high temperatures. The components involved may react violently when water or foam is applied. The tires may explode when reaching extremely high temperatures; parts and debris will travel out from the sides if landing gear explodes. Unstable landing gear should be pinned by authorized personnel.

- *Energized electrical lines* — may injure or electrocute personnel

- *Hydraulic and pneumatic lines* — contain flammable and toxic fluids and gases under very high pressures which may be in excess of 3,000 p.s.i. Some fluids used can deteriorate PPE, as well as irritate exposed skin and eyes. Flight controls, braking systems, thrust reversing systems, landing gear bay doors, cargo door operation, and other necessary systems rely on hydraulic pressure. When the flight control systems and gear bay doors operate, personnel must exercise extreme caution not to be pinched be moving parts.

- *Oxygen systems* — pressurized oxygen systems, chemically generated oxygen, and liquid oxygen systems: each poses a significant risk of explosion when exposed to petroleum products or engulfed in flames; extreme caution must be used at all times when approaching. Cylinders should be removed and secured away from the crash site.

- *Composite fibers* — favored construction material for modern aircraft; dust, smoke, and very small fibers resulting from the cutting or the combustion of the aircraft skin present a skin irritation and respiratory hazard to firefighters. High concentrations can create radio interference to the point that two way radio communication is non existent.

- *Biohazards* — usually bodily fluids of aircraft occupants; may also be present on debris contaminated with lavatory waste or may come from items such as donor blood or organs being shipped onboard an aircraft. All crash sites should be considered biohazard sites until determined otherwise.

- *Pitot Tubes* — sharp and often heated to prevent them from icing; located on the side of the fuselage below cockpit windows and can cause rescuers or evacuees to become injured when sliding from the cockpit window with the aircraft's escape rope. ARFF personnel should avoid and not touch pitot tubes as they may be hot enough to cause burns.

- *Air Bags* — undeployed air bags may pose a hazard to aircraft occupants and ARFF personnel during rescue operations. Passengers, crew, or ARFF personnel may accidentally activate these devices and be jostled about forcefully or injured by a rapidly deploying bag. Airport firefighters should become familiar with each of the various types of air bag systems they may encounter so that they may properly safety these devices following an aircraft crash.

WARNING!
Aircraft have very large electrical systems. Transport aircraft usually have 115-volt AC electrical systems and 24- or 28-volt DC electrical systems.

WARNING!
Pressures in excess of 3,000 psi (21 000 kPa) generate enough energy to sever fingers, hands, and arms. Guard against leaning against moving parts; stay clear of ALL moving parts when working around an aircraft.

Engine Hazards

Both reciprocating engines and jet engines present extreme hazards to ARFF personnel. If responders treat engines casually, lives can be lost even at aircraft scenes that could be considered routine. The two sections that follow discuss the hazards unique to reciprocating and jet engines.

Reciprocating Engine Hazards

A reciprocating engine that is not properly stopped can restart if the propeller is moved. When the propeller is turned, the magneto within the engine turns

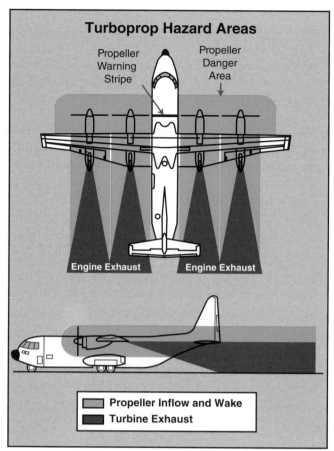

Figure 4.13 Propeller and exhaust hazard areas.

as well and can produce a spark capable of igniting unspent fuel. Once ignited, the propeller may rotate or the engine may restart. In either case serious injury or death may occur.

It is very difficult to see a propeller when it is rotating at high speed. Personnel must possess a situational awareness when approaching a rotating propeller as the aircraft could suddenly move without warning. Even very slow moving propellers can be dangerous. Airport firefighters should not touch or attempt to stop a slow moving propeller! The leading edge of a propeller might be heated to prevent icing - so even if it is not in motion, a propeller may be dangerous to touch. When approaching a propeller, personnel should remain at least 15 feet (5 m) from it **(Figure 4.13)**.

Aircraft that have a variable pitch prop may cause the aircraft to move backwards and produce a prop wash in either direction. The prop is very quiet even at 100% power and ARFF personnel if not cautions could walk into a prop.

Jet Engine Hazards

Jet engines pose a serious threat to ARFF personnel. Even after a crash jet engines may continue to run. These type engines can generate an extreme amount of thrust. Enough thrust to overturn fire apparatus. The air intakes located at the front of the engines are equally dangerous. Large quantities of air are drawn in through the front of the engine to produce thrust. Firefighters near the front of a jet engine while it is running risk the possibility of being sucked into the engine. Being drawn into an engine in this manner will most likely be fatal and could possibly cause the engine to explode.

> **WARNING!**
> Even if a propeller has stopped, do not move it under any conditions. Piston engines that have recently stopped can sometimes cycle, violently rotate, or restart if the propeller is moved.

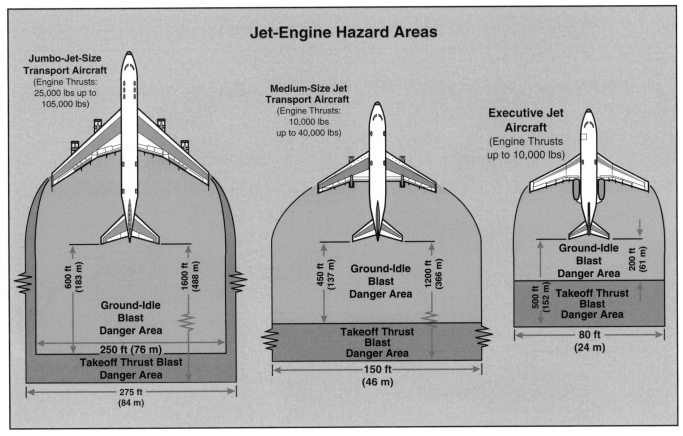

Jet-Engine Hazard Areas

Jumbo-Jet-Size Transport Aircraft (Engine Thrusts: 25,000 lbs up to 105,000 lbs)

600 ft (183 m)

1600 ft (488 m)

Ground-Idle Blast Danger Area

250 ft (76 m)

Takeoff Thrust Blast Danger Area

275 ft (84 m)

Medium-Size Jet Transport Aircraft (Engine Thrusts: 10,000 lbs up to 40,000 lbs)

450 ft (137 m)

1200 ft (366 m)

Ground-Idle Blast Danger Area

Takeoff Thrust Blast Danger Area

150 ft (46 m)

Executive Jet Aircraft (Engine Thrusts up to 10,000 lbs)

Ground-Idle Blast Danger Area

200 ft (61 m)

500 ft (152 m)

Takeoff Thrust Blast Danger Area

80 ft (24 m)

Figure 4.14 Jet engines present both intake and exhaust hazards.

Jet-engine exhaust or blast is superheated and may approach velocities well over 800 miles per hour (1 287 km/h). The exhaust from a jet engine may blow loose objects considerable distances, so personnel should avoid exhaust areas when jet engines are operating. The same awareness to operating jet engines must be practiced when operating an emergency response vehicle. Jet blast can easily upset any vehicle that is driven too close to the rear of an operating jet engine **(Figure 4.14)**.

The intake dangers or suction generated by running jet engines is another severe hazard. To ensure a safe distance, personnel should not approach the front of an engine and should stay at least 30 feet (10 m) away from the front and sides of the engine. It is important to communicate to the pilot, with hand signals or radio, prior to inspecting any system on or under an operating aircraft. When a number of jet engines are operating in a given area, it is often difficult for ground personnel to tell which engines are operating and which ones are not, especially if the personnel are wearing hearing protection. Therefore, firefighters and ground personnel should assume that all engines are operating and be aware of the hazard areas. If the engines are running, the red beacons on the top and bottom of the aircraft will be lit. Smaller aircraft may have one beacon on top of the vertical stabilizer. The suction of a jet engine also poses a hazard to the engine itself. Airport firefighters always should be aware of any objects that could be drawn into jet engines. Foreign Object Debris (FOD) can cause significant damage to engines.

CAUTION

After an accident, a jet engine may continue to run if fuel is still being supplied to it. Even after shutdown, jet engines retain sufficient heat to ignite spilled flammable materials for up to 20 minutes. Also, the rotation of the engine may draw in vapors from spilled fuel and ignite them. When possible, cordon off the area around the engine, and establish a safety zone and keep all personnel clear of this area.

SAFETY AROUND HELICOPTERS

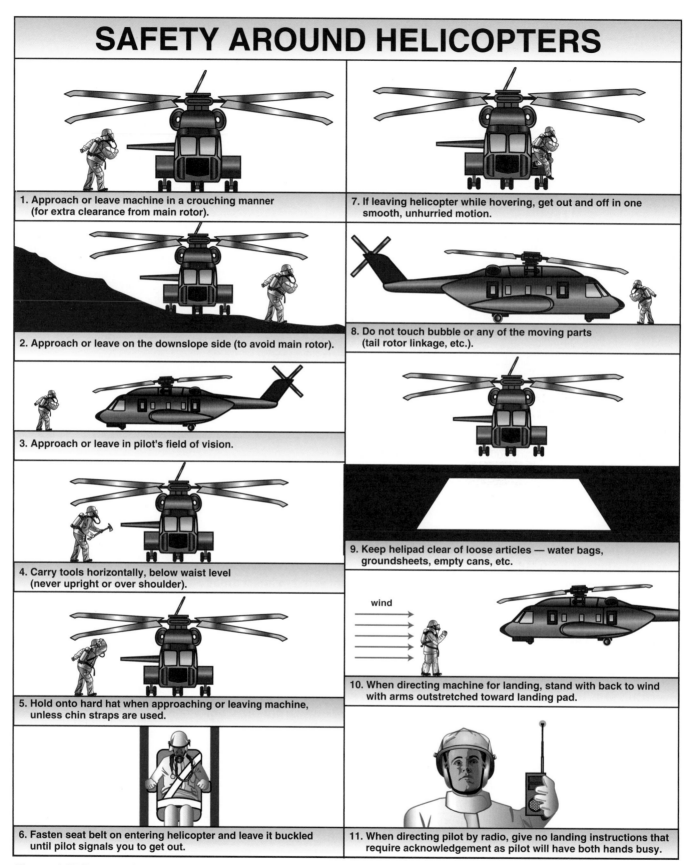

1. Approach or leave machine in a crouching manner (for extra clearance from main rotor).

2. Approach or leave on the downslope side (to avoid main rotor).

3. Approach or leave in pilot's field of vision.

4. Carry tools horizontally, below waist level (never upright or over shoulder).

5. Hold onto hard hat when approaching or leaving machine, unless chin straps are used.

6. Fasten seat belt on entering helicopter and leave it buckled until pilot signals you to get out.

7. If leaving helicopter while hovering, get out and off in one smooth, unhurried motion.

8. Do not touch bubble or any of the moving parts (tail rotor linkage, etc.).

9. Keep helipad clear of loose articles — water bags, groundsheets, empty cans, etc.

wind

10. When directing machine for landing, stand with back to wind with arms outstretched toward landing pad.

11. When directing pilot by radio, give no landing instructions that require acknowledgement as pilot will have both hands busy.

Figure 4.15 Personnel should observe all safety precautions while working around helicopters.

Helicopter Hazards

Helicopters must be approached with caution. The rotors present the greatest hazard and should be avoided at all times. In gusty wind conditions, the main rotor may dip to within 4 feet (1.3 m) of the ground. Because the pilot is most familiar with rotor behavior under various conditions, he or she should decide when it is safe for personnel to approach the helicopter. Therefore, before personnel attempt to approach a helicopter, they should wait until the pilot has them in sight and signals when it is safe to approach the aircraft **(Figure 4.15)**.

The tail rotor rotates at very high speed and is also difficult to see, so personnel should *never* approach a helicopter from the rear. Jet engine exhaust and the radio antenna should also be avoided. Personnel should approach and leave the helicopter in a crouched position and *always* within view of the pilot. On uneven ground, personnel should always approach and leave on the downhill side — *never* on the uphill side.

When approaching a helicopter, personnel must carry all equipment such as shovels, axes, or tools horizontally and below waist level – *never* upright or over the shoulder and always with a tight grip. Any loose articles of clothing must be properly secured before approaching or leaving a helicopter. Personnel should make sure that any gear or cargo is secure and should *never* throw anything in the vicinity of a helicopter.

The selection of an appropriate landing zone is of critical importance in all field situations. A suitable landing area that will accommodate the size of the helicopter must be located and identified for the pilot. ICS facilities, medical, or staging areas, should not be established near helicopter flight paths or landing zones, where noise and prop wash may cause problems. When landing, helicopters must have sufficient clearance of all ground cover within 100 feet (33 m) of the site selected for the landing zone. Use extreme caution and be aware that spotlights and vehicle headlights can blind the pilot. Never point lights at the helicopter. Avoid the use of flares, high beams, and police/caution tape. The operating areas should be kept clear of all personnel, cargo, personal belongings, or other loose articles that may be blown around by the rotor downdraft while the helicopter is approaching or leaving **(Figure 4.16)**. Follow local protocols for establishing LZs.

> ### WARNING!
> Firefighters should wear eye-protection, hearing protection, coat or jacket, bright colored or reflective clothes, and helmets ANY TIME they are around helicopters with running engines, regardless of circumstance (just like a normal landing zone [LZ] operation). The amount of debris rendered airborne by the force of the rotors can cause eye damage and injury.

Prop wash — Current of air created by the rotation of a propeller.

Figure 4.16 A helicopter landing in the landing zone.

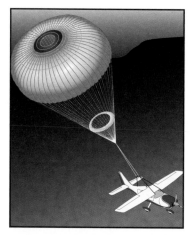

Figure 4.17 An illustration showing an aircraft ballistic recovery system in use.

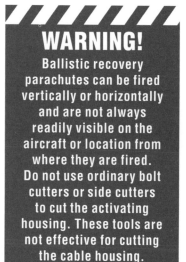

Ballistic Recovery Systems (BRS)

A growing number of general aviation aircraft, ultra-lights, and experimental aircraft, now employ ballistic recovery systems. In the event of a catastrophic emergency or engine failure, these systems are designed to rapidly deploy a parachute that stabilizes the aircraft and slows its descent. While these systems have saved many lives during aircraft emergencies, they can present an extreme hazard to ARFF personnel, particularly if they do not deploy in flight.

On most general aircraft equipped with BRS, such as Cirrus Design System's Cirrus Airframe Parachute System (CAPS), the system is located behind a cover on top of the fuselage just aft of the aircraft's passenger cabin. On smaller aircraft, the entire system is often contained within a canister mounted to the aircraft frame just aft of the pilot's seat.

BRS devices generally consist of a rocket to deploy the parachute, an activation handle, a parachute harness that attaches to the aircraft, a parachute and its lines. When the aircraft encounters an emergency, the pilot pulls on the activation handle causing the rocket to fire. The rocket reaches maximum thrust within a few seconds and deploys the parachute from the aircraft. As the parachute deploys, the harness straps attached to the aircraft and the parachute lines also deploy. The parachute opens and slows the aircraft to a safe speed and orientation for a survivable landing (Figure 4.17).

The presence of a deflated parachute near an aircraft indicates that the BRS has been activated. In this situation, emergency responders should exercise caution as sharp winds at a crash site may cause the parachute to re-inflate and drag or move the aircraft. If the BRS has not deployed, ARFF personnel and other emergency responders should be extremely careful in and around the aircraft because the initiator cable and system are still active and dangerous. The aircraft should only be approached from the front or sides and responders should avoid areas where the rocket might deploy. The safetying of a BRS system should only be done by personnel trained in doing so.

Hazards Associated with Aircraft Cargo

To better facilitate large air cargo transport, large companies have been created which are dedicated solely to cargo transport. These companies use a variety of aircraft, both large craft and small, to transport goods to locations around the world. In addition, commercial flights continue to carry cargo in addition to passengers. The cargo on these commercial and transport flights is often harmless, but frequently cargo is classified as hazardous or dangerous. In these situations, ARFF personnel must take additional precautions when approaching an aircraft incident site.

The term *dangerous goods* (DG) — also referred to as hazardous materials in the United States — is used in the aviation industry to describe hazardous materials. Dangerous goods (hazardous materials) are defined as materials that can harm people, living organisms, property, and/or the environment. The physical property of dangerous goods can be solid, liquid, or gas with hazardous properties such as radioactivity, flammability, explosive, toxic, corrosive, biological, oxidizer, and so on. Aircraft transport large quantities of dangerous goods throughout the world daily, so any air cargo may contain dangerous goods. However, emergency response to incidents involving these aircraft usually remains unchanged from normal aircraft fire fighting procedures.

Because of the materials carried aboard an aircraft for its operation (fuel, hydraulic fluid, etc.) and the combustible metals used in its construction, any aircraft crash could be considered to involve dangerous goods. Technology has advanced aircraft design and construction, incorporating advanced aerospace materials (composites). Exposure to these composites, even in small amounts, may be hazardous to responders, to bystanders, and to electrical/electronic equipment at the scene. Any aircraft subjected to the dynamics of a crash and subsequent fire may release highly harmful substances. Consideration of the possible types and amount of cargo aboard an aircraft suggests a potential for an even greater hazard. ARFF personnel must use proper procedures in response, size-up, and operations to ensure that they are protected from the effects of dangerous goods.

The sections that follow address the laws and regulations that govern the transportation of dangerous goods by air, classifications of dangerous goods, shipment of dangerous goods, product identification and verification, information gathering, and the personal protective equipment ARFF personnel need in situations involving dangerous goods. Also discussed are the safe mitigation and disposition of dangerous goods and lavatory (lav) waste spill incidents and dealing with incidents involving aircraft used in agriculture for applying chemicals.

Laws and Regulations

Transportation of dangerous goods by air is highly regulated. Dangerous goods shipments by civilian aircraft are regulated by the Code of Federal Regulations (CFR) Title 49, Part 175, *Carriage by Aircraft*, in the United States and by the International Air Transport Association (IATA) regulations for international shipments. The IATA regulations are based upon the "Technical Instructions for the Safe Transportation of Dangerous Goods by Air", published by the International Civil Aviation Organization (ICAO). While thousands of chemicals are considered to be hazardous if released from their containers, those chemicals considered hazardous in transport are listed in Table 172.101 of CFR Title 49, *Transportation*. This table also provides information concerning reportable quantities (RQ) of dangerous goods.

Air carriers are required to inspect packages and documents prepared by the shipper to ensure compliance with all appropriate regulations. These procedures, however, do not guarantee that only proper shipments are on board an aircraft. There are many instances in which illegal "undeclared" shipments of hazardous materials are transported by air. Responders must be aware that hazardous materials may be involved whether the accident aircraft is a small private plane or a passenger-carrying jetliner.

> **NOTE:** The required paperwork describing dangerous goods being shipped by aircraft may have a red-and-white candy-striped border. This border should alert ARFF personnel to the presence of these materials aboard **(Figure 4.18, p. 136)**. Required paperwork is more fully discussed in the Product Identification section.

Federal Aviation Regulations CFR Title 14 Part 139 requires initial and recurrent training for airport firefighters on aircraft cargo hazards, hazardous materials, and dangerous goods incidents. Response instructions for hazardous material and dangerous goods incidents, as well as fires at fuel storage areas must be included in the Airport Emergency Plan. Responsibility for

Dangerous Good — any product, substance, or organism included by its nature or by the regulation in any of the nine United Nations classifications of hazardous materials. Used to describe hazardous materials in Canada and used in the U.S. and Canada for hazardous materials aboard aircraft.

Figure 4.18 The red and white striped border on this shipping paper indicates dangerous goods are loaded on this pallet. *Courtesy of John Demyan, LVI Airport.*

planning, preparation, and response to these types of emergencies usually is assigned to the airport fire department. Because airport firefighters are emergency responders, the regulation requires training to the Hazardous Materials Operations Level. Fire Officers should be trained to the Incident Commander Level per NFPA® 472, *Standard for Competence of Responders to Hazardous Materials/Weapons of Mass Destruction Incidents.*

Classification of Dangerous Goods

Dangerous goods may be elements or compounds and may be found as gases, liquids, or solids or in a combination of these physical states. The U.S. Department of Transportation (DOT) defines a *hazardous material* as "a substance that poses an unreasonable risk to the health and safety of operating or emergency personnel, the public, and/or the environment if it is not properly controlled during handling, storage, manufacture, processing, packaging, use, disposal, or transportation." According to Appendix B of NFPA® 402, *Guide for Aircraft Rescue and Fire-Fighting Operations*, dangerous goods are classified by the UN, ICAO, IATA, and the U.S. DOT as follows:

- Class 1 — Explosives
- Class 2 — Gases: compressed, liquefied, dissolved under pressure, or deeply refrigerated
- Class 3 — Flammable liquids
- Class 4 — Flammable solids: substances susceptible to spontaneous combustion; substances that, on contact with water, emit flammable gases
- Class 5 — Oxidizing substances
- Class 6 — Poisonous (toxic) and infectious substances
- Class 7 — Radioactive materials
- Class 8 — Corrosives
- Class 9 — Miscellaneous dangerous goods

Unit Load Devices — Pallets and containers used to facilitate the rapid loading and unloading of aircraft cargo.

Figure 4.19 DOT warning labels can be seen on the packages loaded on this pallet. *Courtesy of Doddy Photography.*

Figures 4.20a and b Two different types of aircraft containers.

Warning labels that have been approved by the U.S. Department of Transportation using the United Nations labeling system are used on shipments within the United States and internationally **(Figure 4.19)**.

Shipment of Dangerous Goods

On cargo-carrying aircraft, hazardous freight is usually placed in containers called *unit load devices* such as aircraft containers or aircraft pallets, either of which may be secured with a net **(Figures 4.20 a and b)**. These containers are then loaded aboard the aircraft. Sometimes loading them requires special equipment, depending upon the size and weight of the particular container. Some air carriers use specially modified unit load devices for transporting certain dangerous goods on the main deck of freighter aircraft. These containers may have special colors and include an integral fire suppression capability.

Unit load devices containing dangerous goods will have a small tag wired to the outside or placed in a plastic window, indicating which of the nine hazard classes, previously listed, is shipped inside. The tag will usually have a red striped border. Special discharge nozzles located inside the container are coupled to a clean agent portable extinguisher by a connection on the exterior of the unit **(Figures 4.21)**. Personnel can manually discharge extinguishing agent into the container without having to open it.

Certain dangerous goods must be accessible to the crew in flight in case of a leak or fire. As a general rule, most dangerous goods on the main deck of cargo aircraft are loaded in the most forward location. Conversely, shipments of radioactive material are usually loaded as far away from the flight crew as possible.

Title 49 and IATA will identify which dangerous goods can only be shipped on cargo aircraft and which can be shipped on both cargo and passenger aircraft. Materials that can only be shipped on cargo aircraft will have "cargo aircraft only" labels on the shipment. ARFF personnel should be familiar with local air cargo loading procedures.

Cargo aircraft have restraining nets or bulkheads to prevent hazardous cargo from shifting. Certain hazardous cargoes are not always transported in specialized containers. These materials, which may be stowed in any aircraft

Figure 4.21 This container for shipping dangerous goods is equipped for fire suppression capabilities. The arrow points to a connection where a hose from a fire suppression system inside the aircraft connects to the container.

CAUTION
Use caution when attempting a rescue through the forward area of cargo-carrying aircraft because of the area's close proximity to any hazardous cargo.

Bulkhead — Upright partition that separates one aircraft compartment from another; may strengthen or help give shape to the structure and may be used for the mounting of equipment and accessories.

cargo compartment, include dry ice and magnetized materials. Passenger aircraft may have dangerous goods shipments loaded in any of the cargo holds.

One possible hazard firefighters might encounter at the scene of an aircraft incident or accident is the presence of undeclared dangerous goods cargo. Undeclared dangerous goods cargo, for whatever reason, is cargo that is not packaged properly, does not have shipping documentation, or has not been handled with the safety precautions required of hazardous shipments. This type of dangerous goods cargo may appear in several forms:

- Dangerous goods improperly shipped through the mail
- Dangerous goods transported in passenger luggage
- Dangerous goods illegally shipped as normal cargo to avoid hazardous cargo shipping charges

Product Identification

One of the most important elements of managing a dangerous goods incident is the proper identification of the product involved. This identification may be challenging in air transport situations because of the wide variety of circumstances in which dangerous goods may be encountered. For example, if an aircraft were involved in a high-impact crash, the probability of the presence of dangerous goods might be high, but rapid identification could be nearly impossible.

> **NOTE:** Certain substances may be shipped only on cargo aircraft and not on passenger aircraft. A package labeled "CARGO AIRCRAFT ONLY" or "DO NOT LOAD ON PASSENGER AIRCRAFT" found aboard an aircraft should alert ARFF personnel that the material is extremely hazardous **(Figure 4.22)**.

If cargo is properly marked and intact, then the recognition and identification of a hazardous shipment is much easier. There are several means of identifying dangerous goods in air transportation. Some of the means of identification and verification are as follows:

Figure 4.22 Packages with this label should only be shipped by cargo aircraft.

- Package markings
- Labels
- UN/NA number (United Nations/North American Systems)
- Container type
- Material safety data sheet
- Shipping papers
- Name of shipper
- Name of receiver
- Name of air carrier

The documentation that accompanies dangerous goods will vary from carrier to carrier. Fire personnel must be familiar with the types of aircraft carrying cargo and cargo operations that frequent their airport. The shipper is responsible for properly packaging, labeling, marking the package and completing the "Shipper's Declaration of Dangerous Goods". Most carriers use a generic international format which has the common haz mat related red striped borders. A few cargo carriers utilize their own unique forms.

The shipper and cargo facility of departure will usually each keep one copy of the "Shippers Declaration". One copy will be affixed to the package, in a clear plastic envelope. If there is more than one package in the shipment, it will be affixed to one of the packages visible from the outside of the shipment.

Federal law requires that the "pilot in command" be provided the shipping paper information for the hazardous cargo on board. The cargo manifest will be kept on the flight-deck. They also must have written documentation regarding the proper shipping name, the UN number, hazard class, quantity, location of the cargo on the aircraft, confirmation that no leaking or damaged packages were loaded, radioactive categories and indexes, "cargo aircraft only" shipments, and any shipments being carried under an exemption. The document(s) is maintained on the flight deck or, on cargo aircraft, may be in a pouch near an exit door — usually the main entry door just aft of the flight deck.

Cargo Manifest — Document or shipping paper listing all contents carried by an aircraft, vehicle, or vessel on a specific trip.

Verification

The initial identification should be verified through multiple sources to ensure accuracy. An error in product identification could be critical and could produce devastating results if the material is consequently handled inappropriately. Therefore, it is recommended that at least three separate sources be used in the identification and verification process. For example, is the product described on the *shipping papers* consistent with the *type of container* and with the *labels* on the container?

Information Gathering (Consulting)

After initial identification and verification have been accomplished, the product must be researched to determine the hazards associated with it. This information gathering helps in the development of a mitigation plan. As in the identification and verification steps, no less than three separate sources of information should be consulted. This procedure helps to ensure the gathering of all information necessary to determine the hazards, to select the personal protective equipment to be used, and to devise a mitigation plan. Some of the common sources of information include the following:

- *Chemical Hazard Response Information System (CHRIS)* — Superintendent of Documents, United States Government Printing Office
- *Hawley's Condensed Chemical Dictionary* — John Wiley and Sons
- *Dangerous Goods Initial Emergency Response Guide* — Transport Canada
- *Sax's Dangerous Properties of Industrial Materials* — Van Nostrand Reinhold Company, Inc.
- *Emergency Response Guidebook* — U.S. Department of Transportation (DOT). This book should be carried on all ARFF vehicles.
- *Emergency Handling of Hazardous Materials in Surface Transportation* — Bureau of Explosives (BOE), division of the Association of American Railroads (AAR)
- *The Firefighter's Handbook of Hazardous Materials* — Baker, Maltese Enterprises, Inc.
- *Fire Protection Guide on Hazardous Materials* — National Fire Protection Association
- *Manual for Spills of Hazardous Materials* — Canadian Government Publishing Centre
- *Pocket Guide to Chemical Hazards* — National Institute for Occupational Safety and Health (NIOSH)

On-scene Verification Resources

A library of information publications should be conveniently and quickly available to response units. Additional data on known chemicals can be obtained on-scene by calling the Chemical Transportation Emergency Center (CHEMTREC®), (800) 424-9300, in the U.S. and calling Canadian Transport Emergency Centre (CANUTEC), (613) 996-6666, in Canada.

Once the materials involved are identified and verified and all their properties and characteristics are known, a mitigation plan may be devised for the disposition of the problem. Based on the known materials regularly transported through the facility, the preparation of pre-emergency plans for specific products or specific situations is recommended. See the IFSTA **Hazardous Materials for First Responders** manual for detailed assistance in developing pre-emergency plans. For more detailed information on handling an actual incident, refer to *Hazardous Materials: Managing the Incident* by Noll, Hildebrand, and Yvorra.

Personal Protective Equipment

Personnel responding to aircraft dangerous goods emergencies need to be protected from the effects of these substances. The responders must ensure they are familiar with the type of PPE being used prior to an emergency situation. The authority having jurisdiction must ensure compliance with NFPA® 1500, *Standard on Fire Department Occupational Safety and Health Program*, and ensure that all steps of identification, verification, and consultation are completed before determining the appropriate level of protection. Protective equipment for any dangerous goods response should be selected following established SOPs and based upon the nature of the incident and the resources available to the department. Under no circumstances should ARFF personnel be assigned tasks or duties for which they do not have adequate protective clothing or training. In situations involving unknown materials, the role of ARFF personnel may be limited to isolating the contaminated area and denying entry until a hazardous materials response team (HMRT) can obtain a sample of the material for analysis.

Dangerous Goods Operations

The first responsibility of units responding to dangerous goods incidents is to isolate the scene and deny entry. This procedure will stabilize the scene and allow for a detailed risk assessment, including determining what rescue efforts may be needed. It is necessary to secure the area, establish control zones, and exclude nonessential personnel as rapidly as possible. ARFF personnel will establish a perimeter. Haz mat team personnel will provide zones, technical references, site safety plans, and incident action plans. Through the use of a systematic size-up procedure and after consulting appropriate references, the incident commander should be able to determine whether evacuation beyond the immediate area of the incident is necessary, and if so, to what extent. ARFF personnel are likely to be involved in the mitigation of the hazardous material release and/or engaged in other essential activities in and around the aircraft. Therefore, a large-scale evacuation, if necessary, will probably become the responsibility of law enforcement or other personnel.

If rescue efforts are necessary, the amount of risk to which ARFF personnel would be exposed must be considered. ARFF personnel trained as technicians and specialists on HAZMAT Operations should not be engaged in rescues or body recoveries at hazardous material incidents. Anytime dangerous goods are involved in aircraft emergencies, a situation that may already be complex and dangerous can become significantly more hazardous for ARFF personnel. The dangerous goods that might be found on or around aircraft are the same as those that could be found on a highway or in a fixed facility. A small amount of a hazardous material confined and concentrated on the inside of an aircraft may be worse than a larger amount spilled in the open on a roadway. The quantities involved in most aircraft accidents tend to be smaller than those in other environments. However, exposure to even minute amounts of some materials may be extremely hazardous to personnel, so all factors involved and the risk/benefit model should always be considered. For more information on dangerous goods incidents, refer to IFSTA's **Hazardous Materials for First Responders** manual or to *Hazardous Materials: Managing the Incident* by Noll, Hildebrand, and Yvorra. Responses to accidents/incidents involving military aircraft are discussed in Chapter 11, Strategic and Tactical Operations.

Lavatory (Lav) Waste Spills

Lavatory waste tanks on air carrier aircraft can range from twenty to several hundred gallons in capacity. These tanks are normally drained and resupplied with fresh blue degerming liquid during aircraft ground servicing. Lav waste is usually disposed of at an airport disposal facility. Spills may occur on the aircraft ramp or enroute to the disposal site.

Spills may contain a considerable amount of toilet paper and solid human waste. Lavatory waste spills are a biohazard and need to be cleaned properly. Like any haz mat or fuel spill, lavatory waste must be prevented from entering storm drains or waterways. Spills should be vacuumed or recovered with absorbents, and the appropriate airport or air carrier personnel should properly dispose of the waste.

Agricultural Application

Agricultural chemicals range from relatively innocuous fertilizers to highly toxic pesticides. Some agricultural chemicals are applied as liquid sprays and others as powders. They are usually shipped to and stored at the aircraft loading point as liquids in drums or as powder in heavy, plastic-lined bags. The materials are usually mixed and diluted prior to being loaded on the aircraft. Different pesticides, herbicides, or fertilizers are sprayed at different times of the year, depending on the life cycle of the pest or the growth stage of the crop.

Agricultural chemicals can be applied with fixed-wing or rotary-wing (helicopter) aircraft. Fixed-wing aircraft are usually loaded at an airport, road, or landing strip as close to the job site as possible **(Figure 4.23, p. 142)**. Helicopters are often trucked to and loaded at the job site. Agricultural spraying or crop-dusting aircraft usually have one or more support vehicles in attendance. These vehicles contain fuel, chemical concentrates, water, mixing hopper, and loading equipment. Helicopters often use saddle tanks to hold the chemical solutions. Fixed-wing aircraft usually have a tank between the engine and the pilot's compartment. The quantities of chemicals carried can range up to several hundred gallons (liters).

These chemicals must be applied at very low altitudes to limit overspray and losses due to wind. Pilots often must fly these aircraft extremely close to

Figure 4.23 An agricultural aircraft (crop-duster) being loaded with agricultural chemicals. *Courtesy of Paul Pestel.*

buildings, trees, power lines, towers, or other types of vertical obstructions. If an accident occurs, the crash site may be very difficult to reach with fire apparatus, and the incident will be complicated by the likelihood of dangerous goods being involved. There is usually no indication on an aircraft of what is being carried. Responders should look for application equipment in the wreckage as an indication that the aircraft was in fact used for spraying/crop-dusting. To determine the chemical being carried, ARFF personnel can contact the owner of the aerial spraying business (the owner may not be the pilot), the owner of the land where the spraying is being conducted, or the local agricultural chemical supplier. *The Farm Chemical Handbook* (Willoughby, US Meister Publishing, 1995) is a valuable reference resource to have available at sites with agricultural application aircraft.

There is a good chance that the pilot, as well as much of the impact area will be contaminated with the spraying material. As with any fire or hazardous material incident, work should be performed from upwind of the accident site.

Although any fire can be extinguished by firefighters operating from a safe distance and in full protective gear and SCBA, the actual recovery of the pilot and control of the spilled material should be accomplished while wearing the proper level of hazardous material protection. As with any haz mat situation, decontaminate any victims prior to transportation to the hospital. Thoroughly decontaminate all personnel and equipment used during the emergency response. Contain any runoff for proper recovery and environmental cleanup.

It should be noted that "agricultural application" may most likely be a problem away from airports because crop duster aircraft often takeoff and land on small airstrips that are not attached to airports. These landing strips may not even be paved and may be no more than a cleared, grassy path on or near farms. Since these strips are often located in rural areas, the first fire department responders on the scene are most likely normal, structural firefighting apparatus and personnel – and are more likely to be staffed by volunteers than departments located in more densely populated areas.

Military Aircraft Hazards

Military aircraft have always had special hazards relating to their mission. Historically, military aircraft experiencing emergencies would be the responsibility of the nearest military installation fire department and only on rare occasions fall under the protection of municipal or airport fire departments. Depending on where the emergency occurs military aircraft may need to use civilian facilities and thus, civilian structural and ARFF personnel should become familiar with the hazards posed by military aircraft.

Special Hazards Associated with Military Aircraft

Some of the unique hazards associated with military aircraft include chaff and flares, Jet Assisted Take-Off (JATO) systems, hydrazine and other chemicals, confined spaces, increased fuel capacities, and the composite materials used in the aircraft bodies and wings. Information on hydrazine can be found in Chapter 3 of this manual while confined spaces were discussed earlier in this chapter. This section will help familiarize an airport firefighter with the remainder of these military aircraft hazards as follows:

- *Chaff* — a radar countermeasure composed of small pieces of aluminum foil or plastic; when released, a cloud of these pieces is formed behind the aircraft which then reflect radar signals back to enemy radar systems showing a group of secondary targets. Caution should be taken around chaff dispensers. An accidental discharge carries sufficient force to knock ARFF personnel off their feet and may cause serious injury.

- *Flares* — countermeasures used to confuse heat seeking missiles by generating an amount of heat similar to that of the engine(s) of an aircraft; when released, they ignite causing an infrared tracking mechanism of an enemy missile to lock onto the flares allowing the pilot to maneuver away from the incoming missile **(Figure 4.24)**. Should flares be accidentally released at a military aircraft crash site, their intense heat can cause fires and burns to human tissue. The light from a flare can cause blindness.

Figure 4.24 Flares being released from a military aircraft. *Courtesy of LCPL Andrew Williams (USMC), Defense Visual Information Center (DVIC).*

Countermeasures — Devices or systems designed to prevent sensor-guided weapons from locking onto and destroying a target.

- *Pyrotechnics* — photoflash cartridges, used for illumination during parachute drops, containing white phosphorous and producing a blinding white light when ignited; *extremely* dangerous and may be found in different locations on many aircraft. Other varieties dispense chaff and high-intensity flares. All readily burn very hot and may ignite surrounding combustibles; once ignited they are very difficult to extinguish because they contain their own oxidizers.

- *Jet Assisted Take-Off (JATO) system* — military aircraft may incorporate a rocket propulsion system used to assist an aircraft in take-off when only limited space is available. The moveable exhaust nozzles on various aircraft pose a significant hazard to personnel approaching from sides of aircraft as well as the usual front or rear of the aircraft. JATO units are not present on all military aircraft.

- *Increased Fuel Capacity* — Military aircraft can have fuel capacities that far exceed emergency responders' expectations. For example a fighter aircraft approximately 50 feet in length can have a fuel capacity in excess of 3,000 gallons; a tanker aircraft may have a fuel load in excess of 50,000 gallons. Increased fuel capacities may require an increase in primary agent necessary to provide/secure rescue paths and control exposure fires; can also contribute to larger areas affected by a fuel spill or hazardous material response. Incident commanders will need to keep fuel capacities in mind when developing action plans to ensure adequate quantities of water and foam are on scene to contain the emergency situation.

- *Composite Wings and Body* — civilian ARFF personnel are not likely to be aware of all the different types of composite materials involved in military aircraft construction. It may be advisable to evacuate the area and contact military representatives as quickly as possible if an unusual environment is encountered or if the fire behavior is not one typically encountered or recognized. The military should be notified every time civilian ARFF personnel encounter any military aircraft emergency or crash.

Emergency Ejection Systems

Accidentally activating ejection seats and canopies may be *extremely* dangerous for ARFF personnel and the aircrew. The catapult containing the explosive charge for the ejection seat may hurl a 300-pound (136 kg) object at an initial rate of 60 feet (20 m) per second. Therefore, it is essential that ARFF personnel know how to safely secure canopies and ejection seats, or avoid them all together, letting trained and qualified military rescue personnel deal with them. Canopies and seats should NEVER be jettisoned indoors as the canopy and crew will impact the roof thus causing severe damage, injury, and possibly death. The sections that follow address ejection seats, canopies, and propellant actuating devices.

Ejection Seats

Ejection seats may be rocket-powered or gas-powered. Some systems fire a single seat, some two seats, and some a complete module from the aircraft. Some systems, referred to as "zero-zero" systems, Zero speed/velocity- zero altitude, may be fired while the aircraft is on the ground and parked. Others require the removal of a hatch before the seat will fire while the aircraft is on the ground. Crew members fire the seats by pulling up on an arm rest, pulling a handle between their legs, or pulling a face curtain from behind their head **(Figure 4.25)**.

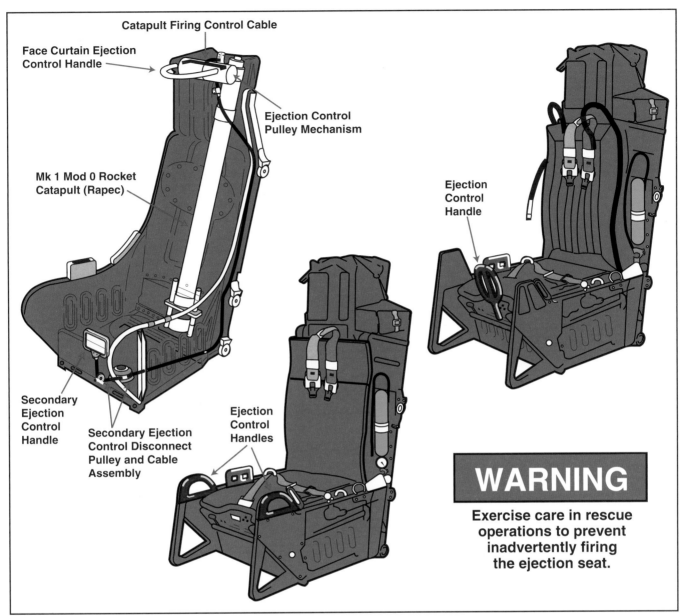

Catapult Firing Control Cable

Face Curtain Ejection Control Handle

Ejection Control Pulley Mechanism

Mk 1 Mod 0 Rocket Catapult (Rapec)

Ejection Control Handle

Secondary Ejection Control Handle

Secondary Ejection Control Disconnect Pulley and Cable Assembly

Ejection Control Handles

WARNING

Exercise care in rescue operations to prevent inadvertently firing the ejection seat.

Figure 4.25 ARFF personnel should use extreme caution when attempting to safety ejection seats as the ejection seat firing mechanisms vary with each type and model of aircraft.

Without proper training, ARFF personnel opening a hatch during an emergency could cause the seat to fire unless it is de-armed and placed in the safe mode. The ejection system may be safetied by interrupting the firing sequence, cutting the initiator hose, or pinning the ejection handles. The pins to safety escape systems, landing gear, guns, EPU, and other aircraft systems may be found in boxes mounted in the main gear wheel wells. However, the specific method of safetying the ejection seat depends upon its manufacturer, the model of the seat, and how it may have been modified **(Figure 4.26, p.146)**. Because several pins may be required to safety a seat or because hoses may have to be cut in several places, hands-on training is the only way to become competent and confident in emergency procedures. Civilian ARFF personnel encountering military aircraft emergency escape systems should not attempt to disarm the system. Military personnel must be contacted to perform this task.

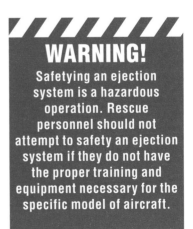

WARNING!

Safetying an ejection system is a hazardous operation. Rescue personnel should not attempt to safety an ejection system if they do not have the proper training and equipment necessary for the specific model of aircraft.

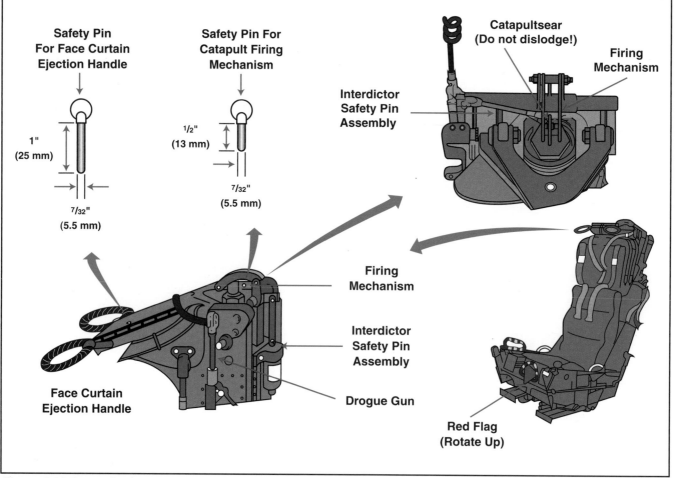

Figure 4.26 Some ejection seats are equipped with an arming/de-arming lever in the middle of the headrest known as the "head knocker."

Canopies

The canopy which encloses the cockpit consists of a metal framework with a transparent covering, usually of Lexan☐ or similar high-impact plastic. It is designed to protect the pilot or crew member while providing them with unobstructed visibility. There are three types of canopies; the clamshell, sliding, and hinged are commonly used on military aircraft **(Figure 4.27)**. Of the three types of canopies, the most common are the clamshell and the sliding types. The sliding canopy is easier to operate during rescues because it does not present as many restrictions as the clamshell canopy.

Canopies are actuated in various ways. Under normal conditions, they may be opened and closed pneumatically, electrically, hydraulically, or manually. In the event of malfunction or mechanical damage to the opening system, power-operated canopies may be opened manually. Once opened, they must be held or propped open with a canopy lock or strut, which prevents the canopy from slamming shut. Canopies weigh several hundred pounds (kilograms). Some canopies are disintegrated with explosives built into the shell or along the canopy frame, and the pilot is ejected through the debris. Because of this disintegration system, only trained, qualified personnel should perform cutting operations to remove pilots.

Most military aircraft with ejection seats have an external means of jettisoning the canopy in an emergency. However, some newer aircraft models are not equipped with such a system. This system consists of a T-handle on

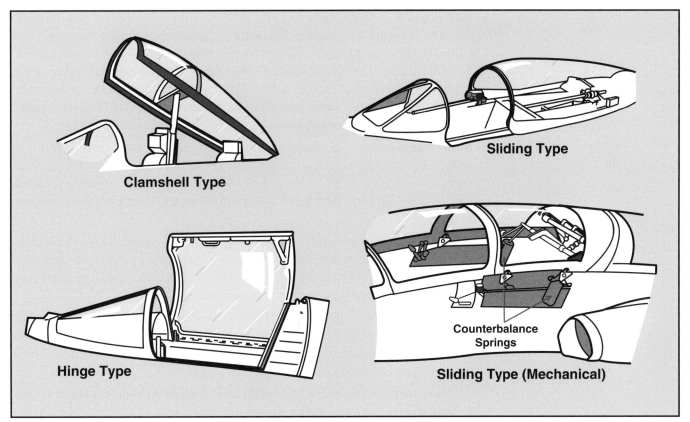

Figure 4.27 The basic types of military aircraft canopies.

the end of a cable and may be fired from either side of the aircraft. The handle and cable will usually be found in a small compartment just below the cockpit and marked "Rescue" with an arrow **(Figure 4.28)**. The canopy is fired by an explosive device that is intended to throw the canopy up and away from the aircraft. Caution should be used when firing this system as the canopy may fall back on the aircraft or rescue personnel after it has been fired. Sometimes jettisoning the canopy will start the seat ejection process. Canopies or hatches should be jettisoned only if absolutely necessary.

Propellant Actuating Devices

Canopy-jettison and seat-ejection systems use explosive charges contained in propellant actuating devices. These devices include canopy removers, initiators, rotary actuators, explosive squibs, thrusters, and seat catapults. Each of these devices is a component of a seat-ejection system. Automatic sequencing of these devices ejects crew members from the moving aircraft, although some systems have zero-zero capabilities that enable crew members to eject while the aircraft is at zero altitude and zero velocity. Detailed descriptions of the propellant actuating devices are as follows:

- **Canopy Removers** — usually gas-pressured telescoping devices that forcibly jettison the canopy in an emergency; when the actuating cartridge is fired, the rapidly expanding gases force the telescoping tubes to extend and jettison the canopy from the aircraft.

CAUTION
Jettisoning the canopy may ignite fuel vapors. When jettisoning the canopy, follow the directions that are printed on the side of the aircraft.

Figure 4.28 The T-handle and cable in this compartment can be used by ARFF personnel to jettison the aircraft's canopy in an emergency. *Courtesy of Edwin A. Jones, USAPR.*

- *Initiators* — cylindrically shaped devices that provide the gas pressure required to start a sequence of events in the emergency ejection process; some fired by gas pressure, others by mechanical pressure, others fire immediately upon actuation, others have a time delay. When the initiator pin is pulled, a firing pin strikes a cartridge, which in turn fires the initiator. The hot gases produced by the burning initiator propellant flow through a tube or hose causing other components to eject the canopy or seat.

- *Rotary actuators* — perform various mechanical functions in aircraft or related equipment; activated by the gas pressure produced by other devices, such as initiators, or by an electrical current. Part of the "canopy remover pad release" system, they forcibly separate the crew member from the seat after ejection.

- *Thrusters* — gas-operated devices that unlock or reposition various units in the escape system during the ejection sequence. For example, thrusters unlock the canopy latches just before canopy jettison, and they move seat and leg guards into position prior to ejection.

- *Explosive Squibs* — small metal tubes closed at one end and plugged with a crimped-in rubber plug at the other end; contains flammable mixtures that produce pressure or provide an ignition source when initiated. There are two types as follows:

  — Flash-vented explosive squibs do not explode but emit a small flame, and they are often used to ignite rocket motors.

  — Closed-end squibs are low-powered explosives that are normally used in explosive bolts, explosive release mechanisms, and fixed fire extinguishing systems.

- *Seat Catapults* — telescoping ejection devices used in the emergency ejection of the aircrew; designed either for upward or downward thrust depending on the type of aircraft. Two types of catapults are used for pilot ejection are as follows:

  — A cartridge catapult propels the pilot and seat with sufficient force to clear the aircraft after the canopy has been jettisoned; used in older aircraft

  — A rocket catapult is more efficient and is employed in more advanced, high-speed aircraft **(Figure 4.29)**. A rocket catapult provides increased thrust to make sure that the crew member successfully ejects, especially in low-altitude situations.

During high-impact crashes and total breakup of military aircraft, all the dangerous components discussed may be scattered throughout the impact area or crash path.

Other Emergency Systems

Because military aircraft often operate in extremely hostile environments, some aircraft have certain emergency systems designed to increase the chances of survival for the aircrew. While some of these systems are typical for any aircraft, some are quite unique to military aircraft. The following emergency systems are unique to military aircraft or have unique configurations on military aircraft:

Figure 4.29 The exhaust of a rocket catapult ejection seat can be seen between the seat and the aircraft as the pilot ejects. *Courtesy of SSgt Bennie J. Davis III (USAF), Defense Visual Information Center (DVIC).*

- ***Emergency Power Unit (EPU)*** — hydrazine-powered; must be safetied before deenergizing electrical power to the aircraft. If this is not done and the power is deactivated before the EPU is secured, the EPU will automatically start. The exhaust produced by a hydrazine-powered EPU is toxic and unprotected personnel coming into contact with the exhaust may become ill or die from the exposure.

- ***Fire protection/detection systems*** — almost all military aircraft have either halon or nitrogen fire extinguishing systems to protect the engines. Much like commercial aircraft, these systems can be activated by T-handles in the cockpit.

- ***Emergency doors/hatches*** — specific locations and operation of these systems vary with each model of military aircraft; some familiarity with the aircraft is necessary to effectively operate them under emergency conditions. Some military aircraft have hatches on the top of the fuselage; some aircraft, such as the C-5, KC-10, C-9, and T-43, have escape slides like those on commercial airliners.

Halon — Halogenated agent; extinguishes fire by inhibiting the chemical reaction between fuel and oxygen.

Weapons and Weapon Systems

In an effort to ensure national security, military aircraft may carry a broad range of weapons and explosives at any time. These armaments may be carried in various forms such as ammunition for machine guns, pyrotechnics, rockets and missiles, and gravity bombs. Unless an aircraft is carrying external weapons, ARFF personnel may have no way of knowing if weapons are on board. Fighter Aircraft in the U.S. must now be considered "armed" until proven otherwise due to their Combat Air Patrols (CAPs) over major cities in the US as a result of the events of September 11, 2001.

While the same fire fighting procedures used on civilian aircraft apply to unarmed military aircraft, there are distinct differences in fire fighting procedures when aircraft are carrying explosives. The primary effort must be directed toward accomplishing a quick knockdown of the fire and cooling of the munitions to maintain a survivable environment. When involved in fire, a weapon or explosive may be expected to detonate within 45 seconds to 4 or 5 minutes, depending on the type of weapon involved. Every effort should be made to extinguish and/or control the fire before the weapons become involved.

The sections that follow provide brief descriptions of the different types of weapons ARFF personnel may encounter on military aircraft.

High Explosive (HE)

While HE itself is not a particular type of weapon, it is present to some degree in all weapons. ARFF personnel must not disturb explosives in any way. A military explosive ordnance disposal (EOD) team should be called to the scene. There are two distinct types of HE, *pressed* and *cast*; and they react somewhat differently when exposed to fire.

Pressed high explosive is pressed into an operational container such as a bomb case. In a fire situation where the ammunition case is not ruptured or broken open, radiant heat or direct-flame impingement will conduct heat through the case to the explosive. This buildup of heat in the explosive may eventually cause a detonation or deflagration of the ammunition. When dealing with confined high or low explosives in an area with fire and/or high heat, detonation most likely will occur.

If the ammunition case is ruptured or broken open, any excessive heat will cause the exposed explosive to burn. This burning explosive could result in a detonation or deflagration. Burning explosives produce flames of various colors. They may be red, greenish-white, yellow, or almost any other color. They normally burn with a very bright, flare-like luminance.

Cast high explosive is heated during the manufacturing process to become a thick liquid that is then poured into the ammunition case, where it slowly cools and re-solidifies. This type of explosive will react the same way as pressed high explosive if the ammunition case is not ruptured or broken open. However, if there is any opening in the ammunition case when it is involved in fire, the HE will melt, run, and resolidify as it cools. Once the explosive resolidifies, it becomes *extremely* sensitive to shock or friction. Driving over or stepping on this resolidified HE may cause it to detonate. Regardless of the type involved, explosives should be expected to be scattered throughout the area in a military aircraft accident.

Ammunition

Fighter and bomber aircraft normally carry internal guns with ammunition drums. This type of ammunition may react violently or discharge when involved in a fire. Guns may be located in the nose section or in the wing roots of fighter and attack aircraft. Personnel and apparatus should not be positioned to put themselves in the line of fire of the gun ports, missiles, or rockets. They should take position at approximately a 45-degree angle off the nose or tail of the aircraft, provided this does not place them in front of or behind underwing rockets or missiles **(Figure 4.30)**.

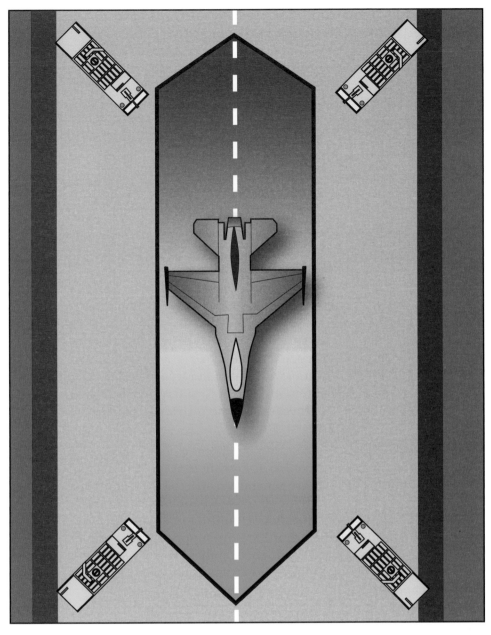

Figure 4.30 ARFF vehicles positioned at a 45-degree angle set-up on a military aircraft.

Rockets and Missiles

Rockets and missiles are self-powered weapons carried on various aircraft. The significant difference between rockets and missiles is that missiles have a guidance-and-control system, and rockets do not. Rockets must be aimed and fired in the direction of a target. However, there is no difference in the explosive potential of either type of weapon. Both types may be carried in internal bays, on wingtips, and on external pylons **(Figure 4.31, p. 151)**. Bomber aircraft may carry cruise missiles in both external and internal mounts.

Gravity Bombs

A significant destructive force can be found in the form of gravity bombs that come in many shapes and sizes. One of the largest bombs currently in the United States inventory is the 2,000-pound (907 kg) MK 84. Although many

Figure 4.31 A F-16 carrying wing mounted missiles, bombs, and external fuel tanks. *Courtesy of SrA Sean Sides (USAF), Defense Visual Information Center (DVIC).*

gravity bombs appear to be similar, they have various capabilities. Some have parachute-ejection devices, some separate and dispense smaller "bomblets," while some carry tear gas. When a bomb is involved in fire and cannot be cooled quickly, the area must be evacuated immediately to no less than 2,000 feet (600 m). If there is a detonation, other weapons in the area may also explode. Water is the agent of choice when attempting to cool a gravity bomb. Foam should not be used because it insulates the weapon and restricts dissipation of heat.

Nuclear Weapons

Nuclear weapons can be affixed to many different types of military aircraft. Nuclear weapons on aircraft are generally restricted to military installations, and aircraft do not usually fly with these weapons aboard unless they are directly involved in a war situation. Handling incidents involving nuclear weapons is the responsibility of military fire suppression personnel who have received specific training and guidance on these weapons systems. Because the chance of a nuclear detonation is extremely remote, the principal hazard of these weapons is the high explosives they contain.

Terrorist Incidents

Airports are mass transit systems with large numbers and concentration of civilians present. Because of this, airports are prime targets for terrorist acts involving chemical, biological, radiological/nuclear, and explosive (CBRNE) weapons of mass destruction (WMD). Airport firefighters need to be trained and prepared to respond to these types of emergencies. Many training programs and sources of information are available on this topic. Indications of a possible terrorist incident involving CBRNE/WMD include:

- Explosions that disperse liquids, mists, vapors, or gas
- Explosions that only destroy a package or bomb device
- Unscheduled and unusual dissemination of aerosol sprays
- Abandoned spray devices or unexplained odors
- Mass casualties without obvious cause or trauma
- Definite pattern of casualties and common symptoms
- Civilian panic in a high-profile target area, such as an airport

Signs and symptoms of nuclear and biological agents typically appear hours to days after the incident. *The Emergency Response Guidebook* can provide information to assist with incidents involving chemical, biological and nuclear agents.

Chemical agents are characterized by a rapid onset of symptoms in minutes or hours, as well as easily observed indicators. Types of chemical agents and their common symptoms include:

- *Blister agents* — red eyes, skin irritation, burning sensation, blisters, upper respiratory damage, cough, and hoarseness

- *Blood agents* — respiratory distress, headache, unresponsiveness, seizures, and coma

- *Choking agents* — irritation to eyes, nose, & throat, respiratory distress, nausea, vomiting, and burning sensations

- *Nerve agents* — pinpoint pupils, extreme headache, severe tightness in chest, dyspnea, runny nose, coughing, salivation, unresponsiveness, and seizures

ARFF personnel on the scene should provide a detailed report on conditions found. This report should include the following information:

- Observed or reported CBRNE indicators

- Wind direction, suggested safe access route, & staging area

- Number, injuries, symptoms, & location of victims

- Control perimeter & command post location

ARFF personnel should follow the procedures outlined in their local emergency response plan for terrorist incidents. Emergency response personnel should utilize procedures similar to those used for hazardous material incidents. Responders should position upwind and uphill, and a safe distance away from the hazard area. They should also establish a perimeter to isolate and deny entry. Emergency decontamination on contaminated or potentially contaminated persons should be performed as well. Additional information regarding responses to terrorist incidents can be found in IFSTA's **Emergency Response to Terrorist Attacks** manual.

Summary

To be able to perform their jobs safely, airport firefighters should be trained in the types and uses of personal protective equipment including self-contained breathing apparatus, personal alert safety systems (PASS), hearing protection, eye protection, and different types of personal protective clothing. They should be thoroughly familiar with firefighter safety while at the fire station, responding to, and at the scene of an emergency. ARFF personnel should anticipate the need to protect mutual aid firefighters that automatically respond to an accident or alert at the airport.

ARFF personnel should be well versed in the general hazards associated with ARFF and the specific hazards aircraft pose to the airport firefighters including the dangers posed by aircraft systems, materials, and cargo. ARFF personnel should have working knowledge of military aircraft hazards. Finally, airport firefighters should be able to identify and respond to terrorist incidents.

Review Questions

1. When does wicking occur?

2. Who should be allowed into the hot zone?

3. When should critical incident stress debriefing (CISD) begin?

4. How might the instability of wreckage affect normally ordinary tasks?

5. When is it acceptable to approach a helicopter from the rear?

6. What is the purpose of a ballistic recovery system (BRS)?

7. What are unit load devices?

8. What is the first responsibility of units responding to dangerous goods incidents?

9. How do flares work on military aircraft as countermeasures to heat seeking missiles?

10. What are explosive squibs?

Fire and Rescue Communications

Chapter Contents

Key Terms

NFPA® references for Chapter 5:

NFPA® 1003 (2010)
  5.2.2
  5.2.3

**NFPA® 1002
(2009 - Chapter 9)**
  9.1.2
  9.2.2
  9.2.3

Federal Aviation Regulations (FAR):

139.319(e)

Fire and Rescue Communications

Learning Objectives

After reading this chapter, students shall be able to:

1. Describe basic airport communication systems. (NFPA® 1003, 5.2.3)

2. Discuss pilot/ARFF Command communications. (NFPA® 1003, 5.2.3)

3. Describe proper radio and telephone communication procedures. (NFPA® 1003, 5.2.3)

4. Identify International Civil Aviation Organization (ICAO) Phonetic Alphabet designations. (NFPA® 1003, 5.2.3)

5. Identify words and phrases unique to the airport environment. (NFPA® 1003, 5.2.3)

6. Discuss the use of computers in airport and ARFF communications. (NFPA® 1003, 5.2.3)

7. Describe light, hand, and other signals used in aircraft accident operations. (NFPA® 1003, 5.2.3)

Chapter 5
Fire and Rescue Communications

Case History

The crash of American Airlines Flight 1420 provides an excellent example of the importance of communications in aircraft rescue and fire fighting operations. The crash occurred at 23:50 hours on June 1, 1999. At approximately 23:52, the control tower at Little Rock National Airport notified the responding airport ARFF crews that an aircraft was down on runway 4R but did not specify which end of the runway (approach or departure). With limited visibility due to high winds and heavy rains, the three responding apparatus went to the approach end of the run to search for the crash site. Not finding the aircraft or debris at the approach end, the driver/operator of one apparatus radioed the control tower and asked the controller if the ARFF apparatus should "sweep the runway" to find the crashed aircraft. A few seconds later, the controller radioed back that the aircraft was located at the departure end of runway 4R and gave the apparatus clearance to proceed down the runway toward the crash site. The ARFF vehicles reached the crash site and began fire fighting operations at approximately 00:08 hours.

Had the tower controller given the location as the departure end of runway 4R, the ARFF crews could have responded directly to that end of the runway. This still would have required a significant amount of time given the severe weather conditions but it would have been far less than the approximately 16 minutes the records show.

When an emergency arises, ARFF personnel should be able to communicate clearly with emergency dispatchers and air traffic controllers in order to locate and respond to an incident site. In some instances, an ARFF Incident Commander may be provided the luxury of talking directly to the flight crew of the aircraft involved in the emergency. The success of incident management depends on clear and understandable communication at all levels. Clearly communicated orders reduce confusion and help to maximize the use of available resources. Clear communication promotes teamwork, reduces the likelihood of freelancing by individual units, and provides the Incident Commander (IC) with an accurate picture of the incident as various operations are being conducted. Because other fire and law enforcement agencies and the local media monitor public safety frequencies, the manner in which communications are handled projects an image of the department.

Each jurisdiction should establish standard operating procedures (SOPs) for dispatch and emergency scene communications. These communications should be coordinated with other agencies within the area. These procedures should include clearly defined lines of communication, specified frequencies, and guidelines for their use. To be most effective, all participating agencies and

Figure 5.1 A dispatcher (telecommunicator) at a dedicated airport dispatch center.

Dispatcher — Person who works in the communications center and processes information from the public and emergency responders.

their individual units should use the established procedures in their day-to-day operations and should exercise the procedures through regular training. The suggested methodology for planning and implementing ARFF communications can be found in the Federal Aviation Administration (FAA) Advisory Circular 150/5210 – 7D, *Aircraft Rescue and Firefighting Communications*.

This chapter provides information regarding ARFF communications and covers airport communication systems such as direct-line telephones, radios, and aviation radio frequencies. The benefits of having communications capabilities between pilots and ARFF incident commanders are also discussed. Chapter 5 also describes proper radio and telephone procedures and provides examples of applicable phonetic alphabet and vocabulary used by the aviation industry and ARFF personnel. An overview is provided of how computer systems are used to communicate critical information to airport firefighters during an incident. Common light and hand signals used during aircraft emergencies are also described.

Airport Communication Systems and Procedures

Depending on the size of an airport, a local fire department located off the airport or a dedicated ARFF dispatch center located on the airport may handle ARFF communications **(Figure 5.1)**. Dispatchers (also called telecommunicators), mutual aid personnel, and all ARFF personnel should be familiar with the terminology common to the airport community and with communication procedures of control tower personnel. Mutual aid and support organizations should be made aware of airport communication procedures in an effort to eliminate confusion when responding to an incident. A communication plan should be established, tested, and implemented if multiple types of radio systems are being used and are not compatible.

At many airports, the activating authority (control tower, flight-service station, airport manager, fixed-based operator, or airline office) communicates

Table 5.1
Categories of Emergency Alerts

FAA	ICAO/NFPA	Description
Alert I - Local Standby Alert	Local Standby	An inbound aircraft with a minor problem or difficulty. At least one ARFF vehicle and crew should standby.
Alert II - Full Emergency Alert	Full Emergency	An inbound aircraft with a major problem or difficulty that requires a full response of ARFF vehicles and crews.
Alert III - Aircraft Accident Alert	Aircraft Accident	An aircraft accident HAS occurred near or on the airport requiring a full response of ARFF vehicles and crews.

directly with the airport fire department and should be able to communicate directly with support agencies such as emergency medical services (EMS), airport maintenance, and police. Airport communication systems for ARFF operations include audible alarms, direct-line telephones, and radios, all of which should be checked daily.

Air traffic control personnel usually provide the following basic information regardless of the method used to notify firefighters of an aircraft incident/ accident. This may vary from airport to airport or at military installations. Personnel taking the information should ask additional questions about the following pieces of information to fully understand the situation.

- Make and model of aircraft

- Name of air carrier

- Response category such as Alert 1 (local standby), Alert 2 (full emergency), or Alert 3 (aircraft accident) **(Table 5.1)**; fire service personnel may elect to upgrade or modify the response based on the information received.

NOTE: Response categories are not standardized.

- Emergency situation

- Number of persons on board

- Amount of fuel on board, usually in pounds, but sometimes in hours of flying time remaining

- Any other pertinent information the reporting party may have knowledge of, such as hazardous cargo on board, non-ambulatory persons aboard, live weapons or ordinance, etc.

Notice to Airmen (NOTAM)
— Bulletin issued by airport personnel notifying aviation interests of issues that can effect normal operations.

Notice to Airmen (NOTAM)

Notice to airmen, commonly called a NOTAM, is information that is issued by the airport operator or air traffic control personnel. A NOTAM addresses important information about airport operations involving runways, taxiways, and essential services. For example, a NOTAM may report pending runway construction and may specify dates, times, or until further notice. Fire personnel should be made aware of, and post, NOTAMs at the time the airport operator issues them. If fire protection apparatus and services fall below the requirements identified in FAR Part 139.319, fire department personnel must notify the airport operator so that a NOTAM can be issued.

The sections that follow discuss the following aspects of ARFF communications:

- Audible alarms and direct-line telephones
- Radio systems commonly used by ARFF departments
- Aviation radio frequencies
- Communications between aircraft pilots and ARFF command personnel

In addition, proper radio and telephone procedures are described as well as explanations of the International Civil Aviation Organization (ICAO) phonetic alphabet and vocabulary words common to ARFF operations.

Figure 5.2 ARFF personnel can receive emergency information of an aircraft emergency over a fire station speaker system.

Audible Alarms and Direct-Line Telephones

When an actual or potential emergency is reported, the appropriate authority will activate audible alarms to alert any or all of the following:

- Airport or facility occupants
- Regular ARFF personnel
- Auxiliary ARFF personnel
- Essential support services, such as airport security, local law enforcement, EMS providers, and others located on or off the airport

Commonly, a direct-line telephone, speaker system, bell, Klaxon□ or similar device, or combinations thereof are used to alert ARFF personnel in the airport fire station **(Figure 5.2)**. When airport auxiliary firefighters or off-duty firefighters are used, they may be notified by pagers, tone-activated radio receivers, cell phones, or a siren/horn that is easily heard above normal noise level.

Direct-line communication used to be limited to that between the control tower and the ARFF station. Since experience has shown the importance of notifying additional resources quickly, direct-line telephone conference circuits have been established between the control tower and multiple emergency agencies. These agencies may include airline station managers, medical transport organizations, area hospitals, and mutual aid fire departments **(Figure 5.3, p. 164)**. Such telephone circuits provide a primary means of aircraft accident/incident notification. To ensure their reliability, these lines should be tested regularly and monitored continuously. A means should be provided for their immediate repair when necessary. This type of system can be used to notify and request resources from multiple organizations at the same time. Some organizations may be provided with a one-way monitor that allows notification of an incident or accident but not two-way conversation.

Radio Systems

The most efficient means for communicating with personnel during emergency scene operations are two-way radios. Radios should have a sufficient number of channels to allow the necessary command, tactical, and support functions to operate on separate channels, and the IC should have the ability to communicate with agencies operating on other frequencies.

Although each agency or group of agencies is assigned a specific radio channel that it may use for routine and emergency messages, all agencies concerned must have one or more common channels for mutual aid operations. Strict radio discipline must also be exercised to facilitate the proper and efficient use of shared radio channels. In addition, emergency agencies should have multi-channel scanning capability in order to monitor local radio channels for critical emergency information.

Clear text language or common terminology should be used in all radio transmissions to eliminate confusion. The use of site specific, slang, local expressions, or esoteric terminology should be suspended particularly during multi-agency operations.

Airport and ARFF management should ensure that fire service radio systems comply with Federal Communications Commission (FCC) *Public Safety and Homeland Security Bureau* and the regulations of the AHJ. Only an FCC

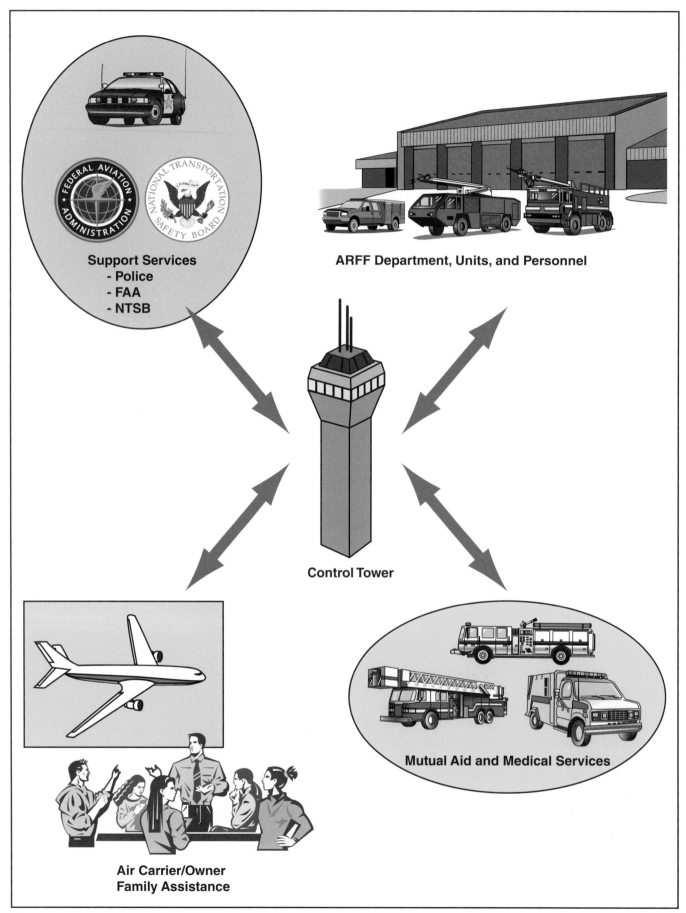

Figure 5.3 The control tower has direct communications with several emergency agencies.

licensed technician is authorized to adjust transmitters, including base station, mobiles, and portables. Radios and communications networks that are not in daily use should be tested regularly to ensure satisfactory operation. Defective units should be repaired or replaced immediately. Personnel are prohibited from transmitting false or misleading information; unassigned call signals; and indecent, obscene, or profane language. Often, computer-monitored systems are used to record and time-stamp verbal communications to help ensure that procedures are followed.

The communications/dispatch center is responsible for ensuring the proper operation of the radio system. Some of the more important functions performed include the following:

- Clearing the air as soon as possible
- Maintaining discipline on the air
- Determining the order of priority for simultaneous transmissions

Aviation Radio Frequencies

ARFF personnel may use or monitor several radio frequencies that are unique to the aviation environment.

> **NOTE:** The exact frequency number for the following radio channels varies from airport to airport.

At controlled airports, which have an active air traffic control tower (ATCT), a ground control frequency is used to obtain clearance for driving on the aircraft movement area during routine and emergency situations. The ground control frequency is also used by aircraft as they move on taxiways and around the ramp area. At uncontrolled airports without ground control radio communications, SOPs should be established by the authority having jurisdiction that describe vehicle and aircraft movement procedures for that airport.

> **NOTE:** The routes and patterns established in the SOPs should illustrate the desired flow of ground traffic for the different runways or airport areas. These routes are designed to keep aircraft away from high-hazard and traffic areas if at all possible.

Another important frequency (or set of frequencies) is assigned to the local control or air traffic control tower. An airport with several runways may have several tower frequencies with each runway having its own frequency. Aircraft turn to this frequency when they enter an airport air traffic control tower's jurisdiction, which is usually approximately ten miles from the airport. Aircraft stay on this frequency until they turn off the runway onto a taxiway at which time they transfer to the ground control frequency.

If it does not interfere with monitoring ground control instructions, firefighters should also monitor the local control/tower frequency during in-flight emergencies and listen to the conversation between the pilot(s) and the tower personnel. Often, responding firefighters are able to hear information of importance and interest to them. Tower personnel usually rebroadcast or convey an edited version of this information on the ground control frequency.

Flight Service Stations (FSS) may operate a radio frequency at airports without an active tower or airport advisory. FSS can provide in-route communications, provide VFR (visual flight rules) search and rescue services, assist lost

Flight Service Station (FSS) — Facility from which aeronautical information and related aviation support services are provided to aircraft; also includes airport and vehicle advisory services for designated uncontrolled airports.

Visual Flight Rules (VFR) — Rules for flight in which the pilot maintains his or her own responsibility for navigation, spacing from other objects, and other flight functions, separate of air traffic control.

Common Traffic Advisory Frequency (CTAF) — Airport radio frequency used for coordination of air and ground traffic between operators when Air Traffic Control is not available.

Automated Terminal Information Service (ATIS) — Continuous automated information which is broadcast over a radio frequency for a specific airport. Typical information in an ATIS report includes weather conditions, active runways, approaches in use, and other pertinent information.

aircraft and aircraft in emergency situations, relay air traffic control (ATC) clearances, and broadcast information and airport advisories. This frequency may be used only during normal working hours.

UNICOM, or unified communications, is a private, nongovernmental frequency that may provide information or access to services and is usually found at general aviation airports. It is sometimes monitored by airport personnel or various airport tenants. Pilots could use UNICOM to declare an emergency.

The Common Traffic Advisory Frequency (CTAF) is used on airports without an operating ATCT or when the tower is closed. The frequency used for this purpose may be UNICOM, FSS, or one of the tower frequencies. Pilots broadcast their positions, intended flight activity (takeoff or land), or ground operation (taxi route) on this frequency. Vehicle operators, such as ARFF firefighters, announce their intended ground operation, such as where they are going or what they are doing.

The Automated Terminal Information Service (ATIS) is a frequency that has a continuous radio broadcast on weather and airfield information. It identifies the runway(s) in use, taxiway closures, and NOTAM information.

Firefighters should continually monitor the appropriate aviation frequencies when responding or operating on aircraft movement areas. If firefighters must communicate on the ground control frequency, they should the following, correct order of information:

- Name of facility being called — "Airport name, Ground"
- Vehicle identity, such as "ARFF 1"
- Firefighter location
- Request of clearance to desired area
- Preferred route to take (optional)

After giving this information, a firefighter should end communication by saying "Over."

Ground control specifies a route if one is not requested. A requested route also may be changed due to aircraft movements or other reasons. ARFF personnel should repeat the tower instructions before acting and should not hesitate to ask for clarification if uncertain of the tower's instructions. If ground control advises of aircraft traffic or a hazard in the area of travel, the firefighter should acknowledge that the aircraft or hazard is in sight. The ARFF vehicle should proceed only after receiving the appropriate clearance, and personnel should inform ground control when they are clear of the aircraft movement area.

NOTE: Because mutual/automatic aid companies responding to an airport emergency may not be equipped with the necessary radio frequencies or may not be familiar with the airport, these units should be escorted to the incident scene by appropriate personnel familiar with the airport layout.

Pilot/ARFF Command Communications

Advancements in communication technology have provided the personnel responsible for flight operations of an inbound emergency aircraft the ability to talk directly to the ARFF incident commander via a discreet frequency between the cockpit and the ARFF IC. This allows the incident commander to provide the flight operations personnel with information regarding the visible condition of the aircraft, status of ARFF equipment, and specifics relating to the emergency. The ARFF incident commander can advise the flight operations personnel of conditions outside the aircraft so that they can make key decisions regarding passenger evacuation. The flight crew may provide information to the ARFF IC such as the number of people on board, amount of fuel remaining, and any hazardous materials that may be carried on the aircraft. Because of the flight crew's workload during the emergency, the pilot should initiate this communication. It is important to remember that the pilot is ultimately responsible for the aircraft and its occupants. ARFF Incident Commanders must remember only to advise the crew of the conditions of the aircraft and not to convey evacuation instructions unless specifically requested. It is important that all parties discuss the guidelines that govern the procedure during pre-incident planning. Guidance for initiating the pilot/ARFF communications procedure can be found in FAA Advisory Circular 150/5210-7C, *Aircraft Rescue and Fire Fighting Communications.*

An alternate system available to ARFF personnel and others to communicate with aircraft crew members is the interphone system. Air carrier maintenance, mechanics, ramp, and pushback personnel use this system to communicate with personnel inside the aircraft during routine operations. Some fire departments use it during emergencies to talk with the pilots. A special headset can be plugged in to an interphone jack location, which is usually found near the flight deck, ground power connection, or nose gear. There are two systems. The flight connection allows communication only with the flight deck and pilots. The service connection allows communication with the flight deck as well as various compartments (air conditioning, accessory, cargo), wheel wells, rear empennage access areas, fueling and APU panels, and other areas on the aircraft.

Proper Radio/Telephone Procedures

ARFF personnel should follow departmental policies and procedures when calling another unit. To aid in clear communication, personnel should observe the following guidelines for proper radio/telephone use:

- Speak directly into the microphone, holding it at a 45-degree angle to and no more than one and one-half inches (40 mm) from the mouth.

- Speak distinctly, calmly, and clearly.

- Pronounce each word carefully, but convey messages in natural phrases — not word by word.

- Use a conversational tone and a moderate speed.

- Speak only as loudly as you would in ordinary conversation. If surrounding noise interferes, speak louder, but do not shout.

- Try to speak in a low-pitched voice because low-pitched tones transmit better than high-pitched tones.

It is important to maintain a calm, clear tone when issuing orders or making reports over the radio. This prevents the need to repeat messages numerous times.

International Civil Aviation Organization (ICAO) Phonetic Alphabet

When atmospheric or other conditions make radio transmissions difficult to hear, it is standard practice to spell out critical information, substituting certain standard words for individual letters of the alphabet. These are often used to indicate an aircraft identification number or a building number or location. This practice reduces the confusion created by certain letters of the alphabet that sound alike. The ICAO phonetic alphabet is used exclusively for this purpose. Also, a specialized vocabulary of words and phrases has been developed to simplify and clarify radio messages as well as keep them brief. Personnel operating radios should use the phonetic alphabet and this vocabulary, when necessary, to help ensure that messages are understood correctly.

Listed below are the letters of the alphabet and their corresponding phonetic names.

A — Alpha (al-fah)
B — Bravo (brah-voh)
C — Charlie (char-lee or shar-lee)
D — Delta (dell-tah)
E — Echo (eck-oh)
F — Foxtrot (foks-trot)
G — Golf (golf)
H — Hotel (hoh-tel)
I — India (in-dee-ah)
J — Juliett (jew-lee-ett)
K — Kilo (key-loh)
L — Lima (lee-mah)
M — Mike (mike)
N — November (no-vem-ber)
O — Oscar (oss-cah)
P — Papa (pah-pah)
Q — Quebec (kwee-beck)
R — Romeo (rom-me-oh)
S — Sierra (see-air-rah)

T — Tango (tang-go)
U — Uniform (you-nee-form or oo-nee-form)
V — Victor (vik-tor)
W — Whiskey (wiss-key)
X — X-ray (ecks-ray)
Y — Yankee (yang-key)
Z — Zulu (zoo-loo)
1 — Wun
2 — Too
3 — Tree
4 — Fow-er
5 — Five
6 — Sicks
7 — Sev-en
8 — Ait
9 — Nin-er
0 — Zero

Sample Vocabulary

Airport operations and aircraft rescue and fire fighting personnel use a number of communications words and phrases that are unique to the airport environment. To be effective in radio communication, personnel must be thoroughly familiar with these terms and their meanings.

The following are only a few of these terms and phrases and the reader should consult **Appendix D** for other words and phrases used in the airport environment.

Air Traffic Control (ATC) — service operated by appropriate authority to promote the safe, orderly, and expeditious flow of air traffic

Base leg — flight path at a right angle to the landing runway off the approach end

Base to final — turning into final approach position

Blind (dead) spot — area from which radio transmissions cannot be received; may also be used to describe portions of the airport not visible from the control tower

Downwind leg — flight path parallel to the landing runway in the direction opposite to landing

ETA — estimated time of arrival

Final approach — portion of the landing pattern in which the aircraft is lined up with the runway and is heading straight in to land

Flameout — unintended loss of combustion in turbojet engines resulting in the loss of engine power

Fuel on board — amount in pounds (6 to 7 lb per gallon [0.7 kg to 0.8 kg per liter]) on aircraft remaining

Gear down — landing gear in down and locked position (have green light in the cockpit)

Go around — maneuver conducted by a pilot whenever a visual approach to a landing cannot be completed

Hold your position — "Do not proceed! Remain where you are."

Hung gear — one or more of the aircraft landing gear not down and locked (no green light indication in the cockpit)

Jet blast — wind and/or heat blast created behind an aircraft with engines running

Low approach — approach over a runway or heliport where the pilot intentionally does not make contact with the runway

Make a 90, 180, or 360 (degree turn) — instructions normally given by the control tower to the aircraft to indicate the degree of turn the pilot is to execute; also frequently used by the control tower to direct vehicles on the ground

Minimum fuel — indicates that an aircraft's fuel supply has reached a state where it can accept little or no delay before landing

Missed approach — maneuver conducted by a pilot whenever an instrument approach cannot be completed into a landing

Overhead approach (360 overhead) — series of standard maneuvers conducted by military aircraft (often in formation) for entry into the airfield traffic pattern prior to landing

Prop or rotor wash — windblast created behind or around an aircraft with engines running

Wind direction and velocity — given to the nearest 10 degrees, and velocity is given in knots. A report of "wind at 330 at 10" would mean the wind was blowing from 330 degrees (30 degrees from north) at 10 knots (12 mph).

Computers

As computers have evolved, so has their use in ARFF. The types of computers vary from laptops to mobile data terminals (MDTs) to global positioning systems (GPS) **(Figure 5.4).** Computers can provide the following information:

- Data on airport layouts
- Prefire plans of airport buildings
- Diagrams and information on various aircraft
- Information on dealing with hazards associated with dangerous goods
- Ability for personnel to give the dispatch center the status and location of ARFF apparatus
- On-screen messaging between apparatus and dispatch

As computer technology continues to develop both in hardware and software, the use of computers will continue to expand as an information tool, a communications system, and a fire scene management system.

Figure 5.4 Some ARFF apparatus are equipped with computer data and communications systems.

Figure 5.5 An air traffic controller signals responding ARFF apparatus with a light gun.

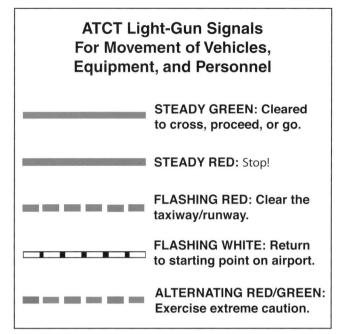

Figure 5.6 Common air traffic control tower light gun signals.

Signals

ARFF personnel also use a variety signals for situations where radio communications fail or it is impossible to hear voice communications. The sections that follow will describe the various signals used in such situations.

Light Signals

Radios represent only one method of communication used for traffic control. The other means of traffic control in aircraft movement areas is through light signals. The tower controller uses a light gun to direct a colored light beam at a vehicle or aircraft **(Figure 5.5)**. Before being allowed to operate a vehicle in aircraft movement areas, operators should memorize the light gun signals and their meanings as described in **Figure 5.6** and in Appendix B, Ground Vehicle Guide to Airport Signs and Markings. The following is a brief description of signal lights:

- A s*teady green light* means that it is clear to cross, proceed, or go.
- A *steady red light* means to stop!
- A *flashing red light* means to clear the taxiway/runway.
- A *flashing white light* means to return to the starting point on the airport.
- *Alternating red and green lights* mean to exercise extreme caution.

Hand Signals

Because of the high noise levels common to aircraft crash scenes, airport fire departments have developed a system of hand signals with which an officer can communicate with a vehicle operator. These signals have been used extensively as a method of communicating when conducting fire-fighting

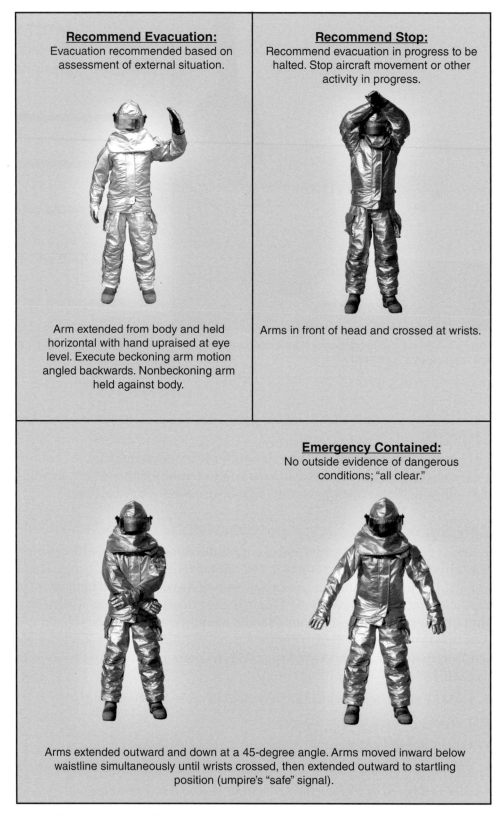

Recommend Evacuation:
Evacuation recommended based on assessment of external situation.

Arm extended from body and held horizontal with hand upraised at eye level. Execute beckoning arm motion angled backwards. Nonbeckoning arm held against body.

Recommend Stop:
Recommend evacuation in progress to be halted. Stop aircraft movement or other activity in progress.

Arms in front of head and crossed at wrists.

Emergency Contained:
No outside evidence of dangerous conditions; "all clear."

Arms extended outward and down at a 45-degree angle. Arms moved inward below waistline simultaneously until wrists crossed, then extended outward to startling position (umpire's "safe" signal).

Figure 5.7 Common ARFF emergency hand signals. *Recommend Evacuation Photo Courtesy of Brian P. Canady, DFWIA Department of Public Safety.*

operations. New signals have been introduced that allow ARFF personnel to communicate with the aircraft's flight crew and with other airline or ramp personnel during emergencies **(Figure 5.7, p. 172)**. These signals are designed to advise the crew of recommendations regarding evacuation operations. Even though advances in portable voice-activated transceivers allow ARFF personnel to incorporate radio communications from under their hoods and helmets, personnel should have a basic knowledge of hand signals in the event that radio communications fail.

It may be necessary for an individual airport fire department to devise additional hand signals to fit its particular procedures and/or apparatus. For example, one department uses one up-raised finger to request that water only be discharged from the turret and two fingers to request that foam be discharged. It is most important that all ARFF personnel within the department know and understand all signals adopted for use by their department. This knowledge can only be acquired with recurrent training and frequent use.

Other Signals for Aircraft Accident Operations

- *Back out or retreat* — sound all audible devices (horns, sirens, etc.) for obviously extended time (1 to 2 minutes)
- *Apparatus is running out of agent* — flash headlights and sound the siren
- *Open or close handline* — tap hand firmly on the desired nozzle barrel
- *Change handline nozzle/stream pattern* — place wrists together and clap hands
- *Advance with handline* — pat shoulder
- *Back out with handline* — tug coattail sharply, or with the hands in front of the chest, give series of pushing motions

Summary

Communications are vital during any emergency and this is true during aircraft emergencies as well. Airport firefighters must be thoroughly trained and proficient in the usage of the communications systems and procedures found at their particular airfield.

This chapter has described importance of the Notice to Airmen issued by airport operators or air traffic control personnel. It has also discussed the types and functions of audible alarms and direct-line telephones used to alert ARFF personnel of an aircraft emergency or incident as well as commonly used radio systems and aviation frequencies used for communications during a response. The benefits of having communications between pilots and ARFF commanders were described. This chapter outlined appropriate radio and telephone procedures to be used by airport firefighters to ensure their communications are clearly understood.

Airport firefighters need to be aware of the growing use of computers to communicate vital information regarding an aircraft incident and some of these uses were described in this chapter. Because ARFF operations can be extremely noisy, other forms of communications such as light, sound, and hand signals are useful at an incident to convey directions and orders to ARFF personnel. A variety of these signals were described in this chapter.

Review Questions

1. Who may handle aircraft rescue and fire fighting communications?

2. How might airport auxiliary firefighters be notified of a situation?

3. What is the most efficient means for communicating with personnel during emergency scene operations?

4. What is the Automated Terminal Information Service (ATIS)?

5. How does an interphone system work?

6. What guidelines should be followed for proper radio/telephone use?

7. Why is use of the phonetic alphabet necessary?

8. What does the phrase "hold your position" mean?

9. What is a mobile data terminal (MDT)?

10. When using light signals, what does a flashing red light mean?

Extinguishing Agents

Chapter Contents

Key Terms

NFPA® references for Chapter 6:

NFPA® 1003 (2010)
5.1.1.3
5.1.1.4
5.3.1
5.3.2
5.3.3
5.3.4
5.3.5
5.3.6
5.3.7
5.3.9

**NFPA® 1002
(2009 - Chapter 9)**
9.1.1

Federal Aviation Regulations (FAR):

139.317 (g)

Learning Objectives

After reading this chapter, students shall be able to:

1. Explain the use of water as an extinguishing agent in aircraft rescue and fire fighting operations. (NFPA® 1003, 5.1.1.3, 5.3.2, 5.3.3, 5.3.4, 5.3.5, 5.3.7)

2. Explain the use of foam as an extinguishing agent in aircraft rescue and fire fighting operations. (NFPA® 1003, 5.1.1.3, 5.3.2, 5.3.3, 5.3.4, 5.3.5, 5.3.7)

3. Identify types of foam concentrates. (NFPA® 1003, 5.1.1.3, 5.3.2, 5.3.3, 5.3.4, 5.3.5, 5.3.7)

4. Describe foam proportioning systems. (NFPA® 1003, 5.1.1.3, 5.3.3, 5.3.4)

5. Discuss portable foam application devices. (NFPA® 1003, 5.1.1.3, 5.3.2, 5.3.3, 5.3.4, 5.3.7)

6. Explain foam application. (NFPA® 1003, 5.1.1.3, 5.3.2, 5.3.3, 5.3.4, 5.3.7)

7. Describe dry chemicals and their applications. (NFPA® 1003, 5.1.1.3, 5.3.1, 5.3.2, 5.3.3, 5.3.4, 5.3.7)

8. Describe clean agents and their applications. (NFPA® 1003, 5.1.1.3, 5.3.2, 5.3.3, 5.3.4, 5.3.7)

Chapter 6
Extinguishing
Agents

Case History

The importance of having adequate extinguishing agents on hand for an emergency can be illustrated by the crash of United Airlines Flight 232. On July 19, 1989, United Airlines Flight 232 (a DC-10) broke apart during an emergency landing at Sioux Gateway Airport in Sioux City, Iowa. Of the 296 people aboard (285 passengers and 11 crew members), 175 passengers and 10 of the crew members survived. The survival of so many aboard Flight 232 was due to the skills of Captain Alfred C. Haynes, his flight crew, and the preparedness and prompt actions of the emergency responders in the Sioux City area.

Sioux Gateway Airport was certified by the FAA as an Index B airport. The Iowa Air National Guard provided the aircraft rescue and fire fighting services at the airport through a joint-use agreement between the City of Sioux City, the State of Iowa, and the National Guard Bureau. DC-10s normally require the fire protection services of Index D airports because they need twice as much firefighting/extinguishing agent as an Index B can provide.

Because of the nature of the aircraft emergency, Sioux Gateway Airport was the only possible landing site for the aircraft. Fortunately, the numerous emergency response agencies in the Sioux City area had entered into cooperative agreements and conducted recent emergency response drills to coordinate their emergency response procedures. When Flight 232 crashed at Sioux Gateway Airport, numerous ARFF and structural apparatus and personnel were on the scene to support the rescue and fire fighting operations.

While rescue operations at this incident were very successful, the fire fighting operations were less so. Due to the lack of adequate quantities of water and foam extinguishing agents, emergency response personnel were unable to extinguish the fire that surrounded the center section of the fuselage.

Airport rescue and fire fighting (ARFF) personnel could encounter Class A, B, C, and/or D fires in any one incident. To be effective, ARFF personnel must have a thorough understanding of fire behavior and extinguishment principles, and the effective use of extinguishing agents. Most airports maintain various types of extinguishing agents, each having a specific use and application. The aircraft fuels, synthetic/composite materials, combustible metals, and other new materials that are constantly being developed and incorporated into modern aircraft, all have specific burning characteristics. Fires involving these materials require the use of specialized extinguishing agents and application techniques. Firefighters must be familiar with new and existing extinguishing agents and their proper application.

In aircraft fire fighting, there are two basic categories of extinguishing agents; primary and auxiliary. (NFPA® 414, *Standard for Aircraft Rescue & Fire-Fighting*

Extinguishing Agent — Substance used for the purpose of controlling or extinguishing a fire.

Two-dimensional fire — Fuel spill that has pooled, having two dimensions, length and width.

Three-dimensional fire — Fuel fire that contains length, width, and height (flowing, spraying, and pouring fuel).

Vehicles uses the term "complementary agents.") Primary agents are those that are designed for mass application and rapid knockdown of a fire. Primary extinguishing agents include water and water-based agents such as the different types of foam, discussed later in this chapter **(Figure 6.1)**. Foaming agents are the primary agents used to combat two-dimensional fires in hydrocarbon fuels such as gasoline, kerosene, heavier oils, and others **(Figure 6.2)**.

When primary extinguishing agents are applied properly and in sufficient quantities, they are effective in extinguishing and/or controlling the flammable liquid fires typical of aircraft accidents/incidents. Occasionally, a three-dimensional (flowing, spraying, pouring fuel) fire may require using auxiliary agents and techniques **(Figure 6.3)**. This type of fire may prove to be very difficult to extinguish with the use of foam agents alone, but it may be quickly knocked down by using auxiliary extinguishing agents such as dry chemical.

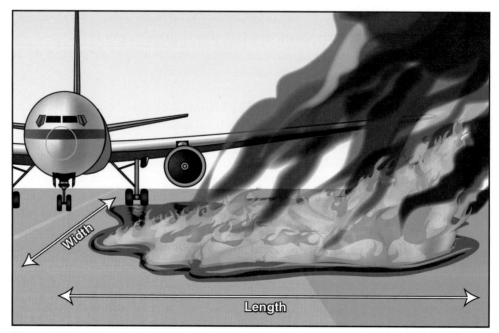

Figure 6.2 An illustration of a 2-dimensional fire.

Figure 6.3 An illustration of a 3-dimensional fire.

Auxiliary extinguishing agents are agents that are compatible with primary agents and are used in conjunction with the primary agent (usually foam) in fire extinguishment. Common auxiliary extinguishing agents for aircraft fire fighting include dry chemical, halons, and halon replacements. In order for an extinguishing agent to be compatible with the primary agent, the agent's chemical composition must not adversely affect the performance of foam. There are other situations where auxiliary agents may be used as the primary agent on specialized fires including fires in wheel wells, engine nacelles, and fires in interior walls and compartments.

Generally, however, auxiliary agents are not effective as primary agents because they are prone to flashback. Dry chemical, for example, provides rapid knockdown of a flammable liquid fire, but if the fire is not fully extinguished and adjacent ignition sources not sufficiently cooled, the entire fire area will "flashback" unless a vapor-suppressing blanket of foam is applied simultaneously. A combined agent vehicle (CAV) can eliminate potential "flash back" issues. A CAV is an airport firefighting vehicle that employs the use of both a primary and one or more auxiliary agents.

Sometimes called "clean" or "clean streaming" agents, halons and halon replacements may prove useful for fires that are inaccessible such as engine fires, fires beneath aircraft, and fires involving a computer system. These agents do have good flooding capability. Fires involving such combustible metals as magnesium, aluminum powder, and titanium must be extinguished using a Class D rated dry-powder combustible-metal extinguishing agent such as MET-L-X˚, G-1 powder, or copious amounts of water.

This chapter focuses on the extinguishing agents commonly used for aircraft fire fighting. The advantages and disadvantages of each agent, as well as the methods of application, are discussed. Special attention is given to foam extinguishing agents as these are the most widely used in ARFF operations.

Some of the most common extinguishing agents are as follows:

- Water
- Foaming agents
- Dry chemicals
- Halogenated agents and halon replacements
- Dry powders

Water and Its Application

Water is by far the most commonly used extinguishing agent in the fire service. However, water alone is generally not a suitable extinguishing agent for large aircraft fuel fires, especially ones in deep pools or pits, unless foaming agents are added to water. By applying water correctly, firefighters may be able to push burning fuel to an area far enough from the aircraft so that an effective rescue can be attempted. This type of fire attack will require a very large quantity of water. Using water on Class B fuel fires may potentially increase the size of the fire, while at the same time moving the fuel to lower locations. When using this method it is imperative that ARFF personnel and apparatus are at a safe location above the fuel.

Water can also be used to cool the aircraft fuselage, thereby reducing the likelihood that the exterior fuel fire could spread into the interior of the aircraft. It can also be used effectively for controlling spot fires and eliminating reignition sources by cooling hot pieces of wreckage. In addition, water can provide an effective heat shield for aircraft passengers and personnel fighting the fire. Class A or B foams would be the preferred agents for extinguishing agents for fires in the interior of aircraft involving Class A materials.

Many procedures for applying water in aircraft fire fighting have been explored. ARFF personnel have been most successful when they have used fog and spray streams. The higher the nozzle pressure, the smaller the water particles become and the more heat the stream absorbs. However, the more finely divided the stream becomes, the more it is subject to the effects of wind and thermal column updrafts; as a result, it may be more difficult to reach the seat of the fire.

When structural apparatus is being used to combat a spilled fuel fire and when water is the only available extinguishing agent, it should be applied from 1½ -inch (38 mm) or larger lines in a fog pattern. Firefighters should avoid using straight streams because they tend to churn and splash the fuel, causing the flammable liquids to spread the fire to other exposures. While structural fire fighting apparatus does not normally carry as much water as ARFF vehicles, its water supply may last long enough for ARFF personnel to effect rescue if the water is judiciously applied.

When using water as an extinguishing agent, ARFF personnel should also keep in mind that there are certain inherent hazards. Water is an excellent conductor of electricity so personnel must take precautions to avoid electrical shock. Water extinguishes primarily by absorbing heat in the process of being converted to steam, but the steam can obscure vision and may scald aircraft occupants and ARFF personnel. This scalding can be significant in fighting fires in the interior of an aircraft. When water converts to steam, it expands at a rate of as much as 1700:1. This high expansion can completely fill the confined interior of an aircraft with steam (especially if ventilation is not

Figure 6.4 Steam generation occurs during interior fire fighting operations.

adequate) **(Figure 6.4)**. The result of this expansion will be steam burns, not only to unprotected victims still inside the aircraft but also to ARFF personnel (even with approved personal protective equipment).

A straight stream may be the best nozzle pattern to use in well-involved, unventilated aircraft interior fires. A straight stream will not upset the thermal layering as much as a fog stream, will generate less steam, and will have better reach to knock down the main body of a fire. As "flashover trainers" used in interior firefighting training show, sometimes short bursts of a fog stream into overhead, super-heated products of combustion can inhibit flashover conditions.

Principles of Foam

Foam is used to combat fires in hydrocarbon fuels such as gasoline, kerosene, crude oil, and others. Foam has lower specific gravity than hydrocarbon fuels; therefore, it floats on the surface of the fuel. In general, foam works by forming a blanket on the burning fuel. The foam blanket excludes oxygen and stops the

Foam — Extinguishing agent formed by mixing a foam concentrate with water and aerating the solution for expansion; for use on Class A and Class B fires; may be protein, synthetic, aqueous film forming, high expansion, or alcohol type.

Figure 6.5 Examples of how foam works.

burning process. The water in the foam is slowly released as the foam breaks down. This release provides a cooling effect on the fuel and surrounding surfaces in contact with the fuel. Foam extinguishes or prevents fire using the following methods **(Figure 6.5)**:

- *Separating* — creating a barrier between the fuel and the fire
- *Smothering* — preventing air and flammable vapors from combining (keeping air out)
- *Cooling* — lowering the temperature of the fuel and adjacent surfaces
- *Suppressing* — preventing the release of flammable vapors (keeping vapors in)

Applying a blanket of foam to burning hydrocarbons cools the fuel and prevents flammable vapors from mixing with air to form a flammable mixture. A good-quality foam blanket should be a homogeneous mass of minute bubbles that will be minimally disrupted by wind, thermal updraft, or flame and hydrocarbon attack.

Firefighters must understand the characteristics of foam to maximize its application and effectiveness. As the foam is applied, it breaks down, and its water content drains out or vaporizes due to the heat and flames. Because of

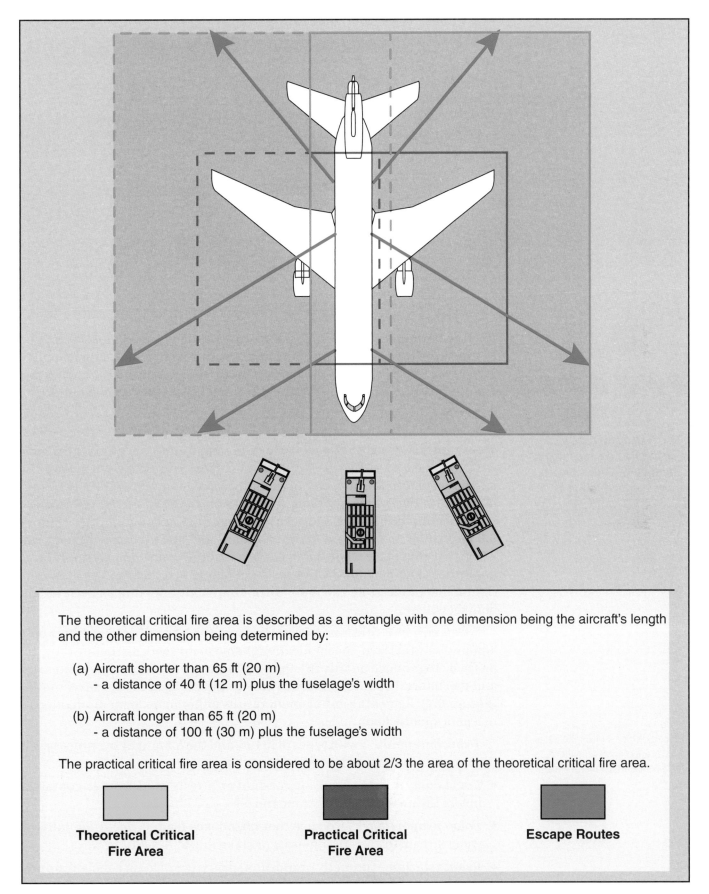

The theoretical critical fire area is described as a rectangle with one dimension being the aircraft's length and the other dimension being determined by:

(a) Aircraft shorter than 65 ft (20 m)
  - a distance of 40 ft (12 m) plus the fuselage's width

(b) Aircraft longer than 65 ft (20 m)
  - a distance of 100 ft (30 m) plus the fuselage's width

The practical critical fire area is considered to be about 2/3 the area of the theoretical critical fire area.

Theoretical Critical Fire Area

Practical Critical Fire Area

Escape Routes

Figure 6.6 The theoretical and practical critical areas relative to an aircraft.

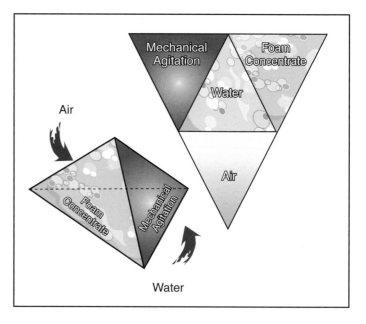

Figure 6.7 The foam tetrahedron illustrates the four components that make up fire fighting foam.

the loss of water through drain out or evaporation, the foam must be applied to a burning surface in sufficient volume, at an adequate rate, and reapplied as necessary to be effective. Applying it in this manner ensures that there is a residual foam layer over the extinguished portion of the burning liquid.

The density and rate of foam application become even more crucial when the *critical area* is considered. The "critical area" also known as "critical fire area" represents a specifically defined region around the aircraft fuselage within which it is feasible to extinguish or control a fire long enough for ARFF personnel to rescue trapped or immobilized occupants. See NFPA 403, *Standard for Aircraft Rescue and Fire-Fighting Services at Airports*, for information on determining this area and respective primary agent quantities **(Figure 6.6 page 185)**. As indicated in this standard, the most serious problem that ARFF personnel face when using foam is that they must quickly apply large quantities of foam to form a fire-resistant blanket on the fire. The larger the flammable liquid spill, the more difficult quickly applying a fire-resistant blanket will be.

Foams currently in use must be proportioned (mixed with water in the proper amounts) and aerated (mechanically agitated to mix with air) before they can be used. To produce quality fire fighting foam, foam concentrate, water, air, and mechanical aeration must be present and blended in the correct ratios **(Figure 6.7)**. Removing any element results either in no foam production or in a poor-quality foam.

To become familiar with types of foams and the foam-making process, it is important to understand the following terms:

- *Foam concentrate* — raw foam liquid as it rests in its storage container before the introduction of water and air

- *Foam proportioner* — device that introduces foam concentrate into the water stream in specific amounts to make the foam solution

- *Foam solution* — properly proportioned mixture of foam concentrate and water before the introduction of air

- *Finished Foam* — completed product after air is introduced into the foam solution (also known as finished foam)

CAUTION
Foam should be re-applied as necessary to maintain the integrity of the foam blanket.

Proportioning — Mixing of water with an appropriate amount of foam concentrate to form a foam solution.

Aeration should produce an adequate amount of bubbles to form an effective foam blanket. The better aerated the foam, the longer the blanket will last. An air-aspirating foam nozzle or nozzle attachment will produced more bubbles than the standard non-air-aspirating fog nozzle.

To be effective, foam concentrates must also match the fuel to which they are applied. Class A foams are not designed to extinguish Class B fires. Class B fuels are divided into two categories: hydrocarbons and polar solvents.

Hydrocarbon fuels, such as crude oil, fuel oil, gasoline, benzene, naphtha, jet fuel, diesel, and kerosene, are petroleum-based and hydrophobic. They will float on water and are insoluble in water. Standard fire fighting foam is effective as an extinguishing agent and vapor suppressant because it can float on the surface of hydrocarbon fuels.

Polar solvents are liquid fuels such as alcohol, acetone, lacquer thinner, ketones, and esters that are flammable and hydrophilic (capable of being mixed in water). Fire fighting foam can be effective on these fuels but only in special alcohol-resistant (polymeric) formulations. It should be noted that many modern automotive fuel blends, which include gasoline with 10 percent or more solvent additives, should be considered polar solvents and handled as such during emergency operations.

Class B foams designed solely for hydrocarbon fires will not extinguish polar solvent fires regardless of the concentration at which they are used. Foams that can be used on polar solvents can also be used on hydrocarbon fires. Polar solvent foams should not be used in ARFF apparatus because the foam concentrate is too viscous to proportion properly.

> **NOTE:** The Federal Aviation Administration forbids the use of alcohol resistant (AR) concentrates in ARFF apparatus purchased with FAA funding. Most ARFF vehicle manufacturers will also void the warranty of apparatus foam systems if this type of foam concentrate is used.

Foam Concentrates

Mechanical foam concentrates can be divided into two general categories: those intended for use on Class A fuels (ordinary combustibles) and those intended for use on Class B fuels (flammable and combustible liquids). The sections that follow contain information on the concentrates in both of these categories and on the common methods for storing them.

Class A Foam

Class A foam has been used since the 1940s; however, only recently has the technology come of age. This agent has proven to be effective for fires in structures, wildland settings, coal mines, tire storage, and other incidents involving similar, deep-seated Class A fuels. However, some jurisdictions may choose to use Class A foams to attack interior aircraft cabin fires or other structural-related fires on airport property.

Class A Foams are essentially wetting agents that reduce the surface tension of water and allow it to soak into combustible materials more easily than plain water. For more information on Class A foam concentrates and their use, see the IFSTA **Principles of Foam Fire Fighting** manual.

Proportioner — Device used to introduce the correct amount of agent, especially foam and wetting agents, into streams of water.

Aeration — Introduction of air into a foam solution to create bubbles that result in finished foam.

Hydrophobic — Incapable of mixing with water.

Insoluble — Incapable of being dissolved in a liquid (usually water).

Polar solvents — Flammable liquids that have an attraction for water, much like a positive magnetic pole attracts a negative pole; examples include alcohols, ketones, and lacquers.

Hydrophilic — Capable of mixing with water.

CAUTION
Failure to match the proper foam concentrate with the proper fuel results in an unsuccessful extinguishing attempt and could endanger firefighters.

Class B Foam

Class B foam is used to extinguish fires involving flammable and combustible liquids and to suppress vapors from unignited spills of these liquids. There are several types of Class B foam concentrates; each type has its advantages and disadvantages.

Class B foam may be proportioned into the fire stream via apparatus-mounted or portable foam proportioning equipment. The foam may be applied either with non-air-aspirating standard fog nozzles (AFFF and FFFP concentrates only) or with air-aspirating foam nozzles (all types). Attachments are available that will convert some fog nozzles into air-aspirating foam nozzles.

In general, different manufacturers' foam concentrates should not be mixed together in apparatus tanks because they may be chemically incompatible. Aqueous film forming foam (AFFF) manufactured to U.S. military specifications (mil spec concentrates) is the exception to the mixing rule. The mil specs are written so that mixing of different manufacturers' mil spec AFFF can be done with no adverse effects. On the emergency scene, concentrates of a similar type (all AFFFs or all fluoroproteins) from different manufacturers, may be mixed together immediately before application. After the incident response is terminated, any remaining mixed, non-mil spec concentrates should be recovered from the apparatus, the foam system thoroughly flushed out, and reloaded with the proper type of concentrate.

NOTE: Although different manufacturers of mil spec AFFF foam concentrates can be mixed together in the same concentrate tank, product quality assurance and accountability is one reason to use only concentrates made by the same manufacturer.

The chemical properties of Class B foams and their environmental impact vary depending on the type of concentrate and the manufacturer. The data sheets provided by the manufacturer provide more information on a specific concentrate. Generally, the runoff and residue from the use of all foam concentrates and solutions is not good for the environment. ARFF personnel should use the minimum amount of foam needed to accomplish extinguishment and prevent ignition. Whenever possible, actions should be taken to contain and recover aircraft fuel and foam runoff.

The sections that follow address foam proportioning, foam expansion, and rates of application.

Proportioning

Today's Class B foams are mixed in proportions from 1% to 6%. The proper proportion for any particular concentrate is listed on the outside of the foam container. Some multipurpose foams designed for use on both hydrocarbon and polar solvent fuels can be used at different concentrations, depending on which of the two fuels they are used. These concentrates are normally used at a 1% or 3% rate on hydrocarbons and 3% or 6% rate on polar solvents, depending on the manufacturer's recommendations.

NOTE: The polar solvent types of foams are not acceptable for use in ARFF apparatus because they are too thick to proportion properly.

Foam Expansion

Foam expansion refers to the increase in volume of a foam solution when it is aerated. This is a key characteristic to consider when choosing a foam concentrate for a specific application. The methods of aerating foam solution result in varying degrees of expansion, which depends on the following factors:

- Type of foam concentrate used
- Accurate proportioning of the foam concentrate in the solution
- Quality of the foam concentrate
- Method of aspiration

Depending on its purpose, foam is either low-expansion, medium-expansion, or high-expansion. Low-expansion foam has an air/solution ratio up to 20 parts finished foam for every part of foam solution (20:1 ratio). Medium-expansion foam is most commonly used at the rate of 20:1 to 200:1 through hydraulically operated, nozzle-style delivery devices. In the high-expansion foams, the expansion rate is 200:1 to 1000:1. Refer to NFPA® 11, *Standard for Low-, Medium-, and High-Expansion Foam,* for more information regarding foam systems.

Rates of Application

The rate of application for fire fighting foam varies depending on any one the following variables:

- Type of foam concentrate used
- Whether or not the fuel is on fire
- Type of fuel (hydrocarbon/polar solvent) involved
- Whether the fuel is spilled or in a tank; if the fuel is in a tank, the type of tank will have a bearing on the application rate

The minimum foam solution application rates for aircraft fuel spill fires are established in NFPA® 403, *Aircraft Rescue and Fire Fighting Services at Airports.* Refer to the IFSTA **Principles of Foam Fire Fighting** manual and to NFPA® 11, *Standard for Low-, Medium-, and High-Expansion Foam,* for fuel tank fire fighting operations, foam proportioning systems, and foam generating systems.

Unignited spills do not require the same application rates as ignited spills because radiant heat, open flame, and thermal drafts do not degrade the finished foam as they would under fire conditions. No specific rate is given by NFPA® 11 for unignited spills. In case the spill does ignite, however, firefighters should be prepared to flow at least the minimum application rate for the specified amount of time based on fire conditions.

Specific Foam Concentrates

Numerous types of foams are selected for specific applications according to their properties and performance. ARFF personnel should consult the applicable Underwriters Laboratories (UL) listing for each specific foam application before selecting the concentrate of choice. Some foams are thick and viscous and form tough, heat-resistant blankets over burning liquid surfaces; other foams are thinner and spread more rapidly. Some foams produce a vapor-sealing film of surface-active water solution on a liquid surface. Others, such as medium- and high-expansion foams, are used in large volumes to flood surfaces and fill cavities. The sections that follow highlight each of the common types of foam concentrates.

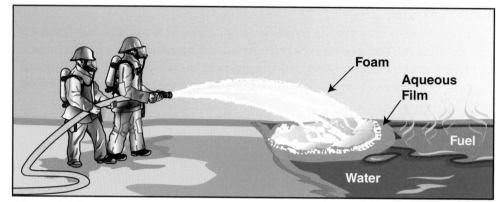

Figure 6.8 The AFFF film floats ahead of the foam blanket.

Aqueous Film Forming Foam (AFFF)

AFFF (commonly pronounced "A triple F") is the recommended extinguishing agent for hydrocarbon fuel fires and is the most commonly used foam at airports today. Aqueous film forming foam (AFFF) is a synthetically produced material. AFFF consists of liquid concentrate that is made from fluorochemical and hydrocarbon surfactants combined with high-boiling-point solvents and water with suitable foam stabilizers. Because the aqueous film in AFFF has a lower specific gravity than hydrocarbon fuels, it floats on the surface of these fuels and, because of its low viscosity, quickly spreads across the fuel surface to form a vapor-suppressing film **(Figure 6.8)**. Furthermore, AFFF has a significant bleeding effect, so as long as the foam blanket of AFFF is maintained on the fuel surface, a cooling film will be continually released.

When AFFF (as well as FFFP, which is discussed later) is applied to a hydrocarbon fire, the following three things occur:

- An air/vapor-excluding film is released ahead of the foam blanket.

- The fast-moving foam blanket then moves across the surface and around objects, adding further insulation.

- As the foam blanket continues to drain its water, more aqueous film is released. This gives AFFF the ability to "heal" over areas where the foam blanket is disturbed.

AFFF is available in 1%, 3%, or 6% concentrates to be mixed with water to form the foam solution. The agent may be used with fresh water, saltwater, or brackish water. It resists breakdown by dry chemicals, making it suitable for use in combination with other agents.

How fast the fire is extinguished depends upon the manner in which AFFF is applied, its application rate, and its density. AFFF may be applied with an aspirating foam or nonaspirating nozzle.

Alcohol-resistant AFFF is available from most foam manufacturers. On most polar solvents, alcohol-resistant AFFF is used at 3% or 6% concentrations, depending on the particular brand used. Alcohol-resistant AFFF can also be used on hydrocarbon fires at a 1% or 3% proportion, depending on the manufacturer, but is not acceptable for use in ARFF apparatus because it is too viscous. Many manufacturers advise that AFFF be stored in a temperature controlled environment and kept in its original container which can result in a shelf life of over 20 years.

Regular Protein Foam (PF) and Fluoroprotein Foam (FPF)

Before the 1970s, protein foam (PF) was used for almost all aircraft fire fighting. PF concentrate consists of a protein hydrolysate plus additives to prevent the concentrate from freezing, to prevent corrosions on equipment and containers, to control viscosity, and to prevent bacterial decomposition of the concentrate during storage. However, due to its corrosiveness, the fact that it is not self-sealing, and other limitations, PF is no longer widely used in ARFF applications. It is still used in some industrial settings.

Fluoroprotein foam (FPF) is a synthetic fluorinated with surfactants added. These surfactants enable the foam to shed, or separate from, hydrocarbon fuels. FPF is not widely used in aircraft fire fighting. However, it is used to protect fuel tanks and petroleum processing facilities because its unique fuel-shedding qualities make it highly desirable for subsurface injection applications. Wherever aircraft operate, bulk fuel storage is present, so ARFF personnel need to be aware of this agent and its capabilities.

Film Forming Fluoroprotein Foam

Film forming fluoroprotein foam (FFFP) concentrate is based on fluoroprotein foam technology with aqueous film forming foam (AFFF) capabilities. FFFP incorporates the benefits of aqueous film for fast fire knockdown and the benefits of fluoroprotein foam for long-lasting heat resistance. FFFP is available in an alcohol-resistant formulation, but as with alcohol-resistant AFFF concentrates, this is not commonly used in ARFF applications.

FFFP is an effective agent on flammable liquid fires. Similar to AFFF, FFFP forms a self-sealing film on the surface of the fuel, continuously suppressing fuel vapors.

FFFP concentrates are available in 3% and 6% solutions that may be applied with non-air-aspirating fog nozzles and air-aspirating foam nozzles. Both fresh water and saltwater (brackish) are suitable vehicles for the foam solution. Additionally, dry chemicals may be used in conjunction with FFFP for successful multiagent applications.

As with AFFF, the effectiveness of FFFP depends upon the application rate, density, and blanketing of the fuel. However, FFFP is not as effective as AFFF in maintaining foam stability. After extinguishment, the foam blanket should be monitored and reapplied as necessary to avoid breakdown and possible reignition hazards.

High-Expansion Foams

High-expansion foams are special-purpose foams and have a detergent base. Because they have a low water content, they minimize water damage. Their low water content is also useful when runoff is undesirable. Fixed, high-expansion foam systems are found in some airport hangars.

High-expansion foams have three basic applications:

- Concealed spaces such as basements, coal mines, or other subterranean spaces
- Fixed extinguishing systems for specific industrial uses such as aircraft hangars, rolled or bulk paper storage, etc.
- Class A fire applications

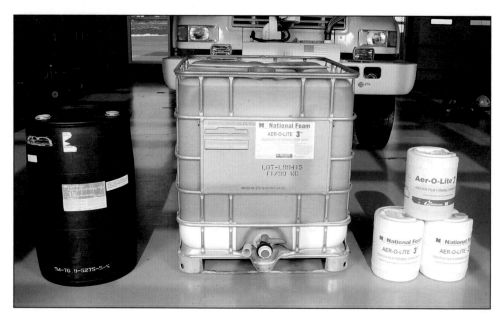

Figure 6.9 From left to right, a foam storage barrel (drum), a tote, and pails.
Courtesy of Doddy Photography.

Figure 6.10 The access cover to the foam tank on an ARFF apparatus.

High-expansion foam concentrates have expansion ratios of 200:1 to 1,000:1 for high-expansion uses and expansion ratios of 20:1 to 200:1 for medium-expansion uses.

How Foam Concentrates are Stored

Foam concentrate is stored in a variety of containers. The type of container used in any particular situation depends on how the foam is generated and delivered. The four common methods of foam concentrate storage are: pails, barrels (drums), intermediate bulk containers (IBC totes) **(Figure 6.9)**, and apparatus tanks **(Figure 6.10)**.

Pails

Five-gallon (20 L) plastic pails are common containers used for shipping and storing foam concentrate. These containers are durable and are not affected by the corrosive nature of foam concentrates. Pails may be carried on an apparatus in compartments, on the side of an apparatus, or in topside storage areas. The containers of alcohol-resistant foams must be airtight to prevent a skin from forming on the surface of the concentrate. Foam concentrate may be educted directly from the pail when using an in-line or foam-nozzle eductor. Plastic pails of foam concentrate should not be stacked more than three high to prevent collapse.

Barrels

Foam concentrate may also be shipped and stored in 55-gallon (220 L) plastic or plastic-lined barrels (drums). Foam concentrate can then be transferred to pails or to apparatus tanks for actual deployment. Some departments have apparatus that are designed to carry these barrels directly to the emergency scene for deployment. Foam concentrate can be educted directly from barrels in the same manner that it is educted from pails.

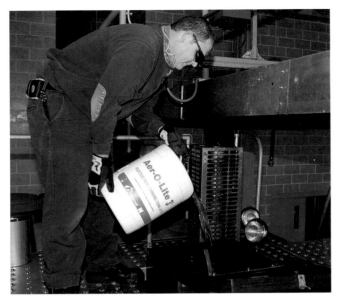

Figure 6.11 An ARFF firefighter adding foam to an apparatus foam tank from a pail. *Courtesy of Doddy Photography.*

Figure 6.12 A foam transfer operation using a side connection fill point. *Courtesy of Doddy Photography.*

Intermediate Bulk Containers (IBC Totes)

Foam concentrate can be ordered in Intermediate Bulk Containers, sometimes called "IBC Totes" or simply totes, which are large plastic tanks inside metal pallets. IBC totes have become more popular in recent years for bulk storage. Totes range in size from 250 to 450 gallons (950L to 1710L) and require a forklift or hydraulic lift to be moved. They are used in much the same way as barrels. Totes can be placed on pickups or flatbed trucks for inexpensive refill capabilities on scene.

Apparatus Tanks

Most ARFF apparatus are equipped with integral, onboard foam-proportioning systems and usually have foam concentrate tanks piped directly to the foam delivery system. This eliminates the need to use separate pails or barrels. Foam concentrate tanks can also be found on municipal and industrial pumpers and on foam tenders. ARFF apparatus will have two methods to transfer concentrate into its foam tank. One is a topside fill location where foam pails can be manually emptied or a fire station overhead foam fill system can be used **(Figure 6.11)**. The other is a side connection, where concentrate from a hose line can be pumped into foam tanks **(Figure 6.12)**.

Foam Proportioning and Proportioning Systems

The process of foam proportioning sounds simple: add the proper amount of foam concentrate into the water stream and an effective foam solution is produced. Unfortunately, this process is not as easy as it sounds. The correct proportioning of foam concentrate into the fire stream requires equipment that must operate within strict design specifications. Failure to operate even the best foam proportioning equipment as designed can result in poor-quality foam or no foam at all. In general, foam proportioning devices operate by one of two basic principles:

- The pressure of the water stream flowing through an orifice creates a venturi effect that inducts (drafts) foam concentrate into the water stream.

- Pressurized proportioning devices inject foam concentrate into the water stream at a desired ratio and at a pressure equal to or higher than that of the water.

This section defines proportioning and details the various types of low-energy and high-energy foam proportioning devices commonly found in portable and apparatus-mounted applications. A low-energy foam system imparts pressure on the foam solution solely by the use of a fire pump. This system introduces air into the solution when it either reaches the nozzle or is discharged from the nozzle. High-energy foam systems introduce compressed air into the foam solution before it is discharged into the hoseline.

Foam Proportioning

The term *proportioning* is used to describe the mixing of water with foam concentrate to form a foam solution. Most foam concentrates are intended to be mixed with either fresh water or saltwater. For maximum effectiveness, foam concentrates must be proportioned at the specific percentage for which they are designed. This percentage rate for the intended fuel is clearly marked on the outside of every foam container. Failure to proportion the foam at its designated percentage results in poor-quality foam that may not perform as desired. Using a 3% concentrate at 6%, for example, will only waste an expensive and limited resource. The FAA recommends that ARFF apparatus foam systems be tested using a refractometer or conductivity meter at least twice a year, to make sure they are proportioning at the proper percentage. FAA Certification Inspectors may ask to see foam testing documentation records when performing annual inspections at FAR Part 139 indexed airports.

Most fire fighting foam concentrates are intended to be mixed with 94 to 99.9 percent water. For example, when using 3% foam concentrate, 97 parts water mixed with 3 parts foam concentrate equals 100 parts foam solution. Similarly, for 6% foam concentrate, 94 parts water mixed with 6 parts foam concentrate equals 100 percent foam solution.

The selection of a proportioner depends on the foam solution flow requirements, available water pressure, cost, intended use (apparatus-mounted or portable), and agent to be used. Proportioners and delivery devices (foam nozzle, foam maker, etc.) are engineered to work together. Using a foam proportioner that is not compatible with the delivery device (even if the two are made by the same manufacturer) can result in unsatisfactory foam or no foam at all. For example, a proportioner that is designed to be used at 95 gpm (380 L/min) must be used with a 95 gpm (380 L/min) nozzle, or the foam will not proportion properly — if at all.

There are four basic methods by which foam may be proportioned:

- Induction
- Injection
- Batch mixing
- Premixing

Refractometer — Device used to measure the amount of foam concentrate in the solution; operates on the principle of measuring the velocity of light that travels through the foam solution.

Induction

The induction (eduction) method of proportioning foam uses the pressure energy in the stream of water to induct (draft) foam concentrate into the fire stream. Induction is achieved by passing the stream of water through a device called an eductor that has a restricted diameter. Within the restricted area is a separate orifice that is attached to the foam concentrate container with a hose. The pressure differential created by the water going through the restricted area and over the orifice creates a suction that draws the foam concentrate into the fire stream (also known as the *Venturi effect*). In-line eductors and foam-nozzle eductors are examples of foam proportioners that use this method. An around-the-pump foam proportioning system, installed on most new ARFF vehicles, uses water pressure off the discharge side of the pump to induct concentrate and produce foam solution, which is then pumped into the intake side of the pump.

Injection

The injection method of proportioning foam uses an external pump or water pressure to force foam concentrate into the fire stream at the correct ratio in comparison to the flow. These systems are commonly employed in apparatus-mounted or fixed-fire protection system applications. Two common types are the direct injection and the balanced pressure proportioners. Many older ARFF vehicles were equipped with balanced pressure foam systems as well as bladder and direct injection systems.

Batch Mixing

By far, the simplest means of proportioning foam is to simply pour an appropriate amount of foam concentrate into a tank of water. This method is called batch mixing or the dump-in method. To do this, an ARFF firefighter pours a predetermined amount of foam concentrate into the tank via the top fill opening at the time when foam is needed. The truck is then pumped normally, and foam is discharged through any hoseline that is opened. The amount of foam concentrate needed depends on the size of the water tank and the proportion percentage for which the foam is designed.

In general, batch mixing is used only with regular AFFF (not alcohol-resistant AFFF concentrates) and Class A concentrates. The AFFF concentrate mixes readily with water, and it will stay suspended in the solution for an extended period of time. When batch-mixing AFFF, the water in the tank has to be circulated for a few minutes before discharge to ensure complete mixing.

The disadvantage of this method is that all the water onboard the apparatus is converted to foam solution. This method does not allow for continuous foam discharge on large incidents, as the stream has to be shut down while the apparatus is replenished. It is difficult to maintain the correct concentrate ratio when refilling unless the water tank is completely emptied each time.

Premixing

Premixing is one of the more commonly used methods of proportioning. With this method, premeasured portions of water and foam concentrate are mixed in a container. Typically, the premix method is used with portable extinguishers, wheeled extinguishers, skid-mounted multiagent units, and vehicle-mounted tank systems.

Eductor — Portable proportioning device that injects a liquid, such as foam concentrate, into the water flowing through a hoseline or pipe.

Around-the-Pump Proportioner — Apparatus-mounted foam proportioner; a small quantity of water is diverted from the apparatus pump through an inline proportioner where it picks up the foam concentrate and carries it to the intake side of the pump; most common apparatus-mounted foam proportioner in service.

Venturi Principle — Physical law stating that when a fluid, such as water or air, is forced under pressure through a restricted orifice, there is an increase in the velocity of the fluid passing through the orifice and a corresponding decrease in the pressure exerted against the sides of the constriction. Because the surrounding fluid is under greater pressure (atmospheric), it is forced into the area of lower pressure.

Balanced Pressure Proportioner — Foam concentrate proportioner that operates in tandem with a fire water pump to ensure a proper foam concentrate-to-water mixture.

In most cases, premixed solutions are discharged from a pressure-rated tank using either compressed inert gas or air. An alternative method of discharge uses a pump and a non-pressure-rated atmospheric storage tank. The pump discharges the foam solution through piping or hose to the discharge device. Premix systems are limited to a one-time application. When used, they must be completely emptied and then refilled before they can be used again.

Portable Foam Proportioners

Portable foam proportioners are the simplest and most common foam proportioning devices in use today at structural fire departments. The three common types of portable foam proportioners are in-line foam eductors, foam nozzle eductors, and self-educting master stream nozzles.

In-Line Foam Eductors

In-line eductors are the most common type of foam proportioner used in the structural fire service; however, they are not commonly used in ARFF applications. This eductor is designed to be either directly attached to the pump panel discharge or connected at some point in the hose lay **(Figure 6.13)**. When using an in-line eductor, it is very important to follow the manufacturer's instructions about inlet pressure and the maximum hose lay between the eductor and the appropriate nozzle.

In order for the nozzle and eductor to operate properly, both must have the same rating in gpm (L/min). The eductor — not the nozzle — must control the flow. If the nozzle has a flow rating lower than that of the eductor, the eductor will not flow enough water to pick up concentrate. For example, a 60 gpm (240 L/min) nozzle combined with a 95 gpm (380 L/min) eductor will not flow enough water to create the desired finished foam.

Foam Nozzle Eductors

A foam nozzle eductor operates on the same basic principle as the in-line eductor. However, this eductor is built into the nozzle rather than into the hoseline. As

Figure 6.13 An inline eductor.

a result, its use requires the foam concentrate to be available where the nozzle is operated. If the foam nozzle is moved, the foam concentrate also needs to be moved. The number of gallons of concentrate required magnifies the logistical problems of firefighter relocation. Because firefighters cannot move quickly and they must leave their concentrate behind if they are required to back out for any reason, use of a foam nozzle eductor compromises firefighter safety.

Self-Educting Master Stream Foam Nozzles
A self-educting master stream foam nozzle is used where flows in excess of 350 gpm (1 400 L/min) are required. These nozzles are available with flow capabilities of up to 14,000 gpm (56 000 L/min) but are not commonly used for ARFF operations. Both foam nozzle eductors and self-educting master stream nozzles have an eductor inside the nozzle. Enough water flows through the eductor to pull sufficient concentrate into the nozzle and mix it into the water steam.

Apparatus-Mounted Foam Proportioning Systems
Foam proportioning systems are commonly mounted on fire boats; structural, industrial, and wildland fire apparatus; as well as on aircraft rescue and fire fighting apparatus. The majority of the following foam proportioning systems can be used for both Class A and Class B foam concentrates:

- Installed in-line eductors
- Around-the-pump proportioners
- Bypass-type balanced-pressure proportioners
- Variable-flow variable-rate direct-injection systems
- Variable-flow demand-type balanced-pressure proportioners
- Batch-mixing

Installed In-Line Eductor Systems
Installed in-line eductors use the same principles of operation as do portable in-line eductors except that these eductors are permanently attached to the apparatus pumping system. The same precautions regarding hose lengths, matching nozzle and eductor flows, and inlet pressures listed for portable in-line eductors also apply to installed in-line eductors. Foam concentrate may be supplied to these devices from either pickup tubes (using 5 gallon [20 L] pails) or from foam concentrate tanks installed on the apparatus.

Around-the-Pump Proportioners
An around-the-pump proportioning system consists of a small return (bypass) water line connected from the discharge side of the pump back to the intake side of the pump **(Figure 6.14 page 198)**. An in-line eductor is positioned on this bypass line. A valve positioned on the bypass line, just off the pump discharge piping, controls the flow of water through the bypass line. When the valve is open, a small amount of water (10 to 40 gpm [40 L/min to 160 L/min]) discharged from the pump is directed through the bypass piping. As this water passes through the eductor, the resulting venturi effect draws foam concentrate from the foam concentrate tank and into the bypass piping. The resulting foam solution is then supplied back to the intake side of the pump, where it is then pumped to the discharge and into the hoseline.

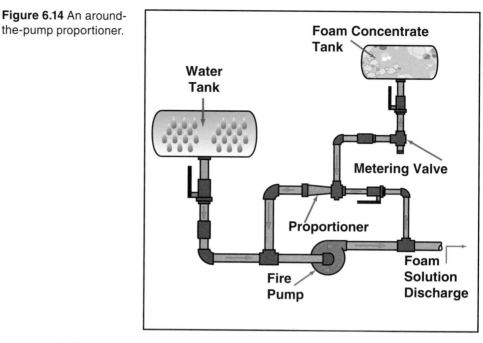

Figure 6.14 An around-the-pump proportioner.

Around-the-pump proportioning systems are rated for a specific flow and should be used at this rate, although they do have some flexibility. For example, a unit designed to flow 500 gpm (2 000 L/min) at a 6% concentration proportions will support 1,000 gpm (4 000 L/min) at a 3% concentration.

A major disadvantage of older around-the-pump proportioners is that the pump cannot take advantage of incoming pressure. If the inlet water supply is any greater than 10 psi (70 kPa), then the foam concentrate will not enter into the pump intake. When resupplying an ARFF vehicle pumping foam from this type of system, ARFF personnel should connect to the tank fill connection and not the pump suction inlet. Another disadvantage is that the pump must be dedicated solely to foam operation. An around-the-pump proportioner does not allow plain water and foam to be discharged from the pump at the same time.

Balanced-Pressure and Direct-Injection Proportioners

Most ARFF apparatus use some type of balanced-pressure or direct-injection foam proportioning system. These systems provide the most accurate proportioning of foam concentrate at large flow rates. There are several specific types of systems used in ARFF apparatus, including: bypass-type balanced-pressure proportioners, variable-flow demand-type balanced-pressure proportioners, and variable-flow variable-rate direct-injection systems.

Apparatus equipped with a *bypass-type balanced-pressure proportioner* have a foam concentrate line connected to each fire pump discharge outlet **(Figure 6.15)**. A foam concentrate pump separate from the main fire pump supplies the foam concentrate line. The foam concentrate pump draws the concentrate from a fixed tank and supplies it to the outlet at the same pressure at which the fire pump is supplying water to its discharge. A hydraulic pressure control valve monitors the pressure from both the fire pump and concentrate pump to ensure that the concentrate pressure and water pressure are balanced.

The primary advantages of a bypass-type balanced-pressure proportioner are as follows:

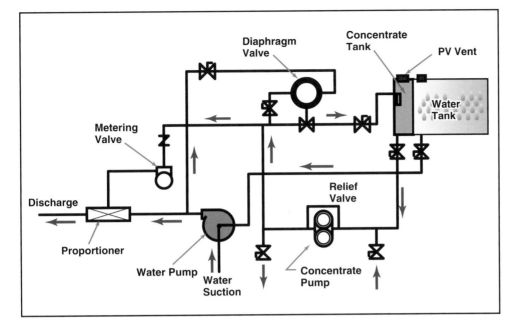

Figure 6.15 A bypass-type balanced-pressure proportioner.

- Ability to monitor the demand for foam concentrate and to adjust the amount of concentrate supplied

- Ability to simultaneously discharge foam from some outlets and plain water from others

Limitations of the bypass-type balanced-pressure proportioner include the following:

- Need for a separate foam pump with power take-off (PTO) or other power source

- Bypass of concentrate in this system can cause heating, turbulence, and foam concentrate aeration (bubble production in the storage tank)

In a *variable-flow demand-type balanced-pressure proportioning system*, a variable-speed mechanism, which is either hydraulically or electrically controlled, drives a foam concentrate pump. The foam concentrate pump supplies foam concentrate to a venturi-type proportioning device built into the water line **(Figure 6.16, p.200)**. When activated, the foam concentrate pump output is automatically monitored so that the flow of foam concentrate is commensurate with the flow of water to produce an effective foam solution.

Advantages of a variable-flow demand-type balanced-pressure proportioning system include:

- Foam concentrate flow and pressure match system demand

- No recirculation back to the foam concentrate tank

- Maintained in a ready-to-pump condition and requires no flushing after use

- Water and/or foam solution can be discharged simultaneously from any combination of outlets up to rated capacity

A limitation of these systems is that the fire pump discharges have ratio controllers (which reduce the discharge area); thus, pressure drops across the discharge are higher than those on standard pumpers.

Variable-flow variable-rate direct-injection systems operate off power supplied from the apparatus electrical system. Large-volume systems may use a

Power Take-off — Rotating shaft that transfers power from the engine to auxiliary equipment.

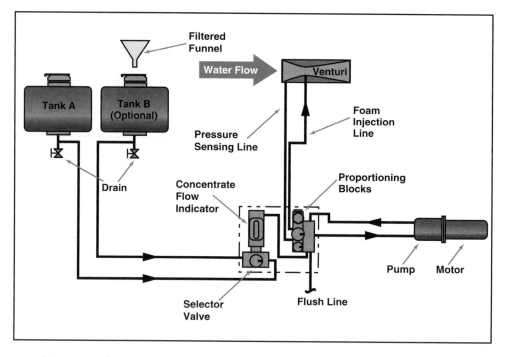

Figure 6.16 A variable-flow demand-type balanced-pressure proportioner.

combination of electric and hydraulic power. The foam concentrate injection is controlled by monitoring the water flow and controlling the speed of a positive displacement foam concentrate pump, thus injecting concentrate at the desired ratio. Because the water flow governs the foam concentrate injection, water pressure is not a factor.

There are several advantages to variable-flow variable-rate direct-injection systems, including:

* Accurately proportion foam concentrate at any flow rate or pressure within the design limits of the system

* Automatically adjusts to changes in water flow when nozzles are either opened or closed

* May have nozzles either above or below the pump, without affecting the foam proportioning

* May be used with high-energy foam systems, which are described later in this chapter

The disadvantage of these systems is that the foam injection point must be within the piping before any manifolds or distribution to multiple fire pump discharges.

High-Energy Foam Generating Systems

High-energy foam systems generally differ from those previously discussed in that they introduce compressed air into the foam solution *prior* to discharge into the hoseline. The turbulence of the foam solution and compressed air going through the piping and/or hoseline creates a finished foam. In addition to simply forming the foam, the addition of the compressed air also allows the foam stream to be discharged considerably greater distances than a regular foam or water fire stream.

This system uses a standard centrifugal fire pump to supply the water. A direct-injection foam-proportioning system is attached to the discharge side of the fire pump. Once the foam concentrate and water are mixed to form a foam solution, compressed air is added to the mixture before it is discharged from the apparatus and into the hoseline. This type of system is commonly called a compressed-air foam system (CAFS).

CAFS systems are most commonly found on structural and wildland fire apparatus. Structural apparatus assigned to an airport facility may have this type of system, but it is not commonly found on other types of ARFF apparatus. For more information on high-energy foam systems, see the IFSTA **Principles of Foam Fire Fighting** manual.

Foam Application

As part of their primary job duties, airport firefighters may be required to operate a foam handline or master stream on a fire or spill. It is important to use the correct techniques when manually applying foam. Using incorrect techniques, such as plunging the foam into a liquid fuel, reduces the effectiveness of the foam.

The sections that follow discuss portable foam application devices, aspirating and non-aspirating nozzles, and foam application techniques.

Portable Foam Application Devices

Once the foam concentrate and water have been mixed together to form a foam solution, the foam solution must then be mixed with air (aerated) and delivered to the surface of the fuel. With low-energy foam systems, the aeration and discharge of the foam are accomplished by a fog nozzle or a foam nozzle, sometimes referred to as a foam maker. Low-expansion foams may be discharged through either handline nozzles or master stream devices. While standard fire fighting nozzles can be used for applying some types of low-expansion foams, it is best to use nozzles that produce the desired result (such as fast-draining or slow-draining foam). This section highlights portable foam application devices.

> **NOTE:** Foam nozzle eductors and self-educting master stream foam nozzles are considered portable foam nozzles, but they are omitted from this section because they are covered earlier in the chapter.

Handline Nozzles

IFSTA defines a handline nozzle as "any nozzle that one to three firefighters can safely handle and that flows less than 350 gpm (1 400 L/min)." Most handline foam nozzles flow considerably less than that figure. The two most common types of handline nozzles used by ARFF firefighters are standard fog nozzles and air-aspirating foam nozzles.

Either fixed-flow or automatic fog nozzles can be used with foam solution to produce a low-expansion, short-lasting foam. It is often referred to as non-aspirated foam. This nozzle breaks the foam solution into tiny droplets and uses the agitation of water droplets moving through air to achieve its foaming action **(Figure 6.17, p. 202)**. Its best application is when it is used with regular AFFF, AFFF-AR, or FFFP. Some nozzle manufacturers have foam aeration attachments that can be added to the end of the nozzle to increase aspiration of the foam solution **(Figure 6.18, p. 202)**.

Figure 6.17 Foam being applied using an automatic nozzle. *Courtesy of John Demyan, LVI Airport.*

Figure 6.18 Foam being discharged through an aeration device. *Courtesy of John Demyan, LVI Airport.*

Air-aspirating foam nozzles are especially designed to provide the aeration required to make the highest quality foam possible and are the most effective appliance for the generation of low-expansion foam. An air-aspirating foam nozzle inducts air into the foam solution by a venturi action. These nozzles provide maximum expansion of the agent. The foam is agitated inside the foam nozzle, which causes a loss of energy and velocity, therefore the reach of the stream from air-aspirating foam nozzles is considerably less than that of a standard fog nozzle.

Turret Nozzles

Turret nozzles are large, pre-plumbed master stream appliances connected directly to a pump that is mounted on a pumper, a trailer, or some airport rescue and fire fighting apparatus. They are capable of sweeping from side to side and designed to deliver large volumes of foam or water. Turrets may be either aspirating, nonaspirating, or a combination of the two, any of which can be used with great success **(Figure 6.19)**. There are several factors to consider when selecting the type. As with any other type of nozzle, better reach and penetration are achieved with nonaspirating turrets, whereas aspirating types produce better-quality foam. Because either type of turret can perform satisfactorily, the type of turret selected is simply a question of preference and local need.

Aspirating Versus Nonaspirating Nozzles

Only film forming foams are suitable for nonaspirating application. The application of protein or fluoroprotein foams requires air-aspirating nozzles. AFFF

Nonaspirating Foam Nozzle — Nozzle that does not draw air into the foam solution stream; foam solution is agitated by the nozzle design causing air to mix with the solution after it has exited the nozzle.

Figure 6.19 These ARFF vehicles have their roof and bumper turrets flowing simultaneously.

may be applied with aspirating or nonaspirating turrets and nozzles. However, there are some important factors that ARFF personnel should consider prior to deciding which type of nozzle to use:

During practical application of AFFF, the advantages of using nonaspirating nozzles are evident. The reach of the stream is greater than with aspirating equipment, and larger areas may be covered with conventional variable stream nozzles. Another advantage of nonaspirating nozzles is that they can generate a wide fog pattern that can also be used for personnel protection. In some instances, extinguishing the fire may be quicker with nonaspirating nozzles than with conventional low-expansion devices. There are less air bubbles in the foam, so it is denser than aerated foams. This allows the foam to better penetrate the fire's thermal updraft or chimney effect, as well produce the aqueous film faster.

The limitations of using nonaspirating nozzles are not as obvious and are often only realized after laboratory and field testing. Nonaspirating devices do not mechanically draw in the air. The foam produced is largely a function of the foam solution properties, nozzle design, setting selected, droplet size, and impact of the stream on the fuel surface. A low-expansion ratio of 2:1 or 3:1 is usually achieved when using nonaspirating devices. This low-expansion ratio limits the foam's ability to seal a fire surface after the fire is out and reduces its effectiveness against reignition and burnback.

Air-aspirating devices are designed to produce good-quality foam. This design requires that all or nearly all the solution be converted into working foam with good properties such as bubble size, uniformity, stability, water retention, and heat resistance. All of these properties are important factors in restricting reignition and burnback. An expansion ratio of 6:1 to 10:1 is commonly associated with low-expansion air-aspirating equipment. Attachments are available for some non-aspirating nozzles to quickly change them into the aspirating type.

Personnel who must write specifications for new vehicles and equipment or develop fire fighting tactics should be aware of the advantages and limitations of nonaspirating and aspirating nozzles.

Foam Application Techniques

Correct application of any extinguishing agent can be as important as the type of agent selected. Approach at the site and application of foam should begin at the farthest reach of a turret at large exterior fires. The principle of "insulate and isolate" explains the general tactics. The initial foam application should insulate the fuselage and protect the integrity of the aircraft skin. Insulating the fuselage will assist in protecting the occupants who may be self-evacuating. The next consideration should be to try to separate (isolate) the fire from the fuselage. While these techniques may have to be modified for any given circumstance or situation, the general principle remains.

Apparatus Placement and Repositioning

Tactically, driver/operators should also consider the correct placement and repositioning of apparatus. It is vitally important to know the effective reach of the turret. Application should begin at the effective reach of the turret. Achieving the accurate distance may be difficult for the driver to judge, having only a limited "one-dimensional" view of the accident. The application may be overshooting, landing short, or not effectively controlling the fire.

To determine whether an apparatus is properly positioned, the turret operator should use a "short burst" application technique. After five to ten second applications of foam, the turret operator should momentarily stop and assess fire conditions. If the application is missing the fire, change the stream pattern or reposition the apparatus. If the fire has been successfully controlled, shut down, redirect the turret, or move the apparatus to attack another area of fire. If available, an officer or other apparatus, placed at a 45-degree angle can view the effectiveness of the turret's reach. At this point, instructions can be given to the driver regarding positioning for turret effectiveness.

Drivers should also reposition apparatus as necessary to apply the agent to the correct areas. ARFF apparatus are built with pump-and-roll capability specifically for this purpose. Care should also be taken to use agent sparingly. The turret can be turned off and on as necessary to produce the most efficient application of the available agent. ARFF personnel should also remember to use a low flow rate application to conserve agent whenever possible.

The sections that follow describe the roll-on, deflection or bank-down, base-of-the-fire, and rain-fall (rain-down) methods of foam application.

Roll-On Method

The roll-on method directs the foam stream on the ground near the front edge of a burning liquid pool. The foam then rolls across the surface of the fuel. ARFF personnel continue to apply foam until it spreads across the entire surface of

Figure 6.20 The roll-on method of foam application being demonstrated. *Courtesy of James Mack, Richmond International Airport.*

Figure 6.21 ARFF personnel demonstrating the deflection or bank-down method of applying foam. *Courtesy of James Mack, Richmond International Airport.*

the fuel and the fire is extinguished **(Figure 6.20)**. It may be necessary to move the stream to different positions along the edge of a liquid spill to cover the entire pool. This method is used only on a pool of liquid fuel (either ignited or unignited) on the ground or pavement.

Deflection or Bank-Down Method

The bank-down method may be employed when an elevated object such as a fuselage, wall, tank shell, wing, or engine is near or within the area of a burning pool of liquid or an unignited liquid spill. ARFF personnel direct the foam stream at the object, allowing the foam to run down or deflect onto the surface of the fuel **(Figure 6.21)**. As with the roll-on method, it may be necessary to direct the stream off various points around the fuel area to achieve total coverage and extinguishment of the fuel.

Base-of-the-Fire Method

AFFF can be applied with the use of a zero-degree, "base-of-the-fire" agent delivery angle to maximize agent effectiveness and minimize extinguishment time. The foam stream is usually applied through a bumper turret; however, a handline can also be effective in delivering foam using the base-of-the fire method **(Figure 6.22, p.206)**

CAUTION
Avoid plunging the foam stream down into the fuel.

Rainfall (Rain-Down) Method

Another foam application method is the 40 degree rainfall or rain-down method. This method extends the reach of the foam stream during initial approach and application. The effect of wind must be considered, used to advantage when approaching an aircraft fire, and continuously considered throughout the fire fighting phase of the operation.

The rainfall method is used when the other methods are not feasible because of either the size of the spill area (either ignited or unignited) or the lack of an object from which to bank the foam. It is also the primary manual application technique used on aboveground storage tank fires. This method directs the stream into the air above the fire or spill and allows the foam to float gently down onto the surface of the fuel **(Figure 6.23, p.206)**. On small fires, the

Figure 6.22 This ARFF apparatus is going to sweep the fire and apply foam using the base-of-the-fire method. *Courtesy of James Mack, Richmond International Airport.*

Figure 6.23 The ARFF vehicle on the far right is using the rain-fall or rain-down method of applying foam.

CAUTION

Avoid plunging the foam stream down into the fuel.

stream is swept back and forth over the entire surface of the fuel until the fuel is completely covered and the fire is extinguished. On large fires, it may be more effective for ARFF personnel to direct the stream at one location to allow the foam to take effect there and then affect the rest of the fuel by flowing from that point.

Dry Chemicals and Their Application

The terms *dry chemical* and *dry powder* are often incorrectly used interchangeably. Dry-chemical agents are for use on Class A, B, or C fires. Dry-powder agents are for Class D fires only. Dry-chemical agents are extremely effective for an initial attack and quick knockdown of a fuel fire, hydraulic fires, pressure fed fuel fires, or lubricant fires. They are also effective for extinguishing three-dimensional or running-fuel fires. Dry-chemical agents are not effective on large spill fires with obstructions in the spill, which is the typical plane crash. However, dry chemicals do not have the vapor-sealing properties or the flashback-preventive characteristics of foam, and reignition may occur due to the lack of cooling effect. Once dry chemicals have accomplished a quick knockdown, a blanket of foam should be applied to prevent fuel vapors from reigniting.

When a dry-chemical agent is discharged into a fire or flames, it inhibits the chemical chain reaction, thereby extinguishing the fire. Multipurpose dry chemical also provides a smothering capability when discharged onto burning, ordinary combustibles. Multipurpose dry chemical leaves a sticky residue on the burning materials, which provides a seal between the material and oxygen. All dry-chemical agents are nonconductive, making them suitable for use on energized electrical equipment.

Dry chemicals used to combat hydrocarbon fuel fires may contain any of a number of different chemical compounds including:

- Sodium bicarbonate
- Potassium bicarbonate
- Urea-potassium bicarbonate
- Potassium chloride
- Monoammonium phosphate

Dry chemicals are compatible with film-forming foams, but dry chemical may degrade a protein foam blanket. Compatibility between foam and dry chemical agents should be confirmed prior to using them together or successively in fire fighting operations.

Dry chemicals are also compatible with water and foam for master stream or turret operations. Dry chemicals alone may not have the reach in windy or terrain restrictive operations. The use of dry chemical, water, and AFFF is referred to as wet chemical or Hydro-Chem. This combination is extremely effective against three dimensional or flowing fuel type fires. The water pattern allows the dry chemical to encapsulate inside the stream for direct seat of the fire applications. Water and dry chemical provide rapid fire knockdown and ahould be followed by AFFF blankets to prevent reigniting.

Multipurpose (ABC) dry chemical fire extinguishers are no longer recommended for use due to their corrosive effects on aircraft materials. Dry-chemical agents are corrosive to metals and can cause damage to electrical equipment and should be used as a last resort if no other suitable agent is readily available. However, under conditions where a three-dimensional or pressure fed fuel fire exists, there is no better agent available. It may be better to use another agent such as halon, halon substitutes, or even carbon dioxide on any electronic equipment or aircraft engines.

Dry chemicals are applied by directing the agent at the base of the fire and sweeping the nozzle back and forth over the fire. Guidelines for applying dry chemicals are as follows:

- Apply dry chemicals from a position upwind of the fire when possible.
- Apply dry chemicals so that the agent will blanket the fire.
- Be aggressive in attacking and extinguishing the fire but do *not* splash or churn the fuel.

- Monitor the fire area for reignition, especially behind the operator, and reapply the agent as necessary.

The dry-chemical agents themselves are nontoxic and generally are considered quite safe to use. However, the cloud of chemicals may reduce visibility and create respiratory problems like any airborne fine particles. Dry chemical can be a minor respiratory irritant, therefore; ARFF personnel should always wear SCBA when applying them.

The sections that follow address dry chemical fire extinguishers and apparatus mounted units.

CAUTION

Never mix or contaminate dry chemicals with any other type of dry chemical because they may chemically react and cause a dangerous rise in pressure inside the extinguisher and reduce extinguishing capabilities.

Extinguishers

Each type of dry chemical extinguishing agent has different extinguishing properties; personnel should consult the applicable Underwriters Laboratories (UL) listing for the fire extinguishing rating for each dry chemical agent before selecting the agent of choice. There are two basic types of dry-chemical extinguishers: regular B:C-rated and multipurpose A:B:C-rated. Regular B:C-rated extinguishers are recommended for fighting aircraft engine fires. Multipurpose A:B:C-rated extinguishers can be used but are not recommended due to the corrosiveness of the agent and the residue left on hot surfaces. Unless specifically noted in this section, the characteristics and operation of both types are exactly the same.

During manufacture, various additives are mixed with the base materials in order to improve their storage, flow, and water-repellent characteristics. This process keeps the agents ready for use even after being undisturbed for long periods, and it makes them free-flowing.

There are two basic designs for handheld and wheeled dry-chemical extinguishers: stored-pressure and cartridge-operated **(Figure 6.24)**. The stored-pressure type contains a constant pressure of about 200 psi (1 400 kPa) in the agent storage tank. Cartridge-operated extinguishers employ a pressure cartridge connected to the agent tank. The agent tank is not pressurized until a plunger is pushed to release the gas from the cartridge. Both types of

CAUTION

The top of a cartridge-operated extinguisher should be pointed away from the firefighter or other personnel when pressurizing the unit. If a cartridge-operated extinguisher is activated, but not used, the pressure will usually bleed off in a few hours.

Figure 6.24 A cartridge operated dry chemical extinguisher and a pressurized dry chemical extinguisher. *Courtesy of Doddy Photography.*

extinguishers use either nitrogen or carbon dioxide as the pressurizing gas. Cartridge-operated extinguishers use a carbon dioxide cartridge unless the extinguisher is going to be subjected to freezing temperatures; in such cases, a dry-nitrogen cartridge is used.

Dry-chemical wheeled units are similar to handheld units but are larger **(Figure 6.25)**. They are rated for regular B:C or multipurpose A:B:C based on the dry chemical in the unit.

The basic designs for wheeled units are similar to handheld extinguishers, stored pressure and cartridge operated, with the only difference being that instead of a cartridge the pressurizing gas is stored in a cylinder. Operating the wheeled dry-chemical extinguishers is similar to operating handheld dry-chemical extinguishers. When the extinguisher is in position at a fire, the hose first should be stretched out completely. This procedure is recommended because removing the hose can be more difficult after it is charged and because the powder can sometimes pack in any sharp bends in the hose. If the extinguisher has an external gas supply the pressurizing gas must be introduced into the agent tank and allowed a few seconds to fully pressurize the tank before the nozzle is opened. The agent is applied in the same way as that described for the handheld, cartridge-type dry-chemical extinguishers.

Figure 6.25 A wheeled dry-chemical extinguisher along a flightline.

Apparatus Mounted Units

Some ARFF apparatus are equipped with dry-chemical or wet-chemical extinguishing systems. These could be skid mounted units for pick-up trucks or built into larger ARFF apparatus. These systems are usually composed of a dry-chemical storage tank, a tank containing a pressurizing gas to expel the dry chemical from its storage tank, the valves and piping to route these materials to a discharge, and sufficient hose and a nozzle for discharging the dry chemical when and where needed **(Figure 6.26)**.

CAUTION

The top of the extinguisher should be pointed away from the firefighter or other personnel when pressurizing the unit. Because of the size of the nozzle, the firefighter should be prepared for a significant nozzle reaction when it is opened and may need assistance.

Figure 6.26 An ARFF firefighter checking the agent level of a vehicle mounted dry-chemical system.

FAR Part 139.317, *Aircraft rescue and firefighting: Equipment and agents*, and AC 150/5220-10D, *Guide Specification for Aircraft Rescue and Fire Fighting Vehicles*, require at least 500 (227 kg) pounds of sodium based dry chemical or 460 pounds (209 kg) of clean agent. Potassium based (Purple K, PKP) can be substituted and requires a minimum of 450 pounds (204 kg). Purple K is twice as effective as sodium bicarbonate. Many ARFF vehicles carry dry chemical, usually Purple K® (PKP), as an auxiliary extinguishing agent. The reason PKP is the dry-chemical agent of choice for multiagent applications is its compatibility with AFFF.

The size of dry-chemical systems on ARFF apparatus usually starts at 500 lb (227 kg) but can be much larger. The dry-chemical is stored on the ARFF apparatus in a manner similar to that of the typical portable fire extinguisher. A large vessel carries the agent and compressed nitrogen stored in a separate cylinder is used to expel the agent. It is very important to be familiar with the type of dry-chemical system on the department's vehicles. These systems require regular attention so that they perform properly when needed.

Dry chemical is dispensed three different ways. The most common method of application is to dispense using a handline stored at some position on the vehicle. Other popular ways include piggybacking and water stream injection. On piggyback systems, the manufacturer has mounted an independent dry-chemical nozzle directly over the water/foam nozzle on the roof or bumper turret. Water stream injection systems work by injecting the dry chemical directly into the water/foam stream of the main turret. This allows the dry chemical to stay inside the water stream of the turret, greatly extending the effectiveness of the agent.

A dry-chemical handline is required to have at least 100 feet of hose. It must flow at least 5 pounds lb/sec and have a range of at least 25 feet. These handlines must have a minimum burst pressure rating of three times the system working pressure. Dry chemical turrets should discharge at 16-22 lb/sec with a no wind range of at least 100 feet. The discharge rate for dry chemicals on an extendable turret is 12-22 lb/sec with at least a 100 foot range.

Dry chemical is often used for three-dimensional fires on aircraft engine nacelles or for running fuel fires. This makes water stream injection effective by applying the dry-chemical to fight the fire and also by supplying the water/foam solution to stop the spill fires associated with three-dimensional fires.

Clean Agents and Their Applications

Clean agents are those extinguishing media that are designed to extinguish fires while leaving little, if no, residue. Traditional clean agents include halogenated agents such as Halon 1211 and Halon 1301. Because of their ozone-depletion potential, halogenated extinguishing agents are included in the *Montreal Protocol on Substances that Deplete the Ozone Layer*, which required a complete phase-out of the production of halogens by the year 2000. The only exceptions allowed under the agreement are for essential uses where no suitable alternatives are available.

Because of the high cost of maintaining clean agent systems, many ARFF agencies are replacing their clean agent systems with dry chemical or wet PKP systems. Other fire departments have aggressive programs to replace halon extinguishers and to use halon replacements where possible. Agents undergo testing and certification by the FAA for approval for use in aviation fire fighting applications. Halon replacement is not a 1 to 1 process as many replacement agents require a higher concentration of agent to extinguish fire than halons do. As a result, larger quantities of the halon replacement agents must be carried on the ARFF vehicle to accomplish extinguishment. The FAA minimum clean agent discharge rates are found in FAR 139.317.

Halotron® I is approved by the U.S. Federal Aviation Authority and the Environmental Protection Agency (EPA) as a "clean agent" replacement for Halon 1211. The FAA has approved the use of Halotron® I at airport gates, on flight lines, and onboard aircraft. When discharged, it is a rapidly evaporating liquid. The agent will not conduct electricity back to the operator, making it suitable for Class C fires.

While headway has been made in replacing halogenated agents in aircraft and on airfields, some aircraft and locations still utilize the halogenated agents. Halogenated extinguishing agents are hydrocarbons in which one or more hydrogen atoms in the molecule have been replaced by halogen atoms. The hydrocarbons from which halogenated extinguishing agents are derived are highly flammable gases; however, substituting halogen atoms for the hydrogen atoms results in compounds that are nonflammable and have excellent flame extinguishment properties. The common elements from the halogen series are chlorine, fluorine, bromine, and iodine. While a large number of halogenated compounds exist, only a few are used to a significant extent as fire extinguishing agents. The two most common halons are Halon 1211 (bromochlorodifluoromethane) and Halon 1301 (bromotrifluoromethane).

Halons are either gases or liquids that rapidly vaporize in fire. Although discharged as a mixture of liquid and vapor, halons extinguish fires best as vapor clouds that chemically interrupt the chain reaction of combustion.

Halogenated vapor is nonconductive and is effective in extinguishing surface fires in flammable and combustible liquids. Similar to dry chemicals, they have almost no flashback-preventive capabilities; but because halons easily penetrate inaccessible areas and have good flooding characteristics, they are effective for fires involving aircraft engines, electronic gear, and other complex equipment. In addition, halons are clean agents that leave no corrosive or abrasive residue that could contaminate sensitive electronic equipment. Although the halons have long been used for the protection of internal combustion engines, their primary modern-day application is for the protection of sensitive electronic equipment such as computers. They are compatible with dry chemicals and AFFF.

Summary

ARFF personnel should be intimately familiar with the common extinguishing agents they will use to fight aircraft fires. Water, foam, dry-chemical, dry-powder, and clean agents all have specific uses in ARFF fire fighting. Foam applications, however, are the most widely used due to their greater ability to extinguish hydrocarbon and polar solvent fuel fires.

ARFF personnel should be familiar with the proportioning process through which fuel concentrate becomes finished foam. In addition, ARFF firefighters must have an understanding of the various eductors and other equipment used in the proportioning process. They should also understand the four methods used to apply foam as well as foam application equipment common to ARFF fire fighting including apparatus-mounted master streams and turrets, handlines, and aspirating and nonaspirating nozzles.

Finally, ARFF firefighters must have a working knowledge of dry-chemical, dry-powder, and clean agent extinguishing agents. In addition to understanding how these agents are applied, personnel must understand the best uses of these agents and the equipment used to apply them.

Review Questions

1. Why is water alone not usually a suitable extinguishing agent for large aircraft fuel fires?

2. What are the methods by which foam extinguishes or prevents fire?

3. How is foam induction achieved?

4. Upon what variables does the rate of application for fire fighting foam depend?

5. What are the three basic applications of high-expansion foam?

6. How does an installed in-line eductor system work?

7. What is a handline nozzle?

8. How does the bank-down foam application technique work?

9. What are the two basic designs for handheld dry-chemical extinguishers?

10. Why are halogenated extinguishing agents being replaced by alternative agents?

Apparatus

Chapter Contents

Key Terms

NFPA® references for Chapter 7:

NFPA® 1003 (2010)

5.1.1.3	5.3.6
5.3.2	5.3.7
5.3.3	5.3.9
5.3.4	
5.3.5	

NFPA® 1002 (2009 - Chapter 9)

9.1.1	9.2.2
9.1.2	9.2.3
9.1.3	
9.2.1	

Federal Aviation Regulations (FAR):

139.317(a)	139.317(e)	139.319(a)	139.319(f)
139.317(b)	139.317(f)	139.319(b)	139.319(g)
139.317(c)	139.317(h)	139.319(c)	139.319(h)
139.317(d)	139.317(i)	139.319(e)	

Apparatus

Learning Objectives

After reading this chapter, students shall be able to:

1. Discuss ARFF apparatus.

2. Describe the types of ARFF apparatus.

3. Identify ARFF apparatus features and options.

4. Describe ARFF apparatus fire suppression equipment. (NFPA® 1003, 5.3.5, 5.3.6)

5. Explain ARFF apparatus agent resupply methods. (NFPA® 1003, 5.3.9)

6. Discuss ARFF apparatus maintenance.

Chapter 7
Apparatus

Case History

Standard fire department pumpers made the earliest fire department responses to airplane crashes. As aircraft fuel loads became larger, the need for greater volumes of extinguishing agents and more effective means of applying these agents became apparent. This was particularly true in the United States Army Air Corps which began researching and developing vehicles specifically tailored to fighting aircraft fires. These, and later, military crash trucks were designed to exacting military specifications (mil specs). One early crash fire rescue truck was the Class 100 Crash Truck. It was equipped with a 375 gallon (1 419 liter) water tank, a 100 gpm (400 l/min) rotary pump, 100 feet (30 m) of 1½ inch (38 mm) hose, a dry powder foam generator, and 200 lbs (91 kg) of carbon dioxide (CO_2).

During the 1930s and 1940s, crash trucks were constructed by building fire fighting equipment onto commercial style trucks frames. During these two decades many of the following new innovations were added to these vehicles:

- Vehicle size was increased to carry greater quantities of water, foam, CO_2, and other extinguishing agents.
- Aircraft specific rescue tools and equipment were added.
- Four- and six-wheel drive capabilities were added for off-road capability.
- Roof and bumper turrets were mounted on the vehicles to increase agent application rates.
- Large capacity pumps (200 and 500 gpm [757 and 1 893 L/min]) and fire fighting fog foam nozzles (developed by the U.S. Navy near the end of World War II).

The 1950s saw the introduction of the second generation of crash fire rescue trucks that were specially designed and built for aircraft fire fighting operations. These included the O-10, O-11A and B, and the O-6 Cardox vehicles. Early versions of the O-10 and O-11 crash trucks experienced mechanical difficulties including electrical and hydraulic failures, broken axles, scabbing tires, and front tire vibrations that snapped steering mechanism bolts. The O-6 carried 4,000 lbs (1 814 kg) of carbon dioxide and was the last USAF crash truck to use CO_2.

A third generation of crash fire trucks came in the early 1960s with the delivery of the FWD P-2 and Oshkosh P-4 vehicles. P-2s were equipped with two six cylinder gasoline engines for traction and pumping and a 1,400 gpm (5 300 L/m) pump. The vehicle carried 2,300 gallons (8 706 L) of water, 200 gallons (757 L) of foam. Years later the P-2s were remanufactured and diesel engines were introduced into crash trucks. The P-4s were equipped with a single diesel engine, a 1,500 gallon (5 678 L) water tank, and 180 gallons (681 L) of foam.

The fourth generation of crash trucks, now called ARFF vehicles or ARFF apparatus, came in the late 1970s up through the 1990s with the introduction of the Oshkosh P-15 and the E-One P-23. The P-15 was specifically designed for larger aircraft with equally large fuel loads. The P-23s replaced the earlier P-2s and P-15s. The P-23 introduced a central tire deflation/inflation system to improve the vehicle's traction in soft sand conditions.

Case History

During these decades, the manufacturers of these mil spec vehicles produced numerous apparatus for civilian airfields. Many of these vehicles were "civilianized" versions of the military trucks while others were developed to new civilian aviation specifications. On many occasions, when a military crash truck was retired from use at a military installation, it would be purchased, refurbished, and put into service at a civilian airport.

A fifth generation of ARFF apparatus began to appear in the late 1990s with many of the following useful and innovative systems:

- Driver's enhanced vision systems (DEVS)
- Vehicle Rear View Backup Camera Systems
- High-mobility suspension systems (independent suspension systems)
- Lateral Acceleration Indicator

With this fifth generation of ARFF vehicles came an interesting change in how the United States military purchased ARFF apparatus. Modern mil-specs for military ARFF vehicles reference the appropriate NFPA® requirements for such apparatus and the military purchases the vehicles "off-the-shelf" for use on military installations around the world.

Aircraft rescue and fire fighting apparatus are the backbone of any ARFF fire department. The airports they serve are as diverse as the vehicles themselves. Aviation industry standards require that ARFF apparatus reach the scene of an aircraft emergency in far shorter time periods than those normally associated with a municipal fire department's response to a structure fire. With the heavy fuel loads and the large numbers of passengers carried by aircraft today, ARFF vehicles must be ready for all conditions and problems. Vehicles used for ARFF operations should be designed as self-contained units with the ability to discharge adequate quantities of extinguishing agents within a short period **(Figure 7.1)**.

This chapter discusses apparatus requirements, types of aircraft rescue and fire fighting apparatus, vehicle options, turret types, handlines, resupply methods, and apparatus maintenance.

Figure 7.1 ARFF apparatus responding during an aircraft emergency.

ARFF Apparatus Requirements

Given the vital role ARFF apparatus play in emergency responses to aviation incidents, there are certain requirements placed upon them. Each airport must identify the appropriate levels of ARFF protection required at that particular location, thus affecting the types and quantities of ARFF apparatus found there. To determine the specifications for the appropriate types of ARFF apparatus to have at an airport, ARFF personnel must identify the level of protection they need and examine the standards created by such agencies as the FAA, ICAO, and NFPA®.

Levels of Protection

The index or category of an airport determines the minimum number and types of ARFF apparatus that are required at that airport. Most airports are categorized or indexed based on the type or length of aircraft using the facility and the daily average number of departures. The FAA, NFPA®, U.S. military, Canada, and ICAO each have their own rating categories and systems **(Table 7.1, p. 220-221)**. Based on its assigned index, set (military equivalent of an index), or category, an airport must maintain certain minimum levels of ARFF apparatus and equipment at all times or sometimes just during air carrier or other type aircraft operations. Should any of the required apparatus or equipment become inoperative at certified airports in the U.S. and an equal replacement is not available within 48 hours, the airport management must notify the Federal Aviation Administration Regional Airports Division Manager and the affected carriers of the reduction in operational readiness. Unless otherwise authorized by the FAA, the airport must limit air carrier operations to the index corresponding with the remaining operative ARFF apparatus.

Although the outcome differs among the organizations, NFPA®, FAA, and ICAO use similar methods to determine the number of vehicles and the amount of extinguishing agent required. Each uses the length of aircraft landing at an airport to determine the ARFF apparatus requirements **(Figure 7.2)**. However, there are some differences in the actual formulas they use. While

Figure 7.2 One factor in determining an airport's index or category is the length of the aircraft that routinely use that airport. *Courtesy of Edwin A. Jones, USAFR.*

Table 7.1
ARFF Requirements by Airport Index
Part I - FAA/NFPA®/ICAO

FAA INDEX	NFPA/ICAO CATEGORIES	Max. Aircraft Length (ft [m])	# ARFF Vehicles Required	Total Fire Fighting Agent Required
GA-1 GA-2 A	1 - 5	< 90 ft (< 28 m)	1	*One vehicle* that carries 500 pounds (227 kg) dry chemical, halon 1211, or clean agent; or 450 pounds (204 kg) dry chemical and 100 gal (379 L) water and a commensurate quantity of AFFF.
B	6	≥ 90 ft and < 126 ft (≥ 28 m and < 38 m)	1 or 2	*One vehicle* that carries at least 500 pounds (227 kg) of sodium-based dry chemical, halon 1211, or clean agent and 1,500 gal (5 678 L) of water and a commensurate quantity of AFFF. **- OR -** *Two vehicles:* - One vehicle that fits the requirements of "A" and a second vehicle that carries at least 1,500 gallons (5 678 L) of water and a commensurate quantity of AFFF.
C	7	≥ 126 ft and < 159 ft (≥ 38 m and < 48.5 m)	2 or 3	*Two vehicles:* One vehicle that carries 500 pounds (227 kg) of dry chemical, halon 1211, or clean agent and 1,500 gallons (5 678 L) of water and commensurate quantity of AFFF and a second vehicle that carries an amount of water and a commensurate quantity of AFFF so the total quantity of water for foam production carried by both vehicles is at least 3,000 gallons (11 356 L). **- OR -** *Three vehicles:* - One vehicle that fits the requirements of "A" and two other vehicles that carry an amount of water and the commensurate quantity of AFFF so the total quantity of water for foam production carried by all three vehicles is at least 3,000 gallons (11 356 L)
D	8	≥ 159 ft and < 200 ft (≥ 48.5 m and < 61 m)	3	*Three vehicles:* - One vehicle that fits the requirements of "A" **- AND -** - Two vehicles that carry an amount of water and the commensurate quantity of AFFF so the total quantity of water for foam production carried by all three vehicles is at least 4,000 gallons (15 142 L)
E	9 - 10	≥ 200 ft (≥61 m)	3	*Three vehicles:* - One vehicle that fits the requirements of "A." **- AND -** Two vehicles that carry an amount of water and the commensurate quantity of AFFF so the total quantity of water for foam production carried by all three vehicles is at least 6,000 gallons (22 712 L)

1) If there are five or more average daily departures of air carrier aircraft in a single Index group servicing that airport, the Index group serving that airport, the longest aircraft with an average of five or more daily departures determines the Index for the airport.

2) When there are fewer than five average daily departures of the longest air carrier aircraft serving the airport, the Index required for the airport will be the next lower Index group than the Index group prescribed for the longest aircraft.

3) The minimum designated index must be Index A.

Table 7.1 (cont.)
Canadian ARFF Requirements
Part II - Canadian

CANADIAN Requirements	Max. Aircraft Length (ft [m])	# ARFF Vehicles Required	Total Fire Fighting Agent Required
1	<29.5 ft long and 6.5 ft wide (<9m long and 2m wide)	1	One ARFF vehicle carrying 61 gallons (230 liters) of water, 99 pounds (45 kilograms) complementary agent, and having a 61 gpm (230 L/min) discharge capacity
2	29.5 ft long but under 39 ft long and <6.5 ft wide (9m but <12m long and 2m wide)	1	One ARFF vehicle with 177 gallons (670 liters) of water, 198 pounds (90 kilograms) of complementary agent, and having a 145 gpm (550 L/min) discharge capacity.
3	at least 12 m long, but less than 18 m, and 3 m wide	1	One ARFF vehicle carrying 317 gallons (1 200 liters) of water, 298 pounds (135 kilograms) of complementary agent, and having a 238 gpm (900 L/min) discharge capacity.
4	at least 18 m long, but less than 24 m, and 4 m wide	1	One ARFF vehicle carrying (2 400 liters) of water, 298 pounds (135 kilograms) of complementary agent, and having (1 800 L/min) discharge capacity.
5	at least 24 m long, but less than 28 m, and 4 m wide	1	One ARFF vehicle, carrying 634 gallons (5 400 liters) of water, 397 pounds (180 kilograms) of complementary agent, and having 793 gpm (3 000 L/min) discharge capacity.
6	at least 28 m long, but less than 39 m, and 5 m wide	2	Two ARFF vehicles, carrying a combined quantity of 2,087 gallons (7 900 liters) of water, 496 pounds (225 kilograms) of complementary agent, and having a combined 1 056 gpm (4 000 L/min) discharge capacity.
7	at least 39 m long, but less than 49 m, and 5 m wide	2	Two ARFF vehicles carrying a combined quantity of 3,197 gallons (12 100 liters) of water, 496 pounds (225 kilograms) of complementary agent, and have a combined 1 400 gpm (5 300 L/min) discharge capacity.
8	at least 49 m long, but less than 61 m, and 7 m wide	3	Three ARFF vehicles carrying a combined quantity of 4,967 gallons (18 800 liters) of water, 992 pounds (450 kilograms) of complementary agent, and have a combined 1,902 gpm (7 200 L/min) discharge capacity.
9	at least 76 m long and 8 m wide	3	Three ARFF vehicles carrying a combined quantity of 6,420 gallons (24 300 liters) of water, 992 pounds (450 kilograms) of complementary agent, and have a combined 2,378 gpm (9 000 L/min) discharge capacity.
10	at least 76 m long and 8 m wide	3	Three ARFF vehicles carrying a combined quantity of 8,534 gallons (32 300 liters) of water, 992 pounds (450 kilograms) of complementary agent, and have a combined 2,959 gpm (11 200 L/min) of discharge capacity.

Where these requirements cannot be met because of personnel shortage or unserviceable equipment (caused by circumstances beyond the control of the airport) which continues for seven days or more, the airport must submit a corrective plan and completion date. The completion date "shall be as early as practicable given the circumstances". If the number of movements or size of passenger aircraft results in a higher category, the airport will have one year to comply. Transport Canada can authorize an airport to cease providing ARFF services if the airport can demonstrate by means of a risk analysis that the cessation of ARFF services will not result in an unacceptable risk to aviation safety.

NOTE: Information compiled from NFPA® Standard 414, *Standard for Aircraft Rescue and Fire-Fighting Services at Airports*; FAR 139.315, Aircraft rescue and firefighting: Index determination: FAR 139.317, Aircraft rescue and firefighting: Equipment and agents; ICAO Airport Services Manual, Part 1, *Rescue and Fire Fighting*; and Canadian Air Regulations (CAR) 303.05, *Aircraft Category for Fire Fighting*, and 303.09, *Extinguishing Agent and Aircraft Fire-fighting Vehicle Requirements*.

FAA limits its requirements to certificated airports that serve aircraft having a certain passenger capacity, NFPA® and ICAO use the length of all aircraft landing at an airport. The United States Department of Defense also has specific requirements pertaining to aircraft sizes and configurations. Military aircraft operations are mostly governed by NFPA® 403, *Standard for Aircraft Rescue and Fire-Fighting Services at Airports*; however, some branches of the military establish ARFF vehicle and manpower requirements based on the type of aircraft being protected. It is important that the appropriate agency requirements be reviewed to ensure compliance.

NFPA® 403 also has requirements for the amount of foam and auxiliary extinguishing agents and number of ARFF apparatus that should be stationed at various sizes of airports. These requirements are based on the NFPA® system of categorizing airports by size.

Apparatus Design

There are a number of agencies and standards that cover the different types of ARFF apparatus, their respective designs, and which types of ARFF apparatus that may be required at any given airport. The following requirements pertain to airport fire fighting vehicles and should be considered when preparing specifications for these vehicles or determining the apparatus necessary to protect a particular airport:

- Federal Aviation Regulations (FAR) Part 139.317, *Aircraft rescue and firefighting: Equipment and agents,* and as outlined in FAA Advisory Circular (AC) 150/5220-10D, *Guide Specification for Aircraft Rescue and Fire Fighting Vehicles*

- International Civil Aviation Organization (ICAO) *Airport Services Manual Part I, Rescue and Fire Fighting*

- NFPA® 403, *Standard for Aircraft Rescue and Fire-Fighting Services at Airports*

- NFPA® 412, *Standard for Evaluating Aircraft Rescue and Fire-Fighting Foam Equipment*

- NFPA®414, *Standard for Aircraft Rescue and Fire-Fighting Vehicles.*

> **NOTE:** Each ARFF apparatus should be painted and/or marked to optimize visibility and should be equipped with appropriate emergency lights.

Aircraft Rescue and Fire Fighting Apparatus

Aircraft rescue and fire fighting apparatus are vehicles that have been specifically designed and manufactured to meet the needs of the aviation industry and airport fire departments. These vehicles must be able to operate effectively in both paved and unpaved areas **(Figure 7.3 a and b)**. In responding to aircraft accidents, ARFF apparatus may have to be driven across terrain that might be difficult to traverse in typical structural fire apparatus. This terrain also may be littered with aircraft wreckage, victims, and both ambulatory and nonambulatory survivors. These vehicles may have to discharge extinguishing agents while moving into or out of fire fighting positions.

Because of the large volumes of fuel involved in aircraft fires, mass application of extinguishing agents may be required very quickly in order to protect

Figure 7.3 a and b ARFF apparatus responding on pavement and off-road. *Off-road photo courtesy of James Nilo.*

the occupants of an aircraft. ARFF vehicles are equipped with turrets, hand-lines, ground sweeps, undertruck nozzles, and extendable turrets to apply the extinguishing agents. Additionally, ARFF vehicles today carry more medical supplies, ladders, and rescue tools and equipment than their predecessors.

For specifying performance criteria of ARFF apparatus and agent systems, NFPA® 414 divides apparatus into the following three different groups based on vehicle water-tank capacities:

● Capacity I: 120 gal to 528 gal (454 L to 1 999 L)

● Capacity II: >528 gal to 1,585 gal (>1 999 L to 6 000 L)

● Capacity III: >1,585 gal (>6 000 L)

The FAA provides a class rating system for ARFF apparatus based on the amount of water and dry chemical or clean agent carried on board. These classes are covered in **Table 7.2.** Each vehicle that carries AFFF should carry sufficient foam concentrate to mix with two tank-loads of water.

Table 7.2
FAA Classes of ARFF Vehicles

Class of Vehicle	Water or Water/Foam Solution		Dry Chemical* or Approved Clean Agent Equivalent	
	Gallons (U.S.)	Liters	Pounds	Kilograms
1	120	454	500	225
2	300	1,136	500	225
3	500	1,900	500	225
4	1,500	5,685	See 14 CFR Part 139, Para 139.317	
5	3,000 to 4,500 in 500 gallon increments	11,360 to 17,035 in 1,900 liter increments	See 14 CFR Part 139, Para 139.317	

* 500 lbs of Sodium based dry chemical or 450 lbs Potassium based dry chemical (i.e. Purple K Powder) or 460 lbs clean agent.

Source: FAA AC 150/5220-10D, Guide Specifications for Aircraft Rescue and Fire Fighting Vehicles.

Figure 7.4 An example of a Rapid Intervention Vehicle (RIV).

In addition to the general description of ARFF vehicles already addressed, the sections that follow describe common ARFF combined agent vehicles (rapid intervention vehicles), structural apparatus, and support vehicles and equipment.

Combined Agent Vehicles (Rapid Intervention Vehicles - RIVs)

Combined agent vehicles are smaller than typical ARFF vehicles and are generally outfitted with combined agent systems. Due to their compact size, these vehicles are designed to respond rapidly to an emergency scene and can also operate in areas that may be unsuited for larger ARFF vehicles **(Figure 7.4)**. RIVs can be equipped with a water pump and tank or a skid unit. Water tank sizes range from 100 to 500 gallon (379 to 1 893 L) and auxiliary agent capacities from 100 to 500 pounds (45 to 228 kg). Combined agent vehicles may be required by FAA regulations depending on airport size and frequency of flights. However, smaller airports may only require the use of a combined agent vehicle to meet their respective ARFF response criteria. ARFF departments should refer to the appropriate regulation or standard to determine if a rapid intervention vehicle is required for their jurisdiction.

Structural Apparatus

Some structural apparatus may be specially adapted and equipped for aircraft rescue and fire fighting applications **(Figure 7.5)**. The modern trend in structural fire fighting apparatus has been to install a fixed foam proportioning system which can be used with either attack lines or piped turrets for foam

Figure 7.5 A structural apparatus configured for ARFF use. *Courtesy of Edwin A. Jones, USAFR.*

Table 7.3
Amount of Concentrate Needed for Various Sizes of Water Tanks

	Foam Concentrate Proportioning %	Water Tank Size in Gallons (Liters)				
		500 (2 000)	750 (3 000)	1,000 (4 000)	1,500 (6 000)	2,000 (8 000)
Concentrate to be added in gallons (liters)	1%	5 (20)	7.5 (30)	10 (40)	15 (60)	20 (80)
	3%	15 (60)	22.5 (90)	30 (120)	45 (180)	60 (240)
	6%	30 (120)	45 (180)	60 (240)	90 (360)	120 (480)

application. These systems may be limited in their capacity to sustain foam fire fighting operations as they typically have smaller foam concentrate storage tanks than do ARFF apparatus. Nevertheless, fixed foam proportioning systems give firefighters more capability than external inline foam eductors because of the friction loss, lack of mobility, and other problems associated with inline foam eductors.

Structural apparatus can also be ordered with all-wheel drive, turrets, aircraft rescue equipment, secondary agent systems, (dry chemical, clean agents, Class D agents) and mass casualty supplies and equipment. Firefighters should be knowledgeable about the capabilities and operation of the apparatus and foam systems in the event of an aircraft accident/incident. Nevertheless, it is very difficult for ARFF equipped structural apparatus to meet the requirements of NFPA® 414. Therefore, ARFF jurisdictions should consult applicable regulations and standards to determine if ARFF equipped structural apparatus will meet their respective needs.

All hose threads and couplings on all structural apparatus must be of the same cut as ARFF apparatus, including mutual aid municipalities or companies. If vehicles have different threads, adapters will have to be obtained to ensure inter-operability between all vehicles otherwise re-supplying of ARFF vehicles will not be possible.

It may be possible to use a structural fire apparatus that is not equipped with a fixed foam proportioning system to produce foam by pouring foam concentrate directly into the apparatus water tank. This method is commonly referred to as *batch mixing*. **Table 7.3** shows the proper amounts of concentrate that are needed for various water-tank sizes. Once the foam concentrate has been distributed throughout the tank, the apparatus fire pump is operated in the standard manner to produce a foam fire stream. This method may be used only with regular AFFF foam concentrates. It is not suitable for use with alcohol-resistant AFFF concentrates. Caution should be used when batch mixing to make sure all the foam has been flushed from the system after the operations are completed. This prevents the vehicle's fire fighting system from becoming damaged by the long-term effects of foam.

Support Vehicles and Equipment

To be successful, ARFF departments must be properly equipped or have agreements in place to expeditiously manage hazards associated with aircraft incidents. Such hazards include but are not limited to mass casualties, mass personnel contamination, technical rescue (confined space, high angle, and

Figure 7.6a An ARFF department command vehicle.

Figure 7.6b An ARFF department heavy rescue vehicle.

Figure 7.6c A set of mobile air stairs dedicated for ARFF department use.

structural collapse), and large hazardous material incidents. To confront hazards associated with aircraft incidents, most ARFF departments operate a host of support equipment, which may include command vehicles, command post vehicles, mobile water supply vehicles, foam supply vehicles and trailers, hazardous materials vehicles and trailers, ambulances, mass-casualty vehicles and trailers, decontamination trailers, heavy rescue apparatus, and even buses.

Some departments have adapted mobile air stairs, food service vehicles, and other such equipment for use as elevated platforms **(Figure 7.6 a–c)**. Modifications such as adding preconnected hoselines, hose reels, ventilation fans, and other innovations make these useful devices. Called "interior access vehicles," these apparatus can be quickly positioned next to an aircraft upright on its landing gear with an interior fire to provide a platform to start interior attack from. For further information refer to NFPA® 414. Vehicles have also been custom designed and ordered new for this purpose. ARFF personnel are limited only by their creativity and ingenuity. These apparatus are intended to meet specific needs for particular airports; however, they are generally not considered as credit towards the minimum ARFF requirements.

Interior Access Vehicles — Fire apparatus designed to provide a raised platform for aircraft fire fighting operations that will elevate fire fighters to an even level with the aircraft compartment.

Apparatus Features and Options

Due to the wide variety of systems, features, and options available in modern ARFF apparatus, today's airport driver/operators have many advantages their predecessors in fire fighting did not have. ARFF vehicle features and options include the following:

- Antilock brake systems
- Central tire inflation/deflation systems
- Driver's enhanced vision systems (DEVS)
- Vehicle Rear View Backup Camera Systems
- Apparatus Mounted Video Cameras
- High-mobility suspension systems (independent suspension systems)
- Monitoring and Data Acquisition System (MADAS)
- Lateral Acceleration Indicator

Antilock Brake Systems

ARFF apparatus are required to have anti-lock braking systems (ABS) in accordance with NFPA® 414. ABS is an electronic system that monitors and controls wheel speed during braking. ABS improves vehicle stability and control by reducing wheel lock during braking.

Antilock brake systems provide the driver with greater control when operating under poor road conditions such as surfaces slick from ice and rain. Antilock brakes keep the vehicle wheels from skidding, which can result in a loss of control. However, this brake system can also give a driver a false sense of security if the driver completely relies on the braking system to prevent the vehicle from losing control. The driver must continue to drive with due caution at all times whether or not the vehicle has antilock brakes.

Central Inflation/Deflation System (CIDS)

This technological advance allows the driver to deflate the vehicle tires while the vehicle is moving or stationary in order to improve the vehicle traction. These systems can be operated at predetermined speeds without interrupting the fire fighting capability of the vehicle. Deflating the tire increases traction and creates greater maneuverability. Deflation also aids in removing mud and debris from the tread, making the aggressive tread of a modern vehicle tires more effective **(Figure 7.7)**. The typical CIDS system is operated from a control panel in the vehicle's cab and has four terrain settings to increase the mobility of the vehicle. The settings are usually highway, off-road (cross country), soft terrain (mud, snow, sand), and emergency. The emergency mode is limited in use to 5 miles distances and speeds less than 5 mph to protect the tires from overheating. As with any advanced system, the tire deflation system can increase downtime for the vehicle when requiring maintenance. The increased ability to respond to incidents in adverse driving conditions greatly outweighs the minor problem of having a vehicle out-of-service for longer than normal periods of time.

Driver's Enhanced Vision System (DEVs)

Most airports experience weather and other vision impairing conditions that can delay ARFF response times. The driver's enhanced vision system (DEVS) allows the ARFF driver to use modern technology to make a safer, quicker response under adverse conditions. Cameras for these systems are mounted on the apparatus exterior (usually on the roof). The display screens are located

Figure 7.7 The box on the upper right portion of the rim of this wheel is part of a central inflation/deflation system.

WARNING!

It is dangerous to be driving an ARFF vehicle at faster speeds with tires inadequately inflated or with different pressures. An accident may occur resulting in vehicle damage and injury to personnel.

Figure 7.8 A forward looking infra-red (FLIR) camera mounted on the roof of an ARFF apparatus.

in the cab and may be mounted to the ceiling near the window or on the dash or, in some cases, may be built into the dash.

The DEVS is composed of the following three subsystems:

- *Night vision* — infrared camera and monitor that enhances vision in smoke, fog, adverse weather, and darkness; the Forward Looking Infra-Red (FLIR) camera can also be used to scan an aircraft and identify hot spots or hidden fire **(Figure 7.8)**

- *Navigation* — differential global positioning system (DGPS) receiver and moving map display inside the cab; GPS is a device which picks up signals from orbiting satellites and determines locations on earth by longitude and latitude reference; an aerial photograph of the airport is digitized so it can be displayed on a computer screen for mapping; if the airport has a Surface Movement Guidance and Control System (SMGCS), this can also be added to DEVS

- *Tracking* — digital radio datalink between the command center and vehicles over which accident information, vehicle position reports, and other messages are sent

This combination of subsystems gives ARFF vehicle driver/operators a distinct advantage when responding under adverse driving and vision conditions. The driver/operator may be able to easily locate a crash site that would otherwise be obscured. The same computer can also display other response information, such as aircraft emergency plans, emergency check lists, phone number lists, and resource data bases, as well as send incident updates and routine messages. As with any other advanced systems, the DEVS requires the driver to train often under the conditions for which the system was designed.

Vehicle Rear View Backup Camera Systems

Many fire and rescue vehicles come equipped with vehicle rear view backup camera systems to assist driver/operators in backing these vehicles more safely. These systems include a camera mounted to the rear of the vehicle that is connected to a small, flat-screen (full-color) monitor in the cab **(Figure 7.9)**. Rear-backing cameras are an invaluable enhancement to ARFF vehicles; however, driver/operators should exercise extreme caution when backing ARFF vehicles and avoid a feeling a false sense of security because of the presence of the cameras.

Figure 7.9 An ARFF driver/operator using the in-cab screen of a backup camera system to watch behind the ARFF apparatus as he backs up the vehicle.

Apparatus Mounted Video Cameras

Front mounted video cameras and remote recording units can be installed on ARFF apparatus. The units can be programmed to start recording when the apparatus is started and record throughout an emergency response. Video images can provide excellent documentation of scene conditions for both training and accident investigation.

High-Mobility Suspension Systems

A high-mobility suspension system gives an ARFF vehicle greater mobility when responding both on and off paved surfaces. This system keeps a vehicle's wheels in as much contact with the surface as possible. Standard straight-axle vehicles have a tendency to lose contact with the surface when encountering extremely uneven terrain. With a high-mobility suspension, each wheel and axle is independent from the others and will articulate over the terrain allowing each wheel to maintain greater contact with the surface. A vehicle with a straight axle crossing a ditch at an angle, for example, would have the possibility of one or more tires losing contact with the surface because the axle is rigid. A high-mobility suspension uses independent drive suspension that would allow the tires to maintain contact with the ground in the same situation.

Monitoring and Data Acquisition System (MADAS)

A MADAS collects minimum vehicle performance measurements. Units can be purchased and programmed to measure the following additional vehicle characteristics:

- Vehicle speed
- Vehicle heading
- Lateral acceleration
- Vertical acceleration
- Longitudinal acceleration
- Engine rpm
- Throttle position
- Steering input
- Braking input (Pedal position and brake pressure)
- Date, time, and location for all data collected

The MADAS must be capable of storing the measurements and time intervals, starting at least 120 seconds before and 15 seconds after any serious accident. The system must not permit the recorded data to be lost due to the use of an emergency shut-off or master electrical disconnect switch.

Lateral Acceleration Indicator (LAI)

This device is intended as an early alert system to assist drivers in recognizing when they are exceeding the safe operating limits of their vehicle and approaching maneuvering limits that are potentially unstable and could cause a rollover accident. The device will not prevent the vehicle from rolling over, however. It is up to the driver/operator to monitor the LAI and drive within its warning limits.

Apparatus Fire Suppression Equipment

ARFF vehicles and their built-in fire pumps are capable of applying various extinguishing agents from turrets, handlines, ground-sweep and under truck nozzles, an extendable turret, or a combination of all or any of these devices.

Fire Pumps

Every major ARFF vehicle has a fire pump rated for that specific vehicle. All ARFF vehicles are capable of delivering large quantities of water to the fire fighting systems. Also, the fire pumps in ARFF vehicles can operate while the vehicle is in motion. This capability allows the operator to attack the fire on initial approach. Because the method of transferring power between the pump and engine during pump-and-roll operations may vary according to manufacturer, ARFF vehicle operators should practice and become familiar with the pump-and-roll characteristics of the vehicle. Refer to the applicable ARFF vehicle technical data and IFSTA's **Pumping Apparatus Driver/Operator Handbook**.

Major ARFF vehicles will have a switch or buttons to activate the fire pump from the cab. The controls will usually give the operator the choice of water or foam. If the apparatus has a structural panel, the operator will also have the choice of pumping in "Crash (pump-and-roll)" or "Structure" mode.

Some ARFF apparatus have structural fire fighting capability **(Figure 7.10)**. This allows the vehicle to be operated as a structural pumper, to draft from a water source, work from a fire hydrant, and operate from the vehicle water

Pump-and-roll — Ability of an apparatus to pump water and foam while the vehicle is in motion.

Figure 7.10 An ARFF driver/operator operating a structural panel on an ARFF apparatus. *Courtesy of John Demyan, LVI Airport.*

tank. The advantages to structural systems on an ARFF vehicle include the ability to better control water pressure when making aircraft interior attacks and the expanded capability of the vehicle when it is used at airports that do not have a dedicated structural pumper. A majority of the manufacturers who provide structural capability usually provide foam to all discharges. The foam delivery systems also vary from one manufacturer to another. Because these systems vary, driver/operators must become familiar with the specific vehicles at their department.

Figure 7.11 An ARFF vehicle's roof and bumper turrets in operation during a training evolution.

Turrets

For mass application of agents during rescue and fire extinguishment, vehicles should have one or more turrets. The turrets may be mounted on the tops of the cabs or on the front bumpers of the vehicles **(Figure 7.11)**. They may be operated either manually or by remote control and should be capable of discharging extinguishing agents in various patterns ranging from straight-stream to fog patterns. Some turrets may also have automatic oscillating features. Vehicles having remote electrical or hydraulic controls for turret operation should also have manual override controls. Driver/operators should become familiar with the capabilities of assigned ARFF vehicle turrets in order to facilitate an effective approach to an aircraft on fire.

Auto-oscillating turrets allow the operator to set the range of sweep, usually 90 degrees each side of center, and the turret automatically sweeps side-to-side. This can often waste a lot of agent. There will be a control to change turret application from straight stream to dispersed or fog stream. Valves may have to be opened, a locking device released, or pins removed to utilize the turret. The joy-stick or manual handle will usually have an on-off button.

The flow or spray of agent from roof mounted turrets can obstruct the ARFF driver/operator's view of the emergency scene to the point that the agent stream from the ARFF vehicle is ineffective. Therefore, some ARFF vehicle manufacturers now offer high flow bumper turrets on the vehicles they produce. These turrets are capable of delivering the same flow as roof turrets and are intended to take the place of the roof mounted turrets. The major benefit of a high flow bumper turret is to provide the driver/operator with improved visibility.

A "dual flow" option can also be ordered to allow selection of low (half, 50%) flow or high (full, 100%) flow discharge from the turret. An example would be a turret that has two flow settings, 350 gpm and 700 gpm (1 325 and 2 650 Lpm). Low flow would be used for close range discharge, agent conservation, and a longer, sustained fire attack. High flow would be used when distance and massive fire knockdown is desired. Dual flow is required when a vehicle only has one turret. The FAA minimum foam discharge rates for turrets are found in FAR 139.317.

Turrets, like all mechanical equipment, are subject to breakdowns and other operational problems. Having two turrets allows for a backup in case of a turret failure. ARFF vehicles may have a second turret mounted on a bumper, on the roof, or on an elevating/extendable device. If there are two or more ARFF personnel on an apparatus, two turrets allow a multidirectional fire attack. Additionally, if two turrets are provided on an ARFF vehicle, one will usually be of a lesser flow.

A secondary turret is often mounted on an apparatus' bumper and is called a "bumper turret." Most are also are operated using a joy-stick and have auto-oscillating capability, with horizontal speed and travel limit control. Bumper turrets can be used in close range applications and to protect the apparatus from fire flare-ups or fuel re-flashes. A bumper turret can usually perform all the tasks under truck and ground sweep nozzles are used for.

Primary turrets must be power-assisted. The amount of force necessary to operate these turrets must be less than 30 pounds. The turret must have an in-cab indicator of the turret's vertical elevation and horizontal direction unless the turret is fully visible to the operator.

Turrets must be capable of being rotated 90 degrees to either side of center, depressed to discharge agent within 30 feet in front of the vehicle using a dispersed stream, elevated at least 45 degrees above the horizontal, have a total horizontal range of not less than 180 degrees.

Handlines

Handlines are needed to extinguish interior fires in the fuselage that turrets cannot reach, to provide protection for rescue personnel, and to extinguish peripheral fires after rescue operations are completed. Most ARFF vehicles are equipped with preconnected noncollapsible booster hose stored on a reel and/ or standard collapsible hose stored in a hose bed (**Figure 7.12**). Both types of hoses must be equipped with variable pattern, shut-off nozzles. Nozzles may be aspirating or nonaspirating.

The longer and larger the hose, the harder it will be to deploy and maneuver around an incident scene. Hose lines may have to be moved around wreckage, on uneven and slippery terrain, or extended via ladders considerable heights into an aircraft. Larger hose requires two personnel to use.

Many preconnect discharge valves on ARFF vehicles require someone to turn the valve on. There are valves that can be remotely operated from the apparatus cab or automatically opened when the hose line is pulled taut. Some newer ARFF units have a cable attached to the last foot of the hose, which is connected to the discharge outlet. This cable is attached to a pin, that when pulled by the deployment of the hose will allow discharge. When hose is deployed, tension in the hose pulls this cable which pulls the pin and allows water

Figure 7.12 ARFF firefighters advancing a handline from the apparatus.

to discharge. This cable/pin system prevents the charging an undeployed hose in a compartment, which could damage the compartment. Some apparatus have sensors that will not increase engine rpms, flow, and pump pressure until the discharge device (nozzle) is open and flowing. Sometimes a blockage, such as a kink or airlock, can delay the charging of the hose line. There may be a momentary throttle override switch that will increase the flow. If foam was used the hose should be flushed with clean water.

Chemical injection systems and nozzles are also available for ARFF hose lines. The foam and dry chemical components can be used separately or in combination. The dry chemical flow is usually 5 pounds per second.

There are also piercing nozzles available for hose lines. Some have built-in ramming devices to force the piercing tip into an aircraft. Other models must be pounded in with a sledge hammer. Still others are simply long applicators that are inserted into a hole made by a forcible entry tool.

A pneumatic or air driven drill is also available that uses a compressed air cylinder or SCBA cylinder to drive a drill bit into an aircraft. Water, foam, or other extinguishing agents can then be discharged through the drill bit.

> ### Auxiliary Agent Delivery Systems
>
> Most major ARFF vehicles carry some type of auxiliary agent. These agents include dry/wet chemical and clean agents. These may be delivered through separate hose reels, twin agent handlines, or piped directly to a dry-chemical injection nozzle.

Ground-Sweep and Undertruck Nozzles

Ground-sweep nozzles are used to lay a blanket or path of foam in front of a vehicle so that it can move into extinguishment and/or rescue positions without endangering the apparatus. Operation of ground-sweep nozzles should be controlled from within the cab of the vehicle.

Figure 7.13 An ARFF apparatus undertruck nozzle in operations during vehicle checkout.

Undertruck nozzles discharge extinguishing agents directly beneath the vehicle chassis **(Figure 7.13)**. They are designed to protect the ARFF vehicle and equipment from the possibility of fuel and flames floating back and igniting beneath the vehicle itself. Controls for the undertruck nozzles are also located inside the vehicle cab.

Extendable Turrets

An extendable turret is capable of attacking a fire at the base of the flames by placing the agent stream where the foam can best attack the fire. The operator has the ability to reposition the primary turret and attachments to a location that enhances the visibility of and access to hard to reach areas, providing the ability to utilize firefighting agents most effectively. Some hard to reach, obstructed, and shielded aircraft areas are wheel wells, landing gear, aircraft interiors, belly areas, and tail mounted engines. Both turrets and piercing nozzles can also be capable of flowing complementary agents, such as dry chemical or clean streaming agents. Because these devices are complicated to operate, driver/operators will require continual training in their operation and in tactics and strategies.

Some extendable turrets also are equipped with a piercing nozzle that is designed to penetrate aircraft skin and apply agent to the aircraft interior without placing firefighters in danger **(Figure 7.14)**. Testing of extendable turret piercing nozzles has shown their impressive ability to contain and control interior fire spread and flashover conditions. The piercing nozzles on extendable turrets can flow in excess of 250 gpm (946 L) through the piercing device. The extendable turret with Forward Looking Infared (FLIR) can be used to locate hidden hot spots in cargo holds or to assist in locating the seat of a fire in a cabin interior. Color video can also be mounted on the boom, nozzle, and penetrator. Color optics must have sufficient resolution to permit overall surveillance of the fire scene when fully extended, as well as provide the operator with the detail needed for placement of the penetrating device. When the extendable turret is top-mounted, the driver/operator must be aware that the vehicle may have a higher center of gravity than other ARFF vehicles and may need to compensate for this when driving.

Elevated Waterways

The most common elevated waterway is an articulating boom design. The boom can be manipulated and agent discharged while the apparatus is in motion (pump and roll). Older booms were not designed to rotate. Newer models will rotate 30 degrees right or left of center. A problem with waterways is the

Figure 7.14 An ARFF apparatus equipped with an extendable turret and piercing nozzle.

amount of left over agent in the piping system. This agent will be dumped on the ground when the waterway is retracted, wasting the agent and potentially causing an otherwise unnecessary environmental hazard.

Air aspirating foam, non-air-aspirating fog, chemical injection, or secondary agent nozzles can also be installed on the boom. The boom on an elevated waterway allows much greater visibility, control, and more efficient application of agent on a fire. Aircraft skin penetrating nozzle (ASPN) can also be installed on the end of the boom. This device may also be referred to as a skin penetrator/agent applicator. The ASPN can also be extended in one foot (0.3 m) increments for deep seated cargo fires. Although it must flow a minimum of 250 gpm (946 L), most ASPNs typically flow 350 gpm (1 325 L) of water or foam. The ideal location to penetrate the skin of cargo aircraft is 24 inches (61 cm) above the cabin windows, between the structural members. Penetrating the passenger aircraft 12 inches (30 cm) above the cabin windows is a best practice because this location will be above the seat backs, but below baggage storage bins. The rivet pattern will indicate where the aircraft structural members are located.

The ASPN will not impede aircraft occupant evacuation. To be effective, it must be inserted between the aircraft occupants and the fire in what is called a "fire stop" or "blocking" attack. The ASPN will provide water extinguishment from ceiling to floor level which will prevent the full growth of the interior fire along the entire length of the interior of the aircraft. Agent application will depend on the location of the main body of fire, so it is important that the operator can determine where this is. Sometimes exterior conditions will indicate where the fire is. The most efficient method is to use a thermal imaging device, preferably mounted on the boom or apparatus, to locate the seat of the fire.

Agent Resupply Methods

When it comes to fighting large fuel-spill fires, rapid resupply can be as important as fighting the fire. All ARFF vehicles should have the ability to quickly resupply with both water and foam concentrate at an emergency scene (**Figure 7.15, p. 236**). Resupply can be critical when operating under large-scale emergency conditions.

Figure 7.15 A rapid resupply operation providing water and foam to an ARFF apparatus responding during a training exercise. *Courtesy of John Demyan, LVI Airport.*

There are several methods associated with agent resupply. These include the following:

- *Rapid Resupply* — tanker establishes a quick water supply to an ARFF vehicle directly involved with the fire fighting effort

- *Sustained Resupply* — water supply is established from a fixed source such as a fire hydrant or pumper fire apparatus to the ARFF vehicle

- *Resupply Point* — ARFF vehicle rotates to a location where fire fighting agent, fuel, or other equipment is provided because these items are not readily available at the incident site

ARFF departments should develop resupply procedures that incorporate all three methods to ensure all operational considerations are taken into account. Each department should spend time training for rapid resupply using whatever method it plans to use in actual incidents.

The sections that follow describe water-fill methods, foam resupply, and auxiliary agent system servicing.

Water-Fill Methods

As with structural fire apparatus, the primary method of refilling an ARFF apparatus water tank is through hose intake connections on the side or rear of the apparatus. These intakes may route water either through the pump or directly into the water tank.

There are also several methods of supplying water to the ARFF apparatus' tank inlets. Water can come directly from a fire hydrant, a mobile water supply, a supply line extended from a pumper, or a fixed, overhead-fill hose found in most fire station apparatus rooms.

All ARFF vehicles also have overhead-fill capability. The overhead-fill method is not as fast or safe as filling from the side of the vehicle. Persons using the top-filling method should use caution when walking on top of the vehicle, as it may be slippery.

Some ARFF apparatus have an auto shut-off system that automatically closes the tank fill valve when the tank is full. Automatic water tank level control is available on some newer ARFF vehicles, that when connected to a hydrant or other water supply, the tank fill valve will automatically open if the tank is less that 70% full and will automatically close when the tank is 95% full. To fully fill the water tank with this system, the fill valve must be manually held open until water flows out of the overflow.

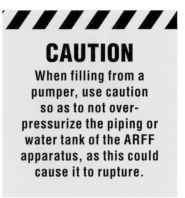

CAUTION
When filling from a pumper, use caution so as to not over-pressurize the piping or water tank of the ARFF apparatus, as this could cause it to rupture.

Foam Resupply

ARFF apparatus can be resupplied with foam concentrate in several different ways, including the following:

- Direct filling from 5-gallon (20 L) containers
- Overhead gravity filling in the fire station
- Mechanical or hand foam concentrate pump transfer from drums, large storage containers, or a foam tender

The least desired method is direct filling with 5-gallon (20 L) containers. This method is slow and requires a large number of personnel. Filling from foam tenders is a more convenient method, allowing a vehicle to be serviced closer to an incident site. Whatever method a department uses must be timely, flexible, and work efficiently when it is needed.

The fill line to the foam tank must minimize foaming of the concentrate. The foam tank should be completely filled and the hatch closed when not in use. Air movement and an air space over the foam concentrate can dehydrate it and cause the foam to gel within the system. At no time should different types of foam concentrate be stored in the same foam tank. Concentrates could react, thicken, and form globules that will deactivate proportioning systems.

The foam tank filler box (on top of apparatus) screen must remain clean at all times to prevent foreign matter from entering the tank. Almost all filler boxes have extremely sharp, knife-like devices used to puncture the bottom of plastic 5-gallon foam containers. A sharp downward motion to set the container over the piercing knife will usually drain the container in 20 seconds or less. Foam bubbles may obscure this knife. Extreme care should be used and gloves worn when cleaning the screen.

There is usually a foam fill connection (1½ inch) on one or both sides of an apparatus. If there is a structural panel, it is usually located near that location. Filling is accomplished with apparatus mounted pumps and portable pumps. Someone should be assigned to watch for a full tank at the top foam tank filler box or at the tank level lights. It is recommended that the foam concentrate tank hatch be open when filling. Personnel must have a container ready to catch excess concentrate as it drains from the filling connection, after the hose is disconnected.

Figure 7.16 A firefighter adding agent to an ARFF apparatus dry chemical system.

Auxiliary Agent System Servicing

Vehicles equipped with auxiliary agent systems typically store the agent in pressurized containers. The most important thing for ARFF personnel to know when refilling is what type(s) of agent their department uses. It is not acceptable to mix different types of agents or expellants. The system should only be filled according to the system manufacturer's directions. At no time should there be deviations from the manufacturer's recommended servicing instructions. Dry-chemical systems should be serviced in a well-ventilated area, and persons filling them should use respiratory protection. It is extremely rare for these systems to be serviced during the course of an incident (**Figure 7.16**).

Although all agent systems should be thoroughly flushed after each use, dry-chemical piping and hoselines must be completely flushed, or blown down, after any discharge.

Dry chemical left in the piping or hoselines tends to attract moisture and cake which could cause the line to become packed and unusable.

Many ARFF vehicles with auxiliary firefighting agents have a built in lift system (electric winch) for reservicing of the pressure cylinders. Familiarization with this system's operating procedures is vital in order to prevent injury to personnel reservicing the system. If no lift system is available on the vehicle or in the station, personnel must exercise the same caution because pressurized cylinders are heavy and awkward to handle.

Apparatus Maintenance

According to FAR Part 139.319 and ICAO Annex 14, all ARFF apparatus must be maintained so that they are always in operational condition during all air carrier operations. Therefore, ARFF apparatus and its equipment should be inspected immediately after shift change and after each use and be serviced as necessary. Ideally, the fire apparatus mechanic should occasionally monitor routine preventive maintenance inspections in order to improve the quality of inspections and to explain mechanical functions and service requirements to ARFF personnel during inspections. It is also good practice to use a detailed inspection checklist so that items are not missed during inspections. Mechanical problems should be reported to apparatus maintenance once they are discovered so that repairs can be accomplished in a timely manner (**Figure 7.17**). Adequate reserve ARFF apparatus should be maintained to ensure that the minimum ARFF protection is provided when first line ARFF vehicles are out of service.

Figure 7.17 An ARFF driver/operator and an ARFF apparatus mechanic discussing a problem with the apparatus.

For each vehicle, personnel should keep a complete record that includes the following information:

- Mileage
- Engine hours
- Fuel and oil consumption
- Tire-replacement information
- Parts information (when required, ordered, and installed)
- Total expenditures and out-of-service time

For each pumper, a record of annual pump performance tests also should be included in these permanent files. Particular attention should be paid to pressure readings on auxiliary firefighting agent pressure cylinders. Many leaks go undetected until the pressure gauge reading is low or empty.

Summary

There are many types of ARFF vehicles. ARFF departments should consider all applicable regulations and standards when designing the type of ARFF apparatus required for their jurisdiction. ARFF departments should take an all hazards approach to determine what support vehicles and equipment are necessary for a successful response outcome. ARFF jurisdictions must provide adequate resources and establish agreements with other agencies as necessary to meet the needs of their airfields. ARFF departments should also develop appropriate procedures and training evaluations to ensure personnel are proficient with ARFF vehicle operations. ARFF personnel must become proficient in the operation of each assigned vehicle; having a thorough understanding of the vehicle and associated systems is vital for successful response and operations.

Review Questions

1. What determines the minimum types of aircraft rescue and fire fighting apparatus required at an airport?

2. What are the specifications of a Capacity II aircraft rescue and fire fighting apparatus?

3. What is batch mixing?

4. What is the purpose of an antilock brake system?

5. What are the three subsystems of a driver's enhanced vision system (DEVS)?

6. What is the purpose of a turret?

7. How are pre-connect discharge valves operated?

8. What is sustained resupply?

9. In what ways can aircraft rescue and fire fighting apparatus be resupplied with foam concentrate?

10. When should aircraft rescue and fire fighting apparatus be inspected?

Rescue Tools and Equipment

Chapter Contents

chapter 8

NFPA® references for Chapter 8:

NFPA® 1003 (2010)
- 5.1.1.3
- 5.3.5
- 5.3.6
- 5.3.7
- 5.3.8
- 5.4.1
- 5.4.2

**NFPA® 1002
(2009 - Chapter 9)**
- 9.1.2

Federal Aviation Regulations (FAR)

139.319 (g)

Learning Objectives

After reading this chapter, students shall be able to:

1. Discuss the use of ARFF rescue tools and equipment.
   (NFPA® 1003, 5.3.8, 5.4.1, 5.4.2)

2. Describe hand tools used in ARFF rescue operations.
   (NFPA® 1003, 5.3.8, 5.4.1, 5.4.2)

3. Describe power tools used in ARFF rescue operations.
   (NFPA® 1003, 5.3.8, 5.4.1, 5.4.2)

4. Discuss lifting and pulling tools and equipment used in ARFF rescue operations.
   (NFPA® 1003, 5.3.8, 5.4.1, 5.4.2)

5. Discuss lighting and electrical equipment used in ARFF rescue operations.
   (NFPA® 1003, 5.3.8, 5.4.1, 5.4.2)

6. Discuss other common types of equipment used in ARFF rescue operations.
   (NFPA® 1003, 5.3.8, 5.4.1, 5.4.2)

Chapter 8
Rescue Tools and Equipment

Case History

The response to the crash of the Columbian Avianca Airlines Flight 52 on January 25, 1990, on Long Island, New York revealed many of the difficulties pertaining to rescuing persons trapped in a crushed and twisted aircraft. The aircraft had run out of fuel and crashed onto a densely wooded hillside. Because of the lack of fuel, there was no post-crash fire. The impact caused all the interior furnishings and finish, including seats, overhead compartments, modular galleys, and lavatories to be ripped from their mountings and thrust upon the passengers. Fuel and lavatory chemical residues created a strong odor around the incident scene. Initial efforts involved making the scene safe for the rescue.

It was nighttime, so generators and portable lighting were utilized to light the impact area. Hand tools and chain saws were the first rescue tools utilized to cut vegetation, gain access, and create safe working areas around the aircraft. The aircraft had broken into several sections on a relatively steep hillside. Each section had to be stabilized to prevent the potential for sliding, rolling, or collapse.

Rescuers first gained access to the aircraft interior through openings created by the crash. Tools and other materials were used to widen and make these openings more effective for rescue operations. Every accessible and still functional door and hatch was opened. As a last resort, numerous other openings had to be cut through the fuselage walls to perform some of the rescues. The four- to six-foot (one to two meters) distance from the ground to the doors and openings made entry and victim removal difficult.

Firefighters initially had to stand on top of wreckage that contained both survivors and fatalities. Ladders were laid on top of the interior wreckage to provide safe footing. Rescue tool power units & lighting were hung from overhead aircraft structural members. Rescue saws had the best success cutting and enlarging openings into the fuselage. Hydraulic and other portable cutting tools were used to systematically disentangle the aircraft occupants from the complicated mix of aircraft debris. Although the police wanted the deceased left in place to aid in the investigation, firefighters had to move some to reach survivors. Firefighters had to rely on creativity, ingenuity, and sheer determination to successfully rescue the eighty-five (85) survivors. Every one of the survivors, as well as each of the seventy-three (73) fatalities during body recovery, had to be physically extricated from the aircraft. The first survivor was transported sixty-five minutes after rescuers first arrived on scene. Rescue tools were used for forcible entry to gain access to the aircraft interior, as well as to separate and disentangle the survivors from the wreckage and debris inside the aircraft. Over one thousand (1,000) responders, ninety-one (91) ambulances, numerous heavy rescue and fire apparatus responded from thirty-seven (37) departments. Every available rescue tool was utilized, from hand tools to power equipment.

Case History

Survivor injuries consisted of multiple lower leg fractures and dislocations, head injuries, hip fractures, spinal fractures, multiple lacerations, and contusions. Rescuers had difficulty keeping pace with the number of victims. There was a short supply of backboards and other immobilization devices. Because of the number of persons and limited working area, most survivors were removed as gently as possible, without first being stabilized. There was also a Spanish language barrier with most of the survivors. Overall, the rescue response was exceptional under the difficult circumstances of fog, rain, and wreckage location. Most of the rescuers participated in critical incident stress management programs in the weeks following the response.

The tools and equipment used for aircraft accidents/incidents vary to some degree from the tools and equipment used in structural fire fighting. However, conventional tools are acceptable for aircraft rescue as are forcible entry tools in most cases. In addition to the tools and equipment covered in this chapter, there are many other tools (such as bolt cutters, wrecking bars, hacksaws, shovels, and door openers) used similarly for both structural and airport rescue and fire fighting. This chapter discusses general tools and equipment as well as those that are unique to aircraft rescue and fire fighting.

The U.S. Federal Aviation Administration (FAA), the National Fire Protection Association (NFPA®), and the International Civil Aviation Organization (ICAO) each recommend the types of tools and equipment to be carried on ARFF apparatus. These organizations understand the limited space and weight restrictions associated with ARFF apparatus and have identified the minimum tools and equipment to be carried on each vehicle in an ARFF department (**Table 8.1**). Aircraft rescue firefighters should be familiar with the tool requirements of the authority having jurisdiction over their airport operations. A dedicated rescue vehicle should be considered to carry specialized rescue equipment.

Using Rescue Tools and Equipment

A number of tools and equipment have been designed specifically for aircraft rescue. Many of these tools are appropriate for a variety of rescue situations and are, therefore, well-known and widely distributed. Other tools are very specialized and are designed for specific applications.

Aircraft rescue tools include both hand tools and power tools (**Figure 8.1, p. 246**). These can be divided into four groups, based on the manner in which they are used: cutting, prying, pushing/pulling, and striking. A rescue tool may belong to more than one of these groups, and many hand tools can be used for prying and spreading as well as for cutting, striking, or even lock-entry work. These tools are often referred to as "multipurpose" or "utility" tools. Some tools may be used in combination with others.

Sometimes, using power tools (i.e., electric, hydraulic, gasoline, battery, or air-powered) is much easier than using hand tools when performing aircraft rescue work because of the tremendous mechanical advantage these tools

Table 8.1
FAA / NFPA / ICAO
Recommended Tools and Equipment

The FAA, NFPA®, and ICAO recognize that weight and space limitations restrict the quantity of tools and equipment ARFF vehicles may carry. The following lists are tools and equipment that are recommended by FAA, NFPA®, and ICAO to be carried on ARFF vehicles or within the ARFF department. The exact descriptions, quantity, and specifications of each tool or piece of equipment vary depending on the referenced agency.

Items found on two or more lists:

FAA	NFPA®	ICAO
Pike pole (12 ft [3.7m])	Hook, grab, or salvage tool	Grab or salvaging hook
Adjustable hydrant wrench	Hydrant wrench	
Sledge hammer (8 lb [3.6kg])	Hammer (4 lb [1.8kg])	Hammer (4 lb [1.8kg])
Extension ladder (2 section, 18 ft [5.5m]) or single section ladder (18 ft [5.5m])	Ground Ladder	Extending ladder (appropriate to aircraft)
Bolt cutters (36 inches [914mm] long)	Bolt cutters (minimum 24 inches [609.6mm])	Bolt cutters (24 inches [61cm])
Electric hand lantern	Handlight (intrinsically safe)	Flashlights/hand lamps
Metal cutting hand axe with insulated handles	Non-wedge type axes	Rescue axes (non-wedge types: 1 large and 1 small)
Pinch point crowbar	Prying tools	Crowbars (37.4 inch [61cm] and 65 inch [1.65m])
Portable gasoline driven metal cutting saw	Gasoline powered rescue saw	Powered rescue saw
First aid kit	First aid kit	Medical first aid kit
"V" blade rescue with spare blades [6]	Harness cutting tools	Seat belt/harness cutting tool
Self contained breathing apparatus	Self contained breathing apparatus	Breathing apparatus and spare cylinder
Smoke ejector Ventilation fans	Fan for ventilation and cooling	
Spanner and hose coupling wrenches	Spanner wrenches	
Air operated metal chisel	Air chisel	
Hydraulic Rescue kit	Hydraulic rescue tools (spreaders, lifters, cutters, or combination tools)	Hydraulic or pneumatic forcing tool
Cold chisel (8 x 1 inch [203 x 25mm])		Cold chisel (2.5cm)
Lineman's pliers with insulated handles (8 inch [203mm])		Pliers - Side cutting (7 inch [17.8cm]) and Slip joint (10 inch [25cm])
	Utility rope (100 ft [30m])	Rope lines (50 ft [15m] and 100 ft [30m])

Table 8.1 (continued)
FAA / NFPA® / ICAO
Recommended Tools and Equipment

FAA	NFPA®	ICAO
	Fire-resistant blanket	Fire resisting blanket
Pistol grip hacksaw (12 in [305mm]) with 12 assorted blades		Metal cutting or hacksaw, heavy duty with extra blades
Sheet metal sheers		Tin snippers
Screwdrivers (variety of flat [1] and phillips head [2])		Set of assorted screwdrivers

Items unique to each agencies list:

FAA	NFPA®	ICAO
Round point shovel	Tank fill hose (1 section minimum diameter of 2½ inches [65mm])	Adjustable wrench
Aircraft cable cutter or equivalent [10cm] high)	Wheel chocks	Chocks (6 inch [15cm] and 4 inch
Double grip screwdriver (12 inch [305mm])	Skin penetrator/agent applicator	Stretcher
Ball peen hammer (1¼ lb [0.6kg])	Portable lights	Flame resistant gloves (unless issued individually)
Wood or rubber plugs [6]	Multipurpose forcible entry tool	Oxygen inhaler
Felt pads (30 x 30 inches x ¼ inch [762 x 762 mm x 6.4mm]) [2]		
Explosion proof flashlights		
Portable electric generator/alternator (1 per department)		
Portable floodlights [2]		
Electrical extension cables with reels [2]		
Dry chemical extinguishers		
Gooseneck wrecking bar with claw		
Dzus key access panel fastening tools [2]		

Sources:

FAA AC 150/5210-6C, *Aircraft Fire and Rescue Facilities and Extinguishing Agents*

NFPA® Standard 402, *Guide for Aircraft Rescue and Fire Fighting Operations*, and NFPA® Standard 414, *Standard for Aircraft Rescue and Fire-Fighting Vehicles*

ICAO Doc 9137-AN/898, *Airport Services Manual, Part 1, Rescue and Fire Fighting*

Figure 8.1 Just a few of the many tools and equipment that are carried on ARFF apparatus.

provide. Some power tools generate over 20,000 psi (140 000 kPa) of mechanical energy. In other cases, due to restricted access and mobility, small hand tools may be needed.

The sections that follow describe safety considerations for use of rescue tools and equipment, hazards presented by flammable atmospheres, and aircraft stability.

Safety

Operating rescue tools and equipment during aircraft rescue operations can be very dangerous. The number of personnel in the operational area should be limited to the minimum number necessary to complete the task. All personnel in the hazard zone should be in full protective gear, especially eye and hand protection. Because rescue tool operations are often very noisy, rescue personnel should wear hearing protection. Personnel should maintain a natural body position and solid footing when using tools and equipment. A low (worker-to-supervisor/safety officer) span of control should be maintained, and rescue teams should coordinate their efforts to avoid adversely affecting each other's efforts. Safety should always be the number one priority.

Manufacturer's recommendations and operating guidelines should be followed at all times. A tool should only be used on those tasks for which it was designed. When any tool is pushed beyond the limits of its design and purpose, tool failure or injury to the user may occur.

Officers in charge of a rescue and extrication operation should be in communication with each other and constantly reevaluate and update operational plans. Often an activity at one end of the aircraft can adversely affect conditions at another area.

Flammable Atmosphere

When choosing tools and equipment to use at an aircraft accident, firefighters should consider the possibility that a flammable atmosphere might exist at the incident site. The forces involved in an aircraft crash often compromise the fuel system, creating a flammable atmosphere. ARFF personnel should carefully consider this and take proper precautions to avoid a "flash" or ignition of any spilled flammable materials. During cutting operations, for example, a saw blade that contacts a steel cable, rivet, or other similar material can cause sparks that may start a fire.

The aircraft incident scene needs to be rendered safe to use rescue tools and equipment. Tool work areas should be constantly monitored with vapor detectors for evidence of flammable fuel concentrations. Fuel leaks should be identified, stopped, or controlled. Leaks can be plugged or patched using a wide variety of materials and techniques. Leaking fuel can be contained by diking or can be captured in portable containers. Spills may also be contained with dirt or other absorbent material, but, the application of dirt may not adequately suppress fuel vapors. Spilled fuel should be covered with a foam blanket — followed by frequent reapplications — as well as dirt or other absorbent materials. ARFF crew members should eliminate obvious ignition sources by shutting down the aircraft power on the flight deck and disconnecting the batteries. Runway or taxiway lighting, if damaged during aircraft impact, should also be shutdown.

WARNING!
ARFF personnel should use a flammable metering device when entering a flammable atmosphere.

Stability of Aircraft

Firefighters always should consider the stability of the aircraft before making entry. Unless stabilized, the aircraft may move, shift, or roll – trapping and possibly injuring occupants and rescuers and causing more fuel to be released. Structural conditions of the aircraft must be constantly monitored. Personnel also must consider the structural integrity of the aircraft when positioning apparatus. Should the aircraft shift, it may contact or impede improperly placed apparatus. For all of these reasons, firefighters must bring the proper stabilizing tools and equipment with them to an emergency scene.

Many tools, equipment, and materials can be used to stabilize an aircraft. Cribbing, airbags, heavy timber, and jacks can be used to prevent the aircraft from rolling, sliding, twisting, collapsing, or shifting. Dirt can be pushed up against the fuselage, or heavy equipment can be parked against it. ARFF personnel can use ropes, cables, and chains to help secure large aircraft wreckage. In addition, shoring, such as wood timbers, hydraulic speed shores, and ladders, can be used to support sections of an aircraft and prevent collapse.

ⓘ Training of ARFF Personnel

ARFF personnel must have hands-on training using rescue equipment. When practical, training should involve an actual aircraft so that firefighters can learn the real capabilities and limitations of these tools. Many techniques that work in auto extrication, for example, do not work as effectively in the aircraft environment and can only be learned through training and practical experience **(Figure 8.2)**.

Figure 8.2 ARFF personnel training on the use of a rescue saw.

Assorted Rescue Tools and Equipment

Many general tools and equipment can be used in ARFF operations. Most conventional tools and equipment commonly used in structural rescue and fire fighting can be adapted to aircraft rescue and fire fighting situations. An assortment of conventional and specialized tools and equipment should be available to carry out ARFF functions. For example, after entry into an aircraft, firefighters may have to cut seat belts or harnesses in order to free occupants. Pads or salvage covers may be needed to cover jagged egress openings that could injure people or damage equipment. Tools and equipment may be needed to plug leaking fuel or oil lines. ARFF personnel should plan ahead so that they have the appropriate tools and equipment available to perform forcible entry and rescue operations in a timely and effective manner. The following sections discuss ordinary and commonly used tools and the primary or most common use for each.

Equipment/Tool Resource Pool

Tools and equipment should be stored on an apparatus in a manner that makes them readily available during rescue operations. For example, if ARFF personnel place the hydraulic rescue tools and equipment on a major ARFF apparatus that may return to the station to refill with water or agent, then personnel must take the rescue equipment off the apparatus so that it can be left at the scene. However, once at the scene, tools should be kept organized and easily accessible as well.

In order to effectively manage equipment and tool resources, a "tool drop" or "equipment resource pool" should be established in an area that is as near to the aircraft as is safely possible. Tarps or salvage covers should be spread on the ground and the equipment and tools set onto them. Those rescue units and fire apparatus that are on scene should be pulled up to this location and their equipment and tools stripped off. Areas should be set up in the resource pool for each type of tool. For example, axes, rescue saws, hydraulic tools, air chisels, air bags, and hand tools. Adequate ARFF personnel should be assigned to staff the resource pool in order to

Figure 8.3 A crash axe.

Figure 8.4 The V-blade harness-cutting knife.

Hand Tools

Hand tools generally can be defined as tools that rely on human force to transmit power directly to the working end of the tool. A standard fire apparatus toolbox holds various hand tools and accessories that can be used for rescue-related tasks, including screwdrivers, Allen wrenches, socket sets, open-end and boxed wrenches, ratchets, drivers, assorted pliers, hammers, handsaws, hammers, chisels, punches, and cutters. The following are examples of some of these tools and how they are often used in aircraft rescue and fire fighting:

- *Dzus fastener key* — screwdriver-like tool designed for tightening or removing dzus fasteners

- *Screwdrivers* — used to open access panels secured with Dzus and other screw type fasteners; recommended that personnel carry screwdrivers, which also may be very helpful in pulling out the handle on a flush-mounted operating lever or for other tasks

- *Pike poles* — useful for pushing and pulling operations such as holding open doors on cargo aircraft; either conventional or specialized crash poles

- *Rescue tool assembly* — equipment typically carried on a rescue belt or in a tool roll: a V-blade harness-cutting knife, linemen pliers, vise grips, rubber mallet, fuel line plugs (hardwood and neoprene), flashlight, hatchet, and other small tools

- *Axes* — used to make holes for inserting the tips of hydraulic spreaders during forcible entry: on almost all commercial aircraft, holes may be made with an axe; a variety are used, but at least one should have a serrated face and insulated handle **(Figure 8.3)**

- *Sledge Hammers* — assists in setting prying tools into position for opening some doors and hatches; with the advent of enhanced flight deck security, may be needed to assist in making entry in many new types of doors

- *Metal cutting saws (hacksaws)* — useful in cutting metal on aircraft

- *Assorted prying tools* — standard crowbars, wrecking bars, and other types of pry bars can be used for leverage and for bending and prying objects; can also be used to force open doors and hatches on light-construction, nonpressurized aircraft

- *Harness-cutting knife* — used to cut seat belts, parachute straps, and webbing **(Figure 8.4)**; usually has a V-blade

- *Cable cutters* — used primarily to sever cables, small hoses, and metal tubing

- *Dearming tool* — used to sever gas-initiator lines and safety some ejection seats, making it safer for personnel to work near them **(Figure 8.5)**

- *Wire and bolt cutters* — useful during aircraft rescue; at least one set should have the capacity to cut up to 0.38 inch (.965 cm) diameter hardened steel bolts

Figure 8.5 A firefighter practices using a de-arming tool to cut an ejection system hose on an ejection seat trainer. *Courtesy of Tinker Fire and Emergency Services.*

- ***Ballistic Parachute Cable Cutter*** — used to cut the cables on ballistic parachute systems
- ***Grappling hook and rope sling*** — used for catching, dragging, and lifting objects

Power Tools

Power tools used during ARFF operations may be gasoline powered, electrical, hydraulic, or pneumatic. Gasoline powered saws are powered by internal combustion engines running on gasoline or a gasoline/oil mixture. Electrically powered tools use stored energy from a battery or convert electrical energy into mechanical energy through an electric motor. Hydraulic tools have pumps that produce and transmit pressure through a liquid (hydraulic fluid) to the working end of the tool. Hydraulic pumps are either hand-operated or powered by gasoline-driven or electric motors. Pneumatic tools use either an air compressor or stored pressurized air to transmit energy to the working end of the tool. Pneumo-hydraulic devices combine both air and liquid force in an air-driven hydraulic pump that generates power for operating the tool. While these power units are safer to use in flammable atmospheres, they are not widely used.

The section that follow describe various saws, drills/drivers, spreaders/cutters, and pneumatic (air) tools used in ARFF rescue operations.

Saws

Power saws commonly used in ARFF operations may include circular saws, rescue saws, chainsaws, and reciprocating saws that are electrical or gasoline-powered. Saws used for aircraft forcible entry operations should be equipped with blades that are capable of cutting metal. Circular saws should be rated heavy-duty and be capable of cutting a variety of materials. Similarly, rescue saws also should be rated heavy-duty and have several 16 inch (41 cm) blades capable of cutting a variety of materials. On large-frame aircraft, personnel may need to use large blades in order to penetrate the fuselage. Many different types of reciprocating saw blades are available. ARFF personnel can use these types of saws and blades in tight quarters or in areas that are difficult to access.

CAUTION

ARFF personnel must be aware of the aircraft construction in order not to cut in areas of the aircraft that may create safety hazards for the rescuers or passengers.

A full assortment of rotary saw blades should be carried for the various types of cutting that may be required. Common types of cutting blades are multipurpose or composite, carbide- and diamond-tipped, and serrated. Blades should be color-coded with a legend clearly posted on the compartment or carrying case to ensure that the proper blade for a designated task can be easily identified. Blades from different saw manufacturers should not be used interchangeably.

Composite blades can wear out quickly, chip, or become pinched on rounded aircraft fuselages because the angle of the cut is constantly changing. Rotary saws are the tool of choice for rapid, clean cuts. Drawbacks to their use include excessive noise and the possibility of sparks when the blade contacts ferrous metals (steel and iron). Blades made of metal should be inspected to ensure cutting or chipping teeth on the blade are present and sharp. Metal blades with missing or dull teeth should be replaced.

All rotary saw blades and surfaces being cut must be simultaneously cooled with a water spray during long cutting operations, such as making an opening for entry. This cooling helps prevent the aluminum being cut from melting and fouling the cutting surface.

If it is not possible to cut all the way through the fuselage structure, an aircraft firefighter should make parallel cuts a few inches wider than the saw guard. Then, as much of the material between the cuts as possible should be removed. Finally, the saw should be inserted into the gap to finish the cut.

Reciprocating saws have a straight blade that moves rapidly back in forth in an action similar to a hand saw. Many types and sizes of blades are available for cutting different types of materials. They are very useful for cutting aircraft skin and structural members. When considering the speed with which a reciprocating blade can make a given cut, a firefighter should remember a simple rule: the heavier the gauge of metal, the slower the cut. A wide variety of metal cutting types and adequate replacements should be available. Reciprocating saws are more controllable, lightweight, and can be used while working from a ladder or confined spaces. A spray bottle applying water and soap during cuts will help the blades to last longer and cut faster than without its use.

Drills/Drivers

Another tool used by ARFF personnel is the drill/driver, which can be battery-powered/electric or pneumatic. When used with a socket drive, they may be used to open a variety of compartments by removing rivets, screws, or nuts and bolts. Rescue workers should use caution not to exceed the recommended revolutions per minute (rpm) of the tool when accessing these compartments, or they may damage the opening mechanisms.

Spreaders/Cutters

Hydraulically operated tools may be used for spreading or forcing apart structural members of an aircraft during extrication operations. The hydraulic pressure can be produced either manually through a hand pump or through a power unit (usually either a gas-driven engine or a pneumatic or battery powered/electric pump. Because these tools are so versatile in their application, they are highly recommended for airport fire departments.

Electric/battery powered, pneumatic, or gasoline-powered hydraulic spreaders and cutters commonly used in auto extrication also have some application in aircraft incidents. Spreaders are primarily used for prying, pushing,

CAUTION

Hydraulic spreaders may project metal fragments in all directions during rescue operations. In addition, some hydraulic tools are heavy and may need to be operated by two rescue personnel.

In flammable areas, rescue workers should consider using hydraulic spreaders and cutters because they do not produce sparks (as opposed to an electric power unit or a gas-driven unit). They also do not produce the type of noise that is associated with a gas-driven unit.

or crushing. With the proper grab hooks and chain accessories, they can also be used for pulling. Spreaders can produce thousands of psi (kPa) pressure at the tips and spread up to and over 30 inches (76 cm). Because spreaders tear aircraft skin as opposed to cutting, personnel may need to make a hole in the aircraft skin between structural members for the tips of a spreader. Sometimes the aircraft skin will roll up or orange-peel ahead of the spreading tips, or the aircraft fuselage metal may be brittle. A technique for quickly opening a large hole in the side of an aircraft is to use a hydraulic spreader in tandem with a hydraulic cutter. As the spreader is used to tear a progressive cut in the skin, hydraulic cutters are used to reach through the cut and sever the structural members underneath.

Figure 8.6 A SPAAT tool ready for use.

Pneumatic (Air) Tools

ARFF personnel may perform numerous cutting tasks with pneumatic (air) tools such as an air chisel (or air hammer) during aircraft rescue operations. An air chisel may be powered by compressed air from a breathing apparatus cylinder, from a compressor or cascade system, or from an air system on ARFF vehicles. An air chisel cuts by applying thousands of short-distance impacts per minute against a metal object. Different tips are available. The relatively light weight and compact size of an air chisel allow the firefighter to use it from a ladder. Air chisels can also be used to chip out some rigid plastic windows.

Another air powered tool is the hand held Skin Penetrating Agent Applicator Tool (SPAAT) used to apply agent to the interior of an aircraft **(Figure 8.6)**. Air pressure drives the SPAAT tools pointed, hollow spike through the aircraft's skin. Once the spike is through the skin, agent flows through the spike and exits through jets or holes near its point. The agent sprays out of these jets in all directions applying the agent into the aircraft's interior.

Lifting and Pulling Tools and Equipment

It is often necessary to perform lifting and pulling tasks to free trapped victims or to gain access to an interior. Rescue and fire fighting personnel should be familiar with all types of tools that can perform these functions. The sections that follow discuss the more common lifting and pulling tools and equipment.

Truck-Mounted Winch

The use of a truck-mounted winch in the aircraft rescue and fire fighting environment is somewhat limited. However, a truck mounted winch can be critical in certain situations such as the following:

- When a piece of wreckage needs to be moved quickly in order to gain access to an area
- When an aircraft or component needs to be stabilized
- When assistance is need to force (such as pulling a door open)

Come-Along

A come-along provides much the same application as the truck-mounted winch, only this device is more portable. Using a ratchet and pulley, a come-along maximizes a lever's pulling ability. The come-along is anchored to a secure object, and the cable or chain is run out to the object to be moved. Once both ends are attached, the lever is operated to pull the movable object toward the anchor point. The most common sizes or ratings of come-alongs are 1 to 10 tons (907 kg to 9 072 kg).

Rope

The use of ropes in the fire service is widespread, and its applications are well-known. In the aircraft rescue and fire fighting environment, the applications are the same. The primary uses include pulling, lifelines, anchoring, rigging, stabilization, movement of tools and equipment (hoisting and lowering), and creating barriers (crowd control). Consult the IFSTA **Essentials of Fire Fighting** manual for more information on the use, application, and care of ropes.

Chains

Chains are used primarily in conjunction with other devices or tools. They are often used to extend the distance for lifting and pulling operations (for example, they can be attached to the spreaders of a hydraulic rescue tool). Chains are stronger than rope and are more suitable for some applications. Steel alloy chains, are resistant to abrasion, and recommended for rescue work. The appropriate sized chain must always coincide with the load being moved or the task being performed.

Webbing

Webbing is usually made of strong synthetic fibers such as nylon that are woven to form flat or tubular strands of varying widths and lengths. Webbing is easily carried by individual ARFF personnel and can be used in confined environments. Commonly used for personnel applications, such as seats or slings, this versatile tool should be carried by all ARFF personnel. An 8- to 10-foot (2.5 m to 3 m) length can be carried in the pocket of turnout gear for easy accessibility. Rope, chain, and webbing also can be used to suspend tools and lights when working inside an aircraft.

Pneumatic Lifting Bags

Pneumatic or air lifting bags are versatile devices that are easily applied to rescue and aircraft stabilization work. Lifting bags transmit the force of compressed air, usually supplied by compressed-air cylinders, throughout the surface of the bag. Although working pressure does not exceed 200 psi (1 400 kPa), the pressure is multiplied over every square inch (centimeter) of the bag, producing enough force to lift or displace enormous objects that cannot be lifted with other lifting equipment.

WARNING!

Operate any truck-mounted winch in accordance with the manufacturer's recommendations. Failure to follow such specifications as the maximum weight limits may cause the winch to fail, injuring or killing the operators or personnel in the immediate area. ARFF personnel should always wear full protective clothing to include gloves and eye protection during winching operations.

Air bag systems consist of an air supply, pressure regulator, controller with relief valve, hoses, and the bag. Gauges are usually provided on the regulator and controller to monitor air pressures. Hoses come in various lengths and colors. System connections are usually fitted with dual-locking, quick-disconnect fittings. Sometimes the regulator may frost up due to condensation caused by the expansion of the compressed air. Pneumatic lifting bags have a wide variety of applications in extrication operations. They can be inserted into openings that are too small for other lifting equipment, and they are relatively quick and easy to use. However, their use is not without some risks. ARFF personnel should follow the manufacturer's safety recommendations when using pneumatic lifting bags. Cribbing should always be used to back up operations utilizing pneumatic lifting bags to prevent collapse should the lifting bag(s) fail.

There are three basic types of lifting bags: high pressure, medium pressure, and low pressure. A fourth type of bag that may be used by ARFF personnel is useful for sealing leaks.

High-Pressure Air Bags. High-pressure bags are constructed of neoprene rubber reinforced with either steel wire or Kevlar® aramid fiber and have a rough, pebble-grained surface to improve purchase. Before inflation, the bags lie virtually flat and are about 1 inch (25 mm) thick. They come in various sizes that range from 6 x 6 inches (150 mm x 150 mm) to 36 x 36 inches (914 mm x 914 mm). The range of inflation pressure of the bags is about 116 - 145 psi (812 - 1 015 kPa). Depending on the size of the bags, they may inflate to a height of 20 inches (500 mm). The largest bags can lift approximately 75 tons (68 040 kg). An air bag's weight-lifting capacity decreases as the height of the lift increases and its maximum lift capacity is generally rated at one inch (50 mm) of lift. For example, a bag rated at 10 tons (9 072 kg) only lifts 5 tons (4 536 kg) to 8 inches (203 mm); one rated at 75 tons (67.5 t) only lifts 37 tons (33.3 t) to 20 inches (508 mm). To ensure the maximum, safe lift, cribbing or another suitable base should be used to position the bag as close as possible to the underside of the object to be lifted. The bag must be protected from possible punctures by placing a protective mat or a piece of conveyor belt material between the bag and the object.

Low- and Medium- Pressure Air Bags. Low- and medium-pressure bags are considerably larger than high-pressure bags and are most commonly used to lift or temporarily stabilize large vehicles or objects **(Figure 8.7, p. 256)**. Their primary advantage over high-pressure air bags is that they have a much greater lifting range. They are also safer than stacking high-pressure bags, and they are easier to repair.

Low- and medium-pressure lifting bags do have the following disadvantages, however:

● Each bag is capable of lifting less weight than a high-pressure bag

● Require twice as much space for insertion between the base and the object being lifted

● More vulnerable to puncture than high-pressure bags

● Do not operate the same as high pressure bags

● Cannot lift a load straight up on their own

● Must have a base or foundation point

Figure 8.7 Air bags can be very helpful during aircraft emergency operations. *Photo provided by Hurst Jaws of Life.*

Depending on the manufacturer, a low- or medium-pressure lifting bag may be capable of lifting an object 6 feet (2 m) above its original position. Low-pressure bags generally operate on 7 to 10 psi (49 kPa to 70 kPa), while medium-pressure bags use 12 to 15 psi (84 kPa to 105 kPa), depending on the manufacturer.

Leak-sealing Bags. Along with their accompanying hardware, leak-sealing bags are designed to be inserted into cracks or holes in low-pressure liquid storage containers or in the open ends of pipes. These bags are constructed much like high-pressure bags but are designed to be inflated at a much lower pressure, usually around 25 psi (175 kPa).

Jacks

Portable jacks can be used for lifting and stabilizing objects. They include screw, ratchet-lever, and hydraulic types. Screw jacks can be extended or retracted by turning a threaded core. Trench screw jacks can be extended up to 6 feet with 2 inch steel pipe. Ratchet lever jacks are also known as high lift jacks. These medium-duty tools are the least stable of all the jacks. They can collapse and the ratchet mechanism can fail under a heavy load. Rated for up to 20 tons or more, a hydraulic jack can be used for heavy lifting operations or as a compression device for shoring and stabilizing operations. Any type of jack should be used on a flat, level footing in conjunction with cribbing. On soft surfaces, a flat board or steel plate should be placed under the jack to distribute the force.

Lighting and Electrical Equipment

During night operations it can become critical to provide additional lighting to carry out tasks safely. The importance of readily available lighting and electricity cannot be overstated. ARFF personnel should know how to quickly set up portable lighting as well as how to operate all lighting sources on the apparatus. When new portable lighting, electrical tools, and generators are purchased, firefighters should ensure that their receptacles match and that their adapters are readily available before being placed in service.

Care should be taken to avoid using portable lighting equipment in a flammable atmosphere as it could provide a source of ignition. Personnel should also use caution to recognize the dangers associated with electricity and practice the necessary safeguards because this equipment often is used in a wet environment. Safety tips that ARFF personnel should follow when working around electricity include the following:

- Maintain a safety zone around the generator, electrical cords, and lighting.

- Guard against electrical shock.

- Treat all wires as "hot" and being of high voltage.

- Use only approved devices in good working condition.

- Wear full protective clothing, and use only insulated tools.

- Exercise care using ladders, hoselines, or equipment near electrical lines and appliances.

- Ensure that all cords and devices have the proper ground wire and are connected to GFCI outlet.

- Do not touch any tool, equipment, or apparatus that is in contact with electrical wires because body contact will complete the circuit to ground resulting in electrical shock.

- Do not drape cords across fences, metal guardrails, or through water or foam.

The sections that follow discuss electrical and lighting equipment that are integral to successful execution of ARFF duties.

Electric Generators

Portable electric generators with floodlights may be used to illuminate forcible entry and rescue points on an aircraft. These generators may also be used to operate electric chain saws, circular saws, reciprocating saws, and various other power tools. Generators that are mounted on apparatus should be removable to allow the generator to be transported to limited-access areas. Generator receptacles should be equipped with ground fault circuit interrupters (GFCI) to prevent electrical shock when working around water. Electrical couplings should be water tight to prevent water or moisture build up within the receptacle contacts.

Portable Lights

Portable lights should be readily available to the airport fire department. Using lights on apparatus does not always provide the direct lighting necessary for interior operations or other areas remote (and perhaps inaccessible) from apparatus. Portable lights and associated equipment, such as cords and stands, should be carried to emergencies, along with a generator having enough capacity to provide power to lights and to any other electrically operated tools and equipment.

Vehicle-Mounted Lights

Most modern ARFF apparatus are equipped with a variety of lighting installed on the apparatus. It is common to see high-powered floodlights mounted in the front of apparatus to light up large areas during approach and subsequent operations. Most apparatus also have side- and rear-mounted lights. Elevating or extending lights can provide additional lighting.

Extension Cords

Extension cords will be needed to provide power to portable equipment. The most common sized cord is a 12 gauge, 3 wire type. Electrical cords may be stored in coils or on reels. Reels can be portable or fixed mounted on apparatus. Electrical cords should be waterproof, have adequate insulation, and have no exposed wires. Junction boxes may be provided with multiple outlets. Outlets should be provided with approved ground-fault circuit interrupters. Outlets can be 3 prong, twist lock, or U-ground. Adapters may be needed to accommodate different types of electrical plugs.

Flashlights

Adequate portable flash lights should also be available. There are a wide variety to choose from. Some have their own stands. Others can be mounted on helmets and other head gear. Some require batteries, while others can be kept in readiness by an apparatus mounted charging unit. Adequate spare batteries and bulbs should also be available. Colored lens attachments are available for using flashlights for marshaling aircraft and other signaling functions.

Other Equipment

There are many other tools, equipment, and devices that can be applied to the aircraft rescue and fire fighting function. The use and applications are limited only by the need, creativity, and the initiative of ARFF personnel. Some of the more common types of other equipment needed to perform ARFF operations are detailed in the sections that follow.

Plugs

Plugs made of wood or rubber are used to plug leaking lines such as fuel lines and hydraulic fluid lines. Rescue crews in most jurisdictions carry a wide variety of shapes and sizes of plugs to ensure that a suitable one is available when needed. Adjustable plugs are available also.

Figure 8.8 ARFF personnel need to become familiar with the use of pins for safetying landing gear and other aircraft components. *Courtesy of Doddy Photography.*

Pins and Other Locking Devices

Some fire departments carry landing gear pins or other devices that can be used to lock and prevent the movement of landing gear assemblies **(Figure 8.8)**. Some military aircraft, especially fighters, have a wide variety of pins for securing guns, canopy jettison systems, seat ejection systems, emergency power units, and other hazardous systems. Munitions safety pins act as a way of securing the aircraft's weapons from accidentally activating while on the ground.

Salvage Covers

Salvage covers may be used to cover jagged openings in order to prevent injury to personnel and passengers. Different-colored salvage covers may be used to designate collection points for equipment and triaged casualties.

Ladders

All types of ladders (ground and aerial) are used for the passage of personnel to and from elevated sections of an aircraft **(Figures 8.9)**. Personnel should consider laddering the leading edge of the wing, all doors, and other access points.

Figure 8.9 ARFF personnel using ladders to gain access to an aircraft's interior by going over a wing. *Courtesy of Doddy Photography.*

Thermal Imaging Cameras (TIC)

Thermal imaging cameras have proven very useful in ARFF operations in the detection of hidden fires and the location of trapped aircraft occupants. Where they are available, ARFF personnel should be trained in the proper use and maintenance of thermal imaging cameras to ensure the devices are used correctly and function properly during an aircraft incident. There are two types of thermal imaging cameras, vehicle mounted and portable (**Figure 8.10**).

Cribbing and Shoring

An adequate assortment of appropriately sized cribbing should be available. It is usually used to stabilize or support an object or load. It should always be used to back up any lifting operation. Wood used for cribbing should be a hardwood, solid, straight, and free of flaws, knots, or splits. The most common sizes are 2 x 4 and 4 x 4, in 18 inch (50 cm) lengths. Except for the ends, wooden cribbing should be left unpainted to prevent slipping when wet. Cribbing can be stacked in apparatus compartments or stored in crates. Plastic cribbing, wedges, blocks, step chocks, and interlocking crib systems can also be purchased.

Figure 8.10 Thermal imaging cameras can be very helpful in identifying the location of an interior aircraft fire.

Power shoring and strut systems are available for stabilizing and supporting unstable and collapsing aircraft wreckage. They either use hydraulic or pneumatic power. Most can be manually put together and extended in varying lengths and with an assortment of footing devices. They have minimal lifting ability and usually can only support loads.

Figure 8.11 A large, vehicle mounted fan unit used for ventilating smoke from an aircraft.

Fans and Blowers

Portable fans may be carried on ARFF apparatus. Some departments have purchased large fan units mounted to heavy trucks for use during aircraft emergencies **(Figure 8.11 page 259)**. Fans may be used to cool hot aircraft brakes and wheels. Another use for these fans is for forced air mechanical ventilation and smoke removal. Fans can be driven by electric, gasoline, or water powered motors.

Cutting Torches

Often overlooked because of the ignition hazard, cutting torches are a rescue tool that could be used in limited applications at aircraft incidents. They are a last resort tool when other options have failed.

Summary

ARFF personnel utilize a wide variety of hand tools and power tools at emergency scenes. All ARFF personnel should be well trained with the tools they will be using. ARFF departments should accurately assess what tools they are likely to need before an incident and ensure that all necessary tools are easily accessible and in working order at all times.

ARFF personnel should always use tools safely and in accordance with the manufacturer's instructions. A special safety consideration for tool use in an aircraft emergency is flammable conditions. Airport firefighters must ensure that their use of power tools and hand tools does not contribute an additional ignition source that might ignite any pooled fuel, leaking fuel, or flammable environments at an aircraft incident.

Lastly, ARFF personnel should understand the safe usage of all portable electrical and lighting equipment needed in ARFF operations. Avoiding electric shocks and preventing electrical equipment from presenting an additional ignition source are measures about which all ARFF personnel should remain vigilant.

Review Questions

1. Into what groups can aircraft rescue tools be divided?
2. What types of tools can be used to stabilize an aircraft?
3. What is an equipment resource pool?
4. Discuss several common hand tools and their uses.
5. When might the use of a reciprocating saw be helpful?
6. How may an air chisel be powered?
7. How is webbing used?
8. What is an advantage of low- and medium-pressure air bags?
9. Discuss several safety tips that aircraft rescue and fire fighting personnel should follow when working around electricity.
10. What is the purpose of a plug?

Driver/Operator

Chapter Contents

chapter 9

Key Terms

NFPA® references for Chapter 9:

NFPA® 1003 (2010)
5.1.1.3
5.1.1.4
5.2.1
5.3.3
5.3.6
5.3.9

**NFPA® 1002
(2009 - Chapter 9)**
9.1.1
9.1.3
9.2.1
9.2.2
9.2.3

Driver/Operator

Learning Objectives

After reading this chapter, students shall be able to:

1. Discuss apparatus inspection and maintenance procedures. (NFPA® 1003, 5.1.1.3)

2. Describe principles of safe vehicle operation. (NFPA® 1003, 5.3.3, 5.3.6)

3. Discuss ARFF vehicle operational considerations. (NFPA® 1003, 5.3.3, 5.3.6)

4. Discuss agent discharge. (NFPA® 1003, 5.3.3, 5.3.6)

5. Discuss resupply. (NFPA® 1003, 5.3.3, 5.3.6, 5.3.9)

6. Describe auxiliary systems and compressed-air foam systems. (NFPA® 1003, 5.3.3, 5.3.6)

Chapter 9
Driver/Operator

Case History

In the mid-1980s, the fire department at Williams Air Force Base received its first Oshkosh P-19 ARFF vehicle to begin the replacement of the aging Oshkosh P-4 vehicles. The United States Air Force sent a mobile training team to conduct a series of vehicle driver/operator classes on the operation of the P-19. Soon after the first group of students graduated, the P-19 was dispatched to its standby position for an in-flight emergency. Responding quickly, the driver executed a sharp right-hand turn at a high rate of speed. The four wheeled vehicle rose on its left tires, wobbled, then settled back on all four tires. Other than scaring the crew (and other responders on the scene), no injuries occurred and the vehicle was not damaged.

The following lessons were learned from this near miss:

- Initial training classes had focused on vehicle familiarization and low speed driving skills. Later classes incorporated more emergency vehicle operations training and hands on driving skills
- Given the situation that day (and on many other occasions), it was not necessary for the driver/operator to drive so fast
- Given the high center of gravity on most ARFF apparatus, driver/operators should make wider turns

An ARFF apparatus driver/operator is responsible for safely transporting firefighters and apparatus to and from the scene of an emergency or other call for service. Once on the scene, the driver/operator must be capable of operating the apparatus properly, swiftly, and safely. A driver/operator must also ensure that the apparatus and the equipment it carries are ready at all times. The driver/operators of ARFF vehicles have the monumental tasks of locating downed aircraft quickly, applying fire suppressants to enhance life safety, and exercising agent conservation **(Figure 9.1, p. 266)**. Driver/operator responsibilities will sometimes grow even larger because a driver/operator may be the only firefighter assigned to an ARFF apparatus.

To perform their duties properly, all driver/operators must meet the requirements established by their respective jurisdictions. In addition, NFPA® 1002, *Standard for Fire Apparatus Driver/Operator Professional Qualifications,* sets minimum qualifications for driver/operators. In particular, Chapter 9 of this standard references ARFF apparatus driver/operators. It requires any driver/operator who will be responsible for operating an ARFF vehicle to also meet the requirements of NFPA® 1001, *Standard for Fire Fighter Professional Qualifi-*

Figure 9.1 ARFF driver/operators positioning their apparatus during a major aircraft incident training exercise.

cations, for Fire Fighter II. For more information on the general qualifications for driver/operator, refer to the IFSTA **Pumping Apparatus Driver/Operator Handbook**.

The driver/operators of ARFF apparatus should also complete any additional training and acquire any special licenses or permits required by the jurisdiction for airfield driving operations. ARFF driver/operators should obey all airfield traffic regulations and observe all airfield security procedures when entering or exiting the airfield or restricted areas.

In general, driver/operators must be mature, responsible, and safety conscious. Because of their wide array of responsibilities, driver/operators must be able to maintain a calm, can-do attitude during stressful emergency situations. Psychological profiles, drug and sobriety testing, and background investigations may be necessary to ensure that a driver/operator is ready to accept the high level of responsibility that comes with the job.

This chapter discusses duties and responsibilities of an ARFF driver/operator, including inspection and maintenance, safe vehicle operation, agent discharge, and familiarization with auxiliary systems and equipment.

Apparatus Inspection and Maintenance

ARFF vehicles are expected to respond to and operate at accidents/incidents on a moment's notice and without delay. A complete apparatus inspection and maintenance program helps keep vehicles in top operating condition at all times.

Each department should have an SOP for the inspection and maintenance of its vehicles. The purpose of this section is not to teach the ARFF firefighter how to inspect the vehicle but rather to teach the importance of a systematic approach to the department's inspection and maintenance program.

The safe and efficient operation of ARFF apparatus will depend in part, on the operator's ability to not exceed the limitations and safety factors of the vehicle design. Driver operators should complete an in-depth study of the operator's manual and have a thorough knowledge of the operating instructions, safety precautions, unit capabilities, and limitations. Vehicle operator's

Table 9.1
Contents of Apparatus Reference Manuals

Manual	Contents	Instructions	Illustrations
Operator	All information required for safe operation of vehicle components, firefighting systems, and integral vehicular options	Descriptions of the vehicle, special equipment, daily maintenance checks, troubleshooting problems, recommended lubrication	Locations and function of all controls and instruments
Service	Repair and overhaul instructions, operating hours, mileage, cycle times; contains an index	Repair and troubleshooting, adjustment procedures, minor and major repairs, overhaul, repair and replacement of assemblies component disassembly and reassembly	Wiring diagrams, special tools needed for overhaul and repair
Parts	Illustrations identifying parts, assemblies, and subassemblies; contains an index	Description and quantity of each item used per vehicle; size, thread dimensions, and special characteristics on all nonstandard nuts, bolts, washers, grease fittings, and similar items.	Illustrations of parts, assemblies, and subassemblies; fully referenced with numbers and parts lists

manuals will have apparatus data, inspection checklists, lubrication charts, and troubleshooting guides. A driver/operator should learn the location of each control, switch, instrument, and gauge, as well as its function and operation. For more information on what is contained in various ARFF apparatus reference manuals, refer to **Table 9.1**.

The sections that follow cover general inspection procedures and safety, and the inspection and testing of foam, dry chemical, and clean agent systems.

General Inspection Procedures and Safety

Each department must create a plan for inspecting its vehicles according to the manufacturers' requirements and the needs of the department. For more details of a model inspection program, see Chapter 3 of the IFSTA **Pumping Apparatus Driver/Operator Handbook**.

The main reason for vehicle inspection is to make sure that the vehicles operate properly when they are needed. Another good reason for daily vehicle inspection is to keep the driver/operators skilled at operating the vehicle. The more practice they have operating their vehicles, the more proficient they are when operating at the scene of an emergency.

Inspection programs greatly differ among departments. A department that rarely uses its vehicles does not need a program requiring inspections as frequently as those of active departments. A daily inspection includes checking all engine fluid levels, checking fire fighting agent levels, setting the mirrors and safety equipment appropriately for the person operating the vehicle, and performing an operational test to make sure the vehicle performs normally **(Figure 9.2 a–d, p. 268)**. All problems should be passed on to the proper authorities to ensure that they are corrected before the vehicle is placed back into service.

Figure 9.2b Checking the extinguishing agent tanks for proper agent level is another ARFF driver/operator task.

Figure 9.2a An ARFF driver/operator checking the oil level and condition for his assigned vehicle's engine. *Courtesy of Doddy Photography.*

Figure 9.2c This firefighter is assisting an ARFF driver/operator by adjusting the angle of one of the apparatus' mirrors.

Figure 9.2d ARFF driver/operators should conduct an operational check of the vehicle's fire fighting systems in accordance with the department's policies.

For airports having only the vehicles required to maintain their operational status, it is a serious concern when a vehicle goes out-of-service due to maintenance problems. A program should be in place to ensure that vehicles are operational and ready at all times so that aircraft will not have to be diverted from the airport because of insufficient protection levels.

Corrosion Control

Cleanliness promotes longer vehicle life. ARFF vehicles should also be washed when returning to the station after off road operation, when used in inclement weather (rain and snow), or anytime abnormally dirty **(Figure 9.3)**. The following guidelines should be followed to ensure vehicles are clean at all times:

- Wash apparatus and rinse thoroughly on a regular basis, usually weekly.
- Wash inside, outside, top, and bottom of the apparatus as needed.
- Use a mild soap to remove dirt and grease.
- Pay particular attention to the wheel wells and undercarriage.
- Rinse and chamois the vehicle dry.
- Periodically blow down the vehicle with compressed air and clean compartments, removing any water.
- Wax the vehicle and steam clean the chassis and undercarriage as necessary.

Figure 9.3 An ARFF apparatus undergoing a routine cleaning.

Inspections must be carried out safely as well as frequently. The following guidelines will ensure safe, injury-free inspections of ARFF apparatus:

- Stop all engine and accessory operations when cleaning, adjusting, servicing, or checking, except when the operation is required for adjustments.
- Chock vehicle wheels.
- Use nonflammable solvent for cleaning that will not damage component parts.
- Keep hands, feet, and loose clothing away from belts, pulleys, and drive shafts when the engine is running.
- Do not smoke while refueling, servicing the fuel system, or working with the batteries.
- Remove rings, watches, and other metallic objects, which may cause shock or burn hazard. Snagged finger rings and watches have caused many serious injuries.
- Wear protective clothing (gloves, apron, eye protection, etc.) approved for the materials, procedures, and tools being used.

Figure 9.4 An example of a foam proportioner on an ARFF vehicle. *Courtesy of Doddy Photography.*

Foam System Inspection and Testing

ARFF apparatus foam systems differ in capacity, application methods, and proportioning systems **(Figure 9.4)**. Inspection of these systems on a daily basis usually consists of making sure that the agent tank is full. At least annually, the inspection includes testing the foam proportioning system to ensure that the appropriate ratio of foam concentrate and water is being discharged from the vehicle. Improper foam concentrate proportioning may result in either one of two problems:

- The foam-to-water mixture may be too lean (not enough foam concentrate in the foam/water solution). This will reduce its extinguishing ability and cause the foam blanket to drain sooner than desired, so the foam blanket will not last as long.
- The foam concentrate may be too rich (too much foam concentrate in the foam/water solution). This will cause expensive and limited available quantities of foam concentrate to be wasted.

NFPA® Standard 412, *Standard for Evaluating Aircraft Rescue and Fire-Fighting Foam Equipment*, allows two methods to be used for testing a foam proportioning system for calibration accuracy:

- Foam solution refractivity testing
- Foam solution conductivity testing

Personnel should follow the apparatus manufacturer's recommended procedures for conducting this testing.

> **NOTE:** Some foam manufacturers recommend simple foam concentrate field tests (agent film quality test) in their engineering manuals.

Foam Solution Refractivity Testing

Foam solution refractivity testing is performed using a device called a *refractometer* to test the quality of a foam solution after the foam proportioning system has created it. This test method is recommended for protein- and fluoroprotein-based and Film Forming Fluoroprotein (FFFP) foam solutions. It is not accurate for synthetic-based foams because they typically have a very low refractive index reading. The conductivity test method can be used for all foams, but is recommended for synthetic-based foams.

When testing proportioning equipment that can be operated at more than one setting, such as an in-line eductor that has 3% and 6% settings, three samples will have to be taken for each proportion and separate charts prepared for each. Refer to NFPA® 412 for procedures for conducting foam testing. Samples of the actual foam solution the system produces should be taken from each pre-connected hose line, turret, and other type foam discharge device for testing. Each discharge device should be adequately flushed with plain water prior to taking a sample. The devices should flow foam at least 30 seconds before sampling to get good representative samples. These samples are tested on the refractometer and then plotted on a graph **(Figure 9.5)**. The results must fall within the parameters identified in the appropriate FAA and NFPA® standards.

Figure 9.5 An ARFF driver/ operator preparing to perform a refractometer test. *Courtesy of John Demyan, LVI Airport.*

Foam Solution Conductivity Testing

Foam solution conductivity testing is used to check the quality of synthetic-based foams that foam proportioning equipment and systems produce. Because synthetic-based foam concentrates are a very light color, the refractivity tests previously discussed are not very accurate for them. Conductivity testing does not rely on the colors of the foam, but rather on their ability to conduct electricity to verify their actual composition.

Conductivity is the ability of a substance to conduct an electrical current. Even though distilled water does not contain enough dissolved solids to conduct electricity, water from domestic water systems and static sources do. Therefore, water used for fire fighting and foam concentrate both conduct electricity. When proportioning foam concentrate into water, the conductivity of the resulting foam solution is somewhere between the figures for plain water and foam concentrate. These figures can be used to measure the amount of foam concentrate in the solution.

There are three methods of performing conductivity testing on foam solution: direct reading conductivity testing, conductivity comparison testing, and conductivity calibration curve testing.

Direct Reading Conductivity Testing. A direct reading conductivity meter directly measures the specific conductivity of a solution and provide a reading on a display. The readout on this meter may or may not indicate the actual percentage of foam concentrate in the solution.

To perform this test, the meter must first be zeroed using plain water. This procedure can be done in either one of two ways:

1. Collect a sample of the water that will be used in the test in a container and immerse the sensor head to zero the meter.

2. Mount the sensor directly into the pump discharge line and zero the meter while flowing water.

Once the meter has been zeroed, obtain a sample of foam solution from the proportioning system. As with the water, a reading may be obtained in either a container or the meter may be mounted directly to the pump discharge. Once the sensor is immersed in the solution, a reading should be taken from the meter. If the meter does not give readings in percentage of foam concentrate in solution, the reading must be plotted on a graph (calibration curve) to get the final results.

Conductivity Comparison Testing. The procedure is fairly simple. First, a reading is taken from the plain water that is to be used for the test. Next, a reading is taken from the foam solution produced by the system being tested. The percentage of foam concentrate in the solution can then be determined using the following formula:

$$\% \text{ of concentrate in solution} = (\text{Conductivity of solution} \div \text{conductivity of water})$$

Conductivity Calibration Curve Testing. *Conductivity calibration curve testing* is performed by using a handheld, temperature-compensated conductivity meter. A calibration curve is developed following the same guidelines as those for refractivity testing. However, in this case the readings will be taken using the conductivity meter. A conductivity meter may need to be calibrated (zeroed) with the apparatus tank water prior to tests. To perform the test, a driver/operator dips the conductivity meter probe into the solution and notes the digital scale reading.

Temperature-Compensated Conductivity Meter — Device designed to measure the conductivity of a solution; it adjusts for conductivity variances at different temperatures.

> **NOTE:** Do not allow foam bubbles to collect on the probe.

Once a calibration curve has been developed, samples of foam solution from the proportioning equipment being tested may be taken and analyzed. The readings from these tests are then plotted on a calibration curve to determine the percent of concentrate in the solution. The tank water may also be contaminated with foam concentrate. The manufacturer's operator's manual will have information on correcting data due to contamination.

It is also possible for the foam concentrate tank contents to be contaminated as well. This is also usually caused by the check or non-return valve in the foam concentrate piping, which prevents a backflow of concentrate or pump water, not seating properly. Refer to the manufacturer's operator's manual to correct this problem. If there is a suspected problem with the tested foam concentrate, then the foam manufacturer should be contacted. Most manufacturers will laboratory test and evaluate a sample of concentrate sent to them.

References on Foam Testing

For more detailed information on foam system testing, including compressed air foam systems, consult Chapters 21 and 22 of NFPA® 1901, *Standard for Automotive Fire Apparatus*. IFSTA's **Pumping Apparatus Driver/Operator Handbook** and **Principles of Foam Fire Fighting** manual also contain detailed information on foam system testing.

Foam Handline Inspection

One other foam system inspection concern is the handline delivery method used for the department's vehicles. Some types of handline delivery are 1½-inch or 1¾-inch (38 mm or 45 mm) hoselines, booster reels, and multiagent handlines. It is important to follow normal maintenance, care, and reloading procedures for these hoses **(Figure 9.6)**.

Figure 9.6 ARFF personnel inspecting a handline. *Courtesy of Doddy Photography.*

Dry-Chemical System Inspection and Testing

On dry chemical systems, the cylinder pressure should be monitored during normal apparatus checks **(Figure 9.7, p. 274)**. The cylinder should usually be replaced or recharged when the pressure is below 1750 to 1,500 psi (12 066 to 10 342 kPa) (per manufacturer's instructions). Pressure in the cylinder can vary with changes in the temperature. Existing pressure readings may have to be adjusted using the temperature correction chart.

Dry chemical is usually added to an agent tank using a funnel and the following filling and safety instructions:

- Wear a dust mask or other respiratory filter when handling dry chemical agent.

- Fill the tank to the manufacturer's rated capacity.

Figure 9.7 A routine pressure check of the dry chemical system's charging cylinder.

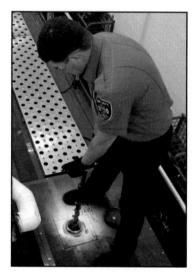

Figure 9.8 A driver/operator fluffing the agent in a dry chemical tank. *Courtesy of Tinker Fire and Emergency Services.*

WARNING!

Firefighters have been killed from improperly servicing pressurized systems. Always follow the manufacturer's instructions whenever servicing any pressurized system.

- Clean fill opening threads and gasket seating surface.
- Examine the gasket for cuts, wear, and elasticity.
- Reset the indicator on top of the tank fill cap, if there is one.

The cylinder shipping cap should always be in place when removing or installing a cylinder. Some manufacturers offer an apparatus mounted davit and winch to raise and lower cylinders from the top of the apparatus.

Testing a dry-chemical system is expensive and time-consuming. The only way to ensure that the system functions correctly is to activate the system on some sort of time schedule. System manufacturers recommend set safety procedures to follow when returning dry-chemical systems to service. Firefighters must not deviate from these procedures.

After a vehicle is driven over a period of time, the dry chemical can begin to settle and pack tightly inside the container. Because of this settling, older dry-chemical systems may require agent fluffing on a regular basis to loosen the dry chemical. Fluffing involves inserting a device (usually made of metal) into the storage cylinder and agitating the chemical **(Figure 9.8)**. Wooden devices are not recommended as they could splinter and block the agent delivery system. Stirring should be done carefully to avoid damaging the agent piping and the internal tank parts.

Humid environments can also contribute to settling due to the high moisture content in the atmosphere at the time the dry-chemical tank is serviced. Servicing under humid conditions can cause the agent to cake and not work properly.

Checking dry-chemical handlines is also important. Handlines should be completely blown out after every use to keep the agent from blocking the hoses and rendering the system useless. Personnel should follow the manufacturer's recommendations when blowing out the hoses and returning the hoses to hose reels.

Clean-Agent Extinguishing System Inspection

Clean agents are usually stored in pressurized vessels on the ARFF apparatus and, like dry-chemical, may be dispensed using other gases such as argon or dry nitrogen. These agents are dispensed through handlines which are part of the clean-agent system mounted on the vehicle. These systems require very little inspection other than checking the agent level, the pressure of expellant gas, and the condition of the handline hose. Because of the high gas pressures involved when servicing these systems, personnel should follow the manufacturer's procedures to the letter.

Principles of Safe Vehicle Operation

After learning a vehicle's capabilities, a driver/operator must take the time to learn how to safely operate the vehicle. ARFF vehicles are larger and heavier than structural fire apparatus and can be dangerous if operated by untrained personnel. Even previously trained drivers may require additional instruction.

NFPA® 1002, *Standard for Fire Apparatus Driver/Operator Professional Qualifications*, Chapter 9, describes required driving skills for the ARFF driver. It is suggested that the operators review these skills and also those that apply to the ARFF driver/operator in the IFSTA **Pumping Apparatus Driver/Operator Handbook**.

Figure 9.9 An ARFF driver/operator practicing driving through a serpentine course. *Courtesy of Doddy Photography.*

NFPA® 1002 specifies a number of practical driving exercises on an obstacle course that the driver/operator candidate should be able to successfully complete before being certified to drive the apparatus **(Figure 9.9)**. The standard requires that driver/operators be able to perform these exercises with each type of apparatus they are expected to drive. Some jurisdictions prefer to have driver/operators complete these evaluations before allowing them to complete the road test on the airport operations area. This ensures that driver/operators are competent in controlling the vehicle before they are allowed to drive it in public.

Personnel who are to drive and operate ARFF apparatus should successfully complete an emergency vehicle operations course (EVOC). Such courses are offered by numerous agencies across the United States and provide the driver/operator with training in techniques that include but are not limited to:

● Vehicle braking and reaction time

● Vehicle rollover awareness and avoidance

● Skid avoidance, control, and recovery

● Safe acceleration and decceleration

Before Leaving the Station

Safe vehicle operation begins before even leaving the fire station. A driver/operator and occupants must wear seat belts! Seat belts do save lives. All heavy objects in the vehicle cab must be secured. A loose piece of equipment such as a portable radio can become a projectile in a vehicle collision. Personnel should take the time to find a place to secure and store these items within the vehicle.

Making sure vehicle safety equipment is set for the driver/operator is important also. Taking the time to adjust the mirrors, seats, steering column, and radio volume can help avoid a collision.

Braking Reaction Times

Driver reaction time can best be described as the time it takes the driver/operator to react to a situation. Reaction time has a direct bearing on braking an ARFF vehicle when quick decision making is necessary. Knowing the braking characteristics of a vehicle can prevent a serious collision. When added to other factors like ice, snow, and water, the friction is reduced under the tires, which makes the vehicle braking even less effective. A driver/operator must be able to react safely and brake safely keeping in mind all adverse conditions and the stopping distance of the vehicle he or she is driving.

Total stopping distance has three component parts: perception distance, reaction distance, and braking distance. The equation used to describe total stopping distance is

$$\text{Perception Distance} + \text{Reaction Distance} + \text{Braking Distance}$$
$$= \text{Total Stopping Distance}$$

Perception distance is the distance the vehicle moves from the time the driver's eyes see a hazard until the driver's brain acknowledges the hazard. The perception time for an alert driver is about ¾ of a second. At 55 mph, a vehicle can travel 60 feet in ¾ of a second. Reaction distance is the distance traveled from the time the driver's brain tells the foot to move from the accelerator until the foot is actually pushing the brake pedal. The average driver has a reaction time of ¾ of a second. At 55 mph, this adds another 60 feet traveled. Braking distance is the distance it takes to stop the vehicle once the brakes are applied. At 55 mph on dry pavement, with good brakes, a heavy vehicle will take 170 feet and 4¾ seconds to stop after the brakes are applied. Thus, at 55 mph, it would take about six seconds to stop and the vehicle would travel about the distance of approximately 290 feet (88 m).

Covering the brake in questionable driving situations can reduce reaction distance and total stopping distance. This consists of removing the foot from the accelerator pedal and holding it over the brake pedal without applying pressure. It may give you that extra edge when a sudden stop may be needed. Be an active operator, ready to react.

Avoiding Rollover

ARFF vehicles have a tendency to rollover due to several factors, one of which is a higher center of gravity than other types of vehicles. Driver/operators must remember that when making a turn onto a taxiway, a 1,500-gallon (6 000 L) four-wheel-drive ARFF vehicle reacts differently than a pickup truck. The water tank is typically on or above the main vehicle frame rails. If the weight is quickly thrown in one direction when the driver/operator oversteers a corner, the vehicle is at risk for rolling over.

Another way of explaining ARFF rollover is to understand the concept that an object in motion tends to stay in motion at a constant velocity unless acted upon by an unbalanced force. This principle holds true when making sharp turns with ARFF vehicles at high rates of speed. If the weight of the vehicle is thrust quickly in one direction, the momentum of that weight will continue in that direction unless an equal or greater force stops it. If the momentum is greater than the resistance posed by the vehicle suspension system, then the

Figure 9.10 A lateral acceleration indicator (LAI) on the dashboard of an ARFF vehicle.

vehicle is likely to overturn. When driver/operators who have experienced vehicle rollovers are asked to recount details of these incidences, they typically remember making a turn but never seem to know at what point the vehicle started to roll.

All new vehicles purchased with FAA funds require a Lateral Acceleration Indicator (LAI) device that indicates to the driver/operator the attitude of the vehicle when making a turn. The driver/operator should take the time to reference this device to better understand the forces the vehicle receives when making a turn **(Figure 9.10)**.

The best way to prevent a rollover is to understand the characteristics of the vehicle — know where the weight is and how the vehicle reacts when making a turn. The more things placed on ARFF vehicles, the heavier they become. This added weight can contribute to the vehicle's reaction during turns at high speeds. The driver/operator should know the vehicle's load factors and drive according to what is safe for that vehicle.

Speed and Centrifugal Force

Speed affects several important factors in driving an ARFF vehicle. When a vehicle is driven in a straight line, its speed has a direct impact on the required stopping distance. Simply put, the faster the vehicle is driven, the longer it will take for it to be brought to a safe stop.

Speed also impacts a vehicle's ability to be turned. The faster a vehicle moves, the more centrifugal force is exerted when the vehicle is turned. As centrifugal force increases, so do the chances of the vehicle overturning if the force exceeds the capabilities of the vehicle suspension system to resist the force. Driving too fast for conditions is a major cause of accidents. Speed is a factor in these accidents and responsible for fatal road accidents.

Conditions are constantly changing so a driver must be able to adapt. The speed of an ARFF vehicle should be reasonable and proper with due regard for actual and potential conditions or hazards. Controlling speed requires constant attention to changing conditions such as type of area, road surfaces, weather, light, site distance, other vehicles, and the physical condition of the vehicle and the driver.

Those airports that rely on emergency access roads for responding to aircraft emergencies must understand what speed and centrifugal force mean to ARFF vehicles. Hopefully, these roads will be engineered to reduce the hazards created by speed and centrifugal force.

Skid Avoidance

Avoiding a skid is sometimes difficult because ARFF vehicles not only are heavy but also travel at high speeds and require a very long distance to stop. In poor weather conditions, avoiding a skid is even more difficult. To avoid a skid, a driver/operator must know the vehicle stopping distances in normal driving conditions. Understanding a vehicle's braking reactions on dry surfaces can help a driver/operator perceive how the vehicle will react when braking on wet or frozen surfaces. Another way is for personnel to take the time to train under the types of adverse conditions commonly encountered in their jurisdiction. This does not mean finding an icy patch on an airfield, racing toward it, and attempting to control the vehicle; this means starting really slowly and then testing the brakes and steering. Understanding how the vehicle reacts under training conditions can pay off in emergency driving conditions.

Avoiding conditions that lead to skidding is as important as knowing how to correct skids once they occur. A skid happens whenever the tires lose their grip on the road. By far the most common skid is one in which the rear wheels lose traction through excessive braking or acceleration. Rear wheel skids occur when the rear drive wheels lock resulting in a loss of directional control. Locked wheels have less traction than rolling wheels, so the rear wheels usually slide sideways in an attempt to catch up with the front wheels. The vehicle will tend to slide sideways into a spin out. Disengaging the brake will let the rear wheels roll again and keep them from sliding any further. When a vehicle begins to slide sideways, a driver should steer into the skid. As the vehicle turns back on course, the driver may have to countersteer carefully to prevent a skid in the opposite direction.

Most front wheel skids are caused by driving too fast for conditions. Lack of tread or not enough weight on the front tires can also cause a front wheel skid. The front end tends to go in a straight line regardless of how much the driver turn the steering wheel. The only way to stop a front wheel skid is to let the vehicle slow down.

When water collects on a road, a vehicle can hydroplane. Hydroplaning is a condition in which directional control is partially or totally lost because of water on the roadway. It is caused when the tires lose contact with the road surface and have little or no traction. Braking and steering may not be possible while hydroplaning. Releasing the accelerator should allow a driver to regain control of the vehicle. When hydroplaning, the brakes will not help the vehicle decelerate. It does not take a lot of water to cause hydroplaning. It can occur at low speeds. Hydroplaning is more likely to occur if the tire pressure is low or the tread is worn **(Figure 9.11)**.

Hydroplaning — Condition in which moving tires (automobile or aircraft) are separated from pavement surfaces by steam and/or water or liquid rubber film, resulting in loss of mechanical braking effectiveness.

Figure 9.11 An illustration of how hydroplaning occurs.

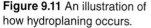

Acceleration/Deceleration

In order to maintain proper control of a vehicle, a driver/operator must first understand the effects of acceleration and deceleration on vehicle control. When responding to an emergency, a driver/operator's main concern is to arrive safely and as quickly as possible. However, a driver/operator must remember that he or she is driving a heavy vehicle moving at speeds of up to 60 miles per hour (97 km/h); these large ARFF vehicles require longer stopping distances than do passenger vehicles driven at the same speed. The driver/operator should anticipate the actions of the vehicle and accelerate accordingly when responding to emergencies.

Another concern of over-acceleration and excessive deceleration is the burden this places on the vehicle engine, transmission, and braking systems. The cost associated with maintaining these systems can be high if drivers do not properly operate vehicles. As usual, when in doubt about the safe operation of ARFF vehicles, personnel should follow the manufacturer's recommendations.

Shifting and Gear Patterns

Most modern ARFF vehicles are equipped with automatic transmissions. Automatic transmissions are far more efficient than manual transmissions and allow the operator to concentrate on driving rather than shifting while responding to emergencies. However, some of the other vehicles used to deliver ARFF services may be equipped with manual transmissions. It is important to learn the proper techniques for operating the vehicles with manual transmissions. Off road operations call for much slower speeds and use of lower gear ranges. For more information on driving vehicles with manual transmissions, see the IFSTA **Pumping Apparatus Driver/Operator Handbook**.

ARFF Vehicle Operational Considerations

Most driving occurs under normal driving conditions. Driver/operators should begin to learn safe vehicle operations in normal conditions, so when faced with adverse surface conditions, such as ice and snow, they are better prepared to deal with these situations.

On the Airport

The majority of driving performed by driver/operators of ARFF vehicles is done while on the airport property. The ARFF driver/operator must be very familiar with all aspects of the airport layout, including taxiways, runways, ramp areas, and service roads. Aircraft parking areas present special challenges to the driver/operator because of the various activities and obstacles that are found there. These include taxiing aircraft, fuel trucks servicing aircraft, ground handling equipment, airline personnel, and, in some cases, airline passengers.

WARNING!
ARFF driver/operators should NEVER, under any circumstances, drive under the wing of a parked or moving aircraft. Doing so places the ARFF crew and vehicle in great danger.

Structural Capability

Some ARFF vehicles are designed with structural fire fighting systems, which allow the vehicle to operate in a structural fire fighting mode. This has become popular with departments who anticipate making interior attacks with their vehicles and fighting structural fires on the airport. Each manufacturer has a different design for its vehicle's structural fire fighting system. The driver/operator should take the time to learn about the vehicle's structural fire fighting capabilities.

Safe operation of the ARFF vehicle is paramount in these situations. Driver/operators must move through these areas with a watchful eye. Many of these dangers may seem to jump out in front of a driver/operator who is not paying attention. Driver/operators should spend enough time driving around the aircraft parking ramps to have a comfortable feel of what to expect while responding to emergencies.

Probably one of the most important driving situations is the route taken when responding to emergencies. Unlike structural firefighters, ARFF crew members do get advanced warning of emergencies from time to time. Predesignated response routes are given for reaching standby parking positions along the runways. The driver/operator must know the route without having to look at a map or without thinking about the best route to take when responding. While situations may change frequently, the majority of responses to the runway standby positions seldom change. Driver/operators should know how to safely enter these areas while working with the air traffic ground controllers, and they should remember that these routes are not designed for making high-speed turns and movements like on highways. ARFF driver/operators should allow ample time to brake and safely corner when responding to emergencies.

Loose or Wet Soil

Beadlocks — Device that secures the bead of a tire to the rim.

Operating on soil and in poor weather conditions are factors that each driver/operator may face when responding to emergencies. Each driver/operator must know the off-road capabilities of his or her vehicle. Tire diameter, width, inflation pressure, and deflection are important elements. Tires can be deflated to improve off road driving. Immediately re-inflate tires to the proper pressure, when returning to hard surfaces and normal driving conditions. Never drive at emergency response speeds with partially deflated or uneven tire pressures. Low inflation pressures also increase the likelihood of hydroplaning on flooded pavements. If tires will be operated at low pressures, beadlocks are recommended.

Advances have been made to improve vehicle handling and operation in off-road conditions. One of these advances is the Central Inflation/Deflation System (CIDS). The CIDS is a system that allows the vehicle operator to deflate the tires to increase the traction surface. This also helps keep the tire tread from filling with mud/dirt and decreasing traction. These systems use an onboard air compressor and are controlled in the vehicle cab. Many airports have chosen this system to help deal with poor off-road conditions.

In rough terrain, safety restraint systems keep the driver behind the wheel and in control. Driver/operators should take the following precautions to ensure safety operations in rough terrain:

- Wear seat and shoulder belts at all times.
- Do not wrap thumbs around the steering wheel because it may jerk suddenly due to tires contacting objects or sudden terrain changes.
- Consider locking the doors and wearing a helmet.
- Secure loose objects, especially in the cab, before driving in off pavement areas.
- Consider having someone walk ahead and guide the apparatus through questionable areas **(Figure 9.12)**.

- Stop the vehicle, get out, and check questionable areas yourself if you are by yourself and unsure.

- Look at conditions before leaving the hard surface and consider the following questions:

  — Has it rained recently?

  — Is the grass green or brown? Color changes may indicate patches of moisture.

- Avoid freestanding water.

- Maintain a steady speed and keep the wheels straight.

- Keep driving if you star losing traction.

- Stop only if you are stuck or need to position the vehicle; stopping for no reason usually results in the vehicle needing to be pulled free of mud, sand, or soft soil.

- Keep headlights and windows clean for maximum visibility.

Parking a vehicle in off-road conditions also requires special precautions such as the following:

- Turn around and stop, facing the way you will be leaving.

- Consider getting out and checking an area before backing into it.

- Make sure there is adequate ground support.

- Walk around vehicle for one last check before leaving it.

Mud and clay type soils can fill the tire tread and significantly reduce traction. The operation of the vehicle in mud is very similar to sand. A driver/operator should take the following actions for successfully navigating muddy or sandy terrain:

- Maintain movement with the least amount of strain on the vehicle, engine, and power train.

- Increase speed going uphill and reduce speed going downhill.

- Consider locking the differentials anytime there are anticipated traction problems or the vehicle must leave the hard surface.

- Maintain a steady and even rate of movement.

- Keep the transmission in one of its lowest ranges and avoid shifting if possible .

- Anticipate and try to avoid difficult spots .

NOTE: The ability to negotiate in mud or sand satisfactorily will come only through experience.

The road, surface, terrain, load, or traffic conditions may make it desirable to restrict the automatic transmission shifting to a lower range. The lower the gear range, the greater the engine braking effect. When climbing a hill or going down a steep grade, shifting the transmission to a lower gear provides adequate driving power and enables the driver to keep the apparatus under control. Gear range 2 is usually used for vehicle speed control up or down steep grades, or other uneven, unusual, or undesirable road conditions. When driving on slippery conditions, such as ice, snow, or mud, any acceleration or deceleration should be made gradually.

The first gear range of an ARFF vehicle automatic transmission is the creeper gear, used for slow, severe load and grade operations, off-road conditions, and pulling through mud and snow. It provides the greatest traction and engine braking action. No up-shift will occur in this position. Drivers should shift into and out of first gear only when the vehicle is stationary. Manually shifting while the vehicle is moving should only be done in gear ranges 2 through 5.

Driver/operators must also understand how to safely return to normal driving after regaining normal traction, for example, when leaving off-road conditions and returning to a hard surface. The following practices allow for the safe transition from off-road to on-road driving:

- Disengage the accelerator, then disengage the differential locking switch; it may be necessary to slowly back-up in order to disengage the system, due to excessive driveline windup.

- Stop and inspect the vehicle, especially under carriage, drive train, axles, wheels, lug nuts, brake lines, firefighting system plumbing and tires for damage.

- Remove mud, stones, or other potential foreign object debris (FOD) before driving on the airport operating area (AOA) **(Figure 9.13)**.

- Make sure all equipment is secure.

Steep Grades
Manufacturers design all major ARFF vehicles to function on steep grades. This does not mean the vehicle can be driven the same as on flat ground. The vehicle's center of gravity changes when it is climbing up and down steep grades. If forced to operate the vehicle on a steep grade, a driver/operator should be extremely cautious and not make sudden changes in direction. Other factors such as mud, snow, or generally poor surface conditions may present an additional safety issue, adding to the danger of operating on these grades. Most apparatus operator's manuals will identify grade-ability, the ability to ascend or descend a specific grade.

Figure 9.13 After driving an ARFF vehicle off-road, the tires should be checked for foreign objects prior to driving on the airport operating area (AOA).

An operator's manual may also identify the vehicle's obstacle climbing ability and side slope stability. Apparatus specs should also address "angle of approach" which is the steepest ramp that a fully loaded vehicle can approach. The "angle of departure" is the steepest ramp from which a fully loaded vehicle can depart. A driver/operator must practice driving assigned vehicles to become acquainted with each vehicle's limitations.

Vehicle Clearance of Obstacles

One of the major contributing factors to a vehicle getting stuck while operating off-road is its catching on something underneath it. ARFF vehicles are designed to allow for maximum ground clearance whenever possible. This, however, does not prevent the vehicle from catching on debris beneath the vehicle. The operator must know the ground clearance of the vehicle and learn to visualize objects to determine if they can be traversed. One way to practice this skill is to set up objects that will not harm the undercarriage of the vehicle, and then cross over them to gain a better understanding of the vehicle's capabilities. Knowing this will help the driver/operator decide whether or not the vehicle may clear objects in its path.

In addition to objects in the roadway, ARFF driver/operators should be able to traverse abrupt changes in surface elevation such as ditches and gullies. The following guidelines should assist drivers when traversing such hazards:

- Cross shallow ditches by using low gear ranges and proceeding slowly.
- Enter the ditch obliquely so that one wheel leaves the ditch as the other wheel on the same axle enters it.
- Use the differential locks if the ditch is deep and use of the locks is advisable.
- Accelerate enough to keep the vehicle rolling after reaching the bottom of a ditch so that the vehicle has enough forward momentum to climb the far side.

Gullies and ravines are natural formations caused by running water. Gullies tend to be deeper than ditches, but many of the previously mentioned guidelines apply to traversing gullies. The following are special considerations for crossing a gully:

- Look these formations over carefully before crossing, in order to pick a good place to cross and ensure the vehicle can get across.

- Approach slowly, in low gear, differential locks engaged, and at a right angle to the edge.

- Ease the front wheels into the gully by using the brakes, being careful to have them strike the bottom at the same time.

- Increase speed when the wheels hit the bottom and accelerate enough to climb when the front wheels touch the opposite bank.

Whether or not a vehicle can effectively and safely cross ditches, gullies, or ravines depends on the depth, width at the top, and top edges. A good driver will wisely judge whether or not his or her vehicle can successfully navigate a given ditch, gully, or ravine; if there is significant doubt of success, then an alternate route should be found. Sometimes it is better to take a little longer to get to a scene, than to risk getting stuck or damaging an apparatus.

Drivers should also proceed slowly in the rocky terrain usually found in gullies. They should also drive around larger obstacles rather than try to "straddle" rocks and risk getting an apparatus stuck on an obstruction.

Limited Space for Turnaround

Many taxiways and aircraft parking areas provide limited space for turning a very large ARFF vehicle. One important lesson to learn during training is the amount of space it takes to turn an ARFF vehicle around. A driver/operator must be capable of visualizing the vehicle's turning radius. By setting out traffic cones or some other nondestructible objects and driving around them, a driver/operator can learn the vehicle's steering pattern. The confined space turnaround exercise required by NFPA® 1002 is also excellent for giving a driver/operator experience in making these maneuvers.

Side Slopes

A serious concern when driving the ARFF vehicle is choosing the correct angle of attack when approaching a steep side slope. A vehicle should be designed to traverse a side slope when operating off-road. A driver/operator not only should know the vehicle's capability of approaching a side slope but also should be able to visualize the approach to a ditch or ravine. How the driver/operator operates on the side slope affects the center of gravity. Rather, he or she should approach side slopes at an acute or sharp angle to reduce the effect on the vehicle's center of gravity. The following actions should help drivers navigate a side slope safely:

- Avoid side-hill situations whenever possible.

- Move extremely slowly to avoid sudden surface changes caused by rocks, bumps, or other terrain features.

- Keep the wheels on the uphill side of the road when driving on a road.

- Steer downhill towards the direction of the slide if the vehicle begins to slide.

- Do not get over confident in a side-hill situation.

Changes in slope are not always apparent and can appear suddenly. The vehicle is more likely to slide when encountering green grass or soft soils.

Depressions, bumps, rocks, and low tire pressures can throw a vehicle on its side. Turning uphill puts weight on the downhill wheels, making the vehicle even more unstable.

Backing a Vehicle

Because the driver cannot see everything behind the vehicle, backing is always dangerous. A driver should avoid backing whenever possible. When stopping or parking, a driver should attempt to stop so the vehicle can pull forward when it is time to move it. When backing is the only option, take the following safety precautions:

● Look at the path or the line of travel.

● Get out and walk around the vehicle if driving alone.

● Back as slowly as possible to correct any steering errors before the vehicle is too far off course.

● Back in the direction that provides the best visibility .

● Use a guide when available and when ever possible, during emergency operations and always during routine operations **(Figure 9.14).**

● Position a second guide at the front of the vehicle on the opposite side of the backing guide if one is available.

A driver is ultimately responsible for backing the vehicle, even with a guide. A driver should always be able to see the guide. A driver should stop backing if he or she loses sight of the guide. Backing can continue when the guide is again in view of the driver.

Similarly, a guide should not leave his or her position until the driver signals. The driver must keep the window rolled down, on the side the guide is on, in order to hear. The guide can also use a portable radio to talk to the driver via the apparatus radio. At night all available lighting, such as vehicle back up lights and rear mounted flood-lights, *should be used* to illuminate the guide.

ARFF apparatus should be equipped with an alarm system that warns others while the vehicle is backing up. Some are equipped with backing sensors

Figure 9.14 A firefighter serving as a spotter as the driver/operator backs an ARFF vehicle into the station. *Courtesy of Doddy Photography*

Figure 9.15 An airfield can look quite different and very confusing at night.

Figure 9.16 An ARFF driver/operator using the night vision screen on the vehicle's dash to check ahead of the vehicle.

that beep louder or faster in the cab as the rear of the vehicle gets closer to an object in its path. A few ARFF vehicles are equipped with rear-mounted video camera that shows a visual cab display of the backing path. Reference points, such as lines painted on the station apron or target marks on the back wall of the apparatus floor are helpful for backing into the fire station garage.

Night Driving

After dark, the airfield appears far different from how it does during the daylight hours. The surfaces of roads, taxiways, runways, and grassy areas, normally visible during the day, become difficult to see and the multitude of lights of various colors lining these areas can be confusing **(Figure 9.15)**. Each driver/operator should access the airfield at night and practice finding his or her way around. Just as pilots practice instrument landings and flying while using only instrumentation, an ARFF driver/operator should practice driving using the driver's enhanced vision system (DEVS) or Forward Looking Infra-Red (FLIR) system on a regular basis. This practice should be performed under driving conditions similar to those they may encounter in adverse weather and in darkness **(Figure 9.16)**.

Off-Airport Responses

Because aircraft accidents can and do occur off of the airport, ARFF driver/operators should be trained and prepared to drive and operate their vehicles under conditions found off-site. ARFF personnel should study the streets and roads around the airport to identify routes that might be used to reach various off-site locations. Street and road layouts, widths, and traffic/parking conditions are critical items of information that can affect the response of large ARFF vehicles. Because of their large size, ARFF vehicles may have limited clearance on one or both sides on off-airport roads or in heavy traffic. Placing a small label listing the vehicle height, weight, and width above the windshield in front of the driver may be a simple way to remind personnel of the limitations of the ARFF Vehicle. Vehicle speed, braking, and maneuvering must be adjusted to the road and traffic conditions to ensure that ARFF vehicles do not cause an accident during a response.

The height and weight limits of bridges surrounding the airport will also influence the selection of off-site response routes. Many ARFF vehicles are quite tall and the addition of roof turret systems increase the risk of striking

Instrument Landing — Landing an aircraft by relying only upon instrument data; may be due to inclement weather or other factors.

overhead obstacles, particularly on low bridges. Also, because of the large volume of water and foam carried by many ARFF vehicles, these vehicles are extremely heavy and may exceed the weight limits for local bridges.

Adverse Environmental or Driving-Surface Conditions

Adverse environmental conditions are commonly contributing factors in delayed ARFF responses to aircraft accidents/incidents. Heavy rainfall, blinding snowfall, fog, smoke, and darkness cause visibility to be diminished and slow the response to an emergency. In such conditions, it can be difficult to see an aircraft that has no lights or that is not burning. Driver/operators must use extreme caution when approaching a suspected accident/incident site to avoid accidentally striking downed aircraft, debris, or people who are fleeing or who have been thrown from it.

Knowing the possible location of the accident/incident helps the driver/operator take the best route, and keeps the responding vehicle out of harm's way. Driver/operators should use all their senses when responding in poor visibility, including slowing down and opening windows to listen for any strange noises.

One more very important part of navigating the route across an airfield is to be very familiar with the layout. Airfield familiarization training during daylight hours will help driver/operators find their way in low-visibility conditions. In addition, knowing the runway and taxiway marking and lighting systems will help driver/operators find their way in poor lighting conditions.

Maneuvering and Positioning ARFF Vehicles on the Accident/Incident Scene

Personnel must consider what they may encounter and what to do when they arrive on scene. Each accident/incident is different. A driver/operator must be alert to the conditions found when arriving on site so as not to further harm any passengers or crew members.

The following guidelines apply to positioning and apparatus:

- Do not get locked into trying to protect a large fuselage and spill fire from a single, parking spot.
- Do not position based solely on tradition or department procedures.
- Position and apply agent based on the situation.
- Do whatever is necessary and move wherever is needed to extinguish all of the fire.

The sections that follow describe emergency scene factors that ARFF driver/operators need to consider during their response.

Wreckage Patterns

The factors that determine the wreckage pattern include direction and speed on impact, weather conditions, size of aircraft, type of crash (high-impact or low-impact), and location of the crash site. Different types of terrain have different effects on the wreckage pattern also.

In addition, the wreckage itself causes problems for personnel approaching the accident/incident site. They should be prepared to find large debris, victims, fire, and hazardous materials. Having some information about the wreckage patterns themselves can provide some insight into the dangers to expect. Aircraft runways and taxiways do not have speed bumps. If an ARFF vehicle is encountering bumps when approaching an emergency scene, the unfortunate truth may be that the bumps are pieces of wreckage or debris, perhaps even victims. Drivers should approach slowly as they near a scene and use a spotter to guide them in whenever possible.

Survivors

When responding to an accident/incident, a driver/operator must always consider where survivors may be found. If the passengers and crew are capable of escaping the aircraft on their own, many of them will be out of the aircraft before the first ARFF units/emergency vehicles arrive. Victims who have escaped on their own will tend to move toward approaching, emergency vehicles which could put them in harms way just when they think they are moving toward safety. Some departments have taken on the practice of deactivating the emergency lights so that the survivors do not move towards their vehicles. When operating powerful turrets, the driver/operator must remember to not directly hit any victims with the stream. At night it may be difficult to spot victims. Personnel should use whatever means possible to light the scene with auxiliary light equipment when working at night.

Aircraft occupant evacuation will also affect the positioning apparatus. Cabin crews are trained to determine outside conditions before opening doors and not utilize exits directly threatened by fire. Unless it is the only option, most people will not try to escape through a fire. Usually, evacuation will be underway at the least threatened exit points, which tend to be on the upwind areas of the aircraft.

Evacuating persons and the aircraft must be protected and isolated from any fuel spill fire. Intact wing fuel cells also need to be protected to prevent additional fuel release and intensification of the fire. The fuel spill fire threatening the aircraft should be controlled within one minute after arrival of ARFF.

Terrain

The type of terrain where an accident/incident occurs definitely affects the driver's approach to the aircraft. Many airports are situated away from metropolitan areas, near mountain regions, at the edge of a body of water, or even in the middle of a city that has grown around the airport. These terrain factors add to the difficult task of positioning the ARFF apparatus. It is important for personnel to be familiar with the terrain of the airport and nearby areas.

> **NOTE:** When positioning at a downed aircraft, stay uphill, upwind, and upstream of the accident/incident site as long as the terrain allows.

Terrain at an incident scene presents some or all of the following problems:

- Mud
- Steep inclines
- Lack of access roads to accident/incident site
- Water crossings
- Poor bridges
- Rocky/hilly areas

All these elements can delay response and make operations very difficult. The key to handling problems with terrain, once again, is anticipating problems and being thoroughly familiar with the airport and surrounding areas.

Agent Discharge

Effective agent application has a definite effect on the outcome of an accident/ incident fire. The driver/operator must be familiar with the extinguishing agents and their characteristics and how to apply them effectively to extinguish fires. Driver/operators should pay particular attention to agent management, effects of wind, and the reach, penetration, and application limitations of ARFF vehicles.

Agent Management

In continuous mass application, most ARFF foam apparatus will exhaust their agent capacity in approximately 90-120 seconds. Unnecessary or ineffective foam application should also be avoided because foam is not good for the environment. The days of hurrying to an aircraft, dumping everything, and racing wildly back to resupply are long gone. A driver/operator must have a thorough familiarization of the agents being used and know how to manage their use. This may be particularly important for personnel working a crash site that is removed from the airport and where resupply may be difficult. Further information regarding extinguishing agents can be found in Chapter 6, Extinguishing Agents, of this manual and in IFSTA's **Essentials of Fire Fighting** or **Principles of Foam Fire Fighting** manuals.

The most important aspect associated with agent management is knowing how much of each agent is carried on each apparatus and what the realistic fire fighting capabilities of that amount of agent are. By training in lifelike scenarios, ARFF driver/operators should be able to develop a sense of the capabilities their vehicles possess **(Figure 9.17, p. 290)**. This training will allow the driver/operators to make good judgments on how and where to use the agent during true emergency conditions. Some general guidelines for agent conservation are as follows:

- Do not waste agent during the approach.

- Get close enough to effectively utilize turrets and reach the fire; if the apparatus is positioned too far away, agent will fall short of the fire and be wasted.

- Utilize the proper turret pattern or flow to get the most amount of agent on the fire.

- Do not overshoot or undershoot the fire.

- Use low flow at close range if an apparatus has dual flow capabilities.

Effects of Terrain and Wind

Just as terrain affects vehicle approach to an aircraft incident, it also affects agent application. If the terrain does not allow an uphill set-up on aircraft, then agent must be applied from a downhill position. This affects the reach of the fire streams and places the crew and apparatus at risk should fuel and the fire spread down the slope from the aircraft. Other terrain factors may prevent direct application of agent by the apparatus turrets and require handlines to be pulled to the site of the fire.

Figure 9.17 ARFF personnel practicing agent application and management during a training evolution.

Similarly, wind has detrimental effects on all types of fire streams. Because airports are wide-open spaces, they tend to be windier than more built-up locations. When discharged into or across the prevailing winds, the agent stream will be broken up and its reach considerably shortened, especially when applying dry chemical or clean agents. These agents are so lightweight that wind easily disperses them and carries them away. Systems that inject the dry chemical into the water/foam stream discharged from a handline or turret can decrease the effect that wind has on dry chemical.

Being directly upwind obviously allows the greatest discharge distance. The more downwind an ARFF vehicle is located, the closer it must be to a fire to successfully apply agent to that fire. Because foam bubbles are being used to extinguish and blanket the fire, the least desirable position for ARFF units is directly downwind. Directly upwind is the best position while 90 degrees or perpendicular to the wind will still work. Again, all fire threatening the entire fuselage needs to be extinguished, so ARFF units may have to work in varying wind directions. The wind will also tend to push the fire. Most of the fire and heat will be at the downwind side of the fuselage. Also, in many low impact crashes, due to wing impact damage and the forward.

Reach, Penetration, and Application

Each major ARFF vehicle has certain characteristics that allow that particular vehicle to achieve a certain agent-application rate, pressure, and distance. A driver/operator must understand the agent-application capabilities of a vehicle. Knowing the vehicle's turret reach allows the driver/operator to judge its effective range and keep the vehicle at a safe distance. If the vehicle gets too close, it could be damaged and possibly catch fire.

The driver/operator must be able to determine how the agent will affect the fire and, as discussed earlier, will have to make sure the agent is actually reaching the fire and extinguishing it. Discharging the agent a few seconds at a time can best do this. This allows the foam to work and spread across the burning fuel and conserves agent.

Each vehicle turret has specific capabilities. The specific gallons (liters) per minute, pressure, and turret location drive these capabilities on the vehicle. Some vehicles are equipped with an extendable turret; this turret has a much farther reach than the conventional roof turret. The extendable turret also has the ability to attack the fire from lower positions and to place the agent closer to the base of the fire, reducing the effects that fire has on breaking up the foam as it is applied.

Application Techniques

Each driver/operator must develop a technique for operating the vehicle's fire fighting systems. One of the most difficult systems to operate is the roof/bumper turret. Reaching the fire with the agent is very important for obvious reasons, but doing so is a skill that requires practice. Because foam must be discharged in order to learn for actual emergencies, environmental concerns can make frequent training difficult.

One way to learn the vehicle's reach is by setting up a course using a traffic cone and a softball. The softball is placed on the traffic cone, and the driver/operator makes "attacks" on the cone in an attempt to use fire stream to knock the ball off the cone. It takes a skilled driver/operator who knows the vehicle's turret reach and control to knock the ball off the cone. By practicing drills such as these, driver/operators can develop their techniques for operating the turrets.

Pump-and-Roll Capability

One feature of all major ARFF vehicles is the ability to pump and roll (sometimes called "modulating") — driving towards a fire and after engaging the fire fighting system, begin fire attack. Pump-and-roll takes practice to gain the skills needed to effectively fight fire **(Figure 9.18, p. 292)**. The movement of the vehicle can make turret control difficult. Once again, practice makes perfect. Each day, morning checkout is a good time to practice pumping-and-rolling by picking a target and attempting to hit it while on the move.

Resupply

The most common agent resupply need during ARFF operations is the need to refill major ARFF vehicles with water because all ARFF apparatus have foam concentrate tanks large enough to produce foam for several tanks of water. For example, an ARFF vehicle with a 200-gallon (800 L) foam concentrate tank and a 1500-gallon (6 000 L) water tank and using 3% foam concentrate uses four tanks of water for each tank of foam concentrate. Because this large amount of foam is useless without a steady supply of water, water resupply is one of the most important factors to ARFF operations **(Figure 9.19, p. 292)**.

Figure 9.18 ARFF personnel practicing pumping-and-rolling. *Courtesy of Edwin A. Jones, USAFR.*

Figure 9.19 An ARFF vehicle being resupplied with water during a training exercise. *Courtesy of Doddy Photography.*

Foam concentrate resupply can be as easy as filling a few gallons (liters) of foam from 5-gallon (20 L) containers or using foam tenders to fill the ARFF vehicles. Each department needs to devise a resupply system that fits its needs. Some departments have central supply points around the airport in order to cut back on the travel time for refilling foam concentrate.

Dry Chemical and Clean Agent Supply

Unlike systems with foam concentrate and water, it is generally not practical to resupply ARFF apparatus dry-chemical or clean-agent extinguishing systems during the course of an incident. Once these systems have been expended, they will not be available for the remainder of the incident. These systems have special servicing requirements that only can be achieved safely under unrushed, nonemergency conditions.

One way to approach foam concentrate and water resupply operations is to call the operation "rapid resupply" and plan ways to decrease the vehicle's out-of-service time. The simple use of cam-lock or Storz fittings cuts the time it takes to connect a water or foam concentrate resupply hose. Using a pump to transfer foam concentrate from a foam tender or other supply source also makes the operation quicker. Preincident planning should prepare for a worst-case scenario fire and establish how much agent is required to extinguish a fire in the largest aircraft that can be expected to land at that airport. Knowing this information helps the department decide what type of resupply system best fits its needs.

Auxiliary Systems and Compressed-Air Foam Systems

Driver/operators must become familiar with the different (and potentially unique) auxiliary systems, equipment, and configurations, of the apparatus to which he is assigned. One example of an auxiliary system is a winterization system, a miniature heating system used to prevent the vehicle from freezing while standing by in extreme cold weather. Auxiliary systems such as these are very diverse and require the driver/operator to be familiar with their inspection and operation.

Another example of equipment used on the vehicle could be an aircraft-skin-penetrating. These devices are used to allow the firefighter to penetrate the aircraft skin and access the fire from a safe environment. These devices are attached to the end of an elevated master stream waterway. They can be designed to use water/foam solutions or other agents through the penetrating nozzle.

Many ARFF vehicles are equipped with compressed-air foam systems (CAFS). The principle behind CAFS is simple. They use either a stored premixed solution of foam concentrate and water or a proportioned foam solution drawn from foam concentrate and water tanks on the apparatus. In either case, compressed air is injected into the foam solution causing the foam solution to become highly aerated, with air-to-agent ratios as high as 20:1. This greatly exceeds the normal average expansion rate of 4:1 to 6:1 created by standard ARFF vehicle low-expansion foam systems. The 20:1 ratio means 30 gallons (120 L) of foam solution will produce an end product of 600 gallons (2 400 L) of finished foam.

The ARFF industry is very interested in this process because of the quality of foam blankets and the extended drain (breakdown) times of this highly expanded foam. This higher air ratio also makes the handlines lighter and has a dramatic effect on extending fire extinguishment times. There are manufactured portable systems in use presently that use a premixed container of agent and a compressed air cylinder with a regulation system. These systems work well on small fuel spills and fires on the flight line.

Summary

ARFF driver/operators are responsible for the vehicles to which they are assigned. Driver/operators should ensure that their vehicles are properly inspected and that all apparatus' extinguishing systems are tested and in working order at all times.

Driver/operators are also responsible for safely getting their vehicles to a scene and positioning their vehicles at the scene. Driver/operators must understand the limitations of ARFF vehicles and drive within those limitations. They must also know how to safely traverse a variety of slopes, terrain, and weather both by day and by night. Also, driver/operators should understand and utilize all of the driving assistance systems on an ARFF apparatus.

Finally, Driver/operators are responsible for administering foam agent from turrets and other outlets on vehicles. They must master agent management and practice frequently to ensure that they can judge the reach and penetration of agent during windy conditions or when pumping-and-rolling.

Review Questions

1. What are the components of a daily inspection?
2. What are the methods of testing a foam proportioning system for calibration accuracy?
3. How is a direct reading conductivity test performed?
4. What filling and safety instructions should be followed when adding dry chemical to an agent tank?
5. How is total stopping distance figured?

6. What is hydroplaning?

7. What is the most important driving situation for ARFF crew members?

8. What are some practices to follow when transitioning from off-road to on-road driving?

9. What guidelines should be followed when positioning an apparatus?

10. What is pump-and-roll?

Airport Emergency Planning

Chapter Contents

chapter 10

Key Terms

NFPA® references for Chapter 10:

NFPA® 1003 (2010)
5.1.1.3
5.2.2
5.3.10

**NFPA® 1002
(2008 - Chapter 9)**
9.2.1

Learning Objectives

After reading this chapter, students shall be able to:

1. Discuss airport emergency plans. (NFPA® 1003, 5.1.1.3, 5.2.2, 5.3.10)

2. Describe primary response considerations. (NFPA® 1003, 5.1.1.3, 5.2.2, 5.3.10)

3. Describe secondary response considerations. (NFPA® 1003, 5.1.1.3, 5.2.2, 5.3.10)

4. Discuss emergency response. (NFPA® 1003, 5.1.1.3, 5.2.2, 5.3.10)

5. Explain training considerations. (NFPA® 1003, 5.1.1.3, 5.2.2, 5.3.10)

Chapter 10
Airport Emergency Planning

Case History

Prior to the crash of United Airlines Flight 232 on July 19, 1989, the numerous city, county, and emergency response agencies in and around Sioux City (fire departments, ambulance agencies, emergency management, hospitals, Air National Guard units, and many others) had entered into cooperative agreements and had recently conducted a drill to test their emergency response capabilities. Upon notification of Flight 232's emergency, these emergency response agencies activated their emergency plans, initiated responses to Sioux Gateway Airport, and began positioning apparatus and personnel in anticipation of the aircraft's arrival. Hospitals in the region called in additional personnel and prepared the medical centers to receive large numbers of injured passengers.

When Flight 232 crashed, the emergency responders at the scene sprang into action. Airport ARFF crews extinguished the numerous fires created by the crash, protecting the passengers, crew, and rescuers from the flames. Some rescuers guided the walking wounded to safe locations where they could be cared for until they could be transported to medical treatment facilities. Other rescuers located severely injured passengers who had been thrown from the aircraft and brought EMS workers to them. Triage was established and the critically injured were placed in ambulances and sent to medical treatment facilities. The airport ARFF crews and local fire department crews searched the wreckage of the aircraft and extricated numerous passengers and aircraft crew. In the end, the planning and teamwork developed through these cooperative agreements between the various agencies in and around Sioux City contributed to the successful rescue of the aircraft crash survivors.

It is the responsibility of airport management to provide for ARFF services at their airport. Airport management personnel at FAA index airports are required to develop, implement and practice a comprehensive plan for handling a variety of emergency related situations. Each indexed airport should develop an Airport Certification Manual (ACM) that explains how the airport will meet the Part 139 certification requirements. The regulations state that the airport emergency plan (AEP) be part of the ACM or a separate document. The AEP should be tested with a full scale exercise at least every 3 years. Airports which are not FAA indexed should also consider developing their own emergency plans as well. The United States Department of Defense also requires each of its installations to have an emergency plan.

In many cases, a single, detailed plan can serve the needs of all agencies involved. In others, a single, all-inclusive plan may be too cumbersome. In these cases, a parent document supplemented by a number of individual elements or annexes may be required, each defining the functions of all agencies under a given set of conditions or the responsibilities of a given agency under all conditions. All plans, whether simple or complex, should identify and reflect potential needs, local resources, and available mutual aid.

Although a number of different formats serve equally well, some general considerations are common to all plans. Sections that should be common to all plans include:

- Introduction
- Aircraft incidents and accidents
- Bomb incidents
- Structural fires
- Mass-casualty and/or fatality incidents
- Natural disasters
- Sabotage/terrorism/hijacking
- Hazardous materials emergencies
- Disabled aircraft removal
- Civil disturbances
- Water rescue situations
- Unauthorized aircraft movements
- Major fuel spill and storage facility fires
- Structural Collapse

Structural fire departments with little or no direct airport responsibility should also plan for the possibility of an aircraft accident in their response area by seeking assistance from airports located in or around their jurisdictions. Response plans should reflect all conceivable contingencies within their boundaries, as well as their role in mutual aid agreements with airport fire departments. Because of the many variables, all agencies involved must recognize the need for validating their plan at least annually through joint training exercises. Structural firefighters providing protection to areas around airports must be knowledgeable in aircraft rescue and fire fighting. They should train with aircraft rescue firefighters on a regular basis and be included in airport emergency planning and exercises.

The airport emergency plan also addresses rescue and fire fighting operations, guidelines for communicating with the news media, the legal obligations of personnel involved, and the joint training necessary to implement and maintain the plan. This chapter discusses airport emergency planning and the many considerations involved in AEP development.

Sources for Joint Action Plans

A joint action plan involving numerous agencies may be based on the information provided in this chapter and the following publications:

- NFPA® 424, *Guide for Airport/Community Emergency Planning*
- NFPA® 402, *Guide for Aircraft Rescue and Fire Fighting Operations*
- NFPA® 1500, *Standard on Fire Department Occupational Safety and Health*

- NFPA® 1561, *Standard on Emergency Services Incident Management System*

- NFPA® 1600, *Standard on Disaster/Emergency Management and Business Continuity Program*

- NIMS, National Incident Management System

- ICAO *Airport Services Manuals*, Part 1, Part 5, and Part 7

- *FEMA Disaster Planning Guidelines for Fire Chiefs*, Federal Emergency Management Agency (FEMA)

- FAR Part 139.325, *Airport Emergency Plan*

- FAA Advisory Circulars 150/5200-12B, *Fire Department Responsibility in Protecting Evidence at the Scene of an Aircraft Accident*; 150/5200-31A, *Airport Emergency Plan*; 150/5210-2A, *Aircraft Rescue and Firefighting Communications*; 150/5210-13B, *Water Rescue Plans, Facilities, and Equipment;* and 150/5210-17A, *Programs for Training Aircraft Rescue Fire Fighting Personnel.*

- DODI 6055.6, Fire and Emergency Services Program

- Air Line Pilots Association (ALPA) *Guide to Accident Survival Factors*

General AEP Considerations

The Airport Emergency Plan (AEP) is an essential part of "risk management" for the airport and should address any event that may disrupt airport operations and services. Such a plan addresses the need for a coordinated response to emergency situations within the airport property including resources from surrounding local jurisdictions. The plan should be as complete and detailed as possible to ensure that all involved agencies are aware of their roles and responsibilities under various conditions **(Figure 10.1)**. The sections that follow describe the variety of conditions that must be considered when developing an airport emergency plan.

Figure 10.1 An airport emergency planning session.

Types of Aircraft Involved

To a large extent, the type and number of aircraft (including cargo aircraft) involved in an accident dictate the kinds and quantities of ARFF resources required. ARFF personnel handle accidents/incidents involving general aviation aircraft in the same way they do those involving commercial aircraft. Incidents/accidents with agricultural aircraft, which are in the general aviation category, may dictate an automatic hazardous materials response because of the potential of a chemical hazard. ARFF personnel should be familiar with the military aircraft that fly in their area, along with military installations and contact numbers in the event of an aircraft accident. Familiarity with and preplanning for the aircraft that frequent the airport will assist in the preparation and development of an effective response plan.

Types of Accidents/Incidents

Understanding the difference between an incident and an accident will help personnel define what equipment is needed and the operations to be conducted. ARFF personnel may respond to aircraft accidents and incidents that are either declared or undeclared prior to the aircraft landing. Some accidents may involve survivors; others will not.

Accidents are defined as low- or high- impact and measured by the severity and angle of impact. In a low-impact crash, if egress is not blocked by fire, fatality rates tend to be low **(Figure 10.2a)**. A high-impact crash is a nonsurvivable

Figure 10.2a An example of a low-impact crash. *Courtesy of District Chief Chris Mickal, New Orleans (LA) FD Photo Unit.*

Figure 10.2b An example of a high-impact crash. *Courtesy of SPC Kyle Davis (US Army), Defense Visual Information Center (DVIC).*

crash resulting in severe structural damage to the aircraft **(Figure 10.2b)**. A high-impact crash will often reduce an aircraft to small pieces and scatter debris over a large area due to the speed of impact. Although a high-impact crash is nonsurvivable by definition, there have been several instances in which individuals have survived such crashes.

In both types of accidents, ARFF personnel should concentrate on the number one goal – life safety/rescue. If ARFF staffing is not sufficient enough to provide hands-on rescue attempts, then emphasis must be placed on fire control in an effort to provide survivors with a means of escape. Providing effective fire control aids in protecting possible survivors while preserving crash-scene evidence.

A large percentage of aircraft accidents result in fire because of the large quantities of fuel and numerous ignition sources that are present. Because aircraft fires spread rapidly, ARFF personnel must respond quickly and take appropriate action to increase the chances of successful rescue and fire fighting operations. As discussed in Chapter 4, "Safety and Aircraft Hazards," aircraft accidents/incidents sometimes involve hazardous materials such as fuel, chemicals, radiological and/or etiological agents, and explosives. ARFF personnel must be prepared to deal with these situations as well as those involving threats of bombs, sabotage, and hijacking.

Critical Phases of Flight

The critical phases of flight for aircraft include the first 5 minutes after take-off, the last 10 minutes of flight before landing, and any time an aircraft is in noncruise flight under 10,000 ft (3 000m). Because these are also the periods when aircraft accidents are most likely to occur, aircraft flight crews and flight attendants exercise the "sterile cockpit rule." This rule requires flight crews and attendants to refrain from excessive talking or performing duties that are not critical to the safe operation of the aircraft during the critical phases of flight. Airport fire department staffing requirements should be maintained during periods when regularly scheduled flights into and out of the airport are in critical flight phases.

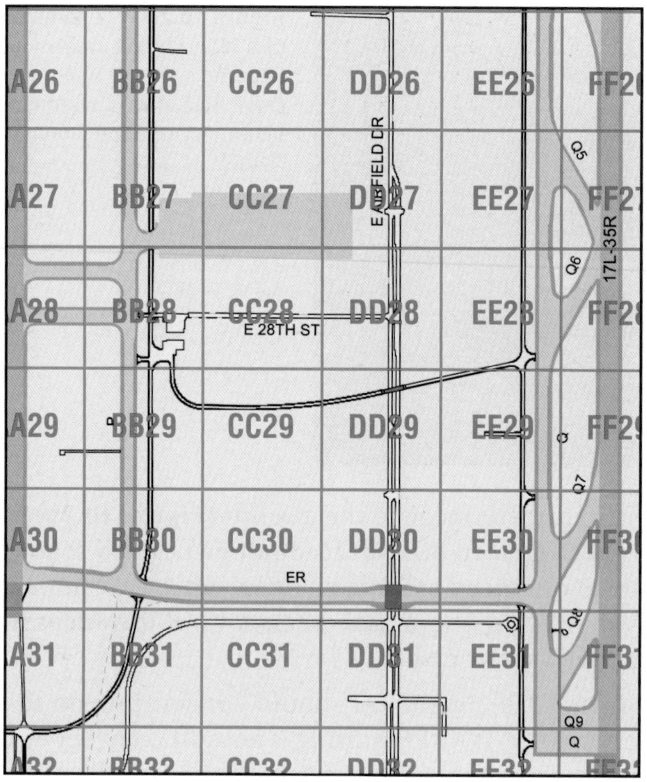

Figure 10.3 Part of an airport grid map. *Courtesy of DFW International Airport - ITS/GIS Department.*

Airport Hazard Assessment — Formal review of the hazards that may be encountered at an airport.

Possible Accident Sites

A high percentage of all aircraft accidents/incidents occur on or near airport property and generally in the threshold or departure area of the runway. In these areas, aircraft may be taxiing, taking off, approaching, and landing while at the same time, other aircraft may be moving about, being fueled, and/or serviced at other locations on the airport. Personnel may determine the areas in which accidents/incidents are likely to occur by studying the arrival and departure traffic patterns. Accidents/incidents on airport property must be anticipated and appropriate plans developed. There is also a need to plan for accidents/incidents occurring away from the airport and in urban, suburban, or rural areas.

Grid maps of the airport and surrounding areas should be prepared as part of airport emergency planning. All agencies concerned with aircraft emergency service rescue and fire protection must have up-to-date, standardized grid maps of the airport and surrounding areas within a 5- to 15-mile (8 km to 24 km) radius. The maps should show access routes and key locations such as water supplies, medical facilities, staging areas, and heliports. They should also identify roads, bridges, perimeter gates, and any other pertinent features of the terrain that could prevent or delay response **(Figure 10.3)**. These maps should also be shared with mutual aid departments responsible for response as part of the emergency plan. Predetermined staging areas can be defined and identified on the maps. Reading of grid maps should be practiced to ensure the accurate location of an accident site is relayed to all responders. GPS locators may be used in assisting with locating downed aircraft.

In addition to grid maps, ARFF fire departments should establish very specific airport hazard assessments. An airfield hazard assessment should include land where certain uses may obstruct the airspace or otherwise be hazardous

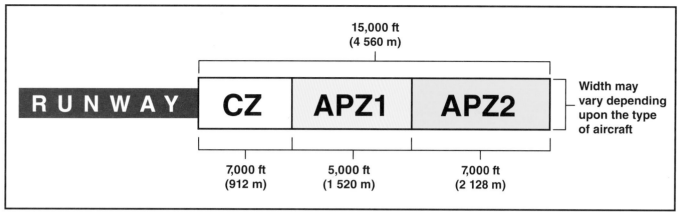

Figure 10.4 An illustration describing Accident Potential Zones (APZ).

to aircraft operations and *Accident Potential Zones (APZ)*, which are land areas immediately beyond the ends of the runways and along primary flight paths that pose a higher risk of aircraft accidents than other areas.

The APZ's encompass an area that extends 15,000 feet (4 572 m) past the ends of the runway(s) **(Figure 10.4)**. The zones are divided as follows:

- *Clear Zone* — area immediately beyond the end of the runway; possesses a high potential for accidents; zone extends 3,000 feet (914 m) past the ends of the runway(s).

- *APZ 1* — area beyond the clear zone having a significant potential for accidents; zone extends 5,000 feet (1 524 m) past the end of the clear zone.

- *APZ 2* — area beyond APZ 1 having a measurable potential for accidents; zone extends 7,000 feet (2 133 m) past the end of APZ 1.

The AEP should provide an outline for fire department responses / actions to aircraft incidents occurring within the Accident Potential Zones (APZ). The Airfield Hazard Assessment should include the following criteria:

- APZ Accessibility

- APZ Runway Ends

- APZ Hazards

> **Accident Potential Zones (APZ)** — Land areas immediately beyond the ends of the runways and along primary flight paths that pose a higher risk of aircraft accidents than other areas.

Bailout and Jettison Areas and Search and Rescue

The AEP should identify predetermined bailout and jettison areas, area maps, and appropriate procedures for military aircrews to bailout or jettison stores at this area in the event of an emergency situation. This area should be one of the first locations included in a search plan in the event an aircraft is reported missing or overdue.

AEPs should establish procedures for the rescue and retrieval of aircrew members as well as establishing a Bailout-Jettison area. The ERP should also identify flight parameters including flight paths and responsible control centers. If a fire department may have to respond to incidents/accidents on or near a military installation, the department should check with the local military installation to identify the location of these Bailout-Jettison areas. The AEP should identify a Search and Rescue Coordinator as the primary contact for search and rescue operations.

There are two types of search and rescue operations (air and ground) that can be activated:

- *Air Search & Rescue* — downed aircraft will normally be reported by receipt of signals from Emergency Locator Beacons (ELB), reports of overdue aircraft, or eye witnesses

- *Ground Search & Rescue (GSAR)* — ground search and rescue operations will normally be initiated by receipt of a signal from a Personal Locator Beacon, or by reports of overdue or missing individuals; volunteer ground search and rescue groups and government or private sector aircraft may provide additional support

GSAR procedures should be initiated once it has been identified that an aircraft is downed, missing, or overdue. All potential agencies should be notified of the nature, location, and requirements for the ground search and rescue operation.

The following agencies should coordinate their own search and rescue efforts:

- Law enforcement agencies
- Local fire departments
- Search and Rescue organizations
- Civil Air Patrol
- Helicopters (Emergency Medical & Private)
- Department of Defense

In both types of search and rescue operations, the immediate launch of search operations will increase the chances of finding individuals early and in good health. In the event an aircraft is lost in-flight, actions must begin to locate possible survivors and initiate rescue efforts. It is critical that responding agencies aggressively locate and rescue downed personnel. Many downed aircrews initially suffer from shock or have delayed reactions to ejection injuries.

Accident Site Accessibility

In a planning survey of potential accident sites, ARFF personnel should check access to areas where crashes are most likely. Obstacles to apparatus response and access to primary and auxiliary water supply sources can be identified through ground and air surveys. Alternative response routes may then be developed to facilitate rescue and fire fighting operations.

The size and condition of roads and bridges may restrict access. Underpasses and bridges may impose height, width, and weight restrictions. There also may be various types of fences and gates that restrict access. For example, apparatus would have difficulty reaching a location that is next to the airport but behind a railroad embankment. Without advance planning, vehicles might have to detour several miles to reach the location and lose valuable time in the process.

A variety of terrain features may exist that may impede response capabilities **(Figure 10.5)**. Routes should be planned to bypass ditches, fenced-in areas, wooded areas, streams, marshes, and swamps that may block or impede the passage of heavy apparatus. The local terrain may also influence how personnel perform rescue operations, as well as which extinguishing methods of agent application they choose.

Figure 10.5 An ARFF vehicle trying to access the "crash site" during an ARFF training exercise. *Courtesy of Robert Lindstrom.*

Advanced planning should include possible routes over areas in which no roads exist. In some cases, personnel can make minor changes during the preplanning stage to permit vehicles to access a site. For instance, grading approaches and stabilizing streambeds may make it possible for vehicles to cross shallow streams. In other situations, it may be necessary to construct roads into inaccessible areas that are likely to be accident sites. Ensuring adequate resources are available prior to an accident will expedite the accomplishment of creating access roads in the event they are needed.

A standard emergency response pattern (SERP) model should be developed for use during each incident. This model should standardize locations for the command post, control zones around the site, and entry and exit corridors **(Figure 10.6, p. 308)**. It should also establish areas for the following purposes:

- Personnel, equipment, and apparatus staging
- Triage, treatment, and transportation of patients
- Rehabilitation of emergency responders
- Helicopter landing zones (helipads)
- Mortuary affairs
- Media/public affairs

Keeping in mind the needs of those participating in an emergency response, transport of patients should be conducted by securing a road into the site and a different road away from the site. This practice may assist in preventing traffic jams from emergency response vehicles.

With the increased use of composite materials in aircraft construction all areas need to be established upwind to stay clear of downwind hazardous contamination.

Climatic Considerations

The effects of various weather phenomena peculiar to the area, especially on substandard roads and off-road areas, should be considered. Climatic conditions such as wind, rain, sleet, and snow may delay or prevent response to an accident site. Terrain that normally accommodates heavy vehicles may turn into a quagmire, causing rescue and fire fighting operations to be bogged down or otherwise hampered. In some cases the use of heavy vehicles and equipment may become impossible.

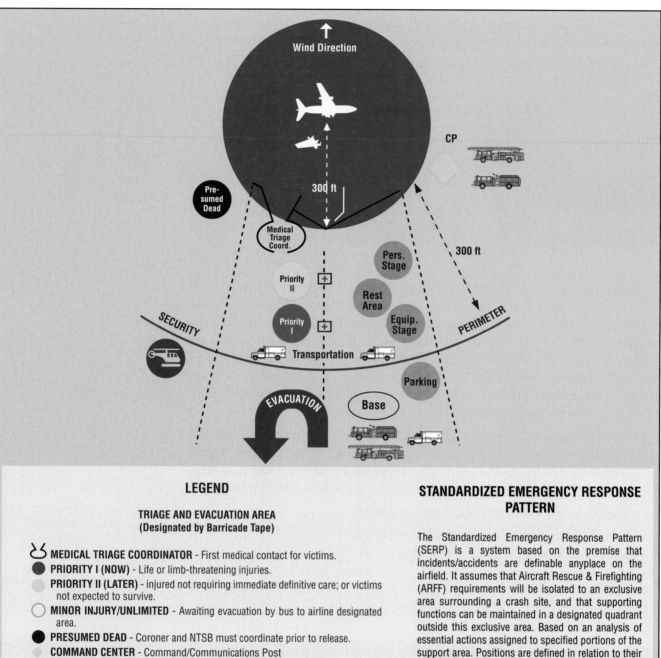

LEGEND

TRIAGE AND EVACUATION AREA
(Designated by Barricade Tape)

MEDICAL TRIAGE COORDINATOR - First medical contact for victims.

● **PRIORITY I (NOW)** - Life or limb-threatening injuries.

○ **PRIORITY II (LATER)** - injured not requiring immediate definitive care; or victims not expected to survive.

○ **MINOR INJURY/UNLIMITED** - Awaiting evacuation by bus to airline designated area.

● **PRESUMED DEAD** - Coroner and NTSB must coordinate prior to release.

◆ **COMMAND CENTER** - Command/Communications Post

⊞ **MEDICAL SUPPLY TRAILERS** - Supplies should be placed 10 ft into Triage area.

EVACUATION - Coned route for ambulances/buses; must not infringe on Triage or Support Areas.

HELICOPTER TOUCHDOWN AREA - Will be marked with reflective materials for night use.

SUPPORT AREA

● **PERSONNEL STAGING** - e.g., volunteer airlines and first aid trained personnel Airfield Maintenance, and local area Emergency services.

● **EQUIPMENT STAGING** - e.g., cranes, vans, light units, various mutual aid agency equipment

● **PARKING** - e.g., Authorized vehicles, VIPS, news media

● **REST AREA** - e.g., portable toilets, temporary shelter for rescue personnel.

STANDARDIZED EMERGENCY RESPONSE PATTERN

The Standardized Emergency Response Pattern (SERP) is a system based on the premise that incidents/accidents are definable anyplace on the airfield. It assumes that Aircraft Rescue & Firefighting (ARFF) requirements will be isolated to an exclusive area surrounding a crash site, and that supporting functions can be maintained in a designated quadrant outside this exclusive area. Based on an analysis of essential actions assigned to specified portions of the support area. Positions are defined in relation to their proximity to each other and in terms of their logistic needs and value to the recovery effort.

The command Post is positioned in a centralized upwind area as far forward as possible without actually entering the ARFF maneuver area; it is the focal point of all support activities. Areas are assigned to each activity on the basis of its proximity to the Command Post and its function within the support quadrant.

Medical requirements include establishment of a triage site, casualty support areas and the positioning of medical supplies and equipment. Other proximity related functional areas include those designated for personnel assembly, rest, parking, press, and security.

Figure 10.6 An example of a standard emergency response pattern (SERP) model.

During plan development, considerations should be made for protecting aircraft occupants along with all emergency responders from harsh weather conditions. Portable shelters may need to be erected at a crash site if extended operations are anticipated. Depending on the conditions, rescue personnel may need to be transported between the crash scene and a climate-controlled rehabilitation area. If weather conditions dictate, blankets and water resistant ponchos or rain gear should be available to occupants, especially if delays in transportation from the site are encountered.

Emergency Response Communications

In addition to the local ARFF department, other agencies, groups, and departments may be involved in the emergency response to an aircraft accident/incident. Emergency planners should identify the methods for alerting emergency response and support personnel: horn, siren, or other audible alarm system; telephone, phone pagers; or radios. Those responsible for completing airport emergency plans should compile an emergency contact list with emergency telephone numbers for key personnel assigned to both the primary or secondary response. Automated dialing systems can be used to initiate an automatic recall of all off-duty fire fighting personnel. Telephone numbers (including pagers) should include those that can be used to reach these personnel at all hours of the day and night, including weekends and holidays. It is critical to keep the personnel recall roster updated to ensure that personnel are able to be located in the event of an emergency. The emergency plan should include recall procedures. The sections that follow present the primary and secondary response groups in an emergency as well as acknowledge the wide variety of other logistical support that may need to be contacted.

Primary Response

The primary response often incorporates those agencies that are notified on the initial call from the air traffic control tower. When the crash phone or crash network is activated, each of these agencies initiate response operations. The nature and magnitude of the emergency often dictate their level of response. In addition to aircraft rescue and fire fighting services, the primary response should include the following personnel and their telephone numbers:

- Law enforcement agencies
- Emergency medical services
- Air carrier/aircraft owner (that is, the tenants concerned or a representative of the aircraft operator)
- Airport Management/Operations

Law Enforcement Agencies

Local, county, and state or provincial law enforcement agencies participate in airport emergency planning to help define and clarify roles and to standardize operating procedures. As part of this planning, ARFF personnel should identify specific concerns that law enforcement agencies should handle relating to ARFF operations.

Crowds of unauthorized persons frequently congregate near the site of an aircraft accident/incident to watch emergency operations, to take pictures, to collect parts of the wreckage as souvenirs, and also to inquire about family members or friends who may have been involved. Because the presence of these individuals may hinder rescue and fire fighting operations, traffic and crowd control are major concerns. A primary concern is to cordon off the immediate crash site to ensure that only authorized personnel are permitted to enter.

Some large airports have hundreds of people working inside the airport fence, some authorized to enter the movement area, some not. These people will tend to converge on an incident scene also. They will interfere and inhibit fire operations unless controlled immediately at the start of the incident. Law enforcement should establish an appropriate scene security perimeter in order to preserve the scene and wreckage, as well as allow for unhampered rescue, medical, and fire operations.

Other airport entry points may have to be guarded or locked. Police may also be tasked with addressing the needs of residents inside the security perimeters or near the crash site. Often, airport maintenance or public works can assist law enforcement with establishing perimeters by providing barricades, traffic cones, portable red lighting, caution tape, and other materials or equipment.

When identifying the Staging Area location, a route should be designated for emergency responders entering the incident site. Law enforcement should close this access to all but authorized persons and emergency equipment. A method of passes or identification will have to be established to allow only authorized persons into the incident scene. These passes may have to be changed daily to keep security tight. Police may also have to route traffic away from or around the incident.

As long as it is safe, police should sweep areas inside the perimeters for unauthorized persons. In addition, law enforcement personnel may have the primary responsibility for conducting large-scale evacuations.

Law enforcement personnel should always be on the lookout for hazardous materials, valuables, mail, money, evidence of criminal activity in the wreckage (guns, drugs, etc.), and hazards to other emergency response personnel. In potential terrorist incidents, these personnel can search for possible secondary and tertiary devices. These personnel can set up barricades and barrier tape around dangerous areas or items that need to be protected, such as the Flight Data and Cockpit Voice Recorders. They may be able to photograph, video, or perform other incident documentation. They can identify and gather information from potential witnesses. Law enforcement agencies may also provide specialized equipment and personnel such as bomb-disposal units as well as accident investigative services and equipment.

Often officials, politicians, and other dignitaries may request tours of an incident scene. Other emergency response organizations may send personnel to evaluate the incident, operations, and gather information. The Federal Aviation Administration and National Transportation Board will need support and assistance during the investigation. Law enforcement can entertain and satisfy the needs of these individuals, freeing key personnel to deal with other incident related needs.

It may take a while to establish effective media relations and control. The media response will usually be large and quick. The media will use every means possible to get into a scene and will be a major problem for perimeter control. Until Information Officers from all the key organizations arrive and set up a formal media organization and area, police officers will have to contain and control the press.

Fire officers should expect to work with a wide variety of law enforcement agencies and organizations during and after an aircraft incident. It is important that fire command officers immediately liaison and co-locate with law enforcement personnel when first arriving on scene to quickly identify areas of responsibility, needs, and an initial action plan. Separate command posts and a lack of communication and coordination between police and fire are common problems identified during aircraft incident critiques.

Emergency Medical Services

Emergency plans should also address emergency medical services needs, including local multicasualty plans. Emergency medical personnel may be needed for triage, emergency care, and transportation of the injured; therefore, planning for emergencies, such as aircraft accidents, requires participation by hospitals and medical response personnel. The airport emergency plan should identify the abilities and limitations of all participating medical facilities to accept patients in various injury categories. A system for determining available hospital bed counts should also be established so transport personnel can track which hospitals are being utilized and where patients are being transported. Arrangements might be made to use an airport facility, such as a hangar or terminal building, to accommodate passengers and crewmembers with minor injuries, keeping in mind that these persons just encountered and survived an aviation accident. Such facilities must be adequate and contain sufficient rest rooms, meeting rooms and private rooms. If such a facility is available, it should be secured, with access limited to authorized persons and family members. Other available locations may include local hotels and schools that often contain the necessary resources to function as a staging area for accident survivors.

Air Carrier/Aircraft Owner

The air carrier is definitely a key player in the management of an aviation disaster. They can provide a wide variety of physical resources, expertise, and information that the response organization needs and should be used where appropriate. Airline personnel can provide precise information regarding the number of occupants, along with known quantities of hazardous materials. In addition, many air carrier organizations have developed airline disaster response and family-assistance resource teams that can be deployed and used as part of an emergency response.

Some airports have provided airline station managers with audio monitors that activate when the crash phone is activated by ATC. This alerts the manager of an impending situation that may necessitate activation of the airline response plan. It should be part of the plan for airline response personnel to report to the airport operations office so that escort services can be provided to and from the crash scene. Depending on the location of the crash site, local law enforcement may need to serve as escorts to the crash scene.

Most major air carriers have safety personnel, investigators, and other personnel that will respond from their corporate headquarters to an incident scene to manage and protect their interests. Local airline personnel may provide assistance in an incident until additional company assistance arrives.

Depending on the location of the incident, this could range from several hours to several days. There are often interline or mutual aid agreements between the airlines at an airport. The incident commander may request a senior air carrier representative be assigned to the command post.

There are benefits to having an airline representative in the command post. Air carriers can provide necessary equipment and expertise. Airlines have air stairs, cherry pickers, baggage loaders, tugs, baggage carts, lighting, buses, and other vehicles and equipment that can be used during an incident. They can provide aircraft mechanics and maintenance personnel to help stabilize aircraft systems, pin gears, support unstable fuselage sections, and provide information about the aircraft. Emergency responders will need copies of passenger and crew manifests, cargo manifests, hazardous material shipping papers, and load plans. An airline representative should be able to provide these documents.

The Aviation Disaster Family Assistance Act of 1996 and the Foreign Air Carrier Family Support Act of 1997 require the affected airline to perform a wide variety of tasks involving the passengers, as well as family and friends of the passengers. Family and friends waiting for the arrival of passengers will need to be collected and sequestered in a secure holding or isolation area. Medical and security assistance may be needed to protect and deal with these persons' needs. Airlines will handle notification of next of kin of deceased passengers and crewmembers, as well as travel and other needs. ARFF personnel should ensure that a plan and agreement is in place with the airline before arriving with accident survivors and friends and families of survivors. Establishing a resource directory of all airline station managers will expedite the contact process.

When authorized and released by the NTSB, the air carrier will be responsible for the removal or salvage of the aircraft. Wreckage may be moved to a hangar or warehouse for long-term component assembly and analysis. This task may require cranes, pneumatic lifting equipment, other heavy equipment, and specialized expertise. Some larger airlines have this capability.

Airport Management/Operations

Airport personnel will obviously be an important part of the management of an aviation disaster, especially on or adjacent to the airport. They will perform many important tasks and provide a wide variety of resources and services. Involved airport personnel may include the manager/director, assistants, operations, clerical staff, engineers, maintenance, and others. Airport management should ensure that airport personnel are trained and prepared to play some role in the management of an incident. After fire and medical personnel have completed their tasks, airport personnel may become the incident commander or share command with law enforcement.

After emergency operations have concluded, the primary goal of airport management personnel will be to resume normal or modified airport operations. They will make the decision to close all or part of the airport runways, taxiways, and other facilities. The airport may issue Notices to Airmen (NOTAMS) regarding restricted use of airport areas. They may work with the airlines and air traffic control to reroute aircraft and passengers to alternate airports.

It is not uncommon to have many helicopters from involved agencies and the news media, as well as private aircraft converge over the incident. They can present a danger to themselves as well as persons on the ground. If aircraft overhead are a problem due to noise, rotor wash, and congestion, ARFF personnel can request an immediate airspace restriction through the nearest Federal Aviation Administration Air Traffic Control Facility (Tower). If it's a water incident, the Coast Guard, Harbor Patrol, Lifeguards, or other marine law enforcement agencies can establish a safety zone around the incident.

Airport management personnel will make a number of required and necessary notifications. They may notify an aircraft operator, government, or military organization of an accident involving one of their aircraft as well as any of the following agencies:

- Federal Aviation Administration Flight Safety District Office (FSDO)
- National Transportation Safety Board (NTSB)
- Federal Bureau of Investigation (FBI)
- Customs
- Immigration
- Agriculture
- Environmental agencies (EPA)
- Health and welfare agencies
- Postal Authorities

Emergency Notification Lists

Regardless of the size and magnitude of a disaster, in order for an emergency plan to be effective, it is critically important that the emergency notification list is kept up-to-date. Individuals on the list move or are reassigned, phone numbers change, and different people assume responsibility for various aspects of the response system. Unless some means is developed for monitoring and disseminating these changes, the list will inevitably become outdated.

Many physical resources may be available from the airport itself. Various divisions at the airport such as maintenance can provide the following resources:

- Trucks, tractors, buses
- Elevating devices
- Portable lights
- Drinking water
- Portable toilets
- Communications equipment
- Runway closing lighted Xs
- Power and hand tools
- Specialized signage to indicate incident areas such as the following:
  — Victim flow
  — Medical areas
  — Staging areas
- Cones, barricades, and barrier tape

Airport personnel would also be good choices for staffing the Logistic Section of the Incident Command System to locate these specialized materials, equipment, supplies, services, contractors, and other specialized resources needed at an aircraft incident. With direction from fire and police, airport personnel can set up inner and outer security perimeters. They can disable access gates and help secure the accident site. They can provide escorts for equipment, without ground frequencies, needing to enter or drive on the Airport Operation Area (AOA). Airport buses can be used to transport uninjured persons or persons with minor injuries to temporary holding areas.

The airport will conduct a damage assessment and inspection of runways, taxiways, structures, and navigational aides. A recovery plan will be developed to coordinate emergency repairs and get the airport back in full service. They can assist with preservation and protection of the wreckage and immediate incident scene. The airport will usually initiate or assume responsibility for removal of the aircraft and wreckage, if not handled by the aircraft operator or air carrier.

Airport personnel are more familiar with the capabilities and resources available from the airlines and airport tenants. Airport management will coordinate and liaison with the air carriers and airport tenants for many of the following resources as well:

- Necessary assistance, personnel, equipment, or use of facilities

- Passenger, crew, cargo, and witness lists

- Private hangars and buildings for use as temporary morgues, holding areas, liaison check-in areas, and media locations

The airport management can obtain weather information and forecast its projected affect on the incident. They can often handle the video and photographic documentation of the incident scene and activities. Fixed airport security cameras often are used for this function.

Secondary Response

As the primary response units arrive on the scene, the secondary response network is activated. Much like the primary response, the secondary response network should expand and contract as dictated by the magnitude of the emergency. The sections that follow include contacts that should be considered essential to any secondary response. Depending on the incident, there may be additional contacts involved in a secondary response.

Mutual Aid Support

Airports should have written mutual aid agreements with surrounding fire and police departments and other emergency service organizations. In an aircraft accident, especially one involving fire, time is of the essence in rescue and fire fighting operations. The amount of resources available quickly may make a significant difference in the final outcome of such an incident **(Figure 10.7)**.

Through prearranged signed agreements, mutual aid fire fighting services can become part of the primary response notification list. As part of the primary response, dispatch and response are automatic. Otherwise, ARFF personnel will need to contact a mutual aid dispatch center and formally request additional manpower and equipment.

Figure 10.7 A mutual aid tanker reservicing an ARFF apparatus. *Courtesy of John Demyan, LVI Airport.*

In order to coordinate the efforts of all those who may be involved, planners should meet with representatives of all entities as a group to define roles, identify resources, and develop procedures. One of the most important products of such meetings should be a comprehensive list of the resources available from the various entities, along with the key emergency phone numbers. All such mutual aid agreements and lists must be periodically reviewed and revised to meet changing conditions and to keep them current.

Available Apparatus, Equipment, and Water Supply

Depending on the situation, the ARFF department may need to call in specialized vehicles and equipment from agencies other than mutual aid fire departments. These other agencies can include equipment rental, construction, and marine companies. In airport emergency planning, the written plan should designate which types of vehicles should respond to each type of accident/incident. Planners should consider the terrain to be encountered when designating heavy, specialized apparatus. Additional considerations are possible needs and sources for other heavy equipment such as bulldozers, cranes, and forklifts plus special-purpose equipment such as lighting, cutting/welding tools, towing/lifting tools, and boats. To ensure availability of such tools and equipment, contractual information should be part of the airport emergency plan so that such agreements do not have to be made after an accident happens. Special emphasis should be placed on identifying possible water supply sources on or near the airfield. Relay pumping or water shuttle operations may need to be considered if hydrants or a sufficient static supply source is not available near the incident.

Rehabilitation Resources

Regardless of the role or task performed, all response personnel should be required to spend time in the rehab area to allow nourishment and hydration. Arrangements should be made with competent vendors, canteen providers, or other similar organizations so that a rehabilitation area can be established

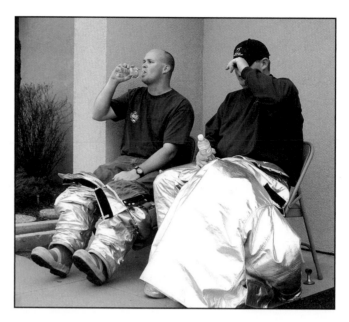

Figure 10.8 Two ARFF personnel rehydrating in a rehab area.

and supplied throughout an incident. An excellent resource for creating a rehabilitation area is the local chapter of the American Red Cross, Salvation Army, or fire service auxiliary groups.

Sufficient resources should be established immediately and are needed to ensure that rescue personnel are provided with an area to where they can retreat from on-scene operations. ARFF personnel must exercise proper decontamination procedures so as not to contaminate the rehabilitation area. The area should be isolated from the emergency site (sights and sounds) while staying clear of triage, staging, and other operational areas. In addition, this area should provide shelter, if required, along with a place to sit or lie down, and warm or cold drinks and fresh fruit or other appropriate foods, should be available **(Figure 10.8, p. 318)**.

NOTE: For more information on this topic, see the FPP/Brady *Emergency Incident Rehabilitation* manual or NFPA® 1584, *Recommended Practice on the Rehabilitation of Members Operating at Incident Scene Operations and Training Exercises.*

Critical Incident Stress Management Team

While working at an accident site, ARFF responders are subjected to a tremendous amount of psychological pressure. This pressure is created when responders are called upon to rapidly handle numerous patients, presenting a variety of injuries, while working in a hazardous environment. Depending on the type of incident, wreckage entrapping many of the victims may require extensive extrication operations. Many injuries are often quite traumatic with responders working in an environment where fatalities may also be present. Rescue workers placed into this type of environment can feel overtaxed and overwhelmed due to the large number of tasks that need to be accomplished.

Fire department, airport operations, law enforcement, and EMS should have as part of their resource directories a list of qualified critical incident stress teams. These teams should provide the ability to respond twenty-four hours a day, seven days a week. They should also be cleared to obtain access to the rehabilitation area in order to provide on-site assistance to all rescue and operations personnel. Confidential emotional support groups should be available and accessible for all persons involved with conducting rescue operations both during and after the incident. It is important to ensure that all personnel are provided the opportunity and encouraged to participate in a critical incident stress program within the first 24 hours. Responders being demobilized from the incident should be defused and provided CISM information, prior to leaving scene.

Other Logistical Support

There are a number of other agencies and organizations that can provide logistical support during an aircraft incident. Emergency response personnel from the military services can provide additional equipment and support. For example, The American Red Cross can provide useful services. Mortuary assistance can be extremely useful during aircraft incidents involving mass casualties. The Department of Defense may be able to provide a quick response medical team along with a team to properly handle the deceased. The sections that follow introduce a variety of agencies, resources, departments, and avenues for additional assistance that may be essential contacts in an emergency.

Government Agencies

The Federal Bureau of Investigations (FBI); the Bureau of Alcohol, Tobacco, Firearms, and Explosives (ATF); and other federal agencies may also assist in a crash investigation. Because even the smallest piece of crash debris may be important evidence, media personnel should be allowed into the scene only with an escort designated by Command, and they must not be allowed to disturb anything. A recommended practice involves placing media personnel on a bus and providing a tour of the crash site. Media personnel should be restricted to the bus while obtaining video footage and pictures from the bus.

To reduce anxiety among relatives and friends of the occupants of an involved aircraft, the investigative authorities may authorize release of the names of those not seriously injured as soon as possible. However, the names of individuals killed or seriously injured are always withheld until next of kin have been notified, and members of the news media are ethically bound to cooperate with this policy.

Military Assistance

Military services, particularly for aircraft and other aerospace vehicle protection, are not necessarily limited to the boundaries of their installations. Public law in the United States allows military funds to be spent for nonfederal, civil, and private interests if the expenditures are in the direct interest of federal agencies or if public disorders or disasters are involved. Military agencies may enter into reciprocal mutual-assistance agreements with surrounding community fire protection organizations to provide many of the services already mentioned. Medevac helicopters, field hospitals, medical support personnel, and additional firefighter personnel are just some of the services that can be pre-arranged **(Figure 10.9 page 318)**. Experience in civil air accidents near military facilities has shown the need for and value of cooperative planning prior to such disasters. Local DOD installations can provide military personnel for the following activities:

Figure 10.9 A military medevac helicopter preparing to land during an ARFF exercise. *Courtesy of AIC L.A. Smith (USAF), Defense Visual Information Center (DVIC).*

- Scene security
- Body recovery
- Documentation
- Fire and hazard control
- Medical services
- Evacuation centers
- Feeding large groups of people

In addition, the military can provide a wide variety of resources from vehicles, heavy lift equipment, divers, vessels, aircraft, tents, and other equipment.

American Red Cross and Salvation Army

Under the "Aviation Disaster Family Assistance Act of 1996", the Red Cross is tasked to work with the National Transportation Safety Board and involved Air Carrier Representatives to provide a wide variety of services after a major passenger aircraft accident. Working in conjunction with the air carrier disaster response team, the Red Cross can provide mental health and counseling services for hospitalized and nonhospitalized survivors. They can help ensure that families are not outnumbered and overwhelmed by well-intentioned organizations and individuals. They can provide mental health resources within the local area while providing childcare services for families who bring young children. The Red Cross coordinates with appropriate representatives of the coroner/medical examiner's office to assist with death notifications and consults with families to arrange suitable nondenominational memorial services just days following the crash, as well as future memorial services for the burial of unidentified remains. The Red Cross can also support a disaster response by providing canteen services, lodging referrals, along with other valuable resources. The Red Cross has a Language Bank to translate for non-English speaking victims. The Salvation Army has disaster programs that are similar to those of the Red Cross.

Mortuary Assistance

Plans for coping with a major disaster should include provisions for a temporary morgue. In a major aircraft accident, the number of fatalities may overwhelm local morgue facilities; planning for some alternate means of maintaining dignified custody of remains is necessary. Representatives of the local coroner, morgue, and mortuaries should meet with fire department planners and representatives of the NTSB/CTAISB to decide on mutually acceptable procedures. Arrangements should be made with a resource that can supply refrigerated trucks as a means of a temporary morgue. On the airport there may be facilities available with equipment that may serve the same purpose.

Federal Aviation Administration (FAA)

The FAA is responsible for investigating all civil aircraft accidents to determine if there have been any violations of federal aviation laws or regulations. Investigations may include scrutinizing any of the following:

- Performance of Air Traffic Control facilities
- Airworthiness of FAA certified aircraft
- Competency of FAA certificated airmen, air agencies, commercial operators, air carriers, or airports

The FAA will also investigate and determine the probable cause of all aircraft accidents/incidents not investigated by the NTSB. They also ensure that all facts and circumstances leading to the accident are recorded and evaluated, and action is taken to prevent similar accidents.

Air Traffic Control Tower (ATCT)

ATCT will immediately notify emergency and airport services of aircraft emergency situation and other observed or reported in progress emergencies involving the airport. It is recommended that the airport emergency services meet with the tower personnel regularly to review and improve operations. The tower will relay radio transmissions received on FAA frequencies related to emergency situations. They will advise all inbound and outbound air traffic of emergency situations affecting their operations at the airport. All tower radio traffic is recorded and these recordings are kept for fifteen (15) days. If there is an accident, the tape will be copied, transcribed, and retained for six months or until the cause is resolved. The Air Traffic Control System (ATCS) will also be investigated by the NTSB as a potential cause of an accident.

Coast Guard

The U. S. Coast Guard has responsibility for all search and rescue missions in the territorial waters of the United States. The Coast Guard can take the following actions in an emergency where their aid is needed:

- Respond to aviation emergencies and ditchings on the high seas, rivers, and other inland water areas

- Coordinate the response of commercial vessels to the location of a downed aircraft
- Use their aircraft to deploy rescue equipment and personnel across a considerable area
- Provide a wide variety of vessels which can be used for search and rescue, floating command posts, and wreckage removal
- Provide emergency plans with extensive resource databases for specialized marine and waterborne resources that would be utilized in an aircraft water incident

Other Waterborne Resources

Harbor masters, Lifeguards, Harbor Patrol, Army Corp of Engineers and other marine organizations have vessels and equipment which may be requested in an aircraft incident including the following, specialized resources:

- Salvage companies
- Marine construction companies
- Divers
- Fireboats
- Vessels
- Sonar
- Underwater, survey equipment

    Private vessel owners have also helped in aircraft water incidents.

Foreign Language Interpreters and Linguists

Local language resources should be identified in emergency plans. Assistance can be obtained via telephone from services such as ALTRUSA International, Inc. Altrusa can be contacted at 312-427-4410 to determine which language bank is best suited for each local. The Altrusa website is located at http://www.altrusa.com/Home/Default.asp.

Religious Organizations and Clergy

Arrangements should be made to contact the clergy to provide comfort to casualties and relatives, as well as perform religious services where and when appropriate. Churches are a good source of volunteers and physical facilities to use for incident command functions such as evacuation centers.

Communications Services

Ham radio organizations can provide additional means of communication when radio frequencies, telephone lines, and cell phone circuits are overloaded. Repeater and antennas can be installed in various airport locations. Ham radio operators can be position in key locations in the incident command structure to provide an additional, backup means of communication. They provide all their own equipment. The telephone and cellular companies can also provide temporary and additional means of communication during an aviation crisis.

Public Works Departments

City and County Public Works Departments can provide a wide variety of vehicles, equipment, and personnel to support an aircraft incident response. State Highway Departments, Water Departments, Gas and Electric Utility Companies may be able to provide similar resources.

Civil Air Patrol

This volunteer organization can provide several aircraft disaster related services. They have aircraft and qualified personnel to search for and locate downed aircraft **(Figure 10.10)**. They can locate and turn off Emergency Location Transmitters (ELTs), which have malfunctioned. Civil Air Patrol units have provided many disaster relief services such as perimeter security and helping in the morgue. This resource is usually provided free of charge and accessed by contacting the Air Force Rescue Coordination Center (AFRCC) at Scott Air Force Base, Illinois, at 1-800-851-3051.

Figure 10.10 A Civil Air Patrol (CAP) aircraft in flight. *Courtesy of Susan C. Robertson, NHQ Photographer, Civi Air Patrol.*

Airport Tenants and Fixed Based Operators (FBOs)

Airport tenants and FBOs may be able to provide a wide variety of resources, equipment, facilities, and specialized personnel. There may be aircraft maintenance and repair facilities with qualified aircraft mechanics, heavy lift capability, and specialized forcible entry and extrication equipment. Airline caterers and restaurants can feed emergency responders, incident scene workers, and other persons associated with the incident. Helicopter contractors, aeronautical/flight schools, rental car, bus companies, and other businesses at the airport may be able to provide resources and assistance. Tenant and FBO facilities can sometimes be used for meeting, work, planning, or holding areas. Airlines and FBOs can assist with defueling damaged aircraft prior to body recovery and accident investigation operations.

Office of Emergency Services/Management (OES/OEM)

City, county, and state Offices of Emergency Services (sometimes called Offices of Emergency Management), their emergency coordinators, and mutual aid coordinators act as a focal point to access many specialized resources and assistance. The Federal Emergency Management Agency (FEMA) is the contact for federal resources during disasters. These agencies may also provide disaster response teams, communication, and command capabilities.

Search and Rescue (SAR) Teams

There are many volunteer, professional, and paid organizations that specialize in certain types of search and rescue. This may involve wilderness, mountain, and desert SAR teams, mounted posses, underwater teams and divers, 4-wheel drive teams, snowmobile teams, and several types of search dog units.

Construction Contractors and Equipment Rental Companies

This is a source of many specialized resources that may be needed such as the following:

- Vehicles (cranes, tractors, trucks, trailers, hoists, forklifts)
- Tools and equipment (cutting torches, saws, electrical generators, lights, jacks)

- Cordoning supplies (tarps, plastic sheeting, fencing, barricades, traffic cones)
- Equipment for survivors and emergency crews (portable toilets, etc)

Other Operational Considerations

Handling communications and dealing with the news media are two other operational considerations that must be addressed during emergency planning for aircraft incidents. The agencies that would be involved in such an incident must resolve any communications difficulties prior to an incident to ensure responding personnel and equipment can communicate during the emergency.

Emergency plans must also address how the emergency response effort will handle news media relations. A Public Information Officer (PIO) is often assigned to brief the news media on the information appropriate for the situation (**Figure 10.11**).

Figure 10.11 An ARFF public affairs officers (PIO) briefing the press during an ARFF exercise.

Communications

In order for multiagency operations to be successful, clear communication is essential. Although each agency or group of agencies is assigned a specific radio channel for transmitting and receiving during day-to-day, routine activities and emergency activities, all agencies concerned must have one or more common channels for mutual aid operations. In addition, they should have multichannel scanning capability in order to monitor local radio channels for critical traffic. The use of radio codes or esoteric terminology must be suspended during joint operations. The use of Clear Text or Plain Text, as specified in the National Incident Management System (NIMS), helps to eliminate confusion.

Multiagency Radio Communication System

A Multi Agency Radio Communication System (MARCS) radio is now available in some states. The MARCS System is a statewide radio system that will give emergency agencies that subscribe to it, the ability to have contiguous communications throughout the state.

Strict radio discipline must also be exercised to facilitate the proper and efficient use of shared radio channels. The use of multiple channels will assist in maintaining communication control of an incident. The Airport Incident Action Plan (AIAP) should address the Incident Communication Plan which specifies call signs, radio frequencies, and command/tactical and EMS channels to name a few.

News Media

By establishing good working relationships with news media personnel before aircraft accidents/incidents occur, ARFF personnel can avoid logistical difficulties during these airport emergencies. Recognizing the importance of media coverage, fire department personnel should meet periodically with representatives of the various news media to discuss mutual concerns about necessary scene security versus the public's right to know. At the same time, they can develop clear procedures that allow both disciplines to perform their respective functions without undue interference from the other.

Newspaper, radio, or television representatives may arrive at an accident scene before investigative authorities arrive. They should be directed to a predetermined site designated for the media. Emergency personnel should see that representatives from the media stay clear of the danger area and should refer them to the Public Information Officer.

The PIO should inform media personnel of any areas where there is a legitimate safety concern, such as those involving hazardous materials or unexploded ordnance, and any other access restrictions by reason of an investigation that is pending or in progress. Beyond that, ARFF personnel should cooperate fully with media personnel as long as it does not interfere with rescue or fire fighting efforts. Should evacuation of the surrounding area be deemed advisable, the broadcast media can be very helpful in notifying the public.

Experience has shown that the public interest is best served when only accurate, factual information is released to the news media. Therefore, ARFF personnel should refrain from making statements and should refer all news media representatives to the public information officer. The PIO should not editorialize or speculate about the incident but should give the media only information that has been confirmed. Should a commercial or military aircraft be involved, the release of information to the media becomes the responsibility of representatives of the carrier and/or the investigative agency once they are on scene.

The law permits photographs to be taken of anything at the scene of a civil aircraft accident as long as no physical evidence is disturbed in the process. Photographs may also be taken at the scene of a military aircraft accident/incident unless classified material is exposed. In that case, military personnel will attempt to cover or remove the material. If they cannot, the PIO should advise photographers that photographs are not permitted. If, after being informed, photographers persist, they will be asked to surrender the film to law enforcement or military personnel. If they refuse, they will be advised that they are subject to penalty under federal law. Willfully retaining a photograph negative or digital image that compromises national security is punishable by a fine, imprisonment, or both.

Emergency Response

Ultimately, an airport emergency plan needs to address specific emergency situations. Events to be prepared for include but are not limited to: building fires, hazardous material incidents, aircraft accident/incident, fuel facility fires, and terrorist activities. The sections that follow address these incidents as well as a number of other, specific emergencies an AEP should include.

Response to Accidents Involving Military Aircraft

An emergency may involve a military aircraft and requiring a military incident commander or representative in the unified command. Only military personnel should deal with delicate, dangerous, and complicated military aircraft systems such as canopies, ejection seats, armament, ordinance, weaponry, and other specialized aircraft characteristics.

Upon notification that an accident involving military aircraft has occurred, the nearest military installation should be called or the National Response Center should be notified.

> **NOTE:** The telephone number for the National Response Center is 1-800-424-8802.

In addition, the regional Federal Emergency Management Agency (FEMA) office should be contacted. After being notified, the military will dispatch assistance teams that usually include the following personnel:

- **Base fire department personnel** — depending on the terms of any existing mutual aid agreement, the ranking officer responding from the base fire department will meet with the civilian IC and either become part of a unified command, act as a technical advisor to the IC, or assume command if the incident is declared a National Defense Area (NDA). While most civilian agencies having mutual aid agreements with federal fire departments usually agree to relinquish control of incidents involving military aircraft, a *unified command* is often appropriate, especially when collateral damage has occurred.

- **Explosive ordnance disposal (EOD) personnel** — EOD personnel disarm, remove, and recover weapons, parts, and residue **(Figure 10.12)**

- **Military police** — may assist the local law enforcement agency as needed; however, they have no peace-officer authority outside of a military installation unless the incident is declared a National Defense Area. In that case, the military police then have full authority over the scene/area control.

- **Medical personnel** — assist with both military and civilian casualties

- **Bioenvironmental personnel** — help with the management of radioactive materials and with decontamination of personnel and equipment

- **Mortuary affairs personnel** — assist with the recovery and identification of human remains

- **Information officer** — either serves as or works closely with the incident PIO to release information to news media representatives

- **Accident Investigation Board personnel** — unless the accident also involves civilian aircraft, only the military Accident Investigation Board investigates the cause of the accident, determines the nature and extent of hazards created by the crash, and attempts to mitigate them

Figure 10.12 A U.S. Air Force explosive ordnance disposal technician during an aircraft crash exercise. *Courtesy of TSgt Douglas K. Lingefelt (USAF), Defense Visual Information Center (DVIC).*

- *Legal officer* — advises and assists citizens in their claims against the federal government
- *Heavy-equipment personnel* —remove the wreckage of military aircraft; however, the owners of any civilian aircraft involved are responsible for removing that wreckage

When military officials arrive at the scene of an aircraft accident, they will need to obtain the following information from witnesses to assist in the investigation of the accident:

- Time of the accident
- Direction in which the aircraft was headed
- Weather conditions at the time of the accident
- Whether anyone was seen parachuting from the aircraft
- Whether there was an explosion in the air prior to the crash

Airport Structure Fires

While the primary focus of aircraft rescue and fire fighting agencies is providing fire protection and rescue services for aircraft incidents, they must often deal with fires in structures on the airport. The FAA requires indexed airports to address structure fires on airport property in the AEP. The AEP will usually only identify what agencies have responsibility for structural firefighting and it is up to those agencies to develop their own SOPs. Terminals, aircraft hangars, control towers, and other ancillary structures are all integral parts of an airfield and require fire protection as well.

Emergency response plans for airport structures should identify evacuation procedures for terminals, hangars, and control towers. These plans should also define the roles and responsibilities of the ARFF agency and local fire and emergency services. On some airfields, the local ARFF agency serves as the primary response agency for the structures on that airfield while the local municipal fire and emergency services agency supports them. On other airfields, the local municipal fire and emergency services agency serves as the primary responder to airport structure fires and the ARFF agency supports them. See IFSTA's **Essentials of Fire Fighting** for more information on structural firefighting procedures.

Response to Hazardous Materials Incidents

The potential for hazardous materials responses is another area which emergency planners need to address in establishing emergency plans. Hazardous materials are often found on airfields in fuel and oil storage areas, aircraft refueling and servicing vehicles, delivery vehicles, aircraft maintenance hangers, and cargo areas. Emergency planners must consider the hazards presented the following substances:

- Aircraft fuels
- Lubricants
- Hydraulic fluids
- Liquid oxygen (LOX)
- Paint solvents
- Non-destructive inspection (NDI) radiation sources

Hazardous material response plans should focus on the hazards commonly found on the particular airfield. The plan must identify which agencies will provide special equipment and personnel and what the procedures are for notifying these response agencies. The AEP will identify the organizations and agencies that are responsible for hazardous material response on the airport, as well as other agencies that will support a response. It is up to those agencies to develop their own SOPs for haz mat response on the airport.

Under SARA Title III, *The Emergency Planning and Community Right-to-Know Act (EPCRA)*, the airport or airport tenants will usually be required to have "Hazardous Material Business Plans (HMBPs)", if they use or have above a certain quantity of solid, liquid, or gaseous hazardous materials at their facility. This plan must be submitted to the administering agency (usually the city or county fire department, or the health department) and must identify responsible persons, contact numbers, employee training, inventory, quantities, and location of hazardous materials.

Contagious Disease Response

The continued growth of commercial passenger air travel has spawned concerns about the potential for an aircraft to carry one or more passengers who are carriers of a contagious disease. Such individuals could spread disease via airborne transmission to their fellow passengers and those passengers could in turn spread the contagion further on connecting flights or throughout a busy airport terminal.

Emergency plans for contagious disease response should identify the procedures for emergency responders to do the following:

- Protect themselves from becoming contaminated.
- Isolate potentially contaminated passengers from those who are not contaminated.
- Provide emergency medical care for those taken ill.
- Provide transportation to medical facilities for those taken ill.
- Contact the local health department or the Centers for Disease Control.

Terrorism Response

Airfields and aircraft have long been targets of terrorists. Hijacked aircraft have been landed at airfields and have created the need for emergency services to respond to these incidents. The potential for individuals to bring sophisticated weapons such as pistols and hand grenades onto aircraft has been reduced over the years due to the use of metal and chemical detectors and baggage screenings. However, terrorists have learned to bring unconventional weapons such as box cutters and binary (two component) explosives on board.

Because hazardous materials may be used in or be released by a terrorist incident, many parts of a terrorist incident response plan will parallel a hazardous materials incident response plan. The danger of secondary events designed to incapacitate the emergency responders and the criminal nature of a terror attack require a different approach.

Airfield emergency planners must develop emergency plans for responding to terrorist incidents that are commensurate with the risks and hazards of that particular airport. A terrorist incident response plan for a general aviation field would be different than one for a large passenger airport because the types of aircraft involved, situations, and hazards are significantly different. Terrorist incident response plans need to include additional agencies, such as the Department of Homeland Security (DHS) and the Federal Bureau of Investigation (FBI), because of the criminal nature of the incident. An aircraft staging area should be identified within the Emergency Response Plan for aircraft involved in potential terrorist activities. The staging area should be in an isolated located away from the terminal and other aircraft.

Response to Mass Casualty Incidents

Crashes involving commercial passenger aircraft can result in a large number of casualties. Emergency responders must be prepared to handle numerous walking wounded, severely injured, and, potentially, deceased passengers at the scene of such incidents **(Figure 10.13, p. 328).**

Mass Casualty Incident (MCI) response plans must identify the procedures for assisting the walking wounded, triaging the severely injured, arranging transportation for those who are injured, and the respectful protection of the deceased. MCI response plans must also define the roles and responsibilities of each agency involved in such a response. Chapter 11 of this manual outlines the specifics for preparing and implementing an MCI plan. Training resources from the National Fire Academy and Federal Emergency Management Agency are available.

Figure 10.13 A mass casualty incident (MCI) exercise at an airport. *Courtesy of William D. Stewart.*

Post-Incident Scene Control

The site of an aircraft incident can be a busy place for some time after the emergency itself is terminated. Fire/rescue personnel, police, and investigators will commonly remain to assist in the investigation phase of the incident. Personnel from the airline, Airline Pilots Association, Association of Flight Attendants, and other agencies may also be on the scene to represent their organizations' interests.

It is important that a plan exists to allow for the presence of such personnel without creating a hazard to them and also ensuring that evidence at the incident scene is not tampered with accidentally or intentionally. The emergency plan should identify the following:

- Potential parties that might come to the post-incident scene
- Procedures for allowing these personnel access
- Credentialing procedures and policies
- Safety precautions and procedures
- Entry control and exit point that all personnel must pass through when conducting business at the crash site
- All the necessities needed to allow the operation to run seamlessly for numerous days

Training

Developing an AEP is not an end in itself, nor is it a guarantee for an effective emergency response. Airport emergency planning does, however, help reduce the confusion that often exists during emergency operations. The efficiency with which an emergency operation is handled may depend upon how well the involved agencies have planned. Beyond planning, the success of the operation depends upon how well those involved understand the plan and how well they execute it. The plan will only be successful if training is designed and conducted to address each part of the plan. This is best accomplished by conducting small exercises that focus on each specific task of response coordination. Upon completion of the small exercises, a large-scale drill should be conducted to exercise the entire emergency plan, noting discrepancies and making modifications to correct suspected deficiencies.

The two sections that follow describe training considerations for including mutual aid agencies, support personnel, and joint training exercises.

Training for Mutual Aid and Support Personnel

Few, if any, fire departments can afford to maintain sufficient numbers of on-duty personnel to handle every contingency within their boundaries without assistance. Most departments are staffed and equipped to handle the usual, day-to-day accidents/incidents; but in a major event or with multiple simultaneous events, mutual aid is often needed. All parties to mutual aid agreements should participate in airport emergency planning, training, and drills.

Because fire department response times may be more critical in an aircraft accident than in other types of more commonly encountered emergencies, mutual aid fire departments and airport support personnel should be sufficiently trained to perform their fire fighting duties quickly and efficiently. This performance can be ensured only through frequent training and evaluation. Nearby structural fire departments should participate with airport fire departments in order to become familiar with the airport and its aircraft. Joint training exercises, drills, and tests should be conducted at the airport. Participation in combined training exercises may help to evaluate airport emergency plans.

Personnel assigned to stations near an airport should become familiar with the airport and with the aircraft that commonly use it. Mutual aid companies should be familiar with the runways, taxiways, apron areas, hydrants and other water sources, and access routes to various airport areas. They should also know airport terminology, control-tower light signals, and other information unique to an airport operation.

Mutual aid training should emphasize the use of structural apparatus and equipment to combat aircraft fires, both in support of airport fire suppression forces and alone if necessary. Emphasis should be placed on rapid resupply so mutual aid personnel can assist in getting ARFF apparatus back in service while on the scene or at the fire station. Firefighters should practice aircraft fire and rescue operations under conditions that are as realistic as possible. Structural firefighters should practice interior aircraft fire fighting operations and should learn to adapt structural techniques to aircraft fire fighting. Conversely, airport fire fighting forces should be equally familiar with the areas surrounding the airport and with how their apparatus and equipment can be used to the best advantage in support of structural fire fighting operations.

If airport support personnel are properly trained, they may be an effective adjunct to regular fire prevention forces in many areas of the airport. Classes for all airport employees should acquaint them with the use of fire extinguishers, fire reporting procedures, and evacuation procedures. With basic fire extinguisher training, support personnel may extinguish incipient fires in aircraft, terminals or other large buildings, fueling areas, hangars, and similar locations.

Joint Training Exercises

Regardless of the amount of thought and effort invested in developing a plan, one or more joint training exercises are needed to test it. Personnel should participate in several full-scale training exercises before they can feel comfortable that the plan will function successfully. The operational priorities in aircraft rescue and fire fighting are the same as in other types of emergencies: rescue, fire control, and loss control. The emphasis here should be on tactical considerations among the participating agencies. Successful execution of joint operations depends on airport emergency planning and cooperation. Identifying and reducing differences in apparatus, equipment, communication systems to include terminology, procedures, and operational styles or philosophies can be of critical importance in the disposition of an actual emergency.

After every exercise, all those involved should participate in a comprehensive, nonthreatening post incident analysis. All facets of the plan should be reviewed objectively, and any deficiencies that emerge should be corrected. The entire plan should be exercised once a year by conducting at least a tabletop exercise. A full-scale disaster drill should be conducted as required by the authority having jurisdiction to ensure that participants are familiar with their roles. Prior to an incident or accident, a thorough plan is the most effective tool. Taking time to develop a complete comprehensive plan has proven to save lives once the plan has been practiced and placed into action. It is important that the plan encompasses all aspects of on-scene and off-scene operations that will be needed. Contacts must be made to ensure the needed materials are available or can be obtained in a short period of time when needed. Constant review and training will help all personnel become more familiar with the plan and also adapt the plan to meet changing needs.

Summary

An airport emergency response plan should include multiple considerations about the airport to which it applies. These considerations include the types of aircraft the airport services, the airport's possible accident sites and their accessibility, as well as information about climate conditions and search and rescue capabilities at the airport. In addition, an AEP should establish all resources available to ARFF personnel, which agencies and organizations should be contacted to obtain those resources, and how communications to resources are coordinated in an emergency.

An AEP must also describe responses to specific emergencies such as terrorist incidents or military aircraft crashes that could occur at an airport. In all cases, every aspect of an AEP should be practiced on a regular basis. Joint training exercises should include all mutual aid support agencies that may respond to an emergency to ensure that all applicable agencies are well practiced in performing their parts of the AEP. This training is as essential to successful emergency termination as the careful planning that must be done to create successful plans for emergency responders to follow.

Review Questions

1. How are accidents defined and measured?

2. What are the types of search and rescue operations that can be activated?

3. What are some common problems identified during aircraft incident critiques?

4. What agencies may need to be notified of an accident by airport management personnel?

5. When is the secondary response network activated?

6. What are some activities for which local Department of Defense (DoD) installations may be called upon for assistance?

7. When are ham radio organizations especially valuable as a means of communication during an ARFF incident?

8. What is the Multi Agency Radio Communication System (MARCS)?

9. What are the duties of military police when called upon for assistance during an ARFF incident?

10. Discuss procedures that must be identified in mass casualty incident (MCI) response plans.

Strategic and Tactical Operations

Chapter Contents

chapter **11**

Key Terms

NFPA® references for Chapter 11:

NFPA® 1003 (2010)
   5.1.1.3
   5.2.2
   5.3.10

**NFPA® 1002
(2009 - Chapter 9)**
   9.2.1

Strategic and Tactical Operations

Learning Objectives

After reading this chapter, students shall be able to:

1. Explain incident management considerations. (NFPA® 1003, 5.1.1.3, 5.2.2)

2. Describe types of in-flight and ground emergencies. (NFPA® 1003, 5.2.4, 5.4.1)

3. Discuss low- and high-impact crashes. (NFPA® 1003, 5.2.4, 5.4.1)

4. Describe response procedures for aircraft emergencies. (NFPA® 1003, 5.2.2, 5.4.1)

5. Explain considerations of responding to accidents involving military aircraft. (NFPA® 1003, 5.1.1.3, 5.2.2, 5.4.1)

Chapter 11
Strategic and Tactical Operations

Case History

There are a wide variety of aircraft emergency situations and accident scenarios. One of the most challenging is the crash of a large passenger aircraft with a post-crash fuel fire. One of these emergencies occurred at Dallas-Fort Worth International Airport on August 31, 1988. Delta Airlines Flight 1141 crashed shortly after takeoff. There were 108 persons on board and 4,446 gallons (16 825 L) of jet fuel. The aircraft came to a stop 3,200 feet (975 m) beyond the departure end of the runway, near the airport boundary fence. It broke into three sections, consisting of the flight deck, main passenger compartment, and tail. Both the forward and aft sections were twisted and leaning significantly to the side. The post-crash fuel spill fire engulfed the right side and rear of the aircraft, eventually spreading to the interior. Survivors evacuated through exits along the left side of the aircraft and breaks in the fuselage.

All available ARFF units responded from the four airport fire stations. The airport was closed for seven minutes to allow emergency vehicles to use taxiways and runways to respond to the scene. Three ARFF units arrived within five minutes of the crash. Turrets were used to quickly control all exterior fuel spill fires threatening the aircraft fuselage. A grass fire was allowed to burn away from the impact area, which was later extinguished by mutual aid fire units. Interior attack hose lines were immediately extended through over-wing exits and openings in the front of the aircraft by the crash. Forward interior fire spread was stopped to allow the rescue of the incapacitated three-person flight crew. The incident commander estimated that majority of the fire was knocked down in the first five minutes. All fires were totally extinguished within forty (40) minutes. Approximately 15,800 gallons (59 790 L) of water and 650 gallons (2 460 L) of foam concentrate were used to extinguish the fires.

Thirteen passengers died of smoke inhalation. One passenger who had successfully evacuated attempted to reenter the aircraft and died of thermal burns. Ten bodies were found in the tail section, where they had tried unsuccessfully to open and exit through the aft galley door. The airport emergency medical services responded with two mobile intensive care units, one mobile rapid response vehicle, and medical triage support trailers. EMS also requested all available mutual aid ambulances. A triage area was set up east of the aircraft. Simultaneously, an off-airport ambulance company and mutual aid fire department had set up another triage area for sixty-nine passengers that had moved away from the accident scene and were not visible in the tall grass. This second triage area initially caused some confusion. There were also two more victims than passengers listed on the manifest due to two unticketed infants.

Overall, the response was timely, aggressive, and effective. As soon as the exterior fires were controlled, interior fire attack and rescue was quickly initiated, resulting in the successful rescue of the flight crew. Many different airport and off-airport organizations and agencies worked efficiently together to get the necessary personnel and equipment to the scene, secure the area, and mitigate this tragic accident.

When seconds count, ARFF responders must be capable of making critical decisions under adverse conditions. Tactical decision-making starts at the time when the tones alert and continues to be made both while enroute and during initial approach to the scene. Size up and correct tactics will need to be implemented in seconds. These decisions include outside agency assistance, emergency medical assistance, and a variety of logistical needs that must be established early for positive results to occur. The best place for the decision-making process to be practiced is the training room prior to an incident. Strategies can be explored, plans can be set, checklists established, and tactics can be reinforced in a controlled environment. It is critical for response crews to conduct scenario-based training in an effort to obtain an idea of the challenges faced at a crash site.

Whether announced or unannounced, the general types of aircraft accidents and/or incidents with which ARFF personnel are confronted are in-flight emergencies or ground emergencies.

Each jurisdiction should have standard operating procedures that address the ARFF response to each of these types of emergencies. These standard operating procedures vary from simply being notified of in-flight emergencies to a full response to a major ground emergency. Historically, the vast majority of in-flight emergencies conclude with the plane landing safely and little, if any, assistance being required of ARFF responders. However, ARFF personnel should not become complacent and must always be prepared for an in-flight emergency to become a ground emergency that requires their immediate intervention.

It is also important to understand the difference between an aircraft accident and an aircraft incident. According to NFPA® 402, *Guide for Aircraft Rescue and Fire Fighting Operations*, an aircraft *accident* involves an occurrence during the operation of an aircraft in which any person involved suffers death or serious injury or in which the aircraft receives substantial damage. An aircraft *incident* encompasses an occurrence other than an accident associated with the operation of an aircraft that affects or could affect continued safe operation if not corrected. An incident does not result in serious injury to personnel or substantial damage to an aircraft. By definition, an aircraft accident is obviously more serious than an incident.

Definitions of ARFF Responses

ARFF personnel respond to accidents, incidents, and emergencies which are each unique and defined in the following ways:

- *Accident* — occurrence associated with the operation of an aircraft where as a result of the operation of an aircraft, any person (either inside or outside the aircraft) receives fatal or serious injury or any aircraft receives substantial damage; not caused by the deliberate action of one or more persons and that leads to damage or injury

- *Incident* — occurrence, other than an accident, associated with the operation of an aircraft that affects or could affect the safety of operations

- *Emergency* — sudden or unexpected event or group of events that require immediate action to mitigate

This chapter deals with the types of accidents, incidents, or emergencies with which aircraft rescue and fire fighting (ARFF) personnel are faced and the actions they should perform. Due to the dynamic nature of each incident, the sequence of events and operations may differ and quite often occur simultaneously.

Incident Management

Airport fire departments are required to adopt and utilize an incident management system for their strategic and tactical operations. Following several terrorist incidents the United States government mandated that all emergency services organizations use common terminology and command structures to improve their interoperability. After this mandate, Homeland Security Presidential Directive/HSPD-5 took the issue a step further stating that all state and local governments and tribal entities MUST adopt the National Incident Management System (NIMS) in order to be eligible for federal funds. Consequently, airport emergency organizations must ensure that their command structure will interface with "outside" organizations during an emergency, as these outside organizations will most certainly adopt NIMS.

In March 2004, the U.S. government officially adopted ICS as part of the National Incident Management System, and all federal agencies or agencies receiving federal funding must use the updated, NIMS-ICS. Additional information on the NIMS-ICS model and its application may be found in the NIMS document itself and the *Model Procedures Guide* series developed by the National Fire Service Incident Management Consortium and published by Fire Protection Publications. NIMS-ICS is designed to be applicable to small, single-unit incidents that may last a few minutes and also to complex, large-scale incidents involving several agencies and many mutual aid units that possibly last for days or weeks. Information regarding NIMS-ICS can be found on the NIMS website at http://www.fema.gov/emergency/nims/.

Components of NIMS-ICS

NIMS-ICS combines command strategy with organizational procedures. It provides a functional, systematic command organizational structure and system. The ICS organizational structure clearly shows the lines of communication and chain of command. NIMS-ICS is designed for single-agency or multiagency use, and it increases the effectiveness of command and personnel safety. The organizational design is applicable to all types of emergency and nonemergency events throughout the airport environment.

NIMS-ICS is the basic operating system for all incidents within each facility or agency. Under NIMS-ICS, the transition from a small-scale to large-scale incident and/or multiagency operation requires minimal adjustment for any of the agencies involved. The following components work together interactively to provide the basis for clear communication and effective operations:

- Common terminology
- Modular organization
- Integrated communications
- Unified command structure
- Consolidated action plans

- Manageable span of control
- Pre-designated incident facilities
- Comprehensible resource management

To understand the application of NIMS-ICS in the aviation setting, ARFF personnel should be aware of the major position descriptions within the NIMS-ICS structure. NIMS-ICS involves the following five major organizational positions:

- Command
- Operations
- Planning
- Logistics
- Finance/Administration

NIMS-ICS also adds another position, Intelligence, which is responsible for gathering information relating to an incident. In some instances, this may actually be part of the Planning function. With the initial response one person will be responsible for establishing some of these functions. If the incident is large and complex these functions may be delegated to responding fire department personnel or other qualified personnel within the airport or mutual/automatic aid organizational structure. All personnel within the airport organization need to ensure that they are familiar with the functions they could be assigned to perform. The Incident Commander retains the responsibility for these functions until they are delegated.

NIMS-ICS Training

It is advantageous for all ARFF personnel to receive NIMS-ICS training as part of their entry level training, recurring proficiency training, and professional development. NIMS-ICS courses are offered through the online resources of the National Fire Academy, the Federal Emergency Management Agency, and many state/tribal and local agencies. **Table 11.1** identifies the appropriate courses for each level of responsibility.

Given the philosophy of ICS and scenario-based training, an Incident Commander (IC) should be able to apply the ICS principles to an aviation response. Scenario-based training allows the IC to work through the decision-making process and to review the order in which decisions need to be made. Scenario-based training will also allow driver/operators, officers, fire fighters and medics to work through their decision-making process as it relates to their delegated duties at a crash site. Support personnel such as airport operations and airport security should also participate in the training to fully understand their roles and their level of interaction. Scenario-based training also allows the IC to make mistakes and learn through trial and error so the mistakes are not made on the real incident. ARFF agencies should incorporate a system that establishes and delegates critical elements of managing an incident.

Table 11.1
NIMS-ICS Courses

Responder	Level Courses
Entry Level Responders And Disaster Workers	FEMA IS-700: NIMS, An Introduction ICS-100: Introduction to ICS (or equivalent)
First Line Supervisors	FEMA IS-700: NIMS, An Introduction ICS-100: Introduction to ICS (or equivalent) ICS-200: Basic ICS (or equivalent)
Middle Management	FEMA IS-700: NIMS, An Introduction FEMA IS-800: National Response Plan (NRP), An Introduction ICS-100: Introduction to ICS (or equivalent) ICS-200: Basic ICS (or equivalent) ICS-300: Intermediate ICS (or equivalent)
Command and General Staff	FEMA IS-700: NIMS, An Introduction FEMA IS-800: National Response Plan (NRP), A Introduction ICS-100: Introduction to ICS (or equivalent) ICS-200: Basic ICS (or equivalent) ICS-300: Intermediate ICS (or equivalent) ICS-400: Advanced ICS (or equivalent)

In-Flight Emergencies

In-flight emergencies include fires as well as other problems that may lead to an aircraft accident/incident. These emergencies include the following:

- System failure
- Hydraulic problems
- Engine failure/fire
- Inoperable or malfunctioning flight controls
- Gear failure (gear retracted or otherwise unsafe for landing), either hydraulic or mechanical
- Special military considerations (explosives becoming dislodged, ejection seat activated, canopy becoming unattached, etc.)
- Loss of cabin pressure
- Onboard fire
- Bird strike
- Structural failure
- Low or no fuel
- Lighting strike, turbulence, wind shear, and icing

> **NOTE:** Although these items are not emergencies in themselves, their effects can cause emergencies.

While in flight, aircraft frequently develop minor difficulties that may or may not be cause for alarm. The majority of these in-flight problems go unnoticed by occupants because they are not serious enough to cause the aircraft to operate abnormally. An example of this type of incident is a minor electrical short or malfunction in one of the warning systems. A malfunction of this type can cause a fire warning light on the instrument panel to indicate a problem when none actually exists. When a fire warning light activates, the crew tries to determine whether there is a fire by making instrument checks and visual observations. If the pilot-in-command is satisfied that the aircraft is safe and airworthy after these checks have been made, the flight continues normally. If a problem actually exists and an emergency is declared, air traffic control notifies the airport fire department, and ARFF personnel respond to their pre-designated standby locations and await the aircraft. Upon landing, the in-flight emergency switches to a ground emergency and depending on the severity may require a full-scale emergency response.

Hydraulic failure or inoperative landing gear may seriously jeopardize the safety of the aircraft and its occupants. Depending on the severity, the aircraft may experience a variety of flight control problems both while flying and once on the ground. This type of emergency may affect aircraft steering, braking, and/or stopping. ARFF responders may want to consider alternate standby locations when dealing with an emergency of this nature so that the safety of the ARFF crews is not jeopardized.

An interior fire aboard an occupied aircraft is a true emergency, particularly if the fire occurs in-flight. Because of the automatic fire detection systems aboard modern aircraft, interior fires are usually detected in their incipient stage.

If the fire is accessible in-flight, the aircraft crew members will usually attempt to extinguish it using onboard fire extinguishers. If the fire cannot be handled with the onboard fire protection equipment or if its location is inaccessible in-flight, it may develop into a serious fire and spread rapidly. In this case, an emergency landing will be attempted immediately.

Depending on the amount of time it takes to make an emergency landing, heat, smoke, and toxic gases may accumulate, creating a deadly threat to the occupants of the aircraft. If the toxic gases build to a sufficient level, flashover or rollover can occur when emergency exits are opened. It is vitally important that rescue workers vent the aircraft as quickly as possible.

Ground Emergencies

Ground emergencies involve aircraft that are conducting operations on the ground. This type of emergency could involve an aircraft and a ground vehicle, a structure, or another aircraft. Operational plans should be developed that address these types of emergencies. These may range from a simple inspection of the aircraft to a multijurisdictional response.

Figure 11.1 This KC-135 tanker aircraft caught fire and exploded while taxiing to parking. *Courtesy of SSgt Michael Z. Moore (USAF), Defense Visual Information Center (DVIC).*

Ground emergencies (from least serious to most serious) that ARFF crews are likely to encounter are as follows:

- Overheated wheel assemblies
- Tire/wheel failures
- Combustible metal fires
- Fuel leaks and spills
- Engine fires or APU fires
- Uncontained engine failures
- Aircraft interior (or "cabin") fires **(Figure 11.1)**

Emergency Evacuation Assistance

Once an aircraft has landed, the flight crew may initiate an emergency evacuation. Arriving ARFF personnel should try to prevent an unnecessary evacuation by immediately contacting the flight crew on the appropriate frequency and giving the flight crew a report on exterior conditions. With most engine, wheel assembly, and other minor exterior emergencies, the situation can be controlled by ARFF personnel, without threatening the aircraft occupants or needing an evacuation. An unnecessary evacuation can endanger and injure the evacuees, as well as complicate and interfere with ARFF operations. The decision to evacuate is always ultimately the call of the pilot in command. ARFF personnel should not impede the egress of occupants and crew in an attempt to enter the fuselage for rescue and/or fire fighting. Personnel must locate and open any other available exits. Additionally, many occupants may not be able to extricate themselves, so ARFF personnel should be prepared to assist after all those who are able have exited.

Discharging agent onto an aircraft with an interior fire wastes agent and creates a hazardous environment for the occupants of the aircraft. The importance lies in opening up the aircraft. This can be accomplished by using all available exits and ARFF crew members assisting occupants from the escape slides by positioning themselves to the side of the slide and lifting occupants to their feet as they approach the bottom of the slide.

When dealing with an exterior fire, personnel should position ARFF apparatus in an effort to extinguish and keep the fire away from the exits being used for egress. Upon making an interior attack, they should use hose streams for ventilation as well as for extinguishment.

Wheel Assemblies

Modern aircraft wheels are commonly equipped with fusible plugs incorporated into the rims. These plugs are designed to melt, automatically deflating the tires when the rim reaches a predetermined temperature, usually from 300°F to 400°F (149°C to 204°C). Releasing the tire pressure reduces the pressure on the wheel, thus reducing the possibility of wheel collapse and fragmentation. Caution must be used as incidents have occurred in which the fusible plugs failed to function properly. Firefighters must approach incidents of this nature from a fore or aft position.

The sections that follow address the two most common hazards related to wheel assemblies: hot brakes and wheel fires.

Hot Brakes

Brakes and wheel assemblies frequently overheat causing ARFF personnel concern during both normal and emergency landings. There are several methods to determine wheel temperature. Thermal imagers and other temperature monitoring devices can be used to determine wheel temperatures from a safe distance. On some newer jet transport aircraft, wheel temperatures can be monitored from the flight deck.

Any time a large transport aircraft lands long, rejects a takeoff, makes a no flap landing, or has problems using engine thrust reversers, ARFF personnel should prepare for a hot brake situation. This type of emergency is usually recognizable by brown colored smoke coming from wheel assemblies. If wheel assemblies are smoking when the aircraft stops, the situation should be monitored because peak wheel temperatures may not be reached until 20 to 30 minutes after the aircraft has come to a complete stop on the ramp.

Acceptable Methods for cooling hot brakes include the following:

- *Continue Taxiing* — will assist in dissipating heat when appropriate; only useful if taxiing can be done without the flight crew applying the brakes; ARFF personnel should monitor this condition until it is determined to be safe

- *Normal Cooling* — wheel assembly cools on its own in a remote area of the airport designated by ARFF personnel; ARFF personnel should monitor this situation until it is determined to be safe

- *Water mist of fog pattern* — cools wheel assembly; water mist or fog pattern in a continuous flow is a suitable alternative and safer than using fans in most cases.

- *Fans* — air cools wheel assembly; suitable method to expedite normal cooling; most ARFF departments use portable fans, and this use places firefighters close to the hazard zone

WARNING!

When responding to a hot brake incident or wheel fire, always approach from forward or aft of the wheel assembly while exercising extreme caution. Never approach from the sides in-line with the axle. In addition, always wear full protective gear including SCBA. The brakes of some aircraft contain beryllium, which produces toxic fumes and smoke.

Wheel Fires

If the wheel assembly is on fire, the safest approach is to use large amounts of water from a distance using turrets. This application keeps the firefighters out of the hazard zone and allows for extinguishment and rapid cooling. Once the fire is out, cooling efforts should be maintained to minimize damage to other components. Handlines can also be used in place of turrets as long as firefighters approach from a fore or aft position. If water is not available, any available agent should be used to extinguish a wheel assembly fire.

The use of combustible metals in the wheel assemblies is declining due to the increased weight of the metals and their tendency to accumulate rust. New generation brakes and wheel assemblies are constructed of Cera-metalic, aluminum alloy, and carbon posing less of a hazard than older generation assemblies, which contained small amounts of magnesium or titanium in their construction. These metals are rarely found in today's commercial and military aircraft. This change should be taken into consideration when addressing department policy in handling these types of emergencies.

Hydraulic failures involving aircraft's flight control systems may contribute to the overheating of wheel assemblies since stopping the aircraft may require applying more brake power than normally required. If the landing gear hydraulic system contains petroleum-based fluids, a fire may start around the hydraulic fittings near the wheel. These fires should be controlled immediately utilizing water and or foam depending on the situation. Failure to do so could allow conducted heat to impinge on the fuselage, allowing the fire to spread to the interior. If Skydrol□ (aviation hydraulic fluid) does ignite, it will thermally decompose at high temperatures, producing toxic vapors. Regardless of what is suspected to be burning during a landing gear fire, ARFF personnel must wear full protective clothing and SCBA.

Combustible Metal Fires

A variety of metals, some of them combustible such as magnesium and titanium, are used throughout modern aircraft.

Magnesium is a lightweight, silvery-white metal. Its ignition temperature is generally considered to be close to its melting point of 1,202°F (650°C). It is classified as a combustible metal, even though as a solid it does not ignite easily. Whether it ignites easily depends upon its mass (thickness and shape). Magnesium is used on most large propeller-driven aircraft and in early transport-type jet aircraft, landing gear, engine mountings, wheel cover plates, and engine components.

Titanium, a silvery-gray metal, is as strong as ordinary steel but is only about 56 percent as heavy. Some titanium alloys are up to three times as strong as the best available aluminum alloys. Titanium's ignition temperature is generally considered to be near its melting point of 3,140°F (1 727°C). It is used in engine parts and nacelles because of its resistance to heat and fire. It is also used in the landing gear assemblies of modern jet transports. Additionally, titanium is being used in greater amounts in new large aircraft.

Combustible metals may introduce additional problems when they become involved in an aircraft fire. When a combustible metal is on fire, water through turret application in heavy, coarse streams provides an accepted method of initial fire control. At first, such streams may intensify the fire and cause the burning metals to spark and shower significantly which must be considered before applying water. Water application is effective, however, because it causes the burning metal to break loose from the aircraft and prevents the unburned metal from reaching ignition temperature. Burning combustible metals around a high impact crash scene can be allowed to burn out, or can be buried with dry powder agents, dirt, or other dry inert materials. Also in some rare instances, smaller quantities of burning metal may be able to be moved to a safer area with a shovel and allowed to burn until all fuel is consumed. SCBA should always be worn to prevent the breathing of smoke from burning combustible metals. The smoke from combustible metals is extremely toxic and may contain particles of metal.

Specialized Class D extinguishing agents such as MET-L-X° and G-1 powder may also be effective in controlling magnesium and titanium fires and should be considered when water is not readily available or has not been effective.

Fuel Leaks and Spills

In some cases, ARFF personnel respond to incidents where aircraft fuel has spilled or is leaking, but it has yet to ignite. At all such incidents, ARFF personnel should take the following precautions:

- Attempt to shut off the fuel at the source or by utilizing emergency fuel shutoff or transfer valves

- Avoid actions that could provide an ignition source

- Evacuate aircraft if the spill poses a threat to occupants

- Keep all nonessential personnel clear of the area

- Make sure that fire fighting personnel are wearing full protective clothing, including SCBA

- If necessary, blanket all exposed fuel surfaces with foam; maintain the foam blanket to prevent release of fuel vapors

- Contain spilled fuel to as small an area as possible

- Prevent leaking or spilled fuel from entering runoffs, storm drains, sewers, buildings, or basements

- Keep apparatus and equipment ready to protect rescue operations in case a fire should occur

- Position apparatus upwind and uphill from the fuel spill

> **NOTE:** The procedures for handling fuel spills described in this section are subject to the regulations and procedures established by the authority having jurisdiction. Information from NFPA® 407, *Standard for Aircraft Fuel Servicing*, was included in the development of this information.

All aircraft spill incidents may be somewhat unique, but certain general principles apply in all cases. Every fuel spill involves several variables such as the following:

- Size of the spill
- Terrain
- Equipment
- Weather conditions
- Type of flammable liquid
- Aircraft occupancy
- Emergency equipment and personnel available

If a fuel leak develops or a fuel spill occurs during aircraft servicing, personnel should act as follows:

- Personnel must stop the fueling operation immediately.
- Nonessential personnel should leave the area until the hazard is neutralized, repairs are made, and the area is safe.
- Safety personnel from the airline and the airport should be notified of such incidents so a determination can be made to allow airport operations to remain in progress or terminate them until the problem has been corrected.

It may be necessary to blanket with foam any spills of aviation fuel that would be considered large spills as previously defined. The severity of the hazard created by a fuel spill depends primarily upon how volatile the fuel is and the proximity to sources of ignition. Aviation gasoline and other fuels with low flash points at normal temperatures and pressures give off vapors that are capable of forming ignitable mixtures with the air near the surface of the liquid. This process is not usually true of kerosene fuels (Jet A or Jet A-1) except where ambient temperatures are at least in the 100°F (38°C) range and the temperature of the fuel has reached the same range. It must be noted that hot pavement can reach temperatures in excess of 140 °F (60°C), therefore, spilled fuel needs to be treated as a flammable liquid in such circumstances.

During any spill or leak, extreme caution must be exercised to avoid actions that could provide ignition sources for the fuel vapors. If fuel is leaking or spilling from a fuel-servicing hose or equipment, the emergency fuel shutoff valve must be closed immediately. If the fuel is leaking or spilling from an aircraft at the filler opening, vent line, or tank seam, fuel delivery must stop immediately. All electrical power to the aircraft should be deenergized, and the aircraft should be evacuated. Maintenance personnel must thoroughly check the aircraft for damage and for flammable vapors that may have entered concealed wing or fuselage compartments before the aircraft is put back into service. Maintenance records that describe the cause, corrective action taken by various personnel, and action taken to prevent recurrence should be kept of each incident or occurrence. This information should also be contained in the fire department's incident report.

Regardless of the size spill, responders may need to evacuate an aircraft in order to safely mitigate an emergency. No one evacuating should be allowed to walk through liquid fuel. Any clothing that is sprayed or soaked with fuel should be removed at once, taking care to avoid additional sources of ignition. Fuel contamination should be washed from skin with soap and water.

Engines both on vehicles and aircraft must create a spark to start and could ignite fuel that has pooled near a vehicle. ARFF firefighters should never start any aircraft, motor vehicle, or other spark-producing equipment in an area before spilled fuel is blanketed or removed. Also, running vehicles or engines should be deactivated if it is safe to do so. The decision to deactivate nearby engines or vehicles needs to be evaluated carefully. If a vehicle engine is running at the time of the spill, it is probably better to drive the vehicle away from the hazard area unless the danger to personnel is judged to be too great. If a vehicle would have to be driven through the spilled fuel to get out of the hazard area, it should probably be left in place without deactivating the engine. Before fuel-servicing vehicles are moved, any fuel hose that was in use or connecting the vehicle and aircraft must be deactivated and safely stowed.

If it is decided that a vehicle with an internal-combustion engine must be shut down within a spill area, the engine speed should be reduced to idle before being turned off in order to prevent a backfire.

If any aircraft engine is operating at the time of the spill, the aircraft should be moved from the hazard area unless the size of the spill would be increased or the prop wash or jet blast would increase the extent of the fuel-vapor hazard.

If fuel has entered sanitary sewers or storm drains, personnel should dam inlets to prevent additional fuel from entering. The responsible utilities supervisor and local environmental health officials should be notified immediately. No further action to dilute or disperse the fuel should be taken until these officials arrive to assess the situation and make recommendations to the IC.

> **NOTE:** Some airport fueling or ramp areas may drain into an oil-water separator system. In this situation, the spilled fuel may be allowed to be flushed into the drainage system. Some jurisdictions may allow the use of emulsifiers to neutralize and break down the fuel, allowing it to be flushed into the storm sewer.

If sewer or storm drain contamination is extensive, steps should be taken to keep sources of ignition, such as operating vehicles and aircraft, away from manholes or storm drain inlets and outfalls until the atmosphere at these sites can be sampled and determined to be within safe limits.

> **NOTE:** See NFPA® 415, *Standard on Airport Terminal Buildings, Fueling Ramp Drainage, and Loading Walkways*, for further information on aircraft fueling ramps designed to reduce the danger resulting from spilled fuel by controlling its flow.

Any aircraft onto which fuel has been spilled should be thoroughly inspected to make sure that no fuel or fuel vapors have accumulated in flap well areas or internal wing sections not designed for fuel storage. It is extremely important that cargo, baggage, mailbags, or similar items that have come in contact with fuel be decontaminated before being placed aboard any aircraft.

WARNING!
Unless ordered to do so by a responsible local official, never flush fuel or other contaminants into sewers or storm drains nor introduce water into these conduits in an attempt to dilute the contaminant. Such actions could increase the possibility of ignition and could expose the airport to significant liability under environmental protection laws.

Engine/APU Fires

In the event of an engine or auxiliary power unit (APU) fire, the cockpit crew may make the first attempt to extinguish the fire by using onboard extinguishing systems. At other incidents, fire personnel may deal with an aircraft that is unoccupied; therefore, airport firefighters must be familiar with aircraft shutdown procedures and the location of external shutdown devices.

When dealing with an engine or APU fire, directing a stream of water or AFFF into the air inlet will not always extinguish the fire. Although some of the agent will go into the core of the engine or APU, the fire very likely involves the accessory section around the outside core of the engine. Clean, gaseous extinguishing agents are the agents of choice when fighting engine or APU fires. Foam may be able to be used if a clean agent is not available. The use of clean agents and foam may allow for an engine to be repaired and reused at a later date. Dry chemical may be used at the discretion of the local ARFF department but may result in engine damage.

The safest method of extinguishment is to operate the engine or APU fire shutdown system from the cockpit or, where provided, from an external fire protection panel. Large-frame aircraft usually have easily identifiable engine and APU fire shutoff handles in the cockpit. Many also have external APU fire protection panels on either the nose landing gear, in the main wheel well, on the belly, or in the tail **(Figure 11.2)**. In addition to arming the extinguishing agent bottles, these systems simultaneously deactivate the power plant's fuel, hydraulic, electrical, and pneumatic connections.

If unable to access or use the aircraft's fire protection system, or if it fails to extinguish the fire, responders may be tasked with opening the engine cowlings or APU access panel doors in an effort to fully extinguish the fire. Because of the potential of residual fuel to pool in the area of the APU during an emergency, the APU cowling should be opened from the lowest point to highest point. Due to the location and configuration of these access panels, firefighters must exercise extreme caution when performing this task. Hot and burning fluids or engine parts may be trapped inside these areas. These could fall onto firefighters when the panels are opened.

If firefighters are unable to safely access the internal components, personnel may want to consider using a piercing tool to apply extinguishing agent prior to opening. This task can be accomplished with a variety of forcible entry tools and should only be attempted after the engine has been deactivated and electrical power has been removed from the engine. The engine should be deactivated and the fuel, electrical, hydraulic, and pneumatic supply removed before using any of the engine fire control techniques discussed in this section.

The key to piercing an engine housing is to know where to penetrate and access the accessory compartment. Piercing the wrong location may miss the compartment and hit another engine component immediately behind the housing. Some aircraft are equipped with fire extinguishing access ports or knock-in panels, which can be used to apply agent directly to the engine. Other means of applying extinguishing agent may include the use of access panel doors around the engine/APU. Doors used to check oil levels or hydraulic levels may also be utilized to gain access into the inner section of the engine.

Figure 11.2 An ARFF firefighter training on APU shutdown procedures. *Courtesy of Doddy Photography.*

Cowling — Removable covering around aircraft engines.

Tail Pipe Fires

A tail pipe fire occurs when too much fuel is ejected into the engine during start-up causing fuel and fuel vapor to be emitted through the engine. Upon reaching the tail pipe assembly, the fuel and fuel vapor ignites because of the high temperatures. Usually, pilots will shut off the fuel and spool-up or rev the engine. This action will blow out the excess burning fuel from the back of the engine, at which time restart procedures can be conducted. Quite often, the fire department is not called unless the pilot is unsuccessful in extinguishing the fire. On occasion, burning fuel may drip out onto the ground from the tail pipe.

Uncontained Engine Failures

An "uncontained engine failure or disintegration" occurs when fan or compressor blades in the engine separate or the turbine section disintegrates. When this happens, fragments may tear through the engine cowling and can penetrate other areas of the aircraft. A similar problem can occur with propeller-driven aircraft when a propeller blade separates. The resulting imbalance can cause disintegration of the engine and loss of control of the aircraft. If the engine shrapnel stays inside the engine housing or cowling, it is a "contained engine failure or disintegration."

The worst-case scenario involves fragments of engine components piercing the fuselage and/or wing structure, causing injuries to occupants, puncturing fuel tanks, severing fuel and hydraulic lines, starting an interior fire, or damaging the flight-control system. Due to the location and configuration of fuel tanks and lines, this type of incident may result in a three-dimensional flowing fuel fire. This may make it necessary for the flight crew to immediately evacuate the aircraft. Firefighters may be forced to make an aggressive interior fire attack in order to support evacuation procedures. Unless the integrity of the passenger compartment has been compromised, an uncontained engine failure can be handled like a normal engine fire.

Aircraft Interior Fires

Major aircraft interior fires have occurred for many reasons. Some have started due to electrical problems. Others have started in lower cargo compartments on passenger aircraft or in containers loaded on cargo aircraft, due to the presence of combustible or reactive materials. Uncontained engine failures have started interior fires. Many fuel spill fires have spread to aircraft interiors after low impact crashes. ARFF personnel should try to get as much information from Air Traffic Control regarding in-flight reports of interior fire situations. Most airport fire departments may not have enough resources to deal with an interior fire on a passenger or cargo aircraft. These departments should activate adequate mutual/automatic aid, as soon as possible. If ARFF personnel wait until it is obvious that additional assistance is needed, that assistance may not arrive in time to be effective.

Occasionally, an aircraft lands and the flight crew reports a strong odor of something burning. The flight crew and passengers may have observed smoke. Most aircraft (the MD-80, for example), include cargo holds below the passenger cabin. Emergencies have been initiated due to smoldering or fuming packages. If a fire develops in the cargo hold, structural members that support the floor can weaken and collapse causing firefighters to become trapped in areas below the floor. Depending on the severity, the pilot and crew have few options once on the ground. Communication between the pilot and the firefighters should be initiated to obtain conditions within the cabin.

Aircraft Attached to the Jetway

Aircraft are often left attached to the jetway during airline arrival and departure operations and during overnight layovers. A fire in either an occupied or unoccupied aircraft could jeopardize the safety of the terminal as well as airport operations. Special considerations should be given to how fire rescue personnel would handle an incident involving a jetway, structure, or multiple structures on the airport. In many cases, electrical power is supplied to the aircraft via an external power cable from the jetway **(Figure 11.3)**. Ground power should be deactivated before disconnecting the plug from the aircraft ground power connection. Also, personnel should disconnect the battery if it can be safely accessed.

To prepare for these types of emergencies, ARFF personnel should develop pre-emergency plans for these structures and conduct training to examine the most effective means for dealing with these structures. The Incident Commander should consider the need for moving the jetway away from the aircraft or the aircraft away from the jetway to eliminate the potential of fire extension.

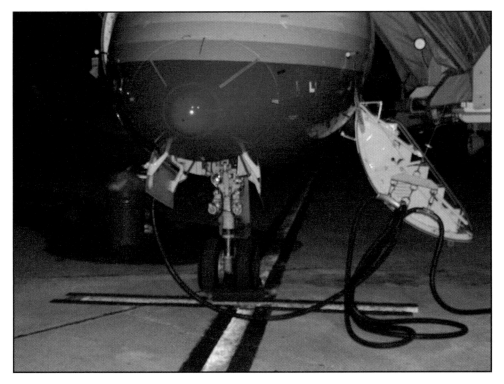

Figure 11.3 An external power cable connects this aircraft to the jetway. *Courtesy of John Demyan, LVI Airport.*

Once it is determined that ARFF personnel will enter an aircraft during an emergency, a rapid intervention team (RIT) should be assigned and standing by in case anything happens to those entering the aircraft. The RIT personnel should be fully dressed in protective clothing and SCBA and ready to assist at a moments notice.

While some ARFF personnel are checking the interior of the aircraft, other ARFF personnel should conduct a thorough examination of the exterior, including the wheel wells, for smoke or signs of charring and blistering. Flames may be visible through aircraft windows especially in well involved interior fires.

If the air traffic control tower or ARFF personnel confirm that a fire exists, the flight crew will most likely initiate an evacuation once the aircraft is brought to a stop. ARFF responders need to assist in evacuation by opening all available exits and assisting passengers off escape slides and away from the aircraft. Wind direction must be taken into consideration before opening exits. If not coordinated, the fire could become larger and spread due to the wind pushing the fire through the cabin. Even if department staffing is limited, all personnel need to assist in evacuation operations. Firefighters should also consider using infrared devices to conduct interior and exterior investigations.

Unoccupied Aircraft

Fires in unoccupied aircraft often develop into major incidents because of delayed detection. An unattended aircraft with all doors closed may sustain a smoldering fire for long periods, resulting in a buildup of smoke and potentially explosive gases that may go unnoticed until the aircraft is opened. Opening an aircraft door under such conditions is extremely hazardous because of the potential for a flashover, rollover, or in rare instances, even a backdraft. As in structural fire fighting, this situation indicates the need for vertical ventilation. Charged hoselines should be in position to immediately respond to the buildup of the fire that occurs when ventilation has been established. Penetrating nozzles may be used to good effect under these conditions. The Incident Commander should evaluate the need to engage in offensive ARFF operations based on the life safety risk.

Common sources and areas of smoke and the odor of something burning aboard aircraft are as follows:

- Overheated fluorescent light ballasts
- Food preparation areas
- Lavatories
- Cockpit area
- Avionics and electronic equipment compartments
- Cargo compartments
- Overheated electrical components

Overheated ballasts in fluorescent lighting fixtures occur as frequently in aircraft as they do in buildings and are usually not serious. But because the consequences of ignoring overheated ballasts could be serious, flight crew personnel who recognize this characteristic odor must not assume that the problem is minor and dismiss it.

As with commercial and domestic kitchens on the ground, food preparation areas aboard aircraft are frequent sources of smoke. ARFF personnel must thoroughly check this area, including all drawers, storage compartments, and hot plate heating elements. Power switches and circuit breakers for galley equipment are located in the cockpit.

Since 1985, smoke detectors have been installed in all lavatories on commercial aircraft, and they should help pinpoint smoke in this location. However, these detectors sound in the local area only and do not transmit an alarm to the cockpit. The cockpit crew may be unaware that a detector has been activated until notified by flight attendant crew members. Lack of awareness on the part of the crew could delay initiation of emergency landing procedures.

Smoke detection systems that alert the flight crew are installed in lower cargo holds on passenger and cargo aircraft. Extinguishing systems that must be activated by the pilots are also provided in lower cargo holds. Cargo freighter aircraft may also have smoke detectors above the main cargo deck, but no extinguishing system.

In the cockpit area, there may be one or more circuit-breaker panels. If any of the electrical systems throughout the aircraft malfunction, the flight crew should be alerted by a tripped circuit breaker. Because of the sensitivity of aircraft circuit breakers, the flight crew may make several attempts to reset a breaker before taking action to correct the problem. Also because of their familiarity with the aircraft, flight crew members may be able to assist ARFF personnel in locating concealed fires. Aircraft system abnormalities and radio interference may also indicate the presence of an interior fire.

Because aircraft interior fires may originate in numerous places in addition to the main passenger cabin, ARFF personnel should understand the structural characteristics of an aircraft fuselage. Fires in concealed spaces may travel between the skin of the aircraft and interior liners, in the overhead access area, through the cargo or belly areas, and may extend the length or width of the aircraft. It may be difficult, under such conditions, to determine either the source of ignition or the extent of the fire spread. If available, portable infrared heat detectors or thermal imagers can be used to locate "hot spots" that indicate concealed fires **(Figure 11.4)**. Other methods of determining the location of concealed fires are to remove sections of flooring, wall panels, and ceilings. On the exterior of the aircraft, paint blistering or discoloration may indicate fire areas. Applying a light water mist and watching for areas where the water turns to steam and evaporates quickly can also pinpoint fire areas.

If there is no sign of evacuation upon landing, ARFF personnel must immediately gain access into the aircraft by using all available doors and hatches and begin rescuing passengers while preparing for fire fighting operations.

Caution is also needed because an interior fire may lack only oxygen; opening the exits allows fresh air into the superheated atmosphere, and a flashover or rollover could occur.

Under *no* circumstances should firefighters entering aircraft impede the emergency exit of occupants. However, allowing occupants to exit the aircraft does not prevent firefighters from opening all available exit doors, hatches, and windows in an attempt to ventilate the aircraft.

Figure 11.4 A firefighter uses a thermal imager to look for hot spots inside an aircraft.

WARNING!
Exercise extreme caution when gaining entry into the aircraft due to the emergency escape slide systems attached to each door and, depending on the aircraft, to over-wing exits as well. If opened from outside, the escape slide may deploy and can seriously injure or kill unsuspecting emergency personnel.

On most aircraft, over-wing exit size will present a challenging entry for ARFF personnel wearing full protective equipment including SCBA. Once inside, advancing down narrow, restrictive aisles — perhaps congested by unconscious or deceased passengers and loose carry-on baggage — may be difficult. Many regional aircraft are configured with over/under wing exits that would make entry extremely difficult. If entry can be safely made, interior aircraft fires should be fought in the same manner as structural fires. Water can be used to fight an interior fire but the extinguishing agent of choice is usually Class A and Class B foam. Most interior aircraft fires will involve Class A combustible materials. When water runs out of an aircraft, it has a tendency to dilute the foam blanket that is serving as a vapor-suppressing agent. Other agents, such as clean agents, and dry chemicals, can be used after occupant evacuation or if occupants are not present. Those making entry must ensure they have a clear escape path to exit the aircraft since interior conditions can change rapidly.

Aircraft ventilation and aircraft cargo present two difficulties specific to ARFF firefighters. These topics are discussed in the sections that follow.

Aircraft Ventilation

Proper ventilation, followed by an interior attack, should be part of a planned and coordinated operation. Ventilation should then be established as soon as ventilating is deemed safe. Initial ventilation may be accomplished by opening as many doors and hatches as possible. Side windows may be able to be knocked in. Firefighters should take advantage of the positive pressure ventilation provided by opening doors, hatches, and windows on the side of the aircraft with the prevailing wind. Hydraulic ventilation may be possible by discharging a fog stream out an opening in the aircraft.

In some cases, vertical ventilation openings can be made in the top of the aircraft while working from an aerial platform **(Figure 11.5)**. ARFF personnel should never stand on top of the aircraft itself. A rescue, rotary, or cutoff saw with a 16 inch cutting wheel will be needed to cut all the way through most commercial aircraft hulls. Any cuts should be cooled with foam during the cutting operation in order to lubricate the cut and prevent molten aluminum from fouling the cutting edge of the blade. ARFF personnel should avoid opening up roof areas that slope towards the nose or tail as these areas are highly reinforced and may not access the main cabin area. If the interior ceiling and luggage bins are intact, vertical openings in the top of the aircraft will only ventilate the overhead access area. There may also be a crew rest area in overhead access area of wide body aircraft.

Early ventilation is important because applying water to an interior fire will quickly cause the limited interior space to fill with smoke and steam. This condition compounds the difficulty of search and rescue efforts and puts occupants and ARFF personnel at risk for steam burns. Once ventilation is started, personnel should gain entry, initiate an immediate search of the interior, and begin the fire attack and rescue from the unburned side. Often the best location to deploy the first interior attack hoseline is at an upwind overwing hatch or door, as long as there is no fire under the wing. The wing provides a platform to stand on while making entry. Because most evacuating passengers will attempt to use doors, overwing hatches are often the first to be available for entry, if applicable. The overwing exits also splits the aircraft in

WARNING!
Never discharge hoseline or turret streams into a hole burned or cut into the top of an aircraft. This will interrupt the vertical ventilation process and push the fire and products of combustion horizontally through the aircraft.

Figure 11.5 ARFF personnel simulating vertical ventilation practices during a training exercise. *Courtesy of Doddy Photography.*

half and can be used to prevent fire spread either direction. On narrow body aircraft, a straight stream will typically reach both ends of the main passenger cabin. Firefighters should use extreme care moving inside the aircraft, because the floor may be weakened or burned through. The ultimate goal is to ensure the safety of ARFF personnel and aircraft occupants; therefore, all doors and hatches should be opened as soon as practical. All viable rescue paths should be established, maintained, and protected as soon as possible.

Fire may spread in the belly of an aircraft; therefore, cargo compartments, electronics bays, and other machinery spaces must be opened and checked for evidence of fire. It may be necessary to unload luggage from cargo holds to check for fire extension and extinguishment. Fire may spread in other concealed areas of the aircraft, such as the overhead access area and side walls. All areas of fire involvement will have to be accessed, extinguished, and overhauled.

> **NOTE:** The structural integrity of the tail may fail in fully-involved, interior aircraft fires. Firefighters should be prepared for this because the rear of the aircraft can suddenly drop to the ground when the tail fails.

Cargo Aircraft

Interior fires in fully loaded cargo aircraft differ significantly from fires in passenger aircraft because of the differences in the number of occupants and in fire load. Hazardous cargo is possible with either type of aircraft; however, cargo aircraft are much more likely to have larger amounts of hazardous cargo/ dangerous goods than passenger aircraft.

In the event of a fire aboard a cargo aircraft on the ground, the flight crew is usually able to exit the aircraft through normal entry doors or through cockpit emergency exits. Once it has been determined that all crew members are out and there is no longer a rescue concern, attention can be focused on fire attack **(Figure 11.6, p. 354)**. If the cargo section doors cannot be opened, a conventional interior attack may be difficult. Cargo containers or loaded pallets can make interior attack difficult. The use of skin-penetrating nozzles may be the best tactic to combat a cargo aircraft interior fire. By using these penetrating nozzles, rescue and fire fighting personnel may locate the hottest point of the fire from the exterior and then penetrate the fuselage at that location. This technique properly applies extinguishing agent onto the fire without exposing ARFF personnel to the hazards of an interior attack.

Figure 11.6 Firefighters entering a cargo aircraft with handlines during a training evolution. *Courtesy of Doddy Photography.*

Some piercing nozzles may not penetrate deeply enough to go through the hull and into the containers. ARFF personnel will still have to access the fire area to completely extinguish the fire and perform overhaul. If piercing nozzles are unable to reach a fire, firefighters should take the following actions to gain access to the fire:

● Determine the area involved in fire with thermal imagers.

● Ventilate by opening up the aircraft above the fire, as discussed previously, or on the downwind side of the aircraft, immediately adjacent to the fire area; in the case of cargo aircraft, sometimes the aircraft can be moved to take advantage of the prevailing wind or to an area that will not affect normal operations or is closer to hydrant water supply.

● Make an opening on the upwind side of the aircraft to make entry to complete extinguishment, prevent fire spread, and perform overhaul.

● Decontaminate after leaving the fire area .

On most fully loaded cargo aircraft, it is virtually impossible to move through the cargo hold. Clearance of only a few inches often exists between the containers and the fuselage. If a small fire is present, it may be possible to unload the cargo to access the fire.

Before making an interior attack, ARFF personnel should attempt to determine the presence, types, and quantities of dangerous goods on the aircraft. Information regarding dangerous goods can be found on the cargo manifest, which can be found in the cockpit or in an area around the main loading door. Other than radioactive materials, dangerous goods have to be accessible by the flight crew and are often stored near the front of the aircraft. Regardless of the amount of dangerous goods presumed to be onboard, a hazardous materials response team should be immediately requested when there is a cargo aircraft emergency. If available, infrared thermal-imaging devices might be used to assist in finding the seat of the fire.

Onboard Fire Suppression Systems

New technology is now being developed utilizing a number of onboard fire suppression systems. High expansion foam automatically discharged from individual penetrating nozzles has shown promising results. External fire department suppression connections may become common place in the future. Heat detector sensors may help identify the exact location penetrating nozzles should be placed. Fire resistant tarps designed to cover cargo pallets can also help suppress fires and prevent them from free burning.

Low-Impact Crashes

Aircraft crashes that do not severely damage or break up the fuselage are likely to have a large percentage of survivors and are generally referred to as low-impact crashes. The aircraft is usually under some degree of control and crashes in a reasonably level and controlled manner. The aircraft fuselage may remain intact or in several large sections. Low-impact incidents often occur on or near an airport. The chance of encountering survivors is very high. These types of incidents may involve fuel fires, although nonfire incidents are not uncommon, especially for aircraft that have exhausted their fuel supply. Regardless, the first priority of ARFF personnel is to ensure the safety of occupants and crew. Although fatalities are possible in low-impact crashes, nonfatal injuries of varying degrees are more likely. While occupants are often able to extricate themselves and walk away from low-impact crashes, rescue operations may have to be performed in conjunction with fire suppression efforts if there are trapped and/or seriously injured occupants.

Even in low-impact crashes, ARFF personnel should initiate extrication operations only after donning full protective clothing and self-contained breathing apparatus. In addition, handline teams should support rescue personnel for protection from a flash fire. Depending on the size of the debris field, handlines will need to be deployed and used during the initial attack of the fire as the turret nozzle stream will be unable to reach the fire area.

The sections that follow detailed the most common varieties of low-impact crashes.

Wheels-Up or Belly Landings

A wheels-up or belly landing may result from a hydraulic system failure or other cause. Fire is not uncommon, although it is not inevitable in these incidents. When an aircraft scrapes along the ground, fuel tanks may rupture, and friction generates tremendous heat and sparks that provide an ignition source.

These hazards are usually greater when the plane lands on airport runways rather than on soft ground. In any event, after a belly landing, suppression efforts to minimize ignition are extremely critical.

There are several combinations of wheels-up type of landings such as the following:

- *Nose gear up with the main gear down* — requires the pilot to approach low and slow to keep the nose up till the last possible moment

- *Single main gear up* — the most dangerous and difficult to control

- *Landing gear down but not locked* — gear can collapse without giving any warning to the flight crew or ARFF personnel

In wheels-up landings, it is almost impossible for the pilot to maintain control of the aircraft. Upon touchdown, the plane may break apart or veer off the runway. ARFF personnel should accept the uncertainty of where the aircraft will come to rest and stage apparatus a safe distance from the runway to avoid being struck. The aircraft should be pursued only after it has passed staged vehicles.

Following such a landing, a large aircraft may remain substantially intact, and a majority of the occupants may be able to leave the aircraft on their own. If fire does occur, an aggressive attack to extinguish and keep the fire clear of the fuselage — especially at the exits — is critical. Egress operations will be hampered due to the final attitude of the aircraft. Escape slides are designed for wheels-down evacuations. When the wheels are up and the aircraft is resting on its fuselage, occupants exiting often crowd together at the bottom of the slide, making egress substantially slower.

Ditching

Another example of a low-impact crash is a wheels-up landing on water, known as *ditching*. In these cases, ARFF personnel can often intervene effectively with rescue boats and personnel trained in water rescue to assist in removing people from the aircraft. Saving occupants from drowning may be a significant challenge for ARFF personnel.

A number of airports have large bodies of water either in their approach/departure patterns or in close proximity. Aircraft accidents/incidents in bodies of water may result when an aircraft skids off a runway, lands short, aborts a takeoff, ditches, or crashes. Such accidents may be dangerous and frustrating for ARFF personnel attempting to extinguish a fire and perform rescue operations. The surface of the water may be covered with fuel, which may or may not be burning. If practical, personnel should apply a blanket of foam to the entire area. If the aircraft is partially in the water and has not ignited, ARFF personnel should remain alert when carrying out rescue operations because fuel rising to the surface may contact heated engine parts and ignite. Survivors and rescue personnel will most likely be contaminated with fuel and will need to be properly decontaminated.

ARFF personnel should also be aware that aircraft wreckage might be floating because of pockets of air trapped in the top of the compartments. Making an opening at a point above the water level may permit the air to escape and cause the wreckage to submerge before occupants have been removed.

Rescue personnel need specialized equipment to perform rescue operations in water. Inclement weather, especially in winter, can bring on hypothermia that can quickly disable aircraft occupants and rescue personnel. Wind chill can cause hypothermia even in warm weather. Depending upon air and water temperatures plus the victim's age, physical condition, and extent of injuries, hypothermia may prove fatal in minutes. In cold water, rescue and fire fighting personnel may use special flotation suits that will support two to three additional people. Neoprene wet suits also may be used by rescue personnel; however, the protection they offer is not as good in cold temperatures as that of the dry suits.

ARFF departments may also need materials such as wool blankets or lightweight Tyvek® coveralls to keep large numbers of survivors dry and warm. Airport shuttle buses may be able to be used to collect and keep survivors warm. For aircraft accidents in swamps, marshes, and tidal flats inaccessible by conventional rescue boats and land vehicles, airboats may be the best alternative. These flat-bottomed, shallow-draft boats need only a few inches of water to operate efficiently, and they are capable of crossing wide expanses of tidal flats on the wet mud. Personal watercraft can be used to tow rafts to move survivors, rescue personnel, and equipment to and from the immediate incident scene.

Water rescue of survivors usually involves surface rescue techniques and equipment. Although helicopters may be effective in some water rescue operations, in others, the rotor downdraft may push rescuers and flotation devices away from victims. Rafts and other types of floatation devices can be dropped and deployed from helicopters. The aircraft escape slides can be disconnected from the aircraft and used as rafts. On a few older narrow body aircraft, the slide may have to be turned over. Each slide has a lanyard to manually hold it to the aircraft as evacuees board. Aircraft seat cushions can be used as floatation devices. If runways, taxiways, and service roads are near bodies of water, ARFF departments should consider carrying water rescue equipment such as personal floatation devices (PFDs), light weight rescue helmets, and lifelines on apparatus.

Rejected Takeoff with Runway Overrun

This type of low-impact crash may result from a sudden loss of power, slippery runway conditions, or the lack of needed runway to stop the aircraft. Again, this type of emergency often leaves the aircraft intact or in large pieces and is usually survivable. Quick response while protecting the egress route is vital to passenger survival. There are far too many scenarios to cover all the reasons for this type scenario. More common reasons include runway incursions, wildlife struck, turbine failure, and migratory bird strikes.

Helicopter Crashes

The use of helicopters in general aviation has increased significantly; as a result, accidents involving helicopters have also increased. Because helicopters are of relatively light construction, they do not withstand the violent forces encountered in vertical impact. The undercarriage, rotors, and tail units usually break apart, leaving the wrecked interior of the fuselage as the main debris **(Figure 11.7, p. 358)**. Rotors, which are usually found close to the passenger area, may continue to spin after a crash. Approaching the aircraft while rotors are still spinning should be avoided. High winds and unlevel terrain may cause the rotors to dip or for rescuers to walk into the path of a spinning rotor.

Figure 11.7 The wreckage of a helicopter crash. *Courtesy of Scott Ramey, S. D. Ramey Photography.*

The main wreckage usually contains the engine and fuel tank and should be approached with caution. The hazards associated with fuel tanks and fuel fires are the same for helicopters as for all other aircraft.

High-Impact Crashes

Aircraft crashes with severe damage to the fuselage (fuselage disintegration) and with a significantly reduced likelihood of occupant survival are generally referred to as high-impact crashes. These are usually high speed, high angle impacts, with little or no control of the aircraft and tend to occur in off-airport areas. At this type of incident, firefighters should see to scene security, protection of evidence, and protection of exposures. By definition, a high-impact crash is an accident in which the fuselage is substantially damaged; the G-forces upon the occupants exceed human tolerance levels; or, the seats and safety belts fail to restrain the passengers during the impact. In high-impact crashes, an aircraft will often break apart upon impact with the ground or trees. Sometimes, hitting obstructions may cause it to cartwheel. If this happens, the main structural components, such as the wings, tail, and undercarriage, may be torn off and scattered over a wide area in the line of approach. Crew members or occupants may be thrown from the aircraft before it comes to rest, so under these conditions, any search for casualties should be thorough and wide-ranging.

In off-airport, high-impact crashes, arriving ARFF personnel may encounter burning structures, vegetation, vehicles, aircraft wreckage, and other Class A combustibles. Wind may be spreading the fire to uninvolved structures.

The airport and its fire department should determine how far off the airport the ARFF equipment will respond and the maximum resources that will be committed. Airport fire departments have been criticized for only responding to accidents within the airport's departure and approach paths and not responding to aircraft crashes off the airport.

Controlled Flight into Terrain

A variety of situations can cause an aircraft to crash. Hydraulics or other systems that keep the aircraft aloft could fail. Poor weather conditions could cause a pilot to lose control of an aircraft. Instruments could be calibrated incorrectly and result in a pilot's inability to navigate accurately. Regardless of the reason for a crash, pilots can often control where a plane will crash even if they cannot prevent the crash entirely. Guiding a crashing aircraft to its destination is known as a controlled flight into terrain.

In an emergency situation, a pilot may have mere seconds to control an aircraft before impact. The pilot may have to choose whether to allow a plane to crash on its present heading into a building or attempt to steer the aircraft into a field or nearby lake or hillside. ARFF personnel must be prepared for any contingency because a controlled flight into terrain could happen on any terrain under any conditions. A controlled flight may also prevent responders from predicting where an aircraft will impact while it is still in flight.

> **Hillside Crashes**
>
> Aircraft fires on hillsides are sometimes so difficult to reach that fire fighting may be limited to preventing fire spread and performing a thorough overhaul. The aircraft fuel usually scatters over a wide area and burns out, leaving only pieces of burning wreckage and vegetation. The slope may spread burning material faster and further than would otherwise be expected.

Crashes Involving Structures

A crash into a building obviously creates a more complex problem than an accident involving only an aircraft. The first-arriving fire officer must attempt to accurately assess the situation, transmit a clear description, and employ available resources as appropriate.

The aircraft may break open upon impact, and flying debris may damage surrounding properties. Damage to the roofs and upper stories of buildings may occur, floors and walls may collapse or be on the verge of failure, and people inside and outside the affected buildings may be injured **(Figure 11.8, p. 360)**. Rescue personnel should search involved properties and evacuate the entire area. Sightseers should be kept as far away from the area as possible.

Almost certainly, the aircraft's fuel tanks will be severely damaged and the contents dispersed. Just after takeoff, new large aircraft may carry as much as 83,290 gallons (315 289 L) of fuel. As soon as possible, ARFF personnel should take steps to prevent fuel from spreading to structures, sewers, and storm drains in the crash area.

Rescue personnel should prohibit smoking and take precautions to eliminate other sources of ignition. Fires may be widely separated and may spread rapidly because of scattered fuel, severed gas lines, and damage to domestic electrical systems.

Figure 11.8 The aftermath of American Airlines Flight 77 striking the Pentagon on September 11, 2001. *Courtesy of JO1 Mark D. Faram (US Navy), Defense Visual Information Center (DVIC).*

Response Procedures

Each jurisdiction must have established procedures for responding to all types of aircraft emergencies. All firefighters must understand their role in the overall operation so that all necessary functions are accomplished rapidly and effectively. While response procedures vary from jurisdiction to jurisdiction, this section highlights some of the more common procedures that most agencies should incorporate into their standard operating procedures (SOP).

Standard Emergency Response

Runway standby positions for ARFF vehicles in anticipation of an emergency should be predetermined, and documented in a SOP **(Figure 11.9).** In the event of an emergency, units should go directly to these positions unless directed elsewhere. Responding units should, if possible, have the following minimum information concerning the accident:

- Make and model of aircraft
- Emergency situation
- Response category
- Amount of fuel on board
- Number and locations of occupants, as well as injured, if known
- Nature and location of any cargo of critical significance
- Location of aircraft (if landing, the runway to be used; if crashed, the site)

While time is essential, ARFF personnel must temper their response with discretion, taking weather, visibility, terrain, and traffic into consideration. Promptness *and* safety are equally important response considerations. The

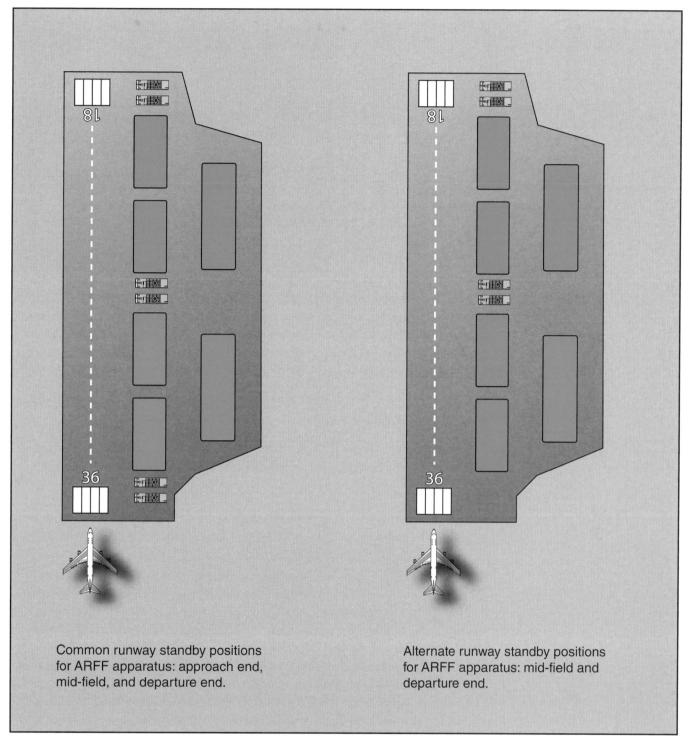

Common runway standby positions
for ARFF apparatus: approach end,
mid-field, and departure end.

Alternate runway standby positions
for ARFF apparatus: mid-field and
departure end.

Figure 11.9 Two examples of predetermined runway standby positions for ARFF apparatus.

Figure 11.10 ARFF driver/operators should avoid driving over debris at crash sites.

fire department section of the airport emergency plan should include response routes to be used unless unforeseen conditions dictate otherwise. This procedure allows all units to anticipate the actions of other units. The following are considerations for selecting these routes:

• Probable accident sites

• Presently available routes (location of frangible crash gates, if available)

• Possible alternative routes

• Design of apparatus (weight, height, width, etc.)

• Load capacity of bridges, ramps, etc.

• Terrain (rough, even, paved, unpaved, flat, hilly, etc.)

• Effects of weather

• Other obstacles

If, for any reason during an emergency response, a driver/operator's vision becomes obscured, the driver/operator should proceed using extreme caution. If visibility becomes obscured when approaching the crash scene, driver/operators should bring their apparatus to a complete stop and only proceed when visibility has been restored to ensure that fleeing occupants are not struck by a responding rescue vehicle. If two people are on board, one person should get out of the vehicle and sweep the area in front of the vehicle to ensure that it is clear and that occupants will not be run over. If the apparatus driver/operator should lose sight of the firefighter on foot, the driver/operator must stop the apparatus immediately to avoid the possibility of running over the firefighter. Response must not be resumed until visual contact has been reestablished. During night operations, forward looking infrared (FLIR) or flashlights may be needed to direct apparatus safely onto the scene.

Responders must also respond in a way that avoids damaging the apparatus and equipment. They should avoid running over aircraft debris scattered throughout the accident scene **(Figure 11.10)**. Hot or sharp aircraft parts could easily damage vehicle tires causing flats which jeopardize the safety of the driver/operator and crew.

During the response and fire fighting operations, ARFF personnel must make every effort to preserve the accident scene and safeguard evidence. Responders should also notice what conditions were encountered upon arrival, who may have entered the scene, and what (if any) evidence has been moved as personnel investigating the scene after the accident will need to know.

Response time to aircraft accidents is critical to initiating an effective rescue effort. The authority having jurisdiction for their respective airport may require the primary airport ARFF apparatus be able to respond from the station to accident/incident site and begin application of extinguishing agent within three minutes of notification. Additional apparatus must be able to respond and begin extinguishment within three and a half minutes. In any case, ARFF personnel should be aware of the standards of response based on the authority having jurisdiction for each respective airport.

> ## Unannounced Emergency Response
> An unannounced emergency is one that occurs without prior warning. With in-flight (announced) emergencies, ARFF personnel are usually given certain preapproach information before the aircraft attempts to land. However, in either case, the available information may be sketchy, such as "Aircraft on fire on the approach end of runway one-seven."

Establish Incident Command and Scene Management

The individual in charge must communicate to all responders the fact that command has been established for the system to function properly. This critical step needs to be done upon arrival while communicating the location of the command post and through the use of a green rotating beacon/strobe light on the vehicle designated as the initial command post. These two functions will serve as indicators to mutual aid responders that someone is in charge and where support functions should report. Unfortunately this step can fail to occur in the excitement of the moment which may lead to no one in charge or multiple agencies claiming to be in charge. As a follow-up, other critical elements involve establishing an operations and logistics section as soon as possible. Quite often the IC is performing these functions by requesting additional support and various services. Many decisions need to be made in a short period of time. It is quite easy to become overwhelmed during the initial response.

Size-Up

As with any other type of incident, size-up at an aircraft incident is one of the most critical parts of the operation. Tasks selected and resources requested during this stage of the operation set the tone for the rest of the incident. Size-up should be examined from four different positions; from the IC's perspective, from the driver/operator's perspective, from the officer/firefighter's perspective, and from an EMS perspective. Quite often in an ARFF response, the IC will accompany responding units which will allow command to be established immediately. If this is not the case, the first unit on the scene must establish command while transmitting a clear report of conditions, summon whatever additional resources may be needed, and describe the plan of action to be implemented. This allows other responding units to envision the scene and prepare for their possible roles. The sooner additional companies and/or specialized units are called, the more successful the operation is likely to be. This process may need to be incorporated as part of an automatic response plan. Rapid size-up also provides the responding chief officers with some of the information they need to assume command upon their arrival. Items to be listed on an IC's check-off list include:

- *Mutual Aid support* — how much is enough
- *Location of staging* — should be preestablished with adequate space; preferably one way in and a different way out
- *Need for buses and blankets* — should be prearranged and available
- *Medical support* — triage, treatment, and transport
- *Rescuer rehab* — resources and location
- *Status report* — to E.O.C. if activated, regarding airport condition (open/closed)

From the driver/operator's perspective, the initial approach and positioning of the first piece of apparatus often dictate the positioning of later-arriving units. It is not practical for the IC to convey setup locations at a crash site unless the safety of the crew and vehicle are in jeopardy. Driver/operators should always attempt to position their apparatus with enough room to pull away from the scene without having to back-up. Tools and equipment placed behind a truck along with people standing to the rear of the truck provide an unseen obstacle for the driver/operator.

With an aircraft crash, immediate emphasis needs to be placed on the rescue of occupants. Fire may burn through an aircraft's skin in as little as 60 seconds, so rapid setup and fire fighting operations need to commence immediately. Because fire fighting agent is often in limited supply, emphasis must be placed on conserving agent during suppression operations to ensure that firefighter safety is not compromised.

An officer's/firefighter's focus should be on a mental review of the aircraft involved by asking the following questions:

- Do the hazards of an escape slide exist?
- Where are the doors and hatches located and how to gain access?
- Is the aircraft equipped with roof hatches that can be utilized to assist in ventilation?
- What types of tools will I need on the scene?

Escape Slide Procedures

An officer/firefighter should review the procedures for assisting passengers down an escape slide as follows:

- Stand to the side of the slide with the slide at mid-thigh level
- Extend an outstretched arm, while assisting passengers to their feet once at the bottom of the slide
- Allow the passenger's forward momentum to assist in the procedure

The EMS focus should be on determining the number of passengers with injuries and the number of medical units that will be needed to transport the injured to local hospitals. Conveying this information forward to the Incident Commander ensures that timely requests can be made to ensure the needed resources are dispatched in an effort to mitigate the emergency. Other factors to examine include the location for a triage area if one is needed. The triage area must be upwind and uphill, accessible by ambulances and mutual aid support. It should also be in the closest safe location to minimize the distance rescuers will have to carry injured persons. EMS providers should attempt to move patients from the crash site, through triage, and transported to area hospitals in less than an hour.

Assuming the first vehicle on the scene has taken a position that affords the greatest route of safety for the aircraft occupants, the later-arriving units should turn off their emergency lights and audible devices as they approach the scene. History has shown that occupants migrate toward the warning devices. By having only one vehicle, in the safest exit path, with operating lights and sirens, confusion is reduced for the occupants.

The sections that follow describe common size-up considerations ARFF personnel must consider during an aircraft emergency.

Priorities

In every emergency situation, whether it is a fire, rescue, medical emergency, or any other type of incident, the priorities are basically the same. These priorities are as follows:

- Life safety (to include the safety of the emergency responders first)
- Incident stabilization
- Property conservation

While the terms may be slightly different in various types of emergencies, the actual priorities remain the same. Life safety is always the first and highest priority, although rescue may not be the first *action* taken by the first-in responders. In some cases, it is necessary to control the hazard before attempting a rescue, and benefits of taking action must be balanced with the risk involved. The second priority is to isolate and/or mitigate the hazard. If a fire can be controlled or a hazardous materials release contained, then the situation can be stabilized and the third priority — conserving property (which includes protecting the environment) — can be addressed. Once the hazard is stabilized and contained, it is no longer a threat to adjacent properties. At the earliest opportunity, an aircraft's various systems should be deactivated. The aircraft batteries should be disconnected to ensure the systems cannot be reenergized but should be accomplished in a manner that does not jeopardize rescue personnel.

Positioning Apparatus

ARFF apparatus and other responding units must be positioned correctly if rescue and fire fighting operations are to be successful. Because ARFF apparatus often respond single file, the first fire apparatus to the accident site often establishes the route for other vehicles and may dictate the approach into their ultimate fire fighting positions. In positioning apparatus, first-arriving crews and the IC should follow certain guidelines:

- Approach the scene with extreme caution so as not to run over any fleeing occupants, wreckage, ground scarring, spilled fuel, or other hazards.
- Do not drive through smoke that obscures escaping occupants.
- Consider the stability of the terrain, slope of the ground, and direction of the wind prior to entering a crash site.
- Attempt to position vehicles uphill and upwind to avoid fuels and fuel vapors that may gather in low-lying areas.

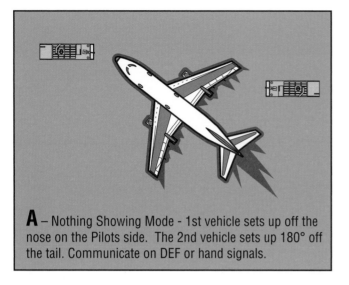

A – Nothing Showing Mode - 1st vehicle sets up off the nose on the Pilots side. The 2nd vehicle sets up 180° off the tail. Communicate on DEF or hand signals.

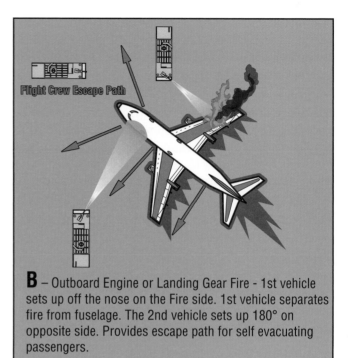

B – Outboard Engine or Landing Gear Fire - 1st vehicle sets up off the nose on the Fire side. 1st vehicle separates fire from fuselage. The 2nd vehicle sets up 180° on opposite side. Provides escape path for self evacuating passengers.

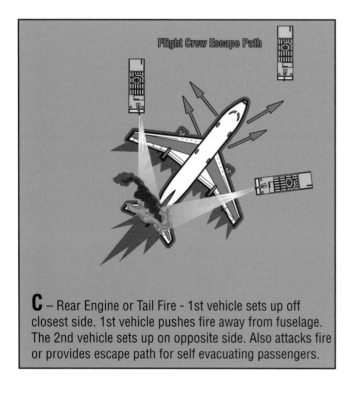

C – Rear Engine or Tail Fire - 1st vehicle sets up off closest side. 1st vehicle pushes fire away from fuselage. The 2nd vehicle sets up on opposite side. Also attacks fire or provides escape path for self evacuating passengers.

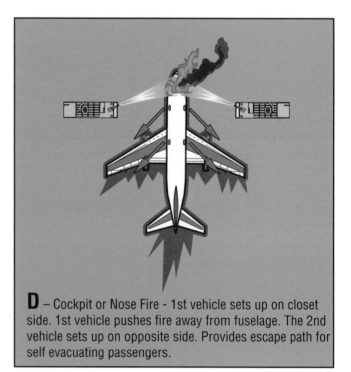

D – Cockpit or Nose Fire - 1st vehicle sets up on closet side. 1st vehicle pushes fire away from fuselage. The 2nd vehicle sets up on opposite side. Provides escape path for self evacuating passengers.

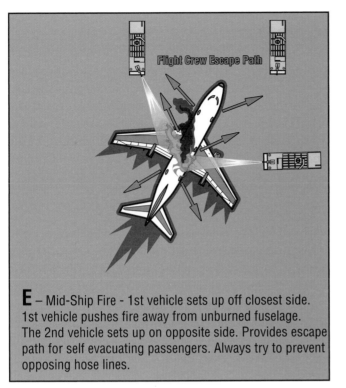

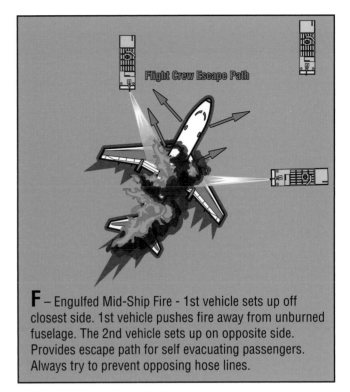

E – Mid-Ship Fire - 1st vehicle sets up off closest side. 1st vehicle pushes fire away from unburned fuselage. The 2nd vehicle sets up on opposite side. Provides escape path for self evacuating passengers. Always try to prevent opposing hose lines.

F – Engulfed Mid-Ship Fire - 1st vehicle sets up off closest side. 1st vehicle pushes fire away from unburned fuselage. The 2nd vehicle sets up on opposite side. Provides escape path for self evacuating passengers. Always try to prevent opposing hose lines.

Figure 11.11 a through **f**　Examples of ARFF apparatus placement based upon: **a.** Nothing Showing, **b.** an Outboard Engine or Landing Gear Fire, **c.** a Rear Engine or Tail Fire, **d.** a Cockpit or Nose Fire, **e.** a Mid-Ship Fire, or **f.** an Engulfed Mid-Ship Fire.

- Do not position vehicles so that they block the entry or exit from the accident site for other emergency vehicles.
- Position vehicles so that they may be operated quickly in the event of flash fire.
- Position vehicles so that they can be used to protect the egress route or rescue operations of persons from the aircraft.
- Position vehicles so that they can be repositioned as easily as possible while limiting maneuvers that require backing the vehicle.
- Position vehicles so that turrets and handlines may be used to maintain the route of egress, if necessary **(Figure 11.11 a - f).**
- Implement the SERP as discussed in Chapter 10 of this manual.

Other factors that must be considered when determining final apparatus placement on the emergency include:

- The number, type, and capabilities of the responding apparatus
- The number and abilities of responding personnel
- The location and condition of the wreckage
- The number and location of survivors
- Fundamentally hazardous areas associated with aircraft emergencies

Wind

While rescue and fire fighting operations can be conducted against the wind, doing so is much more difficult and more hazardous for both ARFF personnel and aircraft occupants. When operating against the wind, smoke obscures vision, heat is more intense, and it is more difficult to reach the fire with extinguishing agents. *Attacking a fire from a position downwind should only be attempted when conditions preclude any other approach.* Operations conducted from upwind are safer and much more efficient because heat and smoke are carried away from the operating area. Attacking with the wind enables extinguishing agents to be applied more effectively, thus reducing extinguishing time. Also, upwind paths of egress for the aircraft's occupants are safer due to the exit corridor being free of heat and smoke. ARFF personnel should make every attempt to use the wind to their advantage. This assists in rescue as well as in fire fighting agent conservation.

Terrain

The influences of some ground features are readily apparent. Soft or muddy soils may stop heavy apparatus and equipment. Steep slopes may be difficult to traverse or climb. Low or downslope areas may become saturated with fuel. Rough or rocky terrain may be impassable. However, other terrain effects may not be so obvious. For instance, fire apparatus should not be driven into gullies or downslope depressions near the aircraft into which fuel may have drained or in which fuel vapors may have collected. ARFF personnel should also consider terrain when establishing a triage area, tool and manpower staging, as well as rehab areas.

Wreckage

The condition and location of wreckage and any hazards it creates must be evaluated. Different methods of attack may be required according to whether the aircraft is intact, broken open, fragmented, or upside-down. More than one apparatus position may be required if the occupied portion of the aircraft is broken and separated into several pieces of wreckage. ARFF personnel should take time to confirm that initial fire fighting efforts are aimed at a portion of the fuselage and not a section of wing or other part of the aircraft that does not contain occupants.

Survivors

The number and location of occupants influences the point at which rescue efforts should begin. If the occupants have not been evacuated and the fuselage is still intact, ARFF personnel should decide upon the rescue entrance (normal loading doors, emergency exits, or emergency cut-in points). If evacuation has begun from the interior of the aircraft, ARFF personnel should protect the exits being used and may be tasked to assist occupants from the escape slides and direct them to safety.

Hazardous Areas

The entire area of an aircraft accident should be considered hazardous, and the following specific areas should be avoided whenever possible:

- *Aircraft propellers* — may be a hazard, even when an engine is not running.
- *Jet and Gas Turbine Engines* — intake and exhaust areas of jet or gas turbine engines are hazardous because the heat that they generate is substantial enough to reach the autoignition temperature of most aviation fuels. When operating — even at idle — jet engine intakes draw large amounts of air into the engine. This suction is substantial enough to draw personnel into the

WARNING!
Bumping or turning a prop may cause the magneto to fire, resulting in the engine trying to start and the prop rotating.

engine. At the opposite end of the engine, exhaust temperatures can be found that could severely burn personnel. Depending on the throttle setting, jet engines emit enough blast to easily blow over a large ARFF vehicle.

- *Line of Fire* — guns and rockets and the rear blast areas of missiles and rockets on military aircraft should always be avoided
- *Wings* — because a wing structure may collapse without warning, do not set up an operation that requires ARFF personnel or others to walk under wings or other overhanging wreckage; whenever possible, the wreckage should be stabilized to prevent collapse of the aircraft's structural components
- *Jagged Metal* — most wreckage will present this hazard
- *Advanced Aerospace Materials* — may involve fires that are extremely hot and difficult to extinguish
- *Biohazards* — human remains and wreckage contaminated by lav waste
- *Radar Systems* — often located in the nose of aircraft; exposure to the waves generated from the system can damage health

Initial Attack/Fire Control

Existing fire and crash conditions govern the placement of fire fighting apparatus for the initial attack. The main objective during this attack is the rescue of occupants trapped within the aircraft. Fires threatening these areas should be extinguished as soon as possible **(Figure 11.12, p. 370)**. Other nonthreatening fires involving unoccupied sections of the fuselage or wing sections may be left for later-arriving units. At times, it is difficult to distinguish between rescue and extinguishment activities because they are interrelated and are often performed simultaneously.

In accidents involving fire or a high likelihood of fire, the initial attack is usually made with one or more units operating both roof and bumper turrets while additional units perform handline operations and interior attack in an attempt to establish a safe area in and around the aircraft exits. This attack is followed by rescue personnel, protected by handlines, making entry into the aircraft. Water supplies must be adequate to support interior fire fighting operations. ARFF personnel should be familiar with the cabin length of the aircraft prior to entry to ensure that ample hose line is taken into the aircraft. In nonfire accidents, the same basic procedures should be followed. Instead of fighting fire, however, firefighters must blanket fuel spills with foam and charged handlines. At the same time, sufficient vehicle turrets must be kept ready in case fire erupts.

If the flight crew has begun evacuating the occupants, the first-arriving unit should establish a safe exit area to permit evacuation to continue and to make sure that the escape chutes remain intact and free of fire impingement. If the fuselage is not intact, more than one rescue area may have to be established.

Utilization of extending booms may assist in extinguishing fires in the confined areas of a crash scene. Application methods consisting of low sweeping patterns and the conservation of agent are critical to ensuring both occupant and firefighter safety. Fuselage sections may need to be stabilized prior to entry by rescue personnel. This can involve using anything from lifting bags and cribbing to securing fuselage sections by tying them off to heavy equipment.

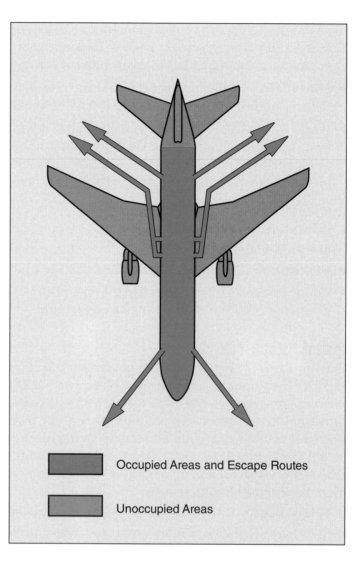

Figure 11.12 The areas in green represent passenger and crew in-cabin locations and common escape routes. Areas in orange are unoccupied areas.

Occupied Areas and Escape Routes

Unoccupied Areas

Quickly controlling an area of fire to establish a safe egress area involves initial mass application of an extinguishing agent. In the case of specially designed aircraft fire fighting apparatus, turrets and ground sweeps should be used to control the fire around the exterior of the fuselage. Handlines should be used for backup, interior attack, and overhaul. The initial attack begins during the approach of the fire fighting vehicles. Roof turrets, bumper turrets, and ground sweeps should be used as soon as the vehicles are within range of the aircraft's occupied sections. However, because limited quantities of extinguishing agents are carried on apparatus, turrets should be used only when the agent can be applied without being wasted. The initial discharge of foam should be made along the fuselage in order to prevent fire from impinging on it and to begin to create an exit corridor or rescue path. Turret operators should use a "short burst" application technique where they apply foam for 5-10 seconds, stop, and reevaluate application effectiveness and fire conditions as follows:

- If the fire is still burning, apply more agent.

- If the application has missed the fire, reposition the apparatus or modify the agent stream.

- If the fire has been extinguished, consider repositioning the apparatus to extinguish fire in other areas .

Although structural apparatus may lack specialized delivery systems, they can still be effective on aircraft fires by using aqueous film forming foam (AFFF). Given an adequate supply of AFFF and additional water available from hydrants, relays, or drafting sources, structural apparatus can sustain an effective attack as long as necessary. Wide coverage and considerable heat absorption can be achieved by using larger handlines and master stream appliances with appropriate fog nozzles.

If fire is confined to the engine nacelles or wings, personnel should attempt to stop the fire at the wing root or engines. Wings may still be full of substantial amounts of fuel and also need to be protected. If the wings fail, additional fuel may be dumped into the fire area. If fuel is leaking from fuel tanks and spreading on the ground, personnel should attempt to keep the fire from the fuselage and egress areas at least until the occupants have been evacuated or rescued.

Aircraft Accident Victim Management

When considering a high-impact crash, emergency medical services' role may be limited to treating rescuers injured while performing body recovery and accident investigation. Depending on the time of year, either heat-related or cold-related medical problems may need to be addressed.

A low-impact crash presents rescuers with the greatest challenge in treating and transporting what could be a very large number of victims. To perform this function efficiently, a system should be utilized that allows rescuers the ability to triage, treat, and transport victims in a short period of time. Factors that weigh into the system include time of day, time of year, location of accident, and availability of resources.

When treating victims, personnel should first ensure personal protection against bloodborne pathogens and then initiate a triage system that can be performed quickly. A colored ribbon or triage tag may be attached to the victim **(Figure 11.13)**. The level of urgency is indicated by the color of the ribbon or tag. Green represents low priority or walking wounded, yellow is medium priority, and red is high priority. Victims who are deceased should be marked with a black ribbon or tag so that they are not rechecked at a later time.

Figure 11.13 An ARFF responder using a triage ribbon during a mass casualty and triage exercise. Courtesy of *SSgt Shelley Gill (USAF), Defense Visual Information Center (DVIC)*.

Simple Triage and Rapid Transport

Many jurisdictions utilize the START (Simple Triage and Rapid Transport) system.

Respiratory (respiration)

    No Respiratory effort----Black

    Breathing ≥ 30-----Red

    Breathing < 30-----Go to Perfusion

Perfusion

    No Radial pulse -----Red

    Pulse Present-----Go to Neurological_

Neurological (mental status)

    Unconscious-----Red

    Altered LOC-----Red

The first action taken by EMS personnel should be to clear the impact area of the ambulatory injured and noninjured according to the following guidelines:

- Use the public address (PA) system on an emergency vehicle or a bull horn to call minor or noninjured persons that have escaped the aircraft on their own to the nearest safe upwind area.

- Try to utilize an area that has a good surface and access, such as a runway, taxiway, or road.

- Place tarps or other covering type materials on the ground for the casualties' comfort.

- Try not to place survivors directly onto wet grass, dirt, or other bare ground areas.

- Use orange traffic cones or other similar devices to delineate this.

As soon as possible, the patients should be covered to maintain their core body temperature. Going into shock is a form of hypothermia and the number one killer of trauma and burn victims. This can occur even on a warm day and is a critical need during cool or wet weather. Having enough blankets or disposable covers, immediately available, is extremely important.

The next action should be to clear the impact area of nonambulatory injured outside of the aircraft wreckage, ambulatory survivors that ignored the initial call to move to a safe area, or persons easy to get to and remove from inside the wreckage. Teams of rescuers should enter the impact area with litters, backboards, or other similar devices to remove these nonambulatory persons. Injured persons may be triaged where they are found or moved to a centralized Triage Area, where they will be properly stabilized, packaged, and triaged.

Adult patients should be moved on litters or backboards. Patients will usually be moved over uneven, slippery terrain and through congested debris and wreckage. Many responders are injured while walking backwards with a backboard due to the number of tripping hazards that exist on a crash site. Wheeled litters or litter carriers are available that permit one to two rescuers to effectively move a patient.

Litters and backboards are often a limited resource initially at multicasualty incidents. An adequate number of litters in caches of emergency medical supplies should be available to handle the potential number of victims that could be encountered on the largest transport aircraft serving the airport or area. Multicasualty litters should have a quick system to secure the patient. When adequate litters are initially lacking at the scene, rescuers need to know basic rescue carries to move patients. These common carries are designed to minimize further injury to the victim and the rescuer. Information on rescue carries are available in the IFSTA **Fire Service Search and Rescue** and **Essentials of Fire Fighting** manuals. Proper lifting techniques should be utilized by rescuers and enforced by safety officers.

Airport Personnel

Personnel needed to move victims through the incident medical organization are a major resource need. Some airports have trained nonemergency personnel to be litter bearers or emergency helpers. They will need to be properly trained regarding blood borne pathogens, incident scene hazards, personal protection, proper lifting techniques, and their assigned duties. They should be provided the proper incident scene identification, clothing, gloves, boots, eye, and head protection.

Once triaged and tagged with their level of priority, victims should be moved to a treatment area, with the high-priority victims being moved first. This process is generally performed by mutual/automatic aid fire department responders while the mutual aid EMS responders assist in establishing a triage area and prepare to transport red tagged victims. It is critical to emphasis to them that victims marked with red are to be moved first.

While the initial rescue and triage is being conducted, other rescuers should be setting up the Treatment and Transportation Areas. Three treatment areas or units will usually be needed. Victims will be separated into the three triage priorities, Immediate, Delayed, and Minor/Non-injured. Like the Triage Area, Treatment Areas should be set up upwind of the wreckage, as close to the Triage Area as is possible, practical, and safe. Utilize the following guidelines when establishing a Treatment Area:

- Place tarps, sheet plastic, or other covering type material on the ground to provide a sanitary area to lay out patients.

- Consider using fire or rescue vehicles to separate the different treatment areas.

- Use tents or other shelters if they are available and the weather is extremely hot, cold, or wet.

- Consider establishing Treatment Areas inside a large structure or vehicle if one is available: either of these may have heating and air conditioning. At these Treatment Areas, patients may receive more advanced trauma care.

At the treatment area, each patient should be reevaluated and placed into the appropriate area for treatment to begin. Once stabilized, patients should be transported to medical facilities at the earliest opportunity. Means of transporting victims to the hospital should be specified in the airport emergency plan and may consist of helicopters, buses, and ambulances. Care must be taken when assigning an area for waiting ambulances that the area is not too close to the treatment area and, if possible, locate the area downwind from the treatment. This can prevent ambulance engine exhaust vapors from affecting the personnel in the treatment area.

Walking Wounded

An area should be identified where the green-tagged victims, or walking wounded, can be transported and treated. Benefits to removing them from the scene include preventing them from returning to the crash site and isolating them from the crash scene for mental health reasons. Victims searching for loved-ones can be extremely persistent in attempting to return to a scene. Victim isolation is also important to ensure the victims are not bothered by members of the press or by attorneys seeking to represent them in legal matters. Someone must stay with these green-tagged victims to make sure they do not wander away.

A temporary morgue may be established for deceased victims. Unless human remains may be further damaged or need to be moved to perform a rescue task, bodies should not be moved. If a body has to be moved prior to formal body recovery operations, be sure to mark the location and document its original position and condition. Any fatalities and significant pieces or concentrations of body parts should be covered in order to minimize the visual stress to emergency workers and other persons at the scene.

Extinguishment

Extinguishment involves the elimination of all surface fire, whether on the ground or inside an aircraft. Even foamed areas should be examined and additional foam applied wherever the foam blanket has been compromised.

The extinguishment phase is an extension of the fire control phase because the control phase includes maintaining an escape exit from fire and, whenever possible, completely isolating the occupied portion of the aircraft. As additional resources become available, either because personnel are no longer needed for rescue operations or because additional units have arrived, the area already secured should be expanded outward to the perimeter of the fire area.

This phase is the final effort prior to overhaul; therefore, extinguishment of surface, interior, and concealed or hard to access fires must be complete in order to avoid further fire damage and to secure the area for overhaul. Complete fire extinguishment should not be attempted if evacuation and rescue operations would have to be reduced. However, conducting the extinguishment phase concurrently with rescue may be justified by the situation and the amount of apparatus and manpower available.

During this phase of the operation, reserve apparatus and equipment may be pressed into service. Additional mobile water-supply vehicles or structural pumpers in relays may be used to replenish depleted water supplies. Special lighting and air-supply units may be needed. After the responsible investigator provides authorization, wreckers and heavy equipment may be used to move parts of the wreckage to ensure thorough extinguishment. Crash debris should only be moved if absolutely necessary for rescue. If possible, it should be photographed or at least documented for future reference before it is moved. Special-purpose vehicles designed to carry mass quantities of medical supplies may also be needed at this time.

Overhaul

After every aircraft incident/accident, a thorough overhaul inspection must be conducted, regardless of whether fire was apparent or not. As always, the on-scene investigating authority should be consulted before overhaul operations begin. During overhaul, ARFF personnel must make sure that all fire is completely extinguished. This phase of aircraft interior fire fighting is one of the most difficult and is also one of the most hazardous. Because toxic gases and fumes are concentrated and other hazards may be present, firefighter safety is a major concern. To protect themselves, ARFF personnel should wear SCBA until the atmosphere in which they are working has been checked with the appropriate gas and particulate detectors and declared safe. In addition, a charged handline must be kept close at hand.

Because of the configuration of aircraft interiors, carpeting, wall panels, partitions, and ceiling coverings may need to be removed to get to deep-seated, concealed fires. During the overhaul phase of the operation, interior crews need to exercise extreme caution to ensure that any fire that has extended into the void space over the ceiling panels is not allowed to extend and come down behind them.

Care should be taken to preserve as much of the interior in its original configuration as is reasonably possible. This process will assist in determining the origin and cause of the fire and will facilitate the investigation. If ARFF personnel must remove wall panels or disturb other items, they should make descriptive notes or take photographs to indicate the original position of the items. If the incident involved a fire somewhere on the aircraft, determining the cause is extremely important. Before overhaul is conducted, the point of origin needs to be identified and protected during overhaul operations.

Firefighters may have to open some parts of the wreckage for complete extinguishment. Whenever the skin of the aircraft is penetrated, however, ARFF personnel should consider the potential hazards of cutting into high-pressure hydraulic lines, compressed gas cylinders, pneumatic lines, and unexploded ordnance on military aircraft. All hot spots should be cooled until extinguishment is complete and reignition no longer occurs.

Preserving Evidence

During overhaul, personnel should avoid disturbing any evidence that may aid investigators in determining the cause of the accident or the extent of damage while ensuring personal protection against bloodborne pathogens. Overhaul personnel should move only those parts of the aircraft that are absolutely essential to complete fire extinguishment. If the aircraft or its parts and controls must be moved because they present a direct hazard to human life, every effort must be made to preserve physical evidence and record the original condition and location of whatever was moved. ARFF personnel should be familiar with their fire department's SOPs that cover this area of operations. The FAA furnishes general guidance for preservation of evidence in Advisory Circular 150/5200-12B, *Fire Department Responsibility in Protecting Evidence at the Scene of an Aircraft Accident*. Also, the National Transportation Safety Board (NTSB) provides general guidelines for handling civil aircraft accidents with which ARFF personnel should be familiar.

Only authorized personnel should remove bodies that remain in wreckage after a fire has been extinguished. Prematurely removing bodies may interfere with identifying them and may destroy evidence required by the medical examiner, coroner, or other investigating authority. If it is absolutely necessary to remove a body prior to the arrival of the medical authority, ARFF personnel should tag each body with a number or secure a stake to note where the body was found. They should note on the tag the location from which the body was removed and also record that information on a drawing of the aircraft accident site in their incident report. This information will be critically important in the accident investigation.

Salvage and Property Conservation

Salvage and property conservation operations involve those actions that recover and protect items such as mail and passenger luggage. Cautious application of firefighting agents by ARFF personnel during extinguishment and overhaul operations can limit property damage.

Incident Termination

Once rescue, extinguishment, and other emergency operations are complete, the IC will terminate the emergency. Aircraft accidents can stretch the limitations of an airport's emergency response plan. Quite often mutual aid from multiple jurisdictions is called in to assist. The IC needs to remember that while mutual aid is assisting, the areas that mutual aid units responded from may become short staffed. Timely release of mutual aid equipment and personnel is important. Quite often off-duty airport fire department personnel can report back to the airport to assist in post accident operations. Important components of incident termination include:

- Decontamination of apparatus, tools, and equipment
- ARFF apparatus resupply with water and foam to get apparatus back in service
- Rehabilitation of emergency responders
- Release of mutual aid resources
- Protection of aircraft wreckage and the accident scene
- Termination reports from the various branches of the ICS
- Conducting a termination meeting with airport officials

Post Incident Responsibilities

After an aircraft incident, there are still numerous responsibilities that ARFF personnel must accomplish or assist in accomplishing. Immediate post incident responsibilities include the following activities:

- Area clean-up
- Determining if any equipment was damaged or lost
- Providing standby, as needed, during any defueling operations on the incident aircraft
- Completing incident reports

Long-term responsibilities may include:

- Resupply of AFFF for FAA required reserve
- Resupply of EMS supplies
- Replacing equipment that was broken or malfunctioned on the crash site
- Supporting aircraft crash investigators with incident cause and fire cause determination
- Post-incident debrief with all responders for lessons learned.

The most critical element of incident termination and post-incident activities involves the mental health of the responders who conducted a variety of duties at the crash site. Aircraft crashes can be quite violent in nature and subject an emergency responder to sights and smells seldom, if ever, encountered on the job. Critical incident stress management is an important part of assisting ARFF personnel in dealing with the stress associated with these incidents. An initial briefing needs to be conducted and follow-up counseling made available to assist responders in dealing with emotional issues that may arise from the experience. History has proven that no one is exempt from emotional issues that may effect the life style and behavior of responders while both on and off duty.

Response to Accidents Involving Military Aircraft

Not all military aircraft accidents occur on military installations. In fact, many occur in or near civilian locations. Civilian ARFF crews responding to a military aircraft incident should take the following actions:

- Approach the accident scene with caution.
- Rescue aircraft personnel.
- Provide emergency medical care for injured personnel.
- Search the wreckage for survivors.
- Protect survivors from further injury or death by removing them from the area if there is danger of fire or explosion.
- Protect civilian personnel and property affected by the accident.
- Notify the nearest military authorities.
- Be prepared to contact local:
  — Fire department
  — Law enforcement
  — Medical facilities
  — Civil Defense
- Guard the wreckage and establish a no-smoking zone around it.
- Refer photographer and news media requests to the appropriate military public affairs representative.

Technical Order (TO) 00-105E-9, "Aerospace Emergency Rescue and Mishap Response Information (Emergency Services)," can serve as a valuable resource for civilian agencies that might respond to a military aircraft accident. Produced by the Department of Defense (DoD), this manual and its supplements provide critical information on the configurations, hazards, emergency egress systems, fire protection systems, crew egress and shutdown procedures, and emergency response requirements for a wide variety of United States and North Atlantic Treaty Organization (NATO) military and aerospace vehicles. Chapter 10 of this manual also contains additional information regarding procedures to follow if faced with a military aircraft accident.

Reporting a Military Aircraft Accident

The nearest military installation should be contacted to report the aircraft incident. This may be accomplished via a collect telephone call or, in some instances, by a radio call to that installation. When the military agency answers and has been informed that this is an aircraft crash notification, the following information should be provided:

- Caller's name and location
- Time at which the aircraft crashed
- Whether or not the aircraft was or is on fire
- How to reach the crash site:
  — Accurate geographical location
  — Road network
  — Compass directions
  — Travel distances
- Whether or not the crew landed with the aircraft or parachuted
- If medical help is needed
- Number of fatalities
- Civilian injuries or private property damage
- Aircraft tail number
- Aircraft type or model
- Where someone can meet the rescue team
- Suitable helicopter landing areas near the accident site

The caller should ensure that the report has been received and understood. The caller should also provide any further information that is pertinent to the incident. Any questions the military agency asks should be answered before hanging up. The caller should always leave a callback number.

After being notified, the military will dispatch assistance teams that usually include the following personnel:

- Base fire department personnel
- Explosive ordnance disposal (EOD) personnel
- Military police
- Medical personnel
- Bioenvironmental personnel
- Mortuary personnel
- Information officer
- Accident Investigation Board
- Legal officer
- Heavy-equipment personnel

When military officials arrive at the scene of an aircraft accident, they will need to obtain the following information from witnesses to assist in the investigation of the accident:

- Time of the accident
- Direction in which the aircraft was traveling
- Weather conditions at the time of the accident
- Whether anyone was seen parachuting from the aircraft
- Whether there was an explosion in the air prior to the crash

Approaching the Site of a Military Aircraft Crash

Military aircraft should be considered somewhat more hazardous than civilian aircraft due to the additional emergency escape and weapons systems and devices found onboard. There are a number of basic safety precautions for approaching the site of a military aircraft crash. ARFF personnel should act as follows:

- Approach from upwind, if possible.
- Exercise caution while approaching the site in a vehicle to avoid striking survivors or armament near the crash site .
- Do not approach the front or rear of any externally carried tanks or pods that can contain rockets or missiles.
- Do not touch or otherwise disturb any armament found near or at the crash site.

Military Aircraft Fuel Hazards

One added hazard involves the fuels used to power and operate these aircraft. Many military aircraft use a varied mixture of jet fuel, which has a flash point significantly lower than civil aviation fuel. Another hazard associated with military aircraft and fuel systems encompasses a fuel described as hypergolic fuel. *Hypergolic fuels* are substances that ignite spontaneously on contact with each other (such as hydrazine with an oxidizer). For example, the F-16 uses H-70, which is 70 percent hydrazine and 30 percent water. Those aircraft that use hydrazine carry a minimum of 7 gallons (28 L). The need for a highly reliable and quickly responsive way of obtaining emergency electrical and hydraulic power aboard aircraft is likely to increase the use of hydrazine. Hydrazine has an odor similar to ammonia, is toxic in both liquid and vapor form, and may explode. It is a strong reducing agent and is hypergolic with some oxidizers such as nitrogen tetroxide and the metal oxides of iron, copper, and lead. Auto-ignition may occur if hydrazine is absorbed in rags, cotton wastes, or similar materials.

WARNING!
Always wear full protective clothing to include SCBA when dealing with hydrazine emergencies as it may be absorbed through the skin. Even short exposures may have serious effects on the nervous and respiratory systems.

One example of equipment in military aircraft that use hypergolic fuels are military EPU units. The EPU may utilize hydrazine, a hypergolic fuel, as the fuel supply for the emergency power unit instead of normal jet fuel. Firefighters may not know whether or not the system was used prior to or during the response. Inhalation, ingestion, and absorption hazards may be present when working with these alternative fuels.

Conventional Weapons/Munitions Fire Fighting Procedures

As stated previously, emergency responders to a military aircraft accident should not approach the front or rear of any externally carried tanks or pods that can contain rockets or missiles. Nor should they touch or otherwise disturb any armament found near or at the crash site. Caution should also be taken to avoid positioning personnel and vehicles in the line of fire of aircraft cannons such as found on the A-10, F-16, and other aircraft. ARFF vehicles should be positioned at a 45° angle to the centerline of the aircraft whenever wind and terrain factors allow.

Response to Aircraft Hazardous Materials Incidents

It is extremely critical that ARFF personnel be able to recognize when hazardous materials are involved in an airport or aircraft incident and take the necessary steps to protect themselves, the public, and the environment. Haz mat incidents may be reported as a medical aid, fire, vehicle or aircraft accident **(Figure 11.14)**. The initial report may not indicate the presence of hazardous materials. Failure to recognize common haz mat warning clues may cause ARFF personnel to become part of the problem, not part of the solution. Refer to the IFSTA **Hazardous Materials for First Responders** manual and other relevant resources for additional information regarding hazardous materials incidents and procedures.

Figure 11.14 ARFF personnel performing decon during a hazmat incident. *Courtesy of SSgt Cecilio Ricardo (USAP), Defense Visual Information Center (DVIC).*

Summary

ARFF personnel should never be hesitant, uniformed, or unprepared for emergency responses. Airport fire departments must implement NIMS-ICS as an organizational tool for emergency response to accidents and incidents on or off the airport. ARFF personnel must understand the difference between accidents and incidents as well as understanding in-flight emergencies, ground emergencies, low-impact crashes, and high-impact crashes.

Properly understanding and following all response procedures is key to successful ARFF operations. Firefighters must understand their respective roles in a response: search and rescue, apparatus positioning, EMS, triage and treatment center establishment, extinguishment, overhaul, command, etc. They must also be able to work within a chain of command and be able to size-up or aid in sizing-up an accident scene quickly and accurately taking all variables into account.

Lastly, ARFF personnel should know how to properly respond to an emergency involving military aircraft even if they are not firefighters at a military installation.

Review Questions

1. What are the five major organizational positions involved in NIMS-ICS?

2. What type of protective gear should be worn when responding to a hot brake incident?

3. What is the safest method of extinguishment when dealing with an engine or auxiliary power unit (APU) fire?

4. What are some common sources of smoke and burning odors on aircraft?

5. Where can information regarding hazardous goods on an aircraft be located?

6. Who should determine how far off the airport ARFF equipment will respond?

7. What are the three priorities of any emergency situation?

8. What guidelines should be followed when establishing a Treatment Area?

9. Who should remove bodies that remain in wreckage after a fire has been extinguished?

10. What are several immediate post incident responsibilities that ARFF personnel must accomplish or assist with?

Appendices

Contents

Appendix A
NFPA Job Performance Requirements (JPRs) With Page References

NFPA® 1003 (2010) JPR Numbers	Chapter References	Page References
4.1	1	15 - 16
4.2.1	1	15, 111
4.2.2	1	15
4.3.1	1	16 - 17
4.3.2	1	16 - 17
4.3.3	1	16 - 17
4.3.4	1	112 - 116
5.1.1	1	17
5.1.1.1	1	17
5.1.1.2	1	7
5.1.1.3	2, 3, 4, 6, 7, 9, 10, 11	20, 48 - 50, 72 - 105, 115 - 115, 119 –121, 123 - 124, 127 - 128, 129 - 142, 179 - 211, 232 - 233, 279 -291, 316 - 317, 369 - 371, 377
5.1.1.4	3, 4, 6, 9, 11	95 - 105, 112 - 118, 137, 182 - 211, 279- 291, 347, 369 - 371
5.1.2	4	111 - 124
5.2.1	2, 9	31 - 50, 274 - 289
5.2.2	2, 3, 5, 10, 11	26 - 52, 57 - 106, 159 - 174, 299 - 330, 337 - 339, 363 - 365
5.2.3	5	156 - 173
5.2.4	4, 9	112 - 123, 274 - 289

NFPA® 1003 (2010) JPR Numbers	Chapter References	Page References
5.3.1	4, 6, 7, 11	127 - 128, 179 - 182, 183 - 210, 232 – 233, 344 - 346
5.3.2	4, 6, 7, 11	127 - 128, 179 - 182, 183 - 210, 232 – 233, 344 - 346
5.3.3	4, 6, 7, 9, 11	127 - 128, 179 - 182, 183 - 210, 231 –232, 234 -235, 289 - 291, 344 - 346, 369 - 371
5.3.4	4, 6, 7, 9, 11	127 - 128, 179 - 182, 183 - 210, 231 – 232, 234 - 235, 289 - 291, 344 - 346, 369 - 371
5.3.5	3, 4, 6, 7, 8, 11	97 - 104, 124 - 128, 182 -183, 201 - 202, 204 - 206, 232 - 233, 244 - 260,348 - 352, 353 - 355, 374 - 375
5.3.6	3, 6, 7, 9, 11	76 - 80, 91 - 93, 96 - 97, 127 - 128, 129 - 131, 204 - 211, 231 - 233, 234 -235, 289 - 291, 346 - 348
5.3.7	3, 4, 6, 7, 11	88 - 89, 129, 182 - 192, 204 - 211, 232 - 233, 342 - 344
5.3.8	3, 8, 11	57, 97 - 104, 244 - 260, 342, 350 - 354, 364
5.3.9	1, 7, 9, 11	22, 235 - 238, 291 - 292, 376
5.3.10	10, 11	310, 362, 375 - 376,
5.3.11	1, 7, 8, 11	112, 232 - 233, 250 - 251, 259, 353 - 354, 359, 370, 365 - 376
5.4.1	3, 4, 8, 11, Appendix C	57 - 76, 80 - 83, 96 - 104, 128 - 152, 244 - 260, 346 - 347, 378, 399 - 409
5.4.2	3, 4, 8, 11	58 - 72, 124 - 152, 244 - 260, 341 - 342, 355 - 357, 365, 368
5.4.3	1, 11	15, 364 - 365, 371 - 374

NFPA® 1002 (2009) JPR Numbers	Chapter References	Page References
9.1	1	15, 17, 23
9.1.1	1, 6, 7, 9	23, 187 - 201, 227 - 235, 238 - 239, 266- 274
9.1.2	1, 2, 4, 5, 7, 9, Appendix B	22 - 23, 31 - 39, 45, 119 - 120, 171, 274 - 279, 287, 397
9.1.3	1, 2, 4, 7, 9	22 - 23, 31 - 39, 45, 119 - 120, 279 -287
9.2.1	7, 9, 11	204, 231 - 232, 234 - 235, 287 - 291, 344, 362, 364 - 369, 379 - 380
9.2.2	2, 3, 5, 6, 7, 9, 11	32 - 39, 58 - 72, 97 - 104, 129 - 134, 143- 152, 171, 182 - 183, 185 - 186, 201 - 206, 230 - 232, 287 - 291, 365 - 368

NFPA® 402 (2009) Competencies	Chapter References	Page References
9.2.3	2, 3, 5, 6, 7, 9, 11	32 - 39, 58 - 72, 97 - 104, 129 - 134, 143- 152, 171, 182 - 183, 185 - 186, 201 - 206, 230 - 232, 287 - 291, 365 - 368
4.1.1	2, 10, 11	39 - 40, 303 - 307, 355 - 359
4.1.2	10	314 - 315, 329 - 330
4.1.3	1, 10	16 - 17, 328 - 330
4.1.4	10, 11	324 - 328, 336 - 339
4.2.1	2, 7, 9	45, 47, 222, 238 - 239, 279 - 287
4.2.2	2, 7, 9, 10	39 - 40, 45, 47, 222, 238 - 239, 279 - 287
4.2.2.1	2	43
4.2.5	2	47
4.2.6	1, 10	17, 41, 304
4.2.8	5, 10	160 - 161, 314 -315
4.2.9	10	304, 329
4.2.10	7, 8, 9	229 - 222, 244 - 247, 249 - 260, 266 -– 269
4.2.11	7, 10	224 - 226, 314
4.3.1	1	15 - 24
4.3.2	1	17 - 24
4.3.3	3, 4	57 - 105, 142 - 153
4.3.4	2	30 - 52
4.4.1	5	163 - 165
4.4.2	5	165 - 167
4.4.4	1, 5, 11	20 - 21, 163 - 165, 166, 322
4.5.1	10, 11	299 - 300, 304, 314 - 315, 321, 322, 324, 328 - 330
4.5.2	1, 10	16, 329
4.5.3	7, 10, 11	224 - 225, 329, 371
4.5.4	10, 11	300, 329
5.1.1	11	341 - 342
5.1.2	1, 11	19, 350, 364
5.1.3	3, 11	101 – 102, 364

NFPA® 402 (2008) Competencies	Chapter References	Page References
5.2.1	5	163 - 173
5.2.2	5	167
5.2.3	5	171 - 173
5.2.4	4, 5	129 – 133, 171
6.1.1	3, 11	81, 364
6.1.2	2, 10	39 – 40, 303 - 307
6.1.3	2, 5, 9, 10	52, 163, 274 – 289, 304, 310, 364,
6.1.6	5	165
6.1.7	2, 10	39 – 40, 303 - 306
6.2.6	7	227 - 228
6.2.7	7	228
6.3.1	11	356 - 357
6.3.3	11	357
7.1.1	4, 8, 11	127 - 128, 248, 348 - 352
7.1.2	4, 10	120 - 121, 309 – 311
7.1.3	11	339 - 355
7.2.1	5	161
7.2.2	5	161
7.2.3	5	161
7.2.4	5	161
7.3.1	9, 11	280, 360 - 363
7.3.2	9	279 - 280
7.3.3	2, 9	41, 280 - 282
7.3.4	9	287 - 289, 362
7.4.1	5, 11	166 - 167, 365 - 367
7.4.2	4, 9, 11	129 - 133, 287 - 289, 365 - 369
7.4.3	3, 11	101 - 102, 367, 369
7.4.4	4	129 - 131

NFPA® 402 (2008) JPR Numbers	Chapter References	Page References
7.4.6	9, 11	288, 355, 365 - 367, 369
7.5.1	4	127 - 128
7.5.2	1, 4	20, 112 - 118
7.5.3	4, 8	125 - 126, 248,
7.5.4	4, 11	134 - 142, 380
7.5.5	3, 11	88 - 89, 342 - 343
7.5.6	4	130 - 131
7.5.7	3, 4	77, 129 - 130
7.5.8	3	92 - 93
7.5.10	4	132 - 133
7.5.11	3, 4, Appendix C	81 - 82, 129, 399 - 409
8.1.1	3	72 - 83
8.1.4	3	88 - 89
8.1.5	3	76
8.2.1	3	80 - 83
8.2.2	3	80 - 81
8.2.3	3	81
8.2.3.1	3, 11	81, 343 - 344
8.2.4	3	81
8.2.5	3, 11	81, 343 - 344
8.2.6	3, 4, Appendix C	81 - 82, 129, 399 - 409
8.2.6.1	Appendix C	399 - 409
8.2.6.2	Appendix C	399 - 409
8.3.1	3, 4	85 - 87,
8.3.1.1	3	85 - 86
8.3.2	3	85
8.3.3	3	85
8.3.4	3	85 - 86
8.3.5	4	127 - 128

NFPA® 402 (2008) JPR Numbers	Chapter References	Page References
8.4.1	3	97 - 104
8.4.3	3	99
8.4.4	3	100 - 102
8.4.5	3	100 - 102
8.4.6	3	101
8.4.7	3	101
8.4.8	3	102 - 103
8.4.9	3	103 - 104
8.4.10	3	62 - 63
9.1.1	11	341 - 342, 350, 351, 368,
9.1.2	3, 11	98, 341 - 342
9.1.3	3, 11	102, 341 - 342, 350, 364, 368
9.1.6	11	368
9.1.7	5, 11	166 - 167, 368 - 369
9.2.1	3	100, 102
9.2.3	3	102
9.2.4	7, 10	226, 312
9.3.1	3, 11	58, 62, 98 - 99, 341 - 342, 350, 351, 356- 357, 364, 368,
9.3.2	3, 6, 7, 11	102, 185 - 186, 201- 202, 232, 368 - 371
9.3.3	3, 11	102, 364
9.3.4	3, 8	258, 103
9.4.1	1, 3, 8	22, 104, 244 - 248
9.4.2	3	104
9.4.3	4, 8	127 - 128, 248, 250 - 253
9.4.4	4, 10, 11	142 - 152, 324 - 325, 377 - 380
9.5.1	11	368
9.5.2	1, 3, 11	22, 97 - 104, 351 – 352, 368
9.5.3	1,	19
9.5.5	8	248

NFPA® 402 (2008) JPR Numbers	Chapter References	Page References
9.5.6	8, 11	248, 374 - 376
9.5.7	10, 11	309, 372 - 373
10.1.1	4	127 - 128
10.1.2	11	364
10.1.4	1, 3, 10	19, 57 - 5896, 100, 302
10.2.1	6	180, 187 - 187, 190 - 191
10.2.2	6	180 - 181, 206 - 211
10.2.3	6	180, 206 - 207
10.2.4	6	181, 207, 211
10.2.5	6	188
10.2.7	6	206 - 207
10.3.2	2	48
10.3.3	10	306
10.4.1	11	364
10.4.2	11	355
10.4.2.1	5	166 - 167
10.4.3	11	369 - 370
10.5.1	11	363 -369
10.5.2	11	363 -369
10.5.3	11	363 -369
10.5.4	11	363 -369
10.5.5	11	363 -369
10.6.2	3, 11	58, 365
10.6.3	11	369
10.6.4	11	369 - 371
10.6.6	4, 11	127 - 128, 344 - 346
10.6.7	6, 7, 9	201 - 206, 231 -233, 289 - 291
10.7.1	6, 7, 9, 11	202, 204 - 206, 231 - 232, 289 - 291, 366 - 367, 369 - 370
10.7.2	11	368 - 370, 374

NFPA® 402 (2008) JPR Numbers	Chapter References	Page References
10.7.3	6, 9, 11	205, 289 - 290, 365 - 368
10.7.4	9, 11	289 - 290, 368
10.7.5	9, 11	288 - 290, 368
10.7.6	6, 7, 9, 11	179 - 182, 231 - 235, 289 - 291, 369 - 371
10.7.7	6, 11	182, 185 - 186, 204, 356, 369 - 370
10.7.8	4, 6, 11	128, 181, 182, 188, 344 - 346
10.8.1	9, 11	287 - 291, 370
10.8.2	9, 11	289 - 290, 365, 367 - 368
10.8.3	11	342
10.8.4	9, 11	289, 364, 366 - 367, 369 - 370
10.8.5	7, 9,	291, 234 - 235
10.9.1	6	183 - 191
10.9.2	6, 7	202 – 204, 232
10.10.1	6	202 - 204
10.10.2	6	202 - 205
10.11.1	11	369 - 370
10.12.1	6, 11	183 - 184, 344 - 246
10.12.2	4, 11	128, 345 - 346
10.12.3	4, 11	128, 345 - 346
10.12.4	4, 8, 11	128, 248 - 249, 345 - 346, 352
10.13.1	11	365
11.1.1	11	348 - 355
11.1.2	11	350 - 351
11.1.3	11	352
11.1.4	11	351
11.1.5	4, 11	115 - 116, 351 - 352
11.1.7	11	350
11.2.1	11	340
11.2.3	11	340

NFPA® 402 (2008) JPR Numbers	Chapter References	Page References
11.2.4	5, 11	161, 340
11.2.5	11	340, 350
11.2.6	11	341 - 342, 351
11.2.7	11	351
11.3.1	11	350
11.4.1	7, 8, 11	235, 253, 350, 353 - 354, 355
11.4.4	8	253
11.4.5	7	235
11.5	11	375
12.2.6	3, 11	81, 343 - 344
12.2.7	11	348
12.3.1	2	48 - 51
12.3.2	11	344 - 346
12.4.1	11	342 - 343
12.4.2	11	342 - 343
12.4.3	11	342
12.4.4	11	343
12.4.5	11	342
12.5.1	11	343
12.5.4	11	343
12.6	11	343 - 344
12.9.1	10	327
12.9.2	10	327
12.9.4	10	327
12.12.1	11	356
12.12.2	11	356 - 357
12.12.7	11	357
12.12.10	11	356
13.1.2	4, 11	111 - 112, 376 - 377

NFPA® 402 (2008) JPR Numbers	Chapter References	Page References
13.1.3	4, 11	127 - 128, 376 - 377
13.1.4	10, 11	328, 375 - 376
13.2.1	11	375 - 376
13.2.2	11	375
13.3.1	11	376
13.3.2	11	376
13.4.1	11	376
13.4.4	4, 11	135, 355, 380
13.5	1	19
14.1.2	6, 10	179 - 211, 300, 314 - 315
14.2.1	10	300, 328 - 330
14.2.2	10	300
14.2.3	1, 4, 10, 11	16, 123 -124, 328 - 330, 377
14.2.4	1, 10	16 - 17, 328 - 330
14.2.6	1, 10, 11	16 - 17, 324 - 325, 328 - 330, 377 - 378
14.2.7	10	328 - 330
14.2.8	1, 3, 4, 10	19, 58 - 76, 89 - 95, 96 - 104, 134, 328 - 330
14.2.11	1, 5	20 - 21, 160, 163, 314 - 315
14.3.1	5, 10	160 - 161, 309
14.3.2	4, 11	111 - 112, 336, 363 - 369
14.3.3	11	355, 367 - 368,
14.3.4	11	336, 360
14.5.1	6, 11	201, 232 - 233, 344 - 346
14.5.2	6, 11	182 - 183, 344 - 346
14.6.1	11	369 - 370
14.6.2	11	369 - 370
14.6.6	4	111, 113
14.7.1	1, 9, 10	22, 291, 315
14.7.4	6, 11	182 - 183,

NFPA® 402 (2008) JPR Numbers	Chapter References	Page References
14.7.6	6	181
14.7.8	2, 6, 11	29, 184, 344, 358, 365,
14.8.1	6	182 - 201
14.8.2	6	201 - 206
14.8.3	6, 7	195 - 196, 225
14.8.4	6, 7	181, 224

NFPA® 403 (2009) JPR Numbers	Chapter References	Page References
4.1.1	10	299
4.1.2	1, 10, 11	16, 299 - 300, 304, 314 - 315, 321, 322, 324, 328 - 330
4.2	4	111
4.2.1	1, 10	23, 299
4.2.2	10	299
4.3.1	2, 7	30 - 31, 219 - 222
4.3.2	2, 7	30 - 31, 219 - 222
5.1.1	6	179 -180, 183 - 192
5.2	6	181, 206 - 211
5.3.1	7	223
5.3.2	7	222 - 223
5.4	6	181
5.5	11	344
5.6.1	6, 7	211, 232
5.6.2	7	232
6.1.2	7	222
6.1.4	9	270
6.2.1	8	226, 244 - 260
6.2.2	7, 8	226, 244

NFPA® 403 (2009) JPR Numbers	Chapter References	Page References
7.1.1	5	159 - 170
7.1.2	5	163 - 166
8.1.4	1	15 - 17
8.2.1	1, 4	20, 112 - 118
8.2.2	1, 4	20, 112 - 118, 120
9.1.1	2	52
9.1.2	2	52
9.1.3	11	363
9.1.4	11	363

FAR 139.315 Line Item Numbers	Chapter References	Page References
139.315(a)	2	30 - 31
139.315(b)	2	31
139.315(c)	2	30
139.315(d)	2	30
139.315(e)	2	30 - 31

FAR 139.317 Line Item Numbers	Chapter References	Page References
139.317(a)	7	220
139.317(b)	7	220
139.317(c)	7	220
139.317(d)	7	220
139.317(e)	7	220
139.317(f)	7	232
139.317(g)	6	210 - 211
139.317(i)	7	210

FAR 139.319 Line Item Numbers	Chapter References	Page References
139.319(a)	2, 7	30 - 31, 219 - 222
139.319(b)	2, 7	30 - 31, 219 - 222
139.319(c)	2, 7	30 - 31, 219 - 222
139.319(d)	2, 7	30 – 31, 219
139.319(e)	5	163 -165
139.319(f)	7	222
139.319(g)	7, 9	238 - 239, 266 - 270
139.319(h)	7, 11	219 - 222, 363
139.319(i)	1, 4	15 -24, 112 - 118
139.319(j)	4	139
139.319(l)	1	10

Appendix B
Ground Vehicle Guide to Airport Signs and Markings

Ground Vehicle Guide to Airport Signs & Markings

U.S. Department of Transportation
Federal Aviation Administration

ATCT Light Gun Signals

Color and Type of Signal	Vehicle and Personnel Movement
STEADY GREEN	Cleared to Cross, Proceed or Go
FLASHING GREEN	Not Applicable
STEADY RED	STOP
FLASHING RED	Clear the Taxiway/Runway
FLASHING WHITE	Return to Starting Point on Airport
ALTERNATING RED/GREEN	Exercise Extreme Caution

Holding Position Markings

ILS Critical Area Markings

Airport Signs — Action and Purpose

4-22 TWY/RWY HOLD POSITION: Hold Short of Runway on Taxiway

Also.... RWY/RWY HOLD POSITION: Hold Short of Intersecting Runway

8-APCH RWY APCH HOLD POSITION: Hold Short for Acft on Approach

ILS ILS HOLD POSITION: Hold Short of ILS Critical Area

⊘ NO ENTRY: Identifies Paved Areas Where Aircraft Entry is Prohibited

B TAXIWAY LOCATION: Identifies Twy on Which Vehicle/Aircraft is Located

22 RUNWAY LOCATION: Identifies Rwy on Which Vehicle/Aircraft is Located

HOLD POSITION BOUNDARY: Exit Boundary of Rwy Protected Areas

ILS CRITICAL AREA BOUNDARY: Exit Boundary of ILS Critical Area

J→ TWY DIRECTION: Defines Direction & Designation of Intersecting Taxiway(s)

↰L RWY EXIT: Defines Direction & Designation of Exit Twy from Rwy

22↑ OUTBOUND DESTINATION: Defines Directions to Take-Off Runways

↖MIL INBOUND DESTINATION: Defines Directions for Arriving Aircraft

TAXIWAY ENDING MARKER: Indicates Twy Does Not Continue

Airport Markings

HOLDING POSITION: Hold Short of Intersecting Rwy Also Land and Hold Short Marking

ILS CRITICAL AREA: Hold Short During IMC Conditions

TAXIWAY/TAXIWAY HOLDING POSITION: Hold Short of Intersecting Runway when Directed by ATC

MOVEMENT AREA BOUNDARY: Defines Boundary of Movement Area and Non-Movement Area

TAXIWAY EDGE: Defines Edge of Usable Full Strength Taxiway Pavement. Adjoining Pavement NOT Usable

DASHED TAXIWAY EDGE: Defines Edge Taxiway where Adjoining Pavement or Apron IS Available for Taxi

1-19 SURFACE PAINTED HOLDING POSITION: Hold Short of Intersecting Runway on Twy

↖B SURFACE PAINTED TAXIWAY DIRECTION: Direction & Designation of Intersecting Twy

K SURFACE PAINTED TAXIWAY LOCATION: Identifies Twy on Which Aircraft is Located

Tower Frequency

Ground Frequency

References: Airman's Information Manual (AIM), and Advisory Circular 150/5340-18C. Standards for Airport Sign Systems

FAA – Airport Certification Program

NSN: 0052-00-918-1000

FAA Form 5280-7 (05-00)

Appendix C
Advanced Composites/Advanced Aerospace Materials (AC/AAM): Mishap Risk Control and Mishap Response

Written By:
John M. Olson, PhD.
January 2000
(updated January 2007)

Overview

Although advanced composites and advanced aerospace materials provide several benefits over other materials options, they do present some important environmental, safety, and health concerns. In their final design state these materials are generally considered safe, inert, and biologically benign. However, when damaged by fire, explosion, or high-energy impact, these materials can be characterized by unique hazards and concerns that require timely and appropriate responses.

The following guidelines are provided as recommended precautions and procedures for dealing with a composite mishap response. However, the hazards are dependent upon the type, quantity, damage extent, and mishap scenario. In most cases, the concentration of the materials present drives the level of risk for the potential injection, inhalation, ingestion, and absorption hazards.

These guidelines address all phases of an aircraft mishap response, including fire fighting, investigation, recovery, clean up, and disposal; however, they can be universally applied to any application or situation involving these materials. Due to the infinite variability of mishap scenarios, this information is general in nature, and should be more specifically tailored to individual mishap scenarios as required. Nevertheless, the purpose of these guidelines is to serve as the basis for the development of consistent and effective procedures and policies throughout the world in order to maximize risk control and minimize the environmental, safety, and health hazards caused by composite mishaps. Ultimately, the user is urged to supplement this information with new and updated research and operational guidance as it becomes available, although the conservative measures outlined within this document are the best course of action in the absence of specific or concrete data.

Composite mishap hazards can, in most cases, be efficiently and effectively mitigated with proper training, precautions, and preparation.

Definitions

Composite Material: A physical combination of two or more materials, generally consisting of a reinforcement and a "binder" or matrix material. Generally, the reinforcements, or load-bearing elements, are fibers, while a resin forms a matrix to hold the fibers and fill the voids. The reinforced matrix structure thereby allows fiber to fiber stress transfer. Composite materials generally consist of laminates of several layers in varying directions. In many cases, a honeycomb core material is sandwiched between two of the laminates. The name of the composite describes its physical makeup: type of fiber/type of resin.

Examples: Fiberglass (Glass/Epoxy, Glass/Polyester)

Advanced Composite Material: A composite material comprised of high-strength, high-stiffness reinforcement (i.e., fibers) in a matrix (i.e., resin) with properties that can include low weight, corrosion resistance, unique thermal properties, and special electrical properties. Advanced Composites are distinguished from traditional composites by their increased relative performance, cost, complexity, and mishap hazard potential.

Examples: Graphite/Epoxy, Boron/Epoxy, Aramid (Kevlar)/Epoxy, FQuartz/Cyanate Ester

Advanced Aerospace Material: A highly specialized material fulfilling unique aerospace construction, environment, or performance requirements.

Examples: Beryllium, Depleted Uranium (DU), Radar Absorbent Material (RAM)

It is essential that a clear distinction be made between Advanced Composites and Advanced Aerospace Materials because of several very specific and unique hazards.

Hazard: A condition or changing set of circumstances that presents a potential for injury, illness, or property damage. Likewise, it can be described as the potential or inherent characteristics of an activity, condition, or circumstance, which can produce adverse or harmful consequences.

Given this definition, the hazards associated with mishap damaged advanced composites and advanced aerospace materials will be addressed with a risk control emphasis.

Risk Control: The process of minimizing accidental and other extraordinary losses by anticipating and preventing unplanned events. It emphasizes the complexities of exposures and encompasses broad areas of risk, which are indicative of a mishap scenario. Effective risk management is comprised of both risk control and risk financing in order to control exposures through knowledge, training, preparation, and an understanding of the factors involved. Loss avoidance must be both a pre- and post-mishap effort.

Background

Damage to Advanced Composites and Advanced Aerospace Materials (AC/AAMs) caused by fire, explosion, and/or high-energy impact in a mishap presents unique environmental, safety, and health hazards. In typical aircraft fires, temperatures reach between 1000°-2000°C. Organic matrix materials (i.e., resins and polymers) burn off around 400°C, creating toxic combustion products and liberating the reinforcement (i.e., fibers). Depending upon the type of composite or aerospace materials, the associated material dynamics and response can vary greatly. For example, glass or aramid fiber reinforcements tend to melt under the extreme heat, whereas the heat can oxidize carbon or graphite fibers, thereby altering their size, shape, porosity, and other characteristics.

The intense thermal and mechanical forces in a mishap generally cause degradation, debonding, and/or "explosive" fracture of the advanced composite structures. While absorbing this fracture energy, the reinforcement, usually stiff and strong, may be broken into particulate fibers, turned to dust, or reduced to a cloth-like consistency. AAMs can produce highly toxic oxides or heavy metal concentrations. Liberated carbon fibers can readily penetrate human skin due to their stiffness, whereas boron fibers can penetrate bone. Furthermore, the adsorbed and absorbed pyrolysis and combustion products (generally toxic) on activated, oxidized fibers can be a very potent injection and inhalation hazard because the toxins can be readily placed and retained in the body. This phenomenon is particularly critical in mishaps involving bloodborne pathogens (i.e., HIV, Hepatitus B) that are present in the debris. In almost all cases, the type, amount, and extent of damage controls the concentration of AC/AAMs at a mishap site, which in turn determines the extent of the hazards. The prevailing weather conditions can also greatly affect the extent of the dispersion of the damaged materials within the vicinity of the mishap.

Fire, coupled with heat, shock, and fragmentation, produces several different types of damage in Advanced Composites (ACs). Effects can range from a simple reduction in strength, to a loss of Low Observable (LO) performance, delamination, debonding, charring, melting, burning, and vaporization. The impact upon AAMs can be just as broad but is highly dependent upon the type of material. For example, Depleted Uranium and Beryllium both produce highly toxic oxides when subjected to intense heat (>700°-800°C).

Although AC/AAMs represent only one of the many hazards associated with an aircraft mishap (i.e., fuels, lubricants, exotic metals, and weapons), they do merit increased awareness and informed precautions because of their increased hazard potential, increasingly widespread use, and persistence or durability. Exposures to potentially harmful vapors, gases, particulates, and airborne fibers generated in a composite mishap need to be controlled because of the combined effects of the dispersion forces and the complex chemical mixtures.

Hazard exposure routes for damaged AC/AAMs include absorption (contact), inhalation (breathing), injection (puncture and tearing wounds), and ingestion (eating, drinking, and smoking). The toxicology of respirable particulates and their disease producing potential is a function of three main variables: 1) the dose or amount of particulates in the lung; 2) the physical dimensions of deposited particulates; and 3) the durability (time) in the lung. Fire-exposed carbon fibers tend to break into shorter lengths and split into smaller diameters with sharp points, thereby increasing their probability for respiration and ease of transport. Dry and windy conditions at a mishap site increase the chances for re-dispersion of particulates. Likewise, whether inhaled or injected, ACs are not easily removed or expelled because of their shape, sharpness, and stiffness. Other potential health and environmental effects from AC/AAMs include dermal and respiratory problems, toxic and allergic reactions, contamination, and radiation exposure for AAMs. These impacts may be acute or chronic, as well as local or systemic, depending upon the circumstances. Mechanical injection or cuts are the most common skin hazard, although sensitization (local and systemic) can occur. Irritation to the respiratory tract is also common, much like a nuisance dust irritation hazard. Off-gassing, toxic products in the smoke plume, smoldering debris, and oxidized (fire-damaged) particulates are the primary respiratory hazards.

Mishaps involving AC/AAMs that are electrically conductive (i.e., graphite or carbon fiber) may present electrical shorting or arcing hazards if very high concentrations exist (usually at the immediate mishap site only). Although rare, this may result in electrical equipment degradation or failure, including communication interference. Research has shown that widespread electrical failure due to environmental release and plume dissipation is highly unlikely, except at the mishap site. Disseminated carbon or graphite fibers are also influenced by the presence of high voltage areas and reduce the local dielectric properties of free air, which could in turn cause equipment malfunctions.

Justification

Given the existing and projected increases in usage and applications of AC/AAMs, it is critical to develop realistic policies and procedures that focus on risk control and minimizing the environmental, safety, and health hazards associated with an advanced composite or aerospace material mishap. As the associated knowledge base grows, procedures and guidelines can be situationally optimized in terms of cost, safety, and performance.

Based upon both existing and uncharacterized mishap hazards associated with AC/AAMs, risk reduction measures are necessary. Administrative controls, including adequate personal protective equipment (PPE), training, and safe practices need to be implemented immediately, as the dynamic field environment is _not_ conducive to engineering controls. Conservative, although situationally optimized, risk control measures are essential. Care and common sense approaches are the best course of action. Because aircraft mishaps occur under extremely diverse weather, terrain, and location conditions, with widely varying degrees of damage, a universally applicable set of risk control precautions is not practical. The many variables require conservative protective measures with a complete material lifetime or "cradle-to-grave" mentality of responsibility. This is true for all phases of a mishap response, ranging from first response and fire fighting, to investigation, recovery, clean up, and disposal.

Major Issues

The major issues currently affecting mishap response which involve Advanced Composites/Advanced Aerospace Materials (AC/AAMs) are:

1. Fiber dispersion and re-dispersion

   –Includes the mishap dynamics, effective response procedures, and hold-down material (fixant) suitability.

2. Synergistic material and combustion effects

   –The combined effects of multiple materials and varying damage extents.

3. Concentrations and compatibility

   –Exposure limits aren't specifically defined. Equipment, procedure, and fire suppression agent compatibility issues also exist.

4. Adsorbed and absorbed pyrolysis and combustion products

   –Impact and extent of the toxin hazard.

5. Site and equipment contamination and decontamination

   –Procedures for effectively and realistically addressing the hazards

6. Clean-up and disposal complications (including potential classifications as Hazardous Materials [Haz-Mat] depending upon the type and damage of the materials)

   –Determine proper disposal methods and classifications of waste debris.

7. Bloodborne pathogens

   –Examine the potential for Hepatitis B and HIV transmission from injection by contaminated debris.

8. Radiation exposure effects

   –Evaluate extent and results of potential exposures to Depleted Uranium and other radioactive AAMs.

9. Acute toxic exposures to beryllium oxide and other highly dangerous AAMs

   –Evaluate protective measures and protective equipment.

Personal Protective Equipment (PPE) Guidelines

As the normal first responders, firefighters are considered the primary response group to a mishap with AC/AAMs and are therefore subjected to the greatest hazard exposures from the materials; however, they are the best protected in all but the most extreme cases. As such, all personnel in the immediate vicinity of an AC/AAM mishap, as well as all personnel subject to the concentrated smoke plume, must wear bunker or proximity suits and Self-Contained Breathing Apparatus (SCBA) until the composite material fires have been <u>completely</u> extinguished, and cooled to a temperature at or below 300°F (149°C) with no intense smoldering.

Personal Protective Equipment (PPE) Requirements	
AC/AAM Mishap Condition	**PPE Recommended**
Burning or Smoldering Materials	1. Full Protective Fire Clothing 2. Self-Contained Breathing Apparatus (SCBA) 3. Do NOT use rubber gloves
Broken, Dispersed, or Splintered Materials (Post-Fire, Explosion, or High-Energy Impact)	1. Protective overalls (Tyvek suit) – coated with hood and foot coverings 2. Full-face respirator with High Efficiency Particulate Air (HEPA) filter (Note: A gas mask with a similar filter may be substituted if equipment or respirator-trained personnel are not present) 3. Hard-soled work boots (steel toe and shank are best) 4. Leather work gloves over nitrile rubber gloves [no surgical gloves]
Minimal or Peripheral Area Material Exposure	1. Long sleeves and long pants for durable work clothing 2. Nuisance dust filter or mask 3. Adequate eye protection (goggles or safety glasses) 4. Hard-soled work boots (steel toe and shank are best) 5. Leather work gloves over nitrile rubber gloves [no surgical gloves]

Movement of the debris to ensure adequate cooling should be accomplished in a manner that limits spreading the particulate matter. It is important to note that the potential exposure to hazards associated with AC/AAM mishaps <u>may</u> be <u>more</u> severe for secondary exposure groups, including all of the subsequent response operations, than for the initial fire fighting activities because of the duration of exposure and generally reduced levels of protection. However, the hazard exposures are minimal if Personal Protective Equipment (PPE) is properly used and good mishap response procedures are diligently followed. All affected personnel need to know both the hazards and the proper response for effective mishap risk control. This makes coordination and communication critical for everyone involved. Preparatory knowledge and training, accompanied by common sense, good judgment, and quick decision making are crucial for success.

Mishap Risk Control Guidelines for AC/AAMs

Immediately after a mishap, the situation should be assessed by answering the following questions:

1) Does the mishap scenario involve advanced composite/advanced aerospace materials?

2) If yes, where are they located, and are they damaged?

3) Who can provide information about the type and content of these materials, and can they be reached for specific questions?

4) How does the environment affect the situation? For example, does the weather impact the response, or does the local geography change the response strategy?

Once these basic questions havbeen addressed, the following steps should be accomplished. The specific response should be tailored to match the extent of the hazards.

1. First responder(s) [usually firefighters] shall conduct an initial mishap site survey for:

   a. Signs of fire, explosion, or high-energy impact damaged Advanced Composite/Advanced Aerospace Materials (AC/AAMs)

   b. Presence of loose/airborne fibers and particulates

   c. Prevailing meteorological condtions/wind direction, including smoke plume assessment (if any)

   d. Degree of site exposure to fire/impact/explosions

   e. Local/proximal equipment/asset damage and hazards, including the debris pattern

   f. Exposed personnel and environmental contamination routes

   Essentially, the first responder will determine the extent of any additional AC/AAM hazards associated with the mishap.

2. Establish control at site with a clear and direct chain of command. If properly protected personnel are not present, avoid the mishap site until appropriately trained and equipped personnel arrive at the scene.

3. Evacuate personnel from areas in the immediate vicinity of the mishap site affected by direct and dense fallout from the smoke plume, along with easily mobile and critical equipment. Continually move fire fighting equipment in

order to avoid the smoke plume, especially in larger scale mishaps involving greater amounts of AC/AAMs. Restrict ALL unprotected personnel from assembling downwind of the mishap site. Use of over-pressurized cab equipped fire vehicles is essential if unable to avoid the smoke plume; however, this will require greater decontamination requirements. Some modern AC/AAM form combustion products that are permeable to the protective membranes for ventilation in contemporary fire suit ensembles. Accordingly, contamination, decontamination, and protection become very important concerns for a small percentage of mishaps, usually involving stealth aircraft. If exposed to either the smoke plume, open fire, or smoldering off-gassing of burned AC/AAMs, firefighters should monitor their bodies as part of the whole system. This would include checking for any potential chemical burns/irritation at heavy perspiration areas such as the armpits and groin. However, this phenomenon is very dependent upon rare material concentrations in confined-space-type environments. Nevertheless, it warrants consideration.

4. Alter or move aircraft and flight operations within the immediately exposed mishap and fallout areas. No ground or flight operations (specifically helicopters) are to be permitted within 500 ft above ground level (AGL) of the site and within 1,000 ft horizontally. (This footprint may be increased depending on concentrations and local conditions).

5. Normal fire fighting mishap response procedures should initially be followed. Once control of any fires is established, the special precautions associated with AC/AAMs should be implemented. Depending upon the type of materials involved, some equipment-related problems might arise. These include: dulling of penetrator tools due to the hardness of some advanced composites, inability to penetrate some areas unless the hard-points and emergency penetration points are known, and internally insulated (imbedded) fires that are difficult to suppress. Complex engine inlets and imbedded exhaust areas are particularly challenging for fire suppression.

6. Extinguish fire and cool AC/AA Materials to below 300°F (149°C). This can be accomplished by spraying a light mist of water or foam on the affected materials once the major fires are extinguished. In some cases, fire suppression agent compatibility will be an issue. For example, dry chemical fire suppressant can destroy some advanced composite components, so care should be exercised with small and isolated fires in order to minimize peripheral material damage. In more extreme cases, known fire suppression agents are somewhat ineffective at extinguishing fires on exotic AC/AAMs. Extreme caution should be exercised in these very rare scenarios.

7. ONLY firefighters equipped with Self-Contained Breathing Apparatus (SCBA) are authorized in the immediate vicinity of a burning/smoldering mishap site until the fire chief declares the area both fire safe and smolder/off-gas hazard safe. If possible, care should be taken to avoid high-pressure water or foam applications due to the high potential for breakup and dispersal of the AC/AA Materials.

8. Avoid dragging fire hoses through mishap debris or contaminated areas, as there is a high potential for abrasion and/or equipment contamination. Gear, including the bunker suits and water/air lines may be snagged by sharp and jagged AC debris. Boots are particularly prone to cuts and penetration where jagged and stiff AC debris is damaged. Likewise, they are big potential sources for contamination from particulates, as well as transfer of these contaminants to other areas beside the immediate mishap vicinity.

9. Cordon or rope off the mishap site and establish a single entry/exit point. Only adequately protected personnel are authorized at the immediate mishap site and peripheral area (contamination reduction zone). The fire chief and bioenvironmental engineer, or the on-scene commander designates the peripheral area in a coordinated effort. As a guide, the peripheral area should be defined as more than 25 feet away from any damaged composite parts, although it will vary based upon local meteorological and geographical conditions.

10. If personnel other than those at the mishap site have been directly and significantly exposed to material and smoke hazards, consult medical personnel for evaluation and tracking. If possible, inform the medical personnel of the type and extent of exposures. Advise and inform the otherwise unthreatened populace of the applicable precautions to take in affected mishap site surroundings or in plume fallout areas. Track patient treatment and outcomes for those involved in the mishap.

11. Coordinate with the on-scene or Incident Commander (IC) to provide necessary access to the mishap site for more thorough survey and investigation. For larger scale mishap response scenarios, especially involving modern, highly unique AC/AAMs, use of a Hazardous Materials Response unit is recommended, because of the added levels of experience and increased capability to control the situation.

12. If possible, toxicology and area studies for dust, inhalable and respirable particulates, and fibers should be conducted by a qualified industrial hygienist or bioenvironmental expert as soon as practical. However, all research personnel must be sufficiently protected. The survey protocol should include a visual observation, personal air, ground, and water sampling, and evaluation of the engineering controls and PPE in use at the scene.

13. Identify specific aircraft and material hazards as soon as possible by inspection of the debris and consultation with applicable, knowledgeable personnel/sources (i.e., crew chief, system managers, reference documents, web sites, contractors, or aircraft specialists). Indicate or point out AC/AAM locations and concentrations to all response personnel, as appropriate.

14. Minimize airborne dispersion of particulates/fibers by avoiding excessive disturbance from walking, working, or moving materials at the mishap site. This includes fire suppression equipment whenever possible.

15. Locate, secure, and remove any radioactive AAMs by using a Geiger counter to find any applicable debris or particulates. Contact relevant authorities and dispose of in accordance with strict policies.

16. Monitor entry/exit from the single Entry Control Point (ECP). The following guidelines apply:

    a. When exiting the mishap site, personnel should follow clearly defined decontamination procedures. Use of a High Efficiency Particulate Air (HEPA) filtered vacuum system is highly desired. If possible, remove AC/AAM contaminants from outer clothing, work gloves, boots, headgear, and equipment. If this type of vacuum is unavailable, efforts must be made to rinse, wipe, or brush off as much particulate contamination as possible.

    b. Clean sites (i.e., tent or trailer) for donning and removal of Personal Protective Equipment (PPE) should be set up as soon as practical.

    c. No eating, drinking, or smoking is permitted within the exclusion and contamination reduction zones, or as otherwise determined by the Incident Commander. Personnel must be advised to wash hands, forearms, and face prior to eating, drinking, or smoking.

  d. Contaminated protective clothing should be properly wrapped, sealed, and disposed.

  e. Personnel should shower in cool water prior to going off-duty to prevent any problems associated with transfer of loose fibers or particulates. Portable showers may need to be provided.

  f. When practical, contaminated outergarments from victims/response personnel should be removed at the mishap site decontamination area in order to protect the subsequent medical staff. Any ill effects believed to be related to exposure to AC/AAMs should be reported immediately. Likewise, the local medical staff should be advised of the incident, along with the potential hazards. Symptoms of effects could include:

  –Respiratory tract irritation and reduced respiratory capacity

  –Eye irritation

  –Skin irritation, sensitization, rashes, infections, or allergic reactions

  g. All contaminated footwear should be cleaned to limit the spread of debris into clean areas and support vehicles.

  h. Materials Safety Data Sheet (MSDS) should be made available to qualified personnel.

  i. Security restrictions may require additional control measures during emergencies.

17. Secure burned/mobile AC/AAM fragments and loose ash/particulate residue with plastic, a gentle mist of water or fire-fighting agent, fixant material, or a tent-like structure in order to prevent redispersion.

18. Consult the specific aircraft authority and/or the investigators before applying a fixant or hold-down material. However, safety concerns at the immediate mishap site may override any delayed application. Fire fighting equipment should be available during fixant/stripper application, aircraft breakup, and recovery. Also, any fires must be completely out and the materials cooled to below 300°F (149°C). Movement of the debris to ensure adequate cooling should be accomplished in a manner that limits spreading the particulate matter. Two types of fixants are generally used: one for burned AC/AA Materials and debris, and the other for land surfaces. Fixant is usually not needed for open terrain and improved surfaces (concrete or asphalt) unless very high concentrations exist.

19. Obtain and mix (if necessary) the fixant or hold-down solution such as Polyacrylic acid (PAA) or acrylic floor wax and water. Light oil is not recommended because it may become an aerosol and collect on equipment, hamper material investigations, and present a health hazard of its own. Generic acrylic floor wax, which is widely available, should be mixed in an approximate ratio somewhere between 2:1 to 10:1, depending upon environmental conditions, damage extent, and criticality of post incident investigation. Use good judgment.

20. Apply (preferably spray) a moderate coating of the fixant solution on all burned/damaged AC/AA Materials and to any areas containing scattered/settled particulate debris. Completely coat the material until wet to ensure immobilization of the material, then allow the coating to dry.

21. **NOTE:** Strip-ability of the fixant coating is required where coatings are applied to debris that must later undergo microscopic chemical and material analysis by incident investigators. Care must be exercised in the use of stripping solutions since they can react with some materials and the process of stripping may damage the parts. PAA may be removed by a dilute solution of household ammonia (about 1% by volume of ammonium hydroxide in water) or trisodium phosphate (approximately one 8 ounce cup of trisodium phosphate per 2 gallons of water).

22. If deemed necessary, agricultural soil tackifiers may be used to hold materials on sand or soil. Most solutions can be sprayed onto the ground at a rate of 0.5 gal/sq yd.

23. Improved hard surfaces (i.e., concrete and asphalt) should be vacuumed (with an electrically protected vacuum) if possible. Sweeping operations should be avoided as they redisseminate the particulates. The effluent from any runoff should be collected via plastic or burlap coated trenches or drainage ditches.

    NOTE: The entire impact or mishap site must be diked to prevent runoff of fire fighting agent (to avoid additional cleanup or environmental contamination).

24. All fixant application equipment should be immediately flushed/cleaned with a dilute solvent to prevent clogging for future use. Likewise, all fire fighting vehicles and equipment must be decontaminated, to the maximum extent possible, at the mishap site. Water and HEPA vacuums may be used.

25. Pad all sharp projections on damaged debris that must be retained so that injuries during handling and analysis can be avoided.

26. Carefully wrap the coated parts and or material with plastic sheeting/film or place them in a plastic bag of approximately 0.006 inches (6 mils) thick. Generic garbage bags are generally inadequate unless they are used as several plies.

27. Conduct all material disposal according to local, state, federal, and international guidelines. Consult with appropriate agencies for relevant procedures and policies for materials that do NOT require mishap investigation analysis or repair. Ensure all parts are released before disposal is authorized. All AC/AAM waste should be labeled appropriately with the type of material followed by the words: "Do Not Incinerate or Sell for Scrap."

28. Complete all necessary soil and surface restoration as required at the mishap site.

29. Place all hazardous waste material in appropriate containers and dispose of properly according to all applicable regulations.

30. If aircraft were subjected to the concentrated smoke plume or debris areas, the following should be accomplished:

    a. Vacuum the air/ventilation/cooling intakes with an electrically protected, HEPA vacuum cleaner.

    b. For internally affected smoke areas, visually and electronically inspect all compartments for debris and vacuum thoroughly.

    c. Prior to flying, perform electrical and systems checks, as well as an engine run-up.

31. For significantly affected structures and equipment, thoroughly clean all antenna insulators, exposed transfer bushings, circuit breakers, and any other applicable electrical components. Inspect air intakes and outlets for signs of smoke or debris and decontaminate if necessary.

32. Continue to monitor affected personnel, equipment, and mishap site.

Rapid Response Checklist

☐ Conduct the Initial Mishap Site Survey

☐ Establish Control at the Mishap Site with a Clear Chain of Command

☐ Evacuate Personnel From the Immediate Mishap Site Vicinity. *Restrict ALL unprotected personnel from assembling downwind of the mishap site.*

☐ Restrict Ground and Flight Operations As Appropriate for Conditions

☐ Extinguish Fire and Cool AC/AA Materials to below 300°F (149°C)

☐ Cordon Off the Mishap Site and Establish a Single Entry/Exit Point

☐ Consult Medical Personnel for Evaluation and Tracking of Exposed Personnel

☐ Coordinate a Thorough Survey of the Mishap Site with an Incident Commander (IC)

☐ Conduct Expert Toxicology and Area Studies With Survey Protocols

☐ Identify Specific Aircraft and Material Hazards

☐ Avoid Excessive Disturbance of the Mishap Site

☐ Locate, Secure, and Remove Radioactive AAMs; Contact Relevant Authorities and Dispose of In Accordance with Strict Disposal Policies

☐ Monitor Entry/Exit from the Single Entry Control Point (ECP)

☐ Secure Burned/Mobile AC/AAM Fragments and Loose Ash/Particulate Residue

☐ Consult Aircraft Authorities Before Applying Fixants or Hold-Down Materials

☐ Obtain and Mix a Fixant or Hold-down Solution

☐ Apply/Spray the Fixant Solution on Burned/Damaged AC/AA Materials

☐ Use Strippable Fixant Coating Where Coatings are Applied

☐ Use Agricultural Soil Tackifiers If Necessary

☐ Vacuum Improved Hard Surfaces

☐ Flush/Clean the Fixant Application Equipment With Dilute Solvent

☐ Pad All Sharp Projections On Damaged Debris

☐ Wrap Coated Parts and/or Material with Plastic Sheeting/Film

☐ Conduct Material Disposal According to Local, State, Federal, and International Guidelines

☐ Complete Soil and Surface Restoration

☐ Dispose of Hazardous Waste Material Appropriately

☐ Continue to Monitor Affected Personnel and Sites

References

"A Composite Picture." *Safety and Health*. Nov 1991. P 38-41.

A Composite System Approach to Aircraft Cabin Fire Safety. NASA Technical Memorandum. Apr 1987.

Advanced Composite Repair Guide. NOR 82-60. Prepared by Northrup Corporation, Aircraft Division, for USAF Wright Aeronautical Laboratories, Wright-Patterson AFB, OH. Mar 1982.

"Aircraft Fire Fighting Procedures for Composite Materials." US Navy/Marine Corps Training Film #112769. Naval Education and Training Support Center, Atlantic. Norfolk, VA. 1993.

American Conference of Governmental Industrial Hygienists. Threshold Limit Values for Chemical Substances and Physical Agents, ACGIH, Cincinnati, OH. 1998.

Baron, P.A. and K. Willeke. "Measurement of Asbestos and Other Fibers." *Aerosol Measurement Principles, Techniques, and Applications*. Van Nostrand-Rheinhold, New York, NY. 1993.

Bickers, Charles. "Danger: Toxic Aircraft." *Janes Defence Weekly*. 19 Oct 1991.

Brauer, Roger L. *Safety and Health for Engineers*. Van Nostrand-Rheinhold, New York, NY. 1990.

Code of Federal Regulations, 29 *CFR* 1910.1000, *Air Contaminants*.

Composite Aircraft Mishap Safety and Health Guidelines. Project Engineer: Capt Keller. USAF Advanced Composites Program Office, McClellan AFB, CA. 18 Jun 1992.

Composite Aircraft Mishap Safety and Health Guidelines. ASCC ADV PUB 25/XX. Air Standardization Coordinating Committee, Washington, DC. 16 Sep 1992.

Composite Material Protective Equipment and Waste Disposal. Memo from 650 MED GP/SGB to 411 TS/CC, Edwards AFB, CA. 14 Oct 1992.

Conference on Advanced Composites, 5-7 Mar 1991. Proceedings. San Diego, CA. 1992.

Conference on Occupational Health Aspects of Advanced Composite Technology in the Aerospace Industry, 5-9 Feb 1989. AAMRL-TR-89-008. Vols I and II, Executive Summary and Proceedings. Wright-Patterson AFB, OH. Mar 1989.

DARCOM/NMC/AFLC/AFSC Commanders Joint Technical Coordinating Group on HAVE NAME (JTCG/HN). *HAVE NAME Guide for Protection of Electrical Equipment from Carbon Fibers*. May 1978.

Faeder, Edward J. and Paul E. Gurba. "Health Effects in the Aerospace Workplace – Some Concerns." SME Conference Proceedings: Composites in Manufacturing 9. Dearborn, MI. 15-18 Jan 1990.

Fire Performance and Suppressibility of Composite Materials. Hughes SBIR Phase II Report HAI 92-1071 DRAFT. 15 Dec 1992.

Fire Safety Aspects of Polymeric Materials, Volume 6: Aircraft: Civil and Military. Report by the National Materials Advisory Board of the National Academy of Sciences. 1977.

Fisher, Karen J. "Is Fire a Barrier to Shipboard Composites?" *Advanced Composites*. Vol 8, No 3: May/Jun 1993.

Gandhi, S. and Richard Lyon. *Health Hazards of Combustion Products from Aircraft Composite Materials*, Draft Manuscript, FAA Technical Center. 1997.

General Advanced Composite Repair Processes Manual. USAF TO1-1-690. McClellan AFB, CA. 1 Aug 1990.

Hetcko, John. "Disposal of Advanced Composite Materials." Defense Division, Brunswick Corporation. Lincoln, NE.

Hubbell, M. Patricia. "Hazard Communication and Composites." McDonnell Douglas Space Systems Company. A3-315-12-1. Huntington Beach, CA 92647.

Kantz, M. "Advanced Polymer Matrix Resins and Constituents: An Overview of Manufacturing, Composition, and Handling." *Applied Industrial Hygiene, Special Issue.* 50(12). P 1-8. 1989.

Mishap Response for Advanced Composites. US Air Force Film. 46th Test Wing Audio-Visual Services, Eglin AFB, FL. Sep 1994.

Morrison, R. General Background on the Filtration Performance of Military Filters. US Army Chemical and Biological Defense Command, Aberdeen Proving Grounds, MD. 1998.

Naval Environmental Health Center, *Advanced Composite Materials*, NEHC-TM91-6. 1991.

Naval Safety Center. *Accident Investigation and Clean up of Aircraft Containing Carbon/Graphite Composite Material Safety Advisory.* Unclassified Telex N03750 from NAS Norfolk, VA. 20 Aug 1993.

Olson, John M. *Aerospace Advanced Composites Interim Technical Mishap Guide.* USAF HQ AFCESA/DF. 22 Mar 1994.

Olson, John M. "Composite Aircraft Mishaps: High Tech Hazards? Part I and II. *Flying Safety Magazine.* Vol 49, No 11 and 12. Nov and Dec 1993.

Olson, John M. *Mishap Risk Control Guidelines for Advanced Aerospace Materials: Environmental, Safety, and Health Concerns for Advanced Composites.* 28 Oct 1993. USAF Advanced Composites Programs Office, McClellan AFB, CA.

Olson, John M. *Safety, Health, and Environmental Hazards Associated with Composites: A Complete Analysis.* 15 Nov 1992.

"Position Paper on the CORKER Program." Oklahoma City Air Logistics Center. 16 Feb 1993.

Revised HAVE NAME Protection Manual. MP 81-266 MITRE MTR 4654. A.S. Marqulies and D.M. Zasada, Eds. Jun 1981.

Risk Analysis Program Office at Langley Research Center. *Risk to the Public from Carbon Fibers Released in Civil Aircraft Accidents.* NASA SP-448. Washington, DC. 1980.

Safe Handling of Advanced Composite Materials. 2nd Ed. SACMA, Arlington, VA. Jul 1991.

Seibert, John F. *Composite Fiber Hazards,* US Air Force Occupational and Environmental Health Laboratory (AFOEHL) Technical Report 90-226E100178MGA. 1990.

Summary of Medical Evaluation of Boeing Employees Working with Composite Materials Who Have Filed Workers Compensation Claims for Illness. Seattle Medical Care, Association for Independent Practitioners. Seattle, WA.

Thomson, S.A. "Toxicology of Carbon Fibers." *Applied Industrial Hygiene, Special Issue.* 50(12). P 34-36. 1989.

Warnock, Richard. "Engineering Controls and Work Practices for Advanced Composite Repair." *Applied Industrial Hygiene, Special Issue,* 50(12). P 52-53. 1989.

Appendix D
Additional Sample Vocabulary

A

Acknowledge — "Confirm that you have received and have understood the message."

Advise intentions — "Explain what you plan to do."

Affirmative — "Yes," "permission is granted," or "that is correct."

Air Traffic Control (ATC) — Service operated by appropriate authority to promote the safe, orderly, and expeditious flow of air traffic.

B

Base leg — The flight path at a right angle to the landing runway off the approach end.

Base to final — Turning into final approach position.

Blind (dead) spot — An area from which radio transmissions cannot be received. May also be used to describe portions of the airport not visible from the control tower.

Broadcast — Transmission of information for which an acknowledgment is not expected.

C

Confirm — "Verify" or "recheck."

Correction — "An error has been made in the transmission, and the corrected version follows."

D

Decontamination — the removal of a foreign substance that could cause harm; frequently used to describe removal of a hazardous material from the person, clothing, or area.

Downwind leg — A flight path parallel to the landing runway in the direction opposite to landing.

E

ETA — Estimated time of arrival.

Expedite — "Prompt compliance is required."

F

Final approach — That portion of the landing pattern in which the aircraft is lined up with the runway and is heading straight in to land.

Flameout — Unintended loss of combustion in turbojet engines resulting in the loss of engine power.

Fuel on board — Amount in pounds (6 to 7 lb per gallon [0.7 kg to 0.8 kg per liter]) on aircraft remaining.

G

Gear down — Landing gear in down and locked position (have green light in the cockpit).

Go ahead — "Proceed with your transmission."

Go around — Maneuver conducted by a pilot whenever a visual approach to a landing cannot be completed.

H

Hold your position — "Do not proceed! Remain where you are."

How do you hear (read/copy) me? — A question relating to the quality of the transmission or to determine how well the transmission is being received.

Hung gear — One or more of the aircraft landing gear not down and locked (no green light indication in the cockpit).

I

Immediately — "Action is required without delay."

I say again — "The message will be repeated."

J

Jet blast — Wind and/or heat blast created behind an aircraft with engines running.

L

Low approach — An approach over a runway or heliport where the pilot intentionally does not make contact with the runway.

M

Make a 90, 180, or 360 (degree turn) — Instructions normally given by the control tower to the aircraft to indicate the degree of turn the pilot is to execute; also frequently used by the control tower to direct vehicles on the ground.

Make your best time — "Expedite."

Mayday — The international radio distress signal.

Minimum fuel — Indicates that an aircraft's fuel supply has reached a state where it can accept little or no delay before landing.

Missed approach — A maneuver conducted by a pilot whenever an instrument approach cannot be completed into a landing.

N

Negative — "No"; "permission not granted"; "that is not correct."

O

Out — "The conversation is ended, and no response is expected."

Over — "My transmission is ended; I expect a response."

Overhead approach (360 overhead) — A series of standard maneuvers conducted by military aircraft (often in formation) for entry into the airfield traffic pattern prior to landing.

P

Prop or rotor wash — Windblast created behind or around an aircraft with engines running.

Proceed — "Go" or "go to."

R

Read back — Repeat the message back to the sender to ensure accuracy.

Received (copied) — "Message has been received and understood."

Repeat — Request operator to say again.

Roger — "Message received and understood."

NOTE: "Roger" *should not* be used to answer a question requiring a "yes" or "no" answer. Use *affirmative* or *negative*.

S

Say again — Request a repeat of last transmission.

Speak slower — Request to reduce rate of speech.

Stand by — The person transmitting will pause, and those receiving transmission should await further transmission.

Stand by to copy — "Prepare to receive detailed information that should be written down."

T

That is correct — Indicates agreement with how message is understood.

U

Unable to — Indicates inability to comply with a specific instruction, request, or clearance.

V

Verify — Request for confirmation of information.

W

Wilco —"Received message, understand, and will comply."

Wind direction and velocity — Wind direction is given to the nearest 10 degrees, and velocity is given in knots. A report of "wind at 330 at 10" would mean the wind was blowing from 330 degrees (30 degrees from north) at 10 knots (12 mph).

Words twice — Indicates that communication is difficult; request that every phrase be said twice.

Appendix E
Additional Information Sources for ARFF Personnel

National Fire Protection Association (NFPA) Standards

NFPA® 1002, *Standard on Fire Apparatus Driver/Operator Professional Qualifications*

NFPA® 1003, *Standard for Airport Fire Fighter Professional Qualifications*

NFPA® 402, *Guide for Aircraft Rescue and Fire-Fighting Operations*

NFPA® 403, *Standard for Aircraft Rescue and Fire-Fighting Services at Airports*

NFPA® 405, *Standard for the Recurring Proficiency of Airport Fire Fighters*

NFPA® 407, *Standard for Aircraft Fuel Servicing*

NFPA® 408, *Standard for Aircraft Hand Portable Fire Extinguishers*

NFPA® 409, *Standard on Aircraft Hangars*

NFPA® 412, *Standard for Evaluating Aircraft Rescue and Fire-Fighting Foam Equipment*

NFPA® 414, *Standard for Aircraft Rescue and Fire-Fighting Vehicles*

NFPA® 415, *Standard on Airport Terminal Buildings, Fueling Ramp Drainage, and Loading Walkways*

NFPA® 422, *Guide for Aircraft Accident/Incident Response Assessment*

NFPA® 424, *Guide for Airport/Community Emergency Planning*

Federal Aviation Regulations (FARs)

Code of Federal Regulations, Title 14, Part 139, Subpart D:

Sec. 121.310, *Additional Emergency Equipment*

Sec. 139.315, *Aircraft Rescue and Firefighting: Index Determination*

Sec. 139.317, *Aircraft Rescue and Firefighting: Equipment and Agents*

Sec. 139.319, *Aircraft Rescue and Firefighting: Operational Requirements*

Sec. 139.325, *Airport Emergency Plan*

Federal Aviation Administration (FAA) Advisory Circulars (ACs)

150/5200-12B *Fire Department Responsibility in Protecting Evidence at the Scene of an Aircraft Accident*

150/5200-18C *Airport Safety Self Inspection*

150/5200-31A *Airport Emergency Plan*

150/5210-5C *Painting, Marking, and Lighting of Vehicles Used on an Airport*

150/5210-6D *Aircraft Fire & Rescue Facilities & Extinguishing Agents*

150/5210-7C *Aircraft Rescue and Firefighting Communications*

150/5210-13B *Water Rescue Plans, Facilities, and Equipment*

150/5210-14A *Airport Fire and Rescue Personnel Protective Clothing*

150/5210-15 Airport *Rescue and Firefighting Station Building Design*

150/5210-17A *Programs for Training of Aircraft Rescue and Fire Fighting Personnel*

150/5210-18 *Systems for Interactive Training of Airport Personnel*

150/5210-19 *Driver's Enhanced Vision System (DEVS)*

150/5220-4B *Water Supply Systems for Aircraft Fire and Rescue Protection*

150/5220-10D *Guide Specification for Aircraft Rescue and Fire Fighting Vehicles*

150/5220-17A Change 1 *Design Standards for Aircraft Rescue and Fire Fighting Training Facility*

150/5220-19 *Guide Specification for Small Agent ARFF Vehicles*

150/5230-4A *Aircraft Fuel Storage, Handling, & Dispensing on Airports*

Emergency Response Telephone Numbers

National Response Center 1-800-424-8802

CHEMTREC® 1-800-424-9300

CANUTEC 613-996-6666 or *666 on Cellular Telephones

Military Shipments:

Explosives/Ammunition Incidents: 703-697-0218

All Other Dangerous Goods Incidents: 1-800-851-8061

Websites

National Fire Protection Association (NFPA):

http://www.nfpa.org

Federal Aviation Administration (FAA):

http://www.faa.gov

U.S. Department of Transportation:

http://www.dot.gov

Aircraft Rescue and Fire Fighting Working Group (ARFFWG):

http://www.arffwg.org

Technical Order 00-105E-9

http://www.robins.af.mil/library/technicalorders.asp

NOTE: To order Technical Order 00-105E-9, contact:
HQAFCESA.CEXF@tyndall.af.mil

Glossary

Glossary of Aviation Terms

NOTE: This glossary is designed to supplement discussions in the text and is not meant to be a comprehensive dictionary of aircraft terms.

A

Abort — Act of terminating a planned aircraft maneuver such as the takeoff or landing; pilots will normally abort a takeoff if any indication of a possible malfunction exists

Accident Potential Zones (APZ) — Land areas immediately beyond the ends of the runways and along primary flight paths that pose a higher risk of aircraft accidents than other areas

Advanced Aerospace Materials — See *Composite Materials*

AEP — Abbreviation for Airport Emergency Plan

Aeration — Introduction of air into a foam solution to create bubbles that result in finished foam

AFFF — See Aqueous Film Forming Foam

Aft/After — Rear or tail section or toward the rear or tail of an aircraft

AHJ — Abbreviation for Authority Having Jurisdiction

Aileron — Movable hinged rear portion of an airplane wing; used to roll or bank the aircraft in flight

Air Bill — Shipping document prepared from a bill of lading that accompanies each piece or each lot of air cargo

Air Traffic Control (ATC) — Federal Aviation Administration (FAA) division that operates control towers at major airports

Aircraft accident — Occurrence during the operation of an aircraft in which any person suffers death or serious injury or in which the aircraft receives damage

Aircraft Familiarization — Area of ARFF personnel training relating to the various aircraft operated in an airport and the features of these aircraft, including fuel capacity, fuel tank locations, emergency exit locations, operation of emergency exits, passenger seating capacity, etc.

Aircraft incident — Occurrence, other than an accident, associated with the operation of an aircraft that affects or could affect continued safe operation if not corrected

Airfoils — Relates to the shape of a wing, propeller blade, or horizontal or vertical stabilizer as it is viewed in cross-section; generate the lift needed for the aircraft to fly

Airport/Airfield — Area on land or water used or intended to be used for aircraft takeoffs and landings; includes buildings and facilities. Aerodrome is the international term with the same definition.

Airport Emergency Plan (AEP) — Plan formulated by airport authorities to ensure prompt response to all emergencies and other unusual conditions in order to minimize the extent of personal and property damage

Airport Familiarization — Knowledge of the locations of airport buildings, runways and taxiways, access roads, and surface features, routes, and conditions that may enhance or obstruct the prompt and safe response to accidents/incidents on the airport and those areas surrounding the airport

Airport Hazard Assessment — Formal review of the hazards that may be encountered at an airport

Aircraft incident — Occurrence, other than an accident, associated with the operation of an aircraft that affects or could affect continued safe operation if not corrected

Airport Operations Area (AOA) — Area of an airport where aircraft are expected to operate such as taxiways, runways, and ramps

Airspeed — Speed of an aircraft relative to its surrounding air mass

AOA — Abbreviation for Airport Operations Area

Approach Lights — System of lights so arranged to assist pilots in aligning their aircraft with the runway for landing

Apron — Defined area on airports intended to accommodate aircraft for purposes of loading or unloading passengers, mail or cargo, refueling, parking, or maintenance; also known as Ramp

APU — Abbreviation for Auxiliary Power Unit

APZ — Abbreviation for Accident Potential Zones

Aqueous Film Forming Foam (AFFF) — Synthetic foam concentrate that, when combined with water, is a highly effective extinguishing and blanketing agent on hydrocarbon fuels

Around-the-Pump Proportioner — Apparatus-mounted foam proportioner; a small quantity of water is diverted from the apparatus pump through an inline proportioner where it picks up the foam concentrate and carries it to the intake side of the pump; most common apparatus-mounted foam proportioner in service

ATC — Abbreviation for Air Traffic Control

ATIS — Abbreviation for automated Terminal Information Service

Authority Having Jurisdiction (AHJ) — Term used in codes and standards to identify the legal entity, such as a building or fire official, that has the statutory authority to enforce a code and to approve or require equipment. In the insurance industry it may refer to an insurance rating bureau or an insurance company inspection department.

Automated Terminal Information Service (ATIS) — Continuous automated information which is broadcast over a radio frequency for a specific airport. Typical information in an ATIS report includes weather conditions, active runways, approaches in use, and other pertinent information.

Automatic Aid — Written agreement between two or more agencies to automatically dispatch predetermined resources to any fire or other emergency reported in the geographic area covered by the agreement. These areas are generally where the boundaries between jurisdictions meet or where jurisdictional "islands" exist.

Auxiliary Power Unit (APU) — Power unit installed in most large aircraft to provide electrical power and pneumatics for ground power, air conditioning, engine start, and backup power in flight. APU also refers to mobile units that are moved from one aircraft to another to provide a power boost during engine startup.

B

Backdraft — Instantaneous explosion or rapid burning of superheated gases that occurs when oxygen is introduced into an oxygen-depleted confined space. The stalled combustion resumes with explosive force. It may occur because of inadequate or improper ventilation procedures. Very rapid, often explosive burning of hot gases that occurs when oxygen is introduced into an oxygen-depleted confined space. It may occur because of inadequate or improper ventilation procedures.

Balanced Pressure Proportioner — Foam concentrate proportioner that operates in tandem with a fire water pump to ensure a proper foam concentrate-to-water mixture

Base Leg — Flight path at a right angle to the landing runway off the approach end. The base leg normally extends from the downwind leg to the intersection of the extended runway line. The aircraft must make a 90-degree turn from the base leg before it can begin its final approach.

Beadlocks — Device that secures the bead of a tire to the rim

Bogie — Tandem arrangement of landing gear wheels with a central strut; swivels up and down so all wheels stay on the ground as the attitude of the aircraft changes or as the slope of the ground surface changes

Breakaway/Frangible Fences and Gates — Fences and gates designed and constructed to collapse when impacted by large vehicles to allow rapid access to accident sites.

Braking Distance — Distance the vehicle travels from the time the brakes are applied until it comes to a complete stop

Bulkhead — Upright partition that separates one aircraft compartment from another; may strengthen or help give shape to the structure and may be used for the mounting of equipment and accessories

C

Cabin — Aircraft passenger compartment that may be separated and may contain a cargo area

Cadet (recruit) Training — Initial training received prior to being assigned to a company

CAFS — Abbreviation for Compressed-Air Foam Ssytem

Canopy — Transparent enclosure over the cockpit of some aircraft

Cargo Manifest — Document or shipping paper listing all contents carried by an aircraft, vehicle, or vessel on a specific trip

CFR — Abbreviation for Code of Federal Regulations

CISD — Abbreviation for Critical Incident Stress Debriefing

CISM — Abbreviation for Critical Incident Stress Management

Clearway/Overrun — Area beyond the end of the runway that has been cleared of nonfrangible obstacles and strengthened to allow overruns without serious damage to the aircraft

Cockpit — Fuselage compartment occupied by pilots while flying the aircraft

Cockpit Voice Recorder (CVR) — Recording device installed in most large civilian aircraft to record crew conversation and communications and is intended to assist in an accident investigation to determine probable cause of the accident

Code of Federal Regulations (CFR) — Formal name given to the books or documents containing the specific United States regulations provided for by law; complete body of U.S. Federal law

Command Post — Command and control point where the incident commander and command staff function and where those in charge of emergency units report to be briefed on their respective assignments

Common Traffic Advisory Frequency (CTAF) — Airport radio frequency used for coordination of air and ground traffic between operators when Air Traffic Control is not available

Composite Materials — Plastics, metals, ceramics, or carbon-fiber materials with built-in strengthening agents; much lighter and stronger than the metals formerly used for such aircraft components as panels, skin, and flight controls. The newer term is Advanced Aerospace Materials.

Compressed-Air Foam System (CAFS) — Generic term used to describe a high-energy foam-generation system consisting of an air compressor (or other air source), a water pump, and foam solution that injects air into the foam solution before it enters a hoseline

Confined Space — Any space or enclosed area not intended for continuous occupation, having limited (restricted access) openings for entry or exit, providing unfavorable natural ventilation and the potential to have a toxic, explosive, or oxygen-deficient atmosphere

Control Tower — Unit (facility) established to provide traffic control service for the movement of aircraft and other vehicles in the airport operations area; contains very sophisticated electronic devices for the control of the flight patterns and airport ground operations

Controlled Airport — Airport having a control tower in operation; the tower is usually, but not always, staffed by FAA personnel

Countermeasures — Devices or systems designed to prevent sensor-guided weapons from locking onto and destroying a target

Cowling — Removable covering around aircraft engines

CRFFAA — Abbreviation for Critical Rescue and Fire Fighting Access Area

Critical Incident Stress Debriefing (CISD) — Counseling designed to minimize the effects of psychological/emotional post-incident trauma on those at fire and rescue incidents who were directly involved with victims suffering from particularly gruesome or horrific injuries

Critical Incident Stress Management (CISM) — Comprehensive crisis intervention system composed of 7 elements: pre-crisis preparation, a disaster or large scale incident, defusing, critical incident stress debriefing, one-on-one crisis intervention/counseling, family/organizational crisis intervention, and follow-up/referral mechanisms. (http://www.icisf.org/inew_era.htm)

Critical Rescue and Fire Fighting Access Area (CRFFAA) — Rectangular area surrounding any given runway; extends 500 feet (150 m) outward from each side of the runway centerline, and 3,300 feet (1 000 m) beyond each runway end; area on an airfield where most accidents are expected to occur

Crosswind Leg — Flight path at right angles to the landing runway off its upwind leg

CTAF — Abbreviation for Common Traffic Advisory Frequency

CVR — Abbreviation for Cockpit Voice Recorder

D

Dangerous Good — Any product, substance, or organism included by its nature or by the regulation in any of the nine United Nations classifications of hazardous materials; used to describe hazardous materials in Canada and used in the U.S. and Canada for hazardous materials aboard aircraft

Decontamination — Removal of a foreign substance that could cause harm; frequently used to describe removal of a hazardous material from the person, clothing, or area

DFDR — Abbreviation for Digital Flight Data Recorder

Digital Flight Data Recorder (DFDR) — Digital recording device on large civilian aircraft to record aircraft airspeed, altitude, heading, acceleration, etc., to be used as an aid to accident investigation; commonly referred to as the "black box"

Dispatcher — person who works in the communications center and processes information from the public and emergency responders

DOT — Abbreviation for United States Department of Transportation

Downwind Leg — Flight path parallel to the landing runway in the direction opposite to landing; normally extends between the crosswind leg and the base leg

Dzus Fastener — Trade name given to a half-turn fastener with a slotted head; used on engine cowlings, cover plates, and access panels throughout the aircraft

E

Eductor — Portable proportioning device that injects a liquid, such as foam concentrate, into the water flowing through a hoseline or pipe

Ejection Seat — Aircraft seat capable of being ejected in an emergency to catapult the occupant clear of the aircraft

Elevator — Hinged, movable control surface at the rear of the horizontal stabilizer; attached to the control wheel or stick and is used to control the up-and-down pitch motion of the aircraft

EMAS — Abbreviation for Emergency Material Arresting Sysystem

Emergency Escape Slide — Escape slides connected to aircraft doors and, in some cases, to overwing exits that when deployed will inflate and extend to the ground; pneumatic in operation; most are automatic by opening the door; some require manual activation, that is, a short pull on a lanyard. Many may be disconnected from the aircraft and used for a flotation device in water.

Emergency Lighting System — Interior and exterior low-power incandescent and/or fluorescent lights designed to assist passengers in locating and using aircraft emergency exits, but not bright enough to assist ARFF personnel in carrying out search and rescue operations

Empennage — See *Tail*

Engineered Material Arresting System (EMAS) — Bed of aerated cement material that is designed to crush under an aircraft's weight to provide a predictable and controlled deceleration

Exhaust Area — Area behind an engine where hot exhaust gases present a danger to personnel

Extinguishing Agent — Substance used for the purpose of controlling or extinguishing a fire

F

FDR — Abbreviation for Flight Data Recorder

Final Approach — Portion of the landing pattern in which the aircraft is lined up with the runway and is heading straight in to land

Fire Suppression — All work and activities connected with fire extinguishing operations, beginning with discovery and continuing until a fire is completely extinguished

Fixed-Based Operator — Enterprise based on an airport that provides storage, maintenance, or service for aircraft operators

Flameout — Unintended loss of combustion in turbojet engines resulting in the loss of engine power

Flaps — Adjustable airfoils attached to the leading or trailing edges of aircraft wings to improve aerodynamic performance during takeoff and landing; normally extended during takeoff, landing, and slow flight

Flash Point — Minimum temperature at which a liquid gives off enough vapors to form an ignitable mixture with air near the liquid's surface

Flashback — Spontaneous reignition of fuel when the blanket of extinguishing agent breaks down or is compromised through physical disturbance

Flashover — Stage of a fire at which all surfaces and objects within a space have been heated to their ignition temperature and flame breaks out almost at once over the surface of all objects in the space

Flight Controls — General term applied to devices that enable the pilot to control the direction of flight and attitude of the aircraft

Flight Control Surface — Devices that enable the pilot to control the direction of flight, altitude, and attitude of the aircraft; includes ailerons, elevator, rudder, flaps and slats, spoilers, and speed brakes

Flight Data Recorder (FDR) — Recording device on large civilian aircraft to record aircraft airspeed, altitude, heading, acceleration, etc., to be used as an aid to accident investigation

Flight Deck — Cockpit on a large aircraft, separated from the rest of the cabin

Flight Service Station (FSS) — Facility from which aeronautical information and related aviation support services are provided to aircraft; also includes airport and vehicle advisory services for designated uncontrolled airports

Foam — Extinguishing agent formed by mixing a foam concentrate with water and aerating the solution for expansion; for use on Class A and Class B fires; may be protein, synthetic, aqueous film forming, high expansion, or alcohol type

FOD — Abbreviation for Foreign Object Debris

Foreign Object Damage — Damage attributed to a foreign object that can be expressed in physical or economic terms that may or may not degrade the product's required safety and/or performance characteristics

Foreign Object Debris (FOD) — Substance, debris or article alien to the vehicle or system which would potentially cause damage

Fore/Forward — Front or nose section of an aircraft or toward that area

FSS — Abbreviation for Flight Service Station

Fuel on Board — Amount in pounds (6 to 7 lb per gallon [0.7 kg to 0.8 kg per liter]) of fuel on aircraft remaining

Fuselage — Main body of an aircraft to which the wings and tail are attached; houses the crew, passengers, and cargo

G

Galley — Food storage and preparation area of large aircraft

Gas Turbine — See *Turbojet*

General Aviation — All civil aviation operations other than scheduled air services and nonscheduled operations for remuneration or hire

Gear Down — Landing gear in down and locked position (have green light in the cockpit)

Global Positioning System (GPS) — System for determining position on the earth's surface by calculating the difference in time for the signal from a number of satellites to reach a GPS receiver on the ground

Go Around — Maneuver conducted by a pilot whenever a visual approach to a landing cannot be completed

GPS — Abbreviation for Global Positioning System

Grid Map — Plan view of an area subdivided into a system of squares (numbered and lettered) to provide quick reference to any point

H

Halon — Halogenated agent; extinguishes fire by inhibiting the chemical reaction between fuel and oxygen

Hazardous Material — Any material that possesses an unreasonable risk to the health and safety of persons and/or the environment if it is not properly controlled during handling, storage, manufacture, processing, packaging, use, disposal, or transportation

Heat Stress — Combination of environmental and physical work factors that make up the heat load imposed on the body. The environmental factors that contribute to heat stress include air, temperature, radiant heat exchange, air movement, and water vapor pressure. Physical work contributes to heat stress by the metabolic heat in the body. Clothing also has an effect on heat stress.

Hold bar — Airport marker for areas on the airport ramp, taxiways, and runways that can be crossed only with permission from the control tower

Hung Gear — One or more of the aircraft landing gear not down and locked (no green-light indication in the cockpit)

Hydraulic System — Aircraft system that transmits power by means of a fluid under pressure

Hydrazine — Toxic, caustic, hypergolic fuel that is a clear, oily liquid with a smell similar to ammonia that poses a health hazard in both the liquid and vapor forms

Hydrophilic — Capable of mixing with water

Hydrophobic — Incapable of mixing with water

Hydroplaning — Condition in which moving tires (automobile or aircraft) are separated from pavement surfaces by steam and/or water or liquid rubber film, resulting in loss of mechanical braking effectiveness

Hypergolic — Chemical reaction between a fuel and an oxidizer that causes immediate ignition on contact without the presence of air

I

ILS — Abbreviation for Instrument Landing System

In-service training — Proficiency training such as classroom study, hands-on skills exercises, and live fire drills conducted within the firefighter's own fire department

Inboard/Outboard — Refers to location with reference to the centerline of the fuselage; for example, inboard engines are the ones closest to the fuselage, and outboard engines are those farthest away

Incursion — Any occurrence in the airport runway environment involving an aircraft, vehicle, person, or object on the ground that creates a collision hazard or results in a loss of required separation with an aircraft taking off, intending to take off, landing, or intending to land

Insoluble — Incapable of being dissolved in a liquid (usually water)

Instrument Landing — Landing an aircraft by relying only upon instrument data; may be due to inclement weather or other factors

Instrument Landing System (ILS) — Electronic navigation system that allows aircraft to approach and land during inclement weather conditions

Intake Area — Area in front of and to the side of a jet engine that might be unsafe for personnel

Interior Access Vehicles — Fire apparatus designed to provide a raised platform for aircraft fire fighting operations that will elevate fire fighters to an even level with the aircraft compartment

Isolation Area — Area used to isolate aircraft carrying hazardous materials or munitions; segregated away from the parking aprons in case an accident or incident should occur

J

JATO — Abbreviation for Jet-Assisted Takeoff

Jet-Assisted Takeoff (JATO) — Rocket or auxiliary jet used to augment normal thrust for takeoffs

Jet Blast — Wind and/or heat blast created behind an aircraft with engines running

Jettison — To selectively discard aircraft components such as external fuel tanks or canopies

Jetway — Enclosed ramp between a terminal and an aircraft for loading and unloading passengers

Jetway eyebrow — Accordion-like canopy that permits the jetway to dock with aircraft that have differing contours in order to protect passengers and crew from the weather during aircraft boarding and deboarding

L

Landing Roll — Distance from the point of touchdown to the point where the aircraft is brought to a stop or exits the runway

Leading edge — Front or forward edge of an aircraft's wings or stabilizers

Low Approach — Approach over a runway or heliport where the pilot intentionally does not make contact with the runway

M

Magneto — Device used in gasoline engines that produces a periodic spark in order to maintain fuel combustion

Mass Casualty Incident (MCI) — Incident that results in a large number of casualties within a short time frame as a result of an attack, natural disaster, aircraft crash, or other cause that is beyond the capabilities of local logistical support

Material Safety Data Sheets (MSDS) — Form provided by the manufacturer and blender of chemicals that contains information about chemical composition, physical and chemical properties, health and safety hazards, emergency response procedures, and waste disposal procedures of the specified material

MDT — Abbreviation for Mobile Data Terminal

Missed Approach — Maneuver conducted by a pilot whenever an instrument approach cannot be completed into a landing

Mobile Data Terminal (MDT) — Mobile computer that communicates with other computers on a radio system

Monopropellant — Chemical or a mixture of chemicals that is stable under specific storage conditions, but reacts very rapidly under other conditions to produce large amounts of energetic (hot) gasses. Monopropellants, such as hydrazine, are commonly used in aircraft emergency power units.

Movement Area — Runways, taxiways, and other areas of an airport that are used for taxiing or hover taxiing, air taxiing, and takeoff and landing of aircraft exclusive of loading ramps and aircraft parking areas

MSDS — Abbreviation for Material Safety Data Sheet

Multiple-Casualty Incident — Incident involving 20 or more transportable patients; may be classified as Extended, Major, or Catastrophic

Mutual Aid — Reciprocal assistance from a neighboring fire and emergency services agency to another during an emergency based upon a prearrangement between agencies involved and generally made upon the request of the receiving agency

N

Nacelle — Housing of an externally mounted aircraft engine

National Defense Area (NDA) — Temporary establishment within the United States of "federal areas" for the protection or security of Department of Defense resources. Normally, NDAs are established for emergency situations such as accidents. NDAs may be established, discontinued, or their boundaries changed as necessary to provide protection or security of Department of Defense (DOD) resources.

NDA — Abbreviation for National Defense Area

Nonaspirating Foam Nozzle — Nozzle that does not draw air into the foam solution stream; foam solution is agitated by the nozzle design causing air to mix with the solution after it has exited the nozzle

NOTAM — Abbreviation for Notice to Airmen

Notice to Airmen (NOTAM) — Bulletin issued by airport personnel notifying aviation interests of issues that can effect normal operations

O

Occupants — Passengers and aircrew aboard an aircraft

On-the-job Training — Learning while performing the day-to-day work requirements under supervision of more experienced firefighters

Ordnance — Bombs, rockets, ammunition, and other explosive devices carried on most military aircraft

Overhead Approach (360 overhead) — Series of standard maneuvers conducted by military aircraft (often in formation) for entry into the airfield traffic pattern prior to landing

Overrun — In military aviation exclusively, a stabilized or paved area at the end of the runway that is the same width as the runway plus the shoulders; used in the event of an emergency that prohibits the aircraft from stopping normally

P

PASS — Acronym for Personal Alert Safety System

PCA — Abbreviation for Practical Critical Fire Area

Perception Distance — Distance the vehicle moves from the time the driver's eyes see a hazard until the driver's brain acknowledges the hazard

Personnel Accountability System — Method for identifying which emergency responders are working on an incident scene

Personal Alert Safety System (PASS) — Electronic lack-of-motion sensor that sounds a loud tone when a firefighter becomes motionless; can also be manually triggered to operate

Petcock — Small faucet or valve for releasing or draining a gas (such as air)

Polar solvents — Flammable liquids that have an attraction for water, much like a positive magnetic pole attracts a negative pole; examples include alcohols, ketones, and lacquers

Power Take-off — Rotating shaft that transfers power from the engine to auxiliary equipment

Prop Wash — Current of air created by the rotation of a propeller

Practical Critical Fire Area (PCA) — Two-thirds of the Theoretical Critical Fire Area (TCA); See also *Theoretical Critical Fire Area*

Proportioner — Device used to introduce the correct amount of agent, especially foam and wetting agents, into streams of water

Proportioning — Mixing of water with an appropriate amount of foam concentrate to form a foam solution

Proximity Clothing — Special personal protective equipment with a reflective exterior that is designed to protect the firefighter from conductive, convective, and radiant heat while working in close proximity to the fire; also called Proximity Suit

Proximity Suit — See *Proximity Clothing*

Pump-and-roll — Ability of an apparatus to pump water and foam while the vehicle is in motion

R

Radial Engines — Internal-combustion, piston-driven aircraft engines with cylinders arranged in a circle

Ramp — Area at airports intended to accommodate aircraft for purposes of loading or unloading passengers or cargo, refueling, parking, or maintenance; also known as Apron

Rapid Intervention Crew (RIC) — See *Rapid Intervention Team*

Rapid Intervention Team (RIT) — two or more fully equipped and immediately available firefighters designated to stand by outside the hazard zone to enter and effect rescue of firefighters inside, if necessary; also known as *Rapid Intervention Crew (RIC)*

Rapid Response Area (RRA) — Rectangular area that includes the runway and the surrounding area extending to but not exceeding the airport property line; extends 500 feet (152 m) outward from each side of the runway centerline and 1650 feet (500 m) beyond each runway end

Reaction Distance — Distance traveled from the time the driver's brain tells the foot to move from the accelerator until the foot is actually pushing the brake pedal

Reciprocating Engines — Internal-combustion, piston-driven aircraft engines with cylinders arranged in opposition

Refractometer — Device used to measure the amount of foam concentrate in the solution; operates on the principle of measuring the velocity of light that travels through the foam solution

Rehabilitation — Allowing firefighters or rescuers to rest, rehydrate, and recover during an incident

Rescue — Saving a life from fire or accident; removing a victim from an untenable or unhealthy atmosphere

Response — Call to respond

RIC — Abbreviation for Rapid Intervention Crew

RIT — Abbreviation for Rapid Intervention Team

Rollover — (1) Condition in which the unburned combustible gases released in a confined space (such as a room or aircraft cabin) during the incipient or early steady-state phase and accumulate at the ceiling level. These superheated gases are pushed, under pressure, away from the fire area and into uninvolved areas where they mix with oxygen. When their flammable range is reached and additional oxygen is supplied by opening doors and/or applying fog streams, they ignite and a fire front develops, expanding very rapidly in a rolling action across the ceiling. Also see Backdraft and Flashover. (2) Involves a vehicle rolling sideways onto its side and possibly continuing onto its top, then the opposite side.

Rotor — Rotating airfoil assemblies of helicopters and other rotary-wing aircraft, providing lift

RRA — Abbreviation for Rapid Response Area

Rudder — Hinged, movable control surface attached to the rear part of the vertical stabilizer and is used to control the yaw or turning motion of the aircraft

Runway — Defined rectangular area on airports prepared for the takeoff or landing of aircraft along its length

S

SCBA — Abbreviation for Self-Contained Breathing Apparatus

Security Identification Display Area (SIDA) — Portions of an airport, specified in the airport security program, in which security measures required by regulation must be carried out; includes the security area and may include other areas of the airport

Self-Contained Breathing Apparatus (SCBA) — Respirator worn by the user that supplies a breathable atmosphere that is either carried in or generated by the apparatus and is independent of the ambient atmosphere; worn in all atmospheres that are considered to be Immediately Dangerous to Life and Health (IDLH); also called Air Mask or Air Pack

Shipping Papers — See *Air Bill*

SIDA — Abbreviation for Security Identification Display Area

Skid Unit — Fire fighting system or systems built on a frame that can be mounted in the bed of a pickup truck or on the bed of a larger vehicle

Skin — Outer covering of an aircraft, which includes the covering of wings, fuselage, and control surfaces

Skin Penetrating Agent Applicator Tool — see *SPAAT*

SOPs — Abbreviation for Standard Operating Procedures

SPAAT (Skin Penetrating Agent Applicator Tool) — Specific type of penetrating nozzle

Special courses and seminars — Extension programs, conferences, short courses, workshops, correspondence courses, or programs in recognized professional schools

Speed brakes — Aerodynamic devices located on the wing or along the rear or underside of the fuselage that can be extended to help slow the aircraft

Spoilers — Movable panels located on the upper surface of a wing and that raise up into the airflow to increase drag and decrease lift

Stabilizer — Airfoil on an airplane used to provide stability; that is, the aft horizontal surface to which the elevators are hinged (horizontal stabilizer) and the fixed vertical surface to which the rudder is hinged (vertical stabilizer)

Staging Area — Prearranged, strategically located area where personnel, apparatus, and other equipment can be held in readiness for use during an emergency

Standard Operating Procedures (SOPs) — Standard methods or rules in which an organization or a fire department operates to carry out a routine function. Usually these procedures are written in a policies and procedures handbook and all firefighters should be well versed in their content. An SOP may specify the functional limitations of fire brigade members in performing emergency operations.

Straight-in approach — Entry into the traffic pattern by interception of the extended runway centerline (final approach course) without executing any other portion of the traffic pattern

Strategy — Overall plan for incident attack and control established by the incident commander

Strut — Aircraft structural components designed to absorb or distribute abrupt compression or tension such as the landing gear forces

T

Tactics — Methods of employing equipment and personnel on an incident to accomplish specific tactical objectives in order to achieve established strategic goals

Tail — Aircraft tail assembly including the vertical and horizontal stabilizers, elevators, and rudders; also called *Empennage*

Target Hazard — Facility in which there is a great potential likelihood of life or property loss

Taxiway — Defined routes used by aircraft on the ground to travel (Taxi)

TCA — Abbreviation for Theoretical Critical Fire Area

Temperature-Compensated Conductivity Meter — Device designed to measure the conductivity of a solution; it adjusts for conductivity variances at different temperatures

Theoretical Critical Fire Area (TCA) — Rectangular area adjacent to an aircraft in which fire must be controlled in order to ensure temporary fuselage integrity and provide an escape route for aircraft occupants

Threshold — Beginning or end of a runway that is usable for landing or takeoff

Three-dimensional fire — Fuel fire that contains length, width, and height (flowing, spraying, and pouring fuel)

Thrust — Pushing or pulling force developed by an aircraft engine

Thrust Reverser — Device or apparatus for diverting jet engine thrust for slowing or stopping the aircraft

Topography — Features of the earth's surface, both natural and constructed, and the relationships among them

Total Stopping Distance — Sum of the driver/operator's perception distance, reaction distance, and the vehicle braking distance

Traffic pattern — Traffic flow that is prescribed for aircraft landing or taking off from an airport

Transportation Area — Location where accident casualties are held after receiving medical care or triage before being transported to medical facilities

Trailing edge — Rearmost edge of an aircraft's wings or stabilizers

Triage — Sorting and classification of accident casualties to determine the priority for medical treatment and transportation

Triage Tagging — Method used to identify accident casualties as to extent of injury

Tug — Specialty vehicle used to move aircraft on the ramp

Turbojet — Jet engine employing a turbine-driven compressor to compress the intake air, or an aircraft with this type of engine; also known as *Gas Turbine*

Turret/Turret Nozzle — Preplumbed master stream appliance on some airport rescue and fire fighting apparatus, capable of sweeping from side to side and designed to deliver large volumes of foam or water

Two-dimensional fire — Fuel spill that has pooled, having two dimensions, length and width

U

Unannounced Emergency — Emergency that occurs without prior warning

Uncontrolled Airport — Airport having no control tower in operation

Undeclared Dangerous Goods Cargo — Cargo that has not received proper packaging, shipping documentation, or safety precautions required of hazardous or dangerous goods shipments

Unit Load Devices — Pallets and containers used to facilitate the rapid loading and unloading of aircraft cargo

United States Department of Transportation (DOT) — Administrative body of the executive branch of the state/provincial or federal government responsible for transportation policy, regulation, and enforcement

Upwind Leg — Flight path parallel to the landing runway in the direction of landing

V

Vector — Compass heading or course followed by or to be followed by an aircraft

Venturi Principle — Physical law stating that when a fluid, such as water or air, is forced under pressure through a restricted orifice, there is an increase in the velocity of the fluid passing through the orifice and a corresponding decrease in the pressure exerted against the sides of the constriction. Because the surrounding fluid is under greater pressure (atmospheric), it is forced into the area of lower pressure.

VFR — Abbreviation for Visual Flight Rules

Visual Approach — Approach to landing made by visual reference to the surface

Visual Flight Rules (VFR) — Rules for flight in which the pilot maintains his or her own responsibility for navigation, spacing from other objects, and other flight functions, separate of air traffic control

Index

Index

Index by Nancy Kopper